Manager's Guide to Making Decisions about Information Systems

Manager's Guide to Making Decisions about Information Systems

Paul Gray

Claremont Graduate University

John Wiley & Sons, Inc.

Acquisitions Editor   *Beth Lang Golub*
Associate Editor   *Lorraina Raccuia*
Production Editor   *Janine Rosado*
Marketing Manager   *Jillian Rice*
Senior Designer   *Maddy Lesure*
Senior Media Editor   *Allison Morris*
Editorial Assistant   *Jennifer Snyder*
Cover Photo   *Comstock/Media Bakery*
Production Management Services   *Ingrao Associates*

This book was set in *Times Ten* by John Wiley Composition Services and printed and bound by R. R. Donnelley and Sons. The cover was printed by Phoenix Color Corp.

This book is printed on acid free paper. ∞

To order books or for customer service please, call 1-800-CALL WILEY (225-5945).

Library of Congress Cataloging-in-Publication Data:

Gray, Paul,
   Manager's guide to making decisions about information systems / Paul Gray.—
1st ed.
         p. cm.
   Includes bibliographical references.
   ISBN-13: 978-0-471-26359-3 (cloth)
   ISBN-10: 0-471-26359-1 (cloth)
  1. Management—Data processing. 2. Information Technology—Management. 3.
Decision making—Data processing. 4. Management information systems. I.
Title.
   HD30.2.G727 2006
   658'.05—dc22

                                                                              2005017559

Printed in the United States of America

10 9 8 7 6 5 4 3 2 1

To Muriel

Preface

This book was written to meet the needs of three types of MBA students for an introduction to information systems (IS):

-those who are enrolled in Executive MBA programs

-those who work full time and therefore deal with information systems on a regular basis

-those who returned to school after years of business experience

In my years of teaching these students, I found that the existing textbooks and the class material available focus on what IS people do, with only occasional looks at how IS can and does affect the business as a whole. Little attempt is made to think about IS from the non-IS manager's point of view. This approach is not unique to IS. Each discipline (be it finance, marketing, operations management) does the same. It is certainly fine if you will be a professional in a given field. However, most MBA's work spans multiple areas because a business involves a team effort. MBAs need to know how each of the functions affects what they do. They also need to know enough about the other fields to be confident that the other specialties are carrying their weight. In a business, everyone is affected by what the firm's information systems can and cannot do.

Managers, be they general managers or in charge of a specialty area, interact with IS all the time. They are called upon to make or approve many important decisions about what IS contributes. Here are some of them:

- What projects should take precedence/priority when resources are scarce, and they always are?

- How do we align IS objectives with business objectives?

- Should our firm undertake a 'big ticket' (i.e., expensive) application such as an Enterprise Requirements Planning (ERP) system or a Customer Relationship Management (CRM) system?

- How do we deal with the nature and educational background of IS people who are different from the business's standard mold? In many firms, IS is the only technically oriented group.

- How should IS interact with the external environment? Government requirements, such as Sarbanes–Oxley and HIPAA, continue to be imposed; worms, viruses, and denial of service attacks increase; lawsuits about IS abound; and other firms are given access to data from your systems.

- Which new technologies should the firm acquire, almost all of which involve digital computing?

- How much capital and operating budget should be allocated to IS compared to other needs in order to compete?

For most of these issues, managers will be (and should be) in the decision-making loop. Both the personal and the organizational level need to be considered. At the personal level:

- Will a particular proposal help me or hinder me in my work?
- How will it affect my people and the processes in which we are involved?

At the organizational level:

- Will it help gain strategic advantage?
- Is it a strategic necessity?

As a manager, you should be able to understand the capabilities that IS offers the organization. This book will help you learn some of which you are not aware, such as the many uses of a data warehouse and gaining business and competitive intelligence.

You will need to learn a little about the various kinds of information systems—both their technology and their applications—so you can understand what they do, so you can understand the seemingly strange language of the IS people, and, perhaps more important, self-defend against the Information System department's superior technical (but not necessarily superior business) knowledge.

You should be aware that there are things that this book does not try to do. It does not discuss the simple things that you do routinely on your personal computer, such as word processing or spreadsheets or PowerPoint presentations. It doesn't try to teach you about computer languages such as Basic or Java or how to find things on the Internet. It doesn't try to make you a techie. However, it does look at what you can do to make your firm's investment in IS pay off.

In short, this book should give you a different view of information systems.

ORGANIZATION OF THIS BOOK.

This book is organized into three parts: (1) overview, (2) big ticket items, and (3) management aspects.

Part 1: Overview

The overview section consists of Chapters 1 and 2 (and backed by the Appendix on software and hardware). Part 1 introduces you to the big picture. It focuses on such issues as the hardware, the software, and the Internet; strategic uses of IS; aligning IS with the business; types of applications; and inter-organizational systems.

Part 2: Big Ticket Applications

Inevitably you will be involved in making decisions on whether to undertake (or upgrade or decommission) large software systems. Each system offers benefits but also introduces costs. In Chapters 3 through 8 we discuss six of these big ticket applications: (1) Electronic Commerce, (2) Enterprise Requirements Planning (ERP), (3) Data Warehousing, (4) Customer Relationship Management (CRM), (5) Knowledge Management, and (6) Business Intelligence. These systems are at different levels of maturity, involve different costs (but all costs are large) and benefits, are better suited to some firms than others, and create different interdependencies. These systems are examples of the many ways in which you can put information systems to use in your firm.

Part 3: Management Aspects

In Part 3 we talk about many of the decisions you will be involved in over time.

We begin with a major issue, outsourcing—both inside the United States and to overseas firms. Why do it or not do it? Systems integration, supply chain, people issues, mergers and acquisitions, infrastructure, and privacy, security, and ethics are the topics of the rest of the chapters in this part.

That's a broad agenda. However, each item involves problems that are bigger than just your IS organization. For example, infrastructure refers to all the services that are provided to everyone—access to the Internet, PCs, large mainframes, and much more. How much infrastructure do you need? How much of your budget should go to it?

ORGANIZATION OF THE CHAPTERS

You will find that each chapter begins with a series of managerial questions and concludes with answers to these questions. In addition, at the end of each chapter, two to four problems expand beyond what is in the book. The problems require you to prepare a short paper. In some, you will be asked for your opinion or to take a position in a debate. In others you will have to go to the Internet and the library to obtain data about the current situation. In still others, you will be asked to look at topics not covered in the book. The idea is to stretch your mind and get you to think beyond what can be put into the pages available.

The meat of each chapter is a discussion of the issues involved, the management considerations, the costs and benefits, and much more. Our assumption is that you are in a U.S. business environment; however, most of the ideas apply worldwide. You should go away from each chapter with a better understanding of what the shouting is about.

GOING BEYOND WHAT IS IN THE BOOK

To go beyond what is in this book, students may access the website of the Communications of the Association for Information Systems (CAIS) whose URL is `http://cais.aisnet.org/ contents.asp`. This website contains cases and articles that cover topics discussed in the text.

INSTRUCTOR'S RESOURCES `www.wiley.com/college/gray`

Instructor's Manual

A brief Instructor's manual is available on the Instructor's Companion Site accessed via www.wiley.com/college/gray. It provides suggested approaches to end-of-chapter exercises, teaching tips, and a list of articles and cases that can be used to supplement the text.

Articles and Cases

Articles and cases are suggested from two sources:

1. Business Extra Select at http://www.wiley.com/college/bxs allows instructors to package the text with cases, articles, and other real-world content from sources such as INSEAD,

Ivey, and Harvard Business School cases, *Fortune, The Economist, Wall Street Journal* and much more. Please contact your Wiley sales representative for more information.

2. The website for the Communications of the Association for Information Systems (CAIS) at `http://cais.aisnet.org/contents.asp` contains cases and articles that cover topics discussed in the text.[1]

PowerPoint Presentation Slides

PowerPoint Slides are available for use in class. Full-color slides highlight key figures from the text, providing a versatile opportunity to add high-quality visual support to lectures. The slides are posted on the Instructor's Companion Site accessed at `www.wiley.com/college/gray`.

---

[1] The articles in the Communications of the Association for Information Systems are available to everyone without password if they are in a volume that is over a year old. All articles, including the most recently published, are available without password in those universities whose libraries subscribe to the journal. Student memberships in the Association for Information Systems, which also provide full access, are available at reduced cost to students.

Acknowledgments

This book's approach was tested with Executive Management Program students at Claremont Graduate University in Southern California. The contributions of my students were immeasurably helpful in creating the final product.

I particularly appreciate the work of Prof. Marlene Davidson, now at Bradley University, who prepared the Appendix to this volume.

The people at Wiley, particularly Beth Golub, Acquisitions Editor, Susan Elbe, Publisher, Lorraina Raccuia, Associate Editor, Jennifer Snyder, Editorial Assistant, Jillian Rice, Marketing Manager, Maddy Lesure, Designer, Jeanine Furino, Production Manager, and Janine Rosado, Production Editor as well as Suzanne Ingrao of Ingrao Associates all contributed to creating the book that you see.

Hugh J. Watson, Professor at the University of Georgia, who is the consulting editor for Wiley's MIS series, encouraged this book, sponsored it, and helped shape it.

The development of this book benefitted from the comments and suggestions of colleagues who teach information systems courses.

I'd like to acknowledge the contributions made by the following individuals:

Stuart John Barnes, University of Bath

Apiwan D. Born, University of Illinois – Springfield

Qiyang Chen, Montclair State University

H. Michael Chung, California State University – Long Beach

Subhasish Dasgupta, George Washington University

Stephen A. Floyd, University of Alabama – Huntsville

Fred Gallegos, California State Polytechnic University

Varun Grover, Clemson University

Rand W. Guthrie, California State Polytechnic University

Patrick J. Hynes, Fordham University

Mark Jeffery, Northwestern University

Leif Johnson, Oklahoma City University

Birsen Karpak, Youngstown State University

Rajesh Mirani, University of Baltimore

Richard Orwig, Susquehanna University

A. Graham Peace, West Virginia University

Erik Rolland, University of California – Riverside

G. Shankar Shankaranarayanan, Boston University

Joseph Sherif, California State University – Fullerton

Jonathan Trower, Baylor University

Hugh Watson, University of Georgia

Jigish Zaveri, Morgan State University

Contents

CHAPTER 2 THE BIG PICTURE: IT AND BUSINESS 15

CHAPTER 3 ELECTRONIC COMMERCE 37

CHAPTER 5 DATA WAREHOUSING   74

CHAPTER 6 CUSTOMER RELATIONSHIP MANAGEMENT   96

CHAPTER 7 KNOWLEDGE MANAGEMENT   117

CHAPTER 12 THE CHIEF INFORMATION OFFICER, PEOPLE ISSUES, PROJECT MANAGEMENT, CHANGE MANAGEMENT   216

Chapter 1

What Is an Information System?

MANAGERIAL QUESTIONS

What is an information system?
What are some major applications of information systems?
How does the Internet fit in?

INTRODUCTION

Why learn about information systems? Aren't they the province of the techies and the nerds, not managers? Surprisingly, the answer is no. Information systems pervade the enterprise. Whether you want to know about your competition, or decide among alternatives, or streamline a business process, or decide where to spend a major portion of your capital budget, you inevitably must think about the information systems you have and the information systems you need. As you progress through the upper ranks of a firm or run a firm of your own, you will be faced periodically with making decisions about the firm's information systems. Your role is multiple. One time you may be a consumer (are they creating what my people and I need?), at another, a member of a steering committee (which projects get priority in this firm within our limited information systems budget?), and still others as a policy maker (should we outsource? should we undertake a major initiative requiring a major new information system?).

You will be involved in information systems decisions whether you are a techie or not. Just knowing how to operate your own personal computer (PC) to send e-mail and surf the Web is not enough. You need to understand what information systems can and cannot do for you. You need to understand, at some level, the technical terms being talked about by the information systems people, by the vendors, and by your colleagues in management. You need to be able to make independent judgments of what your firm needs and what it does not. People trying to convince you that some piece of software or hardware is a silver bullet, whether it is or not. You need to be able to self-defend.

This book is about your role in your firm's information systems. It is written for people like you with managerial experience in companies at the middle and upper levels who are returning to school full- or part-time for an MBA or an executive MBA degree. Since your MBA program tends to be compressed, with much more to cover than can possibly be done in the time available (and usually holding down a full-time job as well), this book concentrates on what you, as a manager, need to know over the next several years.

Information systems is a field in which the technology changes quickly and buzzwords come and go. However, the principles don't change very rapidly. This book, therefore, in addition to describing where information technology is today, we focus on what we know at the conceptual level. Our objective is to make you knowledgeable and able to make decisions about your firm's information systems.

This first chapter begins by explaining information systems and their components. You will inevitably find new things here that you are not familiar with, including the meaning of terms and buzzwords. Since reviewing information systems takes up the entire book, in the first part of this chapter we present only the basics: the hardware, the software, and the Internet.

Throughout this chapter we will refer to other parts of the book where topics mentioned in passing are covered in detail. If that subject is of special interest to you, feel free to skip to it and then return to this chapter.

WHAT IS AN INFORMATION SYSTEM?

> *Definition:* An information system is a combination of technology,[1] people, and processes to capture, transmit, store, retrieve, manipulate, and display information.

Note that an information system is more than just the technology. It includes the people who run it, the people who maintain it, and the executives who manage it. It also includes the business processes that allow people to make use of the data, information, and knowledge that the system creates and maintains.

An information system does not operate in isolation. Rarely, if ever, do people create an information system for its own sake. In business, information systems are used to support specific kinds of work, from the recording of sales in a department store to selecting customer prospects, to analyzing data for business intelligence.

COMPONENTS OF AN INFORMATION SYSTEM

Information systems include hardware and software, and communications.

Hardware includes computers, the printers, the scanners, the displays, the modems, and other physical devices. It also includes the devices that store information.

Software refers to computer programs, that is, lists of instructions to the computer as to what to do. Programs can be divided into those that run the computers (called *operating systems*) and those that record and manipulate data (called *applications*) such as orders, billing, accounting records, sales records, credit data, and more.

Communications includes phone lines, cable lines, wireless, and other modes for transmitting information among computers and people. Communications usually includes local area networks that connect computers close to one another and wide area networks that are dispersed across broad geographic areas.

---

[1] This book is concerned with information systems that incorporate technology, particularly computer technology. Some information systems do not incorporate technology. Many of the same principles, however, apply.

HARDWARE

This subsection examines hardware in terms of the major available business computer types to illustrate some of the hardware categories that exist.

Personal Computers

A personal computer (PC) is what most of us own in our homes and/or have on our desk at work. The personal computer has been with us on a large scale since IBM introduced its Model 51 in August 1981. At the time, the cost was over $3,500 for a unit operating at 1.3 megahertz with two floppy disks and a 12 inch green screen. Nearly 25 years later, the cost of a top-of-the-line system for personal use is still near $3,000 but includes a 2.8 gigahertz or higher clock speed, a unit with a multigigabit hard disk, a 19 inch or larger flat color screen, CD-ROM and DVD writers, and multiple other built-in accessories. The price point for a highly capable unit is under $1,000. Portable and handheld computers are all the rage. Knowledge workers see a PC as part of what comes with their job.

The software to accompany the hardware (see below) also grew. People now have word processing, presentation graphics, spreadsheets, and much more at their fingertips.

The personal computer can be used in stand-alone or networked mode. In stand-alone mode it tends to be relatively secure from hackers, worms, and other attacks (see Chapter 15). As we discuss below in networking, the main use of PCs comes when they can access other computers through networks such as the Internet. However, this access carries with it risks from hostile intruders.

Mainframe Computers

Mainframe computers used to be called "big iron" because they were indeed physically large. Early computers literally occupied large air-conditioned rooms, offered little storage, and had only a few conventional (called dumb) terminals tied to them. Over time, these computers grew smaller in size, added storage and speed, and tied ever more terminals to them. The term mainframe resulted from most companies owning only one for the company or one for each major division. Most manufacturers,[2] led by IBM, produced only such machines from the late 1950s through the 1970s and a few firms, such as IBM, still produce them today.

Initially, these computers ran only in "batch" mode. That is, users would specify which cases they wanted run and the computer would run them all at once. Today's interactive computing, where results are fed back as they occur, did not come into general use until the mid-1970s.

Competition came from new entrants (such as Digital Equipment Corporation (DEC) and Sun) who created smaller computers, called midsized (or mini) computers, that were simply smaller versions of the larger mainframes. Their market was universities and midsized and smaller businesses. Like mainframes, they used dumb terminals. Over time, mainframes were able to connect to PCs.

Today's mainframe computers are quite speedy and offer high capacity and high reliability. Their speed and capacity allows them to process vast amounts of data using both a large internal memory and high-capacity external storage. The machines are workhorses that run uninterrupted for years. If repairs are required, they can often be performed while the machine continues to run. Mainframes can simultaneously support thousands of users. Some mainframes run multiple operating systems and thereby work as if they were several machines (i.e., they are "virtual machines").

---

[2] The eight major computer manufacturers were known as IBM and the seven dwarfs, since IBM was much larger than any of them.

The leading vendors are IBM (which dominates the market), Hitachi, Ahmdahl, and Fujitsu. Prices start at several hundred thousand dollars.

Typical mainframe users are retailers, conglomerates, and banks who are involved in transaction processing.

Client-Server Computers

As PCs became more prevalent and bigger, it became clear that much of the work that was being done on the mainframe could be done on the PC. The client-server model of computing was introduced. In this model, the mainframe (now smaller and called a "server") was used for specific functions. Sometimes it was as a common data storage so that everyone had the same data. Other servers provided specialized services such as telecommunications, e-mail, and printing. The client-server model required duplication of software on the local computers to accomplish the work. Although it was argued that client-server arrangements would be lower cost, on the whole the total cost of ownership was the same or more than mainframes.

Remote Computing Using Application Service Providers, Web Services, and Grid Computing

The next stage in computing hardware was to realize that not all hardware needed to be on the firm's premises and that some computing could be shipped to vendors who specialized in it.

The first stage was the *application service provider*, called ASP for short.[3] Their idea is to ship data for specific applications to an outside firm that does the computing. The ASP provides a data center with the necessary computers, storage capacity, software, bandwidth, and management to run applications. After a run is made, the results are sent back to the requesting firm's computer. The argument is made that, by sharing the ASP's computing capacity, which is larger than the firm's capacity for the application, economy of scale savings can be obtained. Furthermore, if the firm does not maintain the capability at its own facilities, it is not faced with the costs of maintenance and updating the needed hardware and software; the ASP does that.

Web services are interpreted in many ways. The basic idea is that computers can send data to remote computers via the World Wide Web[4] (see below) and receive an answer. This work can be done computer-to-computer (without human intervention) and independent of the particular software used by each participant. The key to making Web services work is that standard methods are used which do not depend on the particular software or hardware. Thus, it is possible for a firm that needs a particular computation to buy use of a module from a Web service by sending input data and receiving the results of the computation over the Web. In effect, the use of the module is shared among many users. From the point of view of the user, they do not know (or care) whether the computation was performed in-house or whether parts or the entire program was run by a service provider out on the Web. Because the software is shared among multiple users, the cost is less than creating or buying the module.

Web services were in an early stage of development in 2005. Web services are a key technology that enables outsourcing (Chapter 9).

---

[3] ASPs are a form of outsourcing. They are discussed further in Chapters 9 and 14. Note that ASPs went through a cycle where they were first in favor, then out of favor, and then again in favor.

[4] The term World Wide Web (abbreviated www) and Internet are used interchangeably in this book since they refer to the same thing.

Grid computing involves the massive integration of multiple computer systems to offer performance unattainable by any single machine. Unlike conventional networks that focus on communication among devices, grid computing harnesses unused processing power of all computers in a network for solving problems too intensive for any stand-alone machine. The concept can be carried down to the level of personal computers, for example. Individual PCs can be hooked together to perform computing tasks that are larger than any one PC could perform on its own. The method saves both money and resources. However, it does require special software that is unique to the computing project for which the grid is being used.

Remote computing, where computers located at and owned by other firms are used to perform the work, involves outsourcing. Outsourcing, which is the subject of Chapter 9, occurs in many more modes than are described here.

SOFTWARE

Hardware, by itself, would be useless unless two kinds of computer programs were available.

- Operating systems
- Applications

Operating Systems

Operating systems are programs that manage and control the computer, telling it where to start, where to stop, where to put results, what computer language to use, how to communicate, and many other things. Typical operating systems include various versions of Windows from Microsoft, MacOS from Apple, UNIX, and LINUX. The choice of an operating system often seems theological rather than an economic judgment, because technical people tend to have strong opinions about small differences. Yet, typically, a computer uses only one operating system and it comes (i.e., is bundled) with the computer.

If multiple applications are running, the operating system schedules them so that they can, in effect, share the computer during a given time. Most computers[5] actually operate in sequence so that only one operation is performed at a time. By interleaving the computer, multiple programs appear to be running at the same time without interfering with one another.

Applications Programs

Applications are computer programs that accomplish a specific task. Examples of generic application programs include word processing, spreadsheets, graphic presentations, e-mail, transaction processing, and accounting. More specialized applications are often created for strategic reasons. We discuss strategic uses of computing later in the next chapter.

Application programs can be as simple as the four instructions for adding 2 and 3 and printing the results that are shown in Sidebar 1, or as complex as requiring millions of lines of code.

---

[5] Powerful, advanced computers operate in parallel. That is, the hardware is replicated and software is configured so that several parts of the problem are actually performed at the same time. These pieces are then brought back together to obtain final results. From the point of view of the user, the computer is much faster but the results are the same. Computers with parallel capabilities tend to be more expensive to buy but offer time and hence money savings in return.

SIDEBAR 1   *A Simple Basic Program for Adding 2 and 3*
and Printing the Result

```
   X = 2
   Y = 3
 SUM = X +Y
PRINT X,Y,SUM
```

Unlike operating systems, which are often bundled (see previous subsection), application programs are obtained one at a time to do specific tasks. For each application program, the firm faces a "build vs. buy" decision, just as it does for buying or building components of its manufactured products or its services.

When computers first came on the scene, computer manufacturers created application programs and bundled them with their machines. With only a few trained programmers in the workforce and firms not skilled in computing, there were no other sources for applications. However, three phenomena led to the creation of a major software industry.

1.   In part because of litigation, IBM and others decided to unbundle their software. They understood that, by not giving software away, they lower their hardware prices (thereby being more competitive) while at the same time selling their software at a profit.

2.   As the number of trained programmers and the size and speed of computers increased, people found additional computer applications. Entrepreneurs started companies that created software to supply these applications. Software is an extreme case of high fixed development cost but very low variable cost to create additional copies. These vendors also understood that by charging maintenance fees they could raise the money for continual improvement that kept them competitive. Of course, the software from vendors was generic so that as many customers could use it as possible.

3.   Individual companies found that not all the applications they wanted were on the market. They therefore needed to write their own application programs. Furthermore, in many cases, if commercial software was purchased, it had to be modified because it did not do things the way the firm did business. The net result was that firms very early started developing in-house teams of programmers who wrote applications.

This set of developments led to trade-offs:

- Buy and install a generic program and change processes to conform to the program's business rules?

- Buy a generic program and modify it to meet the firm's specific needs? This option implies modifying the program[6] for its initial installation and then paying for the same modification over and over each time the vendor updates the program with a new version.

- Create the application in-house, using the firm's own programmers. This approach usually requires more time, greater cost, and greater risk but allows customizing the application to the firm.

---

[6] Usually, the software vendor makes such modifications because the vendor will not release the details of the program to the firm.

In recent years, the size of programs grew larger. In part, this growth was made possible by the availability of large amounts of inexpensive storage, resulting in programs being written less parsimoniously.[7] In part it is due to bundling a number of applications that used to be separate into one package. A simple example of bundling is office software. Where people once bought a word processor, a spreadsheet, and other office applications individually, they now buy an office suite that contains a number of applications compatible with one another. The software allows the user to move data easily between the applications in the suite. A third reason for increasing program size is the creation of new applications, which solve highly complex problems and involve large volumes of data. These applications are often much larger than can be created by the in-house programming staff within the time available.

In Chapters 3 through 8 of this book we consider six types of very large applications programs, each designed for solving a specific problem. Each is expensive to acquire and maintain. Yet each can transform a business.

Electronic Commerce (Chapter 3)

Electronic commerce (or e-commerce for short) software is an application used to market, sell, buy, and service products or services over computer networks such as the Internet. E-commerce can be carried out between firms and consumers (B2C) or between businesses (B2B). It includes the communications and management required for such commerce as well as electronic data interchange (EDI) and automated data collection systems.

ERP (Enterprise Requirements Planning) (Chapter 4)

In the early days of business computing, companies used to custom-write their own software to control their business processes. This approach was expensive because each system required its own program and created its own data. The individual systems were not compatible across business functions or required systems integration (Chapter 10) so that they could communicate. In some cases, it was necessary to re-enter data in the computer to move from one program to another.

Enterprise requirements planning (ERP) extends an earlier software suite called Material Resource Planning (MRP)[8] (which helped run the factory) to cover the entire firm. It provides management and operating information for all the back-office functions across the firm. All functional departments involved in operations or production feed data into and retrieve data from the same computer system. By creating a single source, everyone in the firm uses the same data and the data does not have to be entered and re-entered.

ERP systems are bought in modules, such as finance and human resource management. In addition to manufacturing, ERP systems are used by accounting, human resources, marketing, strategic management, warehousing, and shipping.

ERP software is almost invariably bought from a vendor. Such software is possible because many business processes are common across various types of businesses. Because it consists of common, reusable software, it can provide a cost-effective alternative to custom software. ERP software

---

[7] For example, whereas the PC AT, IBM's newest PC in 1983, provided 5 MB of storage, by 2005 5 gigabytes—a 1000 times larger—was considered small.

[8] MRP came in two versions, first MRP (which was designed for scheduling the factory so that parts and materials were available when needed) and then MRPII (which added cost and other business considerations).

caters to a wide range of industries, from those in service sectors like hospitals and colleges, to manufacturing industries and government departments.

ERP systems integrate and automate many of the business practices associated with the operations or production aspects of a company. Because ERP systems are standardized, they tend to be rigid. That is, processes must be performed according to what the software does. Because customizing the sofware to fit existing processes exactly is quite expensive, implementing ERP almost invariably causes a firm to change many of its business processes. These process changes introduce resistance to change and sometimes lead to implementation failures.

ERP systems are often closely tied to supply chain management systems (Chapter 11). Supply chain management software extends the ERP system to include links with suppliers, often giving suppliers access to the firm's future requirements.

Data Warehousing (Chapter 5)

A data warehouse is a dedicated database system that is separate from a firm's online transaction processing systems. Unlike transaction systems, which are concerned with the current state of affairs, the data warehouse covers a long time horizon. The primary purpose of a data warehouse is to support the organization's decision making.

The data warehouse brings together information stored in many other systems, typically "legacy systems"; that is, computer systems for special purposes that, as their name implies, were created some time ago but are still in use. The data in legacy systems usually do not fully agree with one another. The idea of a data warehouse is to combine the legacy data (usually automatically) into a "single version of the truth" so that endless time is not wasted trying to decide which system provides the correct data. Reconciliation of multiple systems is automated though a series of applications called extract, transform, and load (abbreviated ETL).

Unlike a transaction system, which changes as events (e.g., purchases, payments) occur, once data enters the warehouse it does not change. The warehouse is optimized for answering complex management queries[9] both from users and from other applications, whereas transaction systems are optimized for speed of response.

Data warehouses can be quite large, sometimes holding terabytes of data[10]. In addition to their use for decision making, the data warehouse is the data source for such applications as customer relationship management (Chapter 6), knowledge management (Chapter 7), decision support systems and business intelligence (Chapter 8), and data mining (included in Chapter 5).

Customer Relationship Management (Chapter 6)

For most of the twentieth century, firms focused on mass marketing, a movement that is in decline. The last several years saw the rise of customer relationship management (abbreviated CRM) as a way to return to the world of personal marketing. In this one-to-one approach, information about a customer (e.g., previous purchases, needs, and wants) is used to frame offers that are more likely to be accepted. This approach is made possible by CRM software.

CRM is a broader concept than marketing because it covers marketing management, manufacturing management, human resource management, service management, sales management, and

---

[9] For example, how many small widgets were sold through agents in the Northeast region during the third quarter?

[10] A terabyte is approximately a million megabytes (= 1024 gigabytes = 2^{40} bytes).

research and development management. Thus, CRM requires organizational and business level approaches which are customer centric.

CRM involves all of the corporate functions required to contact customers directly or indirectly. "Touch points" is used to refer to the many ways in which customers and firms interact. Where ERP is a back-office solution, CRM is a front-office solution because it is concerned with customers.

CRM software is a suite of products that is an outgrowth of two pieces of software called Sales Force Automation and Customer Service. The former dealt with providing computer support to sales people in the field by giving them data about their clients, while the latter focused on supporting what we now refer to as the call center.

In addition to being a sales force management and customer service system, CRM is used to support marketing for gathering and aggregating personal information and information about the sales environment. It keeps track of customer preferences, buying habits, demographics, and sales staff performance. One way of looking at CRM is that it creates an ever-expanding database.

The downside for CRM systems is concern about customer privacy (Chapter 15). Not only does CRM make better use of existing data, it is used for gathering and accumulating new data. The extent of the database itself turns out to be a basic privacy concern.

Knowledge Management (Chapter 7)

Why is knowledge important to businesses? Thomas Davenport and Lawrence Prusak give the answer[11]:

> *"In a global economy, knowledge may be a company's greatest advantage."*

Often it may be the company's only advantage because the firm knows how to do something that other firms don't. To understand knowledge management, we need to define three terms: knowledge, knowledge management, and knowledge management systems:

- *Knowledge* refers to ideas that lead to action. It is distinguished from data (individual facts like the details of a transaction) and information (data put into context). Knowledge may be explicit (you can write it down and put it on a computer) or tacit (in the heads of people but difficult to explain or write down).

- *Knowledge management* is the organizational process for acquiring, organizing, and communicating tacit and explicit knowledge.

- *Knowledge management systems* are information systems designed to facilitate creating, gathering, organizing, and disseminating an organization's *knowledge* rather than its *information* or its *data*.

The claims for knowledge management are quite strong. It is believed that organizations will be more flexible, more responsive to market changes, more innovative, and improve decision making.

Information technology does NOT, by itself, create knowledge, or guarantee that knowledge will be generated or promote knowledge sharing in a culture that does not favor knowledge sharing. It is possible to create a knowledge management system [e.g., for the London Taxi Cabs (Chapter 7)] that does not use computers at all.

---

[11] T. Davenport and L. Prusak, *Working Knowledge,* Cambridge, MA: Harvard Business School Press, 1997.

A key characteristic of knowledge management is that it encourages sharing among people in the organization. To do so, many firms create a separate knowledge base on their computers to which people contribute based on their work and from which people retrieve knowledge they need. Note that only explicit knowledge can be tapped in this way.

Although tacit knowledge remains in people's heads, several means are used to make tacit knowledge explicit. One approach is to create a directory of people that lists each individual's specialties and can be searched by topic and by person. Another, a little more exotic, is to go through the e-mail in the firm regularly and deduce employees' specialized knowledge areas.

Business Intelligence (Chapter 8)

While the term business intelligence (BI) is relatively new, computer-based business intelligence systems appeared, in one guise or other, close to 40 years ago.[12] BI as a term replaced decision support, executive information systems, and management information systems. In brief, BI systems combine data gathering, data storage, and knowledge management with analytical tools to present complex and competitive information to planners and decision makers.

Implicit in this definition is the idea (perhaps the ideal) that business intelligence systems provide actionable information delivered at the right time, at the right location, and in the right form to assist decision makers. The objective is to improve the timeliness and quality of inputs to the decision process, hence facilitating managerial work.

Sometimes business intelligence refers to online decision making. Most of the time, it refers to shrinking the time frame so that the intelligence is still useful to the decision maker when decision time comes. In all cases, use of business intelligence is viewed as being proactive.

Some of this information is structured and some unstructured. Structured information can easily be kept in conventional "databases," that is, rows and columns of information such as are found in spreadsheets. Unstructured information is typified by text and documents.

What Does BI Do?

BI converts data into useful information and, through human analysis, into knowledge. Some of the tasks performed by BI are

- Creating forecasts based on historical data, past and current performance, and estimates of the direction in which the future will go.
- "What-if" analysis of the impacts of changes and alternative scenarios.
- Ad hoc access to the data to answer specific, nonroutine questions.

All of these tasks lead to strategic insight.

The next direction in business intelligence appears to be *business performance measurement*, abbreviated BPM. As its name implies, BPM focuses on the internals of the business and its processes. It tries to find ways to make business units, such as finance and materials resources, more effective. To do so, it uses computer programs that consolidate information from a variety of sources and tries to find ways to improve processes such as planning and forecasting.

The main approach is to provide continuous and real-time feedback that allows risk analysis so that problems are found before they occur. BPM works with key performance indicators to monitor

---

[12] For a history of business intelligence, see the website http://dssresources.com/history/dsshistory.html.

actuals against targets. Such analyses typically look at project performance against forecasts and targets. These analyses can be effective, providing action is also taken. However, they require that data be quite current (preferably close to real time) so that the insights can be applied while they still can do some good.

THE INTERNET

The Internet is a wonderful thing. The Internet is a terrible thing. Both viewpoints exist. From a business point of view, the Internet (also called "The Web" or the "World Wide Web") is a world-wide network that allows the firm to send and receive communications (e.g., e-mail) and to create an electronic location (called a website) where it can post information about itself for others to consult. Started by a Defense Advanced Research Project Agency (DARPA) project, the logical outcome of work going back to the 1960s, the Internet became available for commercial use in the mid-1990s. In the intervening years since then, it became a universal capability through which large and small firms and individuals could be reached.

The Internet introduces new problems to the firm because it opens access to internal data and systems. Should users be able to receive or send personal messages via e-mail? Who owns the e-mail? How do you keep your computers and the data you have on your computers safe from hackers? How do you keep your employees from surfing the Internet during work hours or using the Internet to play games? Does your investment in using the Internet pay off?

This subsection[13] discusses a number of issues about the Internet that are important to managers.

Websites

A website is a collection of documents accessible on the Internet through specialized software called a web browser.[14] Any site on the Web is accessible by typing its name (called a URL, an abbreviation for universal resource locator) in a specific location on the browser. The URL reaches a home page which, in turn, serves as a portal[15] for reaching individual pages. For example, typing http://www.wiley.com reaches the home page of the publisher of this book.

Business websites are used to promote the firm and/or to conduct electronic commerce (Chapter 3). A business website may also contain information (such as white papers, organization charts, press releases, and a listing of subsidiaries), catalogs, order forms, and more. The website often looks like an advertisement or a brochure which can be explored by the user. The content of a website is constrained by the hosting computer's power, and also legally, for example, by copyright and other laws.

Connectivity

From the early simplicity of narrowband phone lines to the broadband connectivity of today, connectivity to the Web keeps increasing. The problem is one of "right sizing," that is, choosing the bandwidth (from phone line to wideband T1 line to fiber optics) appropriate for the firm's operations. Although sending content over the Internet remains free, the connections to the Internet still require payment for the bandwidths used.

---

[13] Some of the material on websites is adapted from http://guide.darwinmag.com/ technology/web/.

[14] Browsers come with a PC, for example, at no cost.

[15] Portals are defined and discussed later in this chapter.

Finding Things Using Search Engines

Search engines, such as Google and Excite, are computer programs that help find and then access websites that contain information stored on the World Wide Web. They allow users to define a set of words or a phrase that serves as a search criterion (e.g., mainframe computers) and receive back a large number of locations that contain information specified by the criterion. Unlike an index that organizes all topics in a book or a directory, a search engine looks for locations only in response to a request. Because of the vast size of the Internet, data collection is automated. While a great help, search engines tend to list many more possibilities (often in the thousands or even millions) than can be examined by an individual. To deal with this problem, search engines use criteria for ordering their findings. Unfortunately, these criteria can be (and are) gamed by people in an effort to have their site appear near the top of the list.

Search engines are also used within a firm's individual website to help visitors find items that are available at that site. They are particularly useful when searching within a complex website such as those of a newspaper, a magazine, or of a medium or large size firm.

Content Management

In creating a corporate website it is not enough to create a good-looking, friendly site using cutting-edge technology. It must offer content that people, particularly customers, can use or else they never come back. You can't expect to set up your site so that it will be sufficient forever. Someone or some group must look after it so that it remains useful and current.

Intranet/Extranet

Intranets and extranets are private networks used to communicate. They use the technology of the Internet but differ from it in that access is limited only to people within the company (intranet) or to specific people inside and outside the company and specific external partners (extranet). Creating an intranet or an extranet is more than just throwing a Web interface around stale corporate data. Intranets need to be kept current and reflect the needs of the people who use them.

Privacy

Privacy (Chapter 15) of electronic information can be a paramount issue because different people have different ideas about personal privacy and how far they will go to protect it. Privacy includes both e-mail and information submitted over the Internet to your firm. Although some firms make money selling lists of customers and personal information about them, firms that develop a reputation for poor privacy protection can rapidly lose their good reputation.

Privacy regulations differ between the United States and the rest of the world, with greater restrictions about privacy abroad. The result is that care must be taken in data moved across borders.

Security

No one likes a thief—especially an invisible one who enters digitally to peruse or destroy sensitive corporate data files or disrupts e-mail. The threats to security come from both disgruntled and unknowing employees and from outside the organization via the Internet. Security is discussed together with privacy in Chapter 15.

Corporate Portals

As the name implies, a portal is a gateway. Corporate portals are really websites that contain links to specific portions of the company's data. They provide corporate information to a specific group such as employees, customers, suppliers, or the public at large. Separate portals may be supplied to each group so that users gain access only to information that they need to know. Portals are usually characterized by a good, easy to navigate indexing scheme that allows people to find information quickly.

Individuals or user groups can customize the portal page to each user's preferences and their need to know. Furthermore, portals usually eliminate the need for users to identify themselves over and over, remembering different names and passwords. Rather, once the portal accepts a user, the user is given access to all places where they are entitled to go from that portal.

When used internally, a portal lets people reach not only the specific data sets they work with but also other information such as corporate news and health care benefits. Some firms are starting to use portals as the entry to business intelligence and competitive intelligence information. Because portals can be customized to define users of particular knowledge, some firms, for example, now post their latest competitive information for use by sales and marketing people.

Portals also serve as a customer connection that allows direct access to portions of the firm's computer base and, in the case of e-business, allows the customer to complete transactions. In a sense, portals dumb down the knowledge required of the customer by simplifying the interaction.

In summary, portals continue to expand in functionality and in targeting access to information. In a sense, internally they apply the principles of customer relationship management to workers in the firm.

Website Development

If a website is difficult to find or to navigate, intended customers may leave before learning anything about a company, its vision, or its products. To keep a website fresh, its content must continually be updated. Such features as

- a "what's new" section,
- a search engine (for large sites) or a site map (for small sites),
- a feedback section that allows users to interact with the site and contact people in the company.

Although a portal is a wonderful invention, it does not come cheap. Multimillion dollar installations are common; for example, this amount was spent by the University of Maryland's School of Business.

Website Traffic Analysis

How do you know your site is a success? Typically, site effectiveness is measured by analyzing its traffic, usually by the number of hits, that is, the number of times the site is accessed. More sophisticated measures involve tracking page requests, unique visitors, or orders.

ANSWERS TO MANAGERIAL QUESTIONS

What is an information system?

An information system is a combination of technology, people, and business processes to capture, transmit, store, retrieve, manipulate, and display information. The information is used in accomplishing work.

What are some major applications of information systems?

Information systems are used to keep track of transactions, in performing back-office functions such as accounting and billing, in supporting sales and marketing, in making decisions, and in deciding on business strategy. Large-scale systems such as enterprise requirements planning, data warehouses, customer relationship management, and business intelligence are information systems applications that are used to do these tasks.

How does the Internet fit in?

The Internet provides communications with other firms and with customers. It is the backbone on which e-commerce and e-mail operate. E-commerce can be business-to-business (B2B) or business-to-customer (B2C). Care must be taken to make Internet connections secure.

Chapter 2

The Big Picture: IT and Business

MANAGERIAL QUESTIONS

When does an information system become strategic?

How can I evaluate the strategic ability of the information systems I have?

What are examples of strategic use?

Is creating strategic advantage easy?

Why should I worry about business–IT alignment?

What are the economics of information technology?

Does information technology matter?

What kinds of information systems are there?

What are interorganizational systems and what can I do with them?

What are the key IT issues in the years ahead?

INTRODUCTION

Information systems are one of the many functions that make up a business. Like each of the other functions, it is vital to the modern business. To run even a small one or two person business requires some information technology, if only to keep records of transactions for tax purposes. Yet, unless IS is being used strategically or is intimately tied into a business process, many business people consider it a form of overhead cost that needs to be minimized.

In this chapter we consider the big questions in information systems. As described in the Managerial Questions above, they include the strategic use of IS, the alignment of IS with the business, the economics of information, the argument about whether IT matters at all in a business, and the key issues in the years ahead.

STRATEGIC ADVANTAGE VERSUS STRATEGIC NECESSITY

The strategic use of information systems can be divided into two groups: those that offer help with obtaining a strategic advantage and those that result from strategic necessity. Strategic advantage refers to obtaining a sustainable competitive edge over competitors. That is, the ability to obtain a greater than normal return on investment. A strategic necessity is a system that must be installed to remain competitive and, often, to stay in business.

Strategic advantage can be obtained from being the first (or dominant) mover to introduce an innovation. It can come from consolidating a first mover position by increasing the barriers to entry such as cost to enter or locking in such a large market share that the remaining market is too small to be worthwhile. It may result from seizing an opportunity from a discontinuity such as bank deregulation.[1]

Sustainable competitive advantage is difficult to achieve through information systems because they can be copied. Even with patent or trade secret protection, competitors can eventually achieve the same functionality. A strategic advantage does give a firm a period of time where it is ahead of the competition and thereby provides the opportunity to keep innovating to stay ahead. And innovating it must do to maintain the advantage.

Just as for other initiatives, competitive advantage does not necessarily go to the first mover for an information system. Although the first mover can usually obtain benefits such as higher market share and product prices, customer loyalty, retention through switching costs, enhanced reputation from being a leader, and many more, the first mover also faces some disadvantages. Disadvantages include development risk because product demand is not known, higher development costs, free rider effects by followers, emergence of a dominant design in the market, and shifts in technology. An example is the early PC makers who were eliminated when IBM entered the market.

Strategic advantage lasts for a finite amount of time because strategic advantages turn into strategic necessities. Classic examples of this change can be found in the following:

1. The automatic teller machine (ATM) which was introduced by the Citizens and Southern National Bank in Atlanta, Georgia,[2] in 1971 without connectivity to the bank's computer system. It rapidly added connectivity and then network capabilities (you can tap into your account from machines worldwide) and swept the world as banks introduced them in an effort to gain strategic advantage. However, once nearly all banks (and other stores such as groceries) had them, they became a bank's strategic necessity to stay in business.

EXAMPLE OF COMPETITIVE ADVANTAGE AND COMPETITIVE NECESSITY

The classic case of strategic advantage was American Airline's SABRE reservation system. An airline needs to know which seats are filled and which are still for sale. When an airplane takes off, all unsold seats are lost revenue. American's original automated system goes back to an installation in New York in 1945.[3] Over the years this system grew to cover the entire network, including information on all flights, not just its own. Moreover, American offered terminals connected to its flight information to travel agents, at a fee. SABRE eventually grew to where it was generating more profit than the operation of the airline that requires large capital investment in airplanes. Clearly, American achieved a major strategic advantage. However, this success was not immediate. It took many years for the system to grow to its full capabilities.

American's competitors were faced with a strategic necessity. They either had to license American's capability or build one of their own. For example, United Airlines built its Apollo system and began competing with American Airlines. Other systems (e.g., Galileo, Amadeus) arose. Today, SABRE is only the third largest reservation system for airlines. However, its many spin-offs (e.g., into railroad reservation systems) provide additional revenue.

The impact of American Airlines' competitive advantage from SABRE can be seen from the impact on European airlines. They were at a competitive disadvantage from, among other things, their lack of an automated reservation system.

---

[1] For example, Merrill Lynch's Cash Management Account, discussed below.

[2] Source: http://www.premiumatm.com/atm_history.html. Last consulted 10-12-03.

[3] H. H. Goode and R. E. Machol, Systems Engineering, p. 14, New York: McGraw-Hill, 1958.

2.   Department stores used to close by 5:30 or 6 P.M. except once a week when they stayed open until 8:30 or 9 P.M. When one department store in a city went to daily 9 P.M. closing, all the others competed by going to late closing. The net effect was that late closing time became the norm rather than being an advantage.

Continual Improvement

To try to maintain strategic advantage, firms undertake continual improvement projects. They use the time gained by their initial advantage to stay ahead. This tactic implies that the strategic advantage can be improved over time. However, some innovations (such as ATMs) reach their limits early and cannot continue to be improved on.

It is important to be aware that the gains from continual improvement are not usually from making the information system more efficient. They come from leveraging other resources of the firm. Here are some examples of continuing improvement:

> *Merrill Lynch Cash Management Accounts.* Information systems are incidental. Determinants are service quality, creating new products that use the accounts, and switching costs.
>
> *American Hospital Supply ASAP.* Customizing the system to the needs of individual hospitals extended this system for customer ordering of hospital supplies.
>
> *McKesson and Robbins Economost.* This order entry system for pharmacies moved from advantage to necessity because, like the ATM, it became the norm for the industry. Although it increased financial results, it did not achieve sustainable higher than average profitability. McKesson was not able to improve Economost at a sufficient rate to stay ahead.

Introducing Strategic Information Systems

Many strategic information systems come about almost accidentally. A firm creates a system to help it internally (e.g., American Airlines to record its seat inventory), finds additional uses for it, and then figures out that their system might be marketed to others and bring revenue. No unique answer, no magic formula exists to ensure successful introduction of a strategic information system. Some generalizations, however, evolved out of experience.

Before discussing these generalizations it is necessary to remember that strategic systems can be built around information or around information technology. Information technology is often the way these systems are tied together. For example, Denny's coffee shops used a standard hardware platform.

EXAMPLE: FEDEX

FedEx, a major package delivering service, started with an automated tracking system that recorded the location and delivery status of every package. Package tracking systems rapidly became a strategic necessity for its competitors.

EXAMPLE: OTISLINE

OTISLINE, a maintenance system introduced by Otis Elevator Company, is an example of continuous improvement. The seemingly innocuous system differentiated Otis from its competitors. It started out by recording the time between when a service call was received and when it was completed.[4] The data helped reduce the time the customer had to wait for service, thereby improving satisfaction. The company centralized its service data and added service performance, cost estimates, and elevator and building information. With this information it was able to determine frequency of breakdown by elevator type and even by elevator. By identifying weak and strong components, the spare parts inventory could be adjusted and incipient failures could be identified. Furthermore, elevator designers could improve failure-prone components both for new systems and for replacement parts.

Otis did not stop there. It expanded the system to give repair people handheld terminals that would bring up the history of the elevator, the building, and the elevator's previous repairs. They increased the priority of emergency calls from elevators stuck between floors.

The next step was to install a microprocessor with communications in every elevator; that is, create a remote elevator monitoring system, which logged performance and communicated elevator problems. Technicians were now dispatched before an elevator went out of service.

In creating a new strategic information system, the following are important:

1. *The Vision.*

   Vision is not a synonym for creativity. Vision does not specify the solution to the problem. Many strategic systems are actually quite mundane.[5] However, both senior management and IS must buy into it.

2. *The People Involved.*

   Not only must the CEO and the Chief Information Officer (CIO, see Chapter 12) buy into the vision, but so must the system's champion[6] and key end users whose work life will be affected.

3. *Catalysts and Barriers to Overcome.*

   Depending on whether they are favorable or unfavorable, the same attributes can be a catalyst or a barrier. Examples are clarity of objectives, technical expertise in IS, the relations between the IS department and the rest of the organization, cost–benefit analysis, incentives (long-term vs. short-term), planning, organizational politics, organizational bureaucracy, and management support. Of particular importance is the alignment of IS with the business, a subject discussed later in this chapter.

4. *Implementation.*

   Strategic information systems are generally large projects and hence quite visible. Implementing them is a major chore. Here are some things for IS in particular (but also the rest of the firm) to look out for:

---

[4] The total time from receiving the call to arrival was an hour and a quarter, and the average service time was also an hour and a quarter. These times are phenomenal, given that Otis operates less than 400 service locations in North America.

[5] For example, Bob Smith, the VP of Otis Elevator said: "When elevators are running well, people do not notice them.... Our objective is to go unnoticed."

[6] A champion is a senior, well-respected person in the organization who acts as the sponsor and advocate for the system, has sufficient "clout" that people respect his/her opinion, and controls some or all of the funds and resources involved. IS projects, particularly strategic ones, without a champion usually die.

- Measure the benefits anticipated in terms of the business objectives that the system supports.
- Make sure the technical infrastructure is integrated into the mainstream. Form partnerships among the departments involved.
- Support the champion just as the champion supports the system.
- Keep management on board. Strategic information systems typically are long-term projects rather than showing results every quarter.

Risks

The previous discussion described various aspects of strategic information systems without considering risk. Yet strategic systems, because of their complexity and their tendency to include innovation, are much riskier than most IS systems. Unfortunately, data on failed systems is difficult to find because no corporate PR group likes to brag about them as they do about the firm's successes.

All information systems, be they strategic or not, encounter intrinsic risks such as over budget, over promised time, failure to meet technical specifications, and scope creep. Strategic information systems add extrinsic risk, the risk of not meeting business objectives.

Among extrinsic risks are

- *Being First.* Although being the first mover with a new system can offer strategic advantage, competitors are given a model on which to improve (e.g., American Airlines' SABRE reservation system). They therefore do not incur as great a development cost. While American Airlines was first and enjoyed a lead for some time, it is only third today because competitors caught up.
- *The Basis for Competition Changes.* A strategic system gains an advantage for a period of time, usually by changing the basis for competition. Yet a change in competition is also a risk because, by technology improvements and new ideas, competitors can change the situation once again. Many firms, once they gain the advantage, tend to stay with their way of doing things while competitors are busy finding ways to change the marketplace. Creating a new information system is one way of changing the basis for competition.
- *Lowering Customer Switching Costs.* Although unintentional, customers may find it cheaper to switch when they need only to switch terminals. To counter this risk, American Hospital Supply kept improving its product to provide services before its competitors could.
- *Legal Intervention.* Given companies' tendency to sue and government antitrust actions, innovations are subject to lawsuits. Patent protection can help but outcomes are always uncertain.
- *Lack of Customer Acceptance.* Like dog foods that dogs won't eat, creating strategic information systems that customers do not buy (e.g., because added infrastructure is needed or they don't see the benefit) is a risk. Unfortunately, you don't find out about such risks until after you've made a large up-front investment.

BUSINESS–IT ALIGNMENT

In recent years, considerable attention has been given to the alignment of information systems with the rest of the business.[7] As information technologies evolve and business strategies change, it is easy for them to get out of alignment. But align they must if the business is to obtain maximum value from its information technology investments.

In thinking about proposed investments, the IS group needs to ask whether the investment makes sense in terms of the company's strategy. Similarly, management needs to examine new IS products and services to see where alignment can be improved. That is, both business appreciation of IT and IT awareness of the business are needed.

Alignment is multidimensional and involves six categories of maturity:

1. Communications
2. Competency/value measurement
3. Governance
4. Partnership
5. Technology scope
6. Skills

We discuss each of these six categories in turn.

- Communications maturity refers to the understanding between executives and IS. Automating ineffective processes or implementing technology for its own sake does not improve the organization's bottom line or improve the view of IS.

- Ways of measuring the contribution of IS should be in place and presented in terms that business people can understand.

- Governance implies a joint decision process between senior executives and IS. The principal shared decisions are project selection and setting priorities.

- Partnership means an equal role for IS with other functions in defining business processes and strategies. For example, IS capabilities determine whether and how processes can be improved.

- In technology, IS's role is to evaluate new technologies, provide and support a flexible infrastructure (Chapter 14), and create or obtain software solutions for the firm. For many companies (particularly in service industries) IS is the only group with technical skills in the firm. An atmosphere of trust must exist between IS and executives on technical matters.

- IS skills need to match the strategy requirements for the firm. For example, if a firm's strategy is to use its data resources in a data warehouse (Chapter 5) for competitive advantage, it needs people skilled in both data warehousing technology and in the analysis of the data produced. When an application innovation is introduced such as, say, customer relationship management (Chapter 6), individuals in IT should be provided a culture and a structure that supports the initiative.

---

[7] For detailed discussions of this topic see J. Luftman, "Assessing IT/Business Alignment" and other articles in a special issue of *Information Systems Management* 20(4): pp. 5-42, Fall 2003.

Assessing the Alignment Maturity Level

Since evaluating business alignment involves multiple criteria, it is inevitable that a firm will be at different levels of maturity on each of the criteria. The evaluation will inevitably be biased unless both business and IT executives evaluate each category. Typically, the evaluation process will produce divergent answers. It is this divergence that indicates where the alignment problems (and opportunities) are. However, after several iterations, the assessment should move toward convergence.

Table 1 shows the summary rating sheet proposed by Luftman.[8] Don't worry at this point if you don't understand all the terms used. Most of them will become clear as you proceed through this book. The important point is for you to see that it is possible to create numeric values for measuring alignment for each category. The numbers correspond to five levels of alignment:

Level	Alignment
1	No alignment
2	Beginning process
3	Establishing process
4	Improved process
5	Complete alignment

Assessment is a four-step process:

1. Form a team of IT and business executives. For large firms, between 10 and 30 people are involved.

2. Gather information either with all people in the same room or via a questionnaire.

3. Decide on individual scores. The purpose of this step is not the number but to understand where the firm stands. Average the scores in each category.

4. If you believe categories should not be weighted equally in your firm, get agreement on relative weights. Average the weighted scores.

ALIGNMENT CONSIDERATIONS

The overall alignment score serves two purposes:

- It is a benchmark that can be used to determine improvement over time.
- It can be used for comparison with other firms.

Fortune 1000 firms running this alignment assessment the first time tend to obtain an overall alignment at Level 2, although they score at Level 3 for a few alignment practices.

Alignment when Strategy Changes

Companies change their strategy from time to time. For example, emphasis may change from internal cost efficiency to providing superb customer service. Such strategy changes create IT alignment problems. The tighter the alignment, the more complex and costly it usually is to change IT so that

---

[8] J. Luftman, op. cit.

Table 1   SUMMARY RATING SHEET FOR MEASURING IT ALIGNMENT WITH BUSINESS STRATEGY

Practice Categories	Practices	Averaged Scores 1 1.5 2 2.5 3 3.5 4 4.5 5	Average Category Score
Communications	1 Understanding of business by IT		
	2 Understanding of IT by business		
	3 Organizational learning		
	4 Style and ease of access		
	5 Leveraging intellectual assets		
	6 IT–business liaison staff		
Competency/ value measurement	7 IT metrics value		
	8 Business metrics measurements		
	9 Link between IT and business metrics		
	10 Service level agreements		
	11 Benchmarking		
	12 Formally assess IT investments		
	13 Continuous improvement practices		
Governance	14 Formal business strategy planning		
	15 Formal IT strategy planning		
	16 Organizational structure		
	17 Reporting relationships		
	18 How IT is budgeted		
	19 Rationale for IT spending		
	20 Senior-level IT steering committee		
	21 How projects are prioritized		
Partnership	22 Business perception of IT		
	23 IT's role in strategic business planning		
	24 Shared risks and rewards		
	25 Managing the IT–business relationship		
	26 Relationship/trust style		
	27 Business sponsors/champions		
Technology scope	28 Primary systems		
	29 Standards		
	30 Architectural integration		
	31 How IT infrastructure is perceived		
Skills	32 Innovative, entrepreneurial environment		
	33 Key IT HR decisions made by:		
	34 Change readiness		
	35 Career crossover opportunities		
	36 Cross-functional training and job rotation		
	37 Social interaction		
	38 Attracting and retaining top talent		

Your Alignment Score:_____

Source: J. Luftman, "Assessing IT/Business Alignment," *Information Systems Management,* p. 14, Exhibit 2 Tally Sheet, Boca Raton, FL: Taylor and Francis Group, LLC, Fall 2003. Used by permission.

it is in harmony with the new strategy, goals, and needs. In our example, a cost-efficient firm might minimize IT costs. Yet, when trying to please the customer, a customer relationship management (Chapter 6) software package may be needed that introduces major expense. Changing strategy implies considering the implication of the change on the IT function.

INFORMATION ECONOMICS

Some years ago, my Dean (the person for whom I worked) asked me: "Is IS a bottomless money pit?" I assured him that it was.

Information systems in organizations are beset by a multiplicity of issues:

1. Information systems are inherently not cheap nor can new systems be provided quickly.

2. Information systems people are well paid (because they possess special skills) but many of them are more interested in their technology than they are in their firm. Labor costs are a major portion of ongoing IT expense.

3. No matter how much IT service and capability is provided, people in other departments want more and they want the latest hardware and software. Of course, they assume that someone else would pay for acquisition, training, and maintenance.

The net effect is an economic love–hate relationship between the people in the firm and the information systems group.

The situation is no better at a macro level. In 1987, Nobel Prize MIT economist Robert Solow said, "We see the computer age everywhere except in the productivity statistics." This statement was enshrined as "the productivity paradox" and economists spent the next decade trying to obtain data to support or refute it. The outcome was that the so-called paradox was disproved, although as you will see below in the discussion of the Carr article, it does not go away. At the national level, Alan Greenspan, Chairman of the Federal Reserve Bank, hailed productivity growth and stated it was due to the use of computers in the economy.

The Search for Productivity

Information systems are installed to gain productivity, whether it is in manufacturing, services, or decision making. Initially (and often still yet), the computer is used to gain productivity by substituting for human labor.

Productivity, at the simplest level, is a measure of the output per worker per unit input of that worker. Although this definition sounds simple, it is difficult to determine, particularly because output is difficult to measure for knowledge workers who use computers.

Productivity is measured in two ways[9]:

1. labor productivity, which considers the output per man-hour,

2. total factor productivity (TFP) that takes into account how effectively both labor and capital are used.

To individuals, labor productivity matters because it determines their standard of living.[10] For economists, however, TFP growth is the key number because they see it as a costless way of

---

[9] Source: "Solving the Paradox," *The Economist,* September 21, 2000.

[10] It is reported that the productivity of U.S. workers increased by a factor of 7 during the twentieth century and that this productivity gain is reflected in the U.S. living standard.

increasing growth without increased use of scarce inputs. Faster TFP growth automatically increases labor productivity.

Labor productivity can be increased through IT in three ways:

1. by increasing the amount of capital invested per worker,

2. by speeding up the growth in TFP in industries that produce IT because of technical improvements, and

3. by speeding up the growth of TFP in sectors that use IT.

Clearly, the growth in the IT producing industry was large since 1980; however, that by itself was not sufficient to be reflected in the national productivity statistics.

Time Lag Effects[11]

Analysis of previous major technological changes, the steam engine and electricity, shows a 40 year lead time between the introduction of the technology into business and its major effects on productivity.[12] Computing, which was introduced into business in the 1960s, does not appear to be an exception.

Growth in productivity refers to the increase in output per worker per unit input. Using data from the U.S. government's Bureau of Labor Statistics, the annual growth in productivity in different periods was

- 2001–2003   4%/year
- 1996–2000   2.6%/year
- Prior to 1996   1.5%/year

The argument made is that the massive investment in computers in the 1990s started paying off in the last several years. The reason for the lag is that just installing equipment and software is not enough. People need to be trained; they need to learn how to use what they have, and over time find innovative ways to use their new capabilities.

The Micro Level

The data at the national economy level are made up of the experience of individual firms. Brynjolfssonn at MIT and Hitt at the Wharton School looked at 600 large U.S. firms in the 1987 to 1994 period and found that computers resulted in productivity gains.[13] On a TFP basis, computers boosted annual growth by 0.25% to 0.5%. Furthermore, the productivity gains increased in individual firms over time, confirming the lag effect. Firms that decentralized were able to achieve the greatest gains.

---

[11] The numbers are based on T. Hoffman, "The Lag Effect," *Computerworld,* p. 40, January 12, 2004.

[12] The leading analyst of this effect is Paul A. David an economist at Stanford University. See, for example, P. A. David, "The Dynamo and the Computer: A Historical Perspective on the Modern Productivity Paradox," *American Economic Review Papers and Proceedings* 1(2): pp. 355-361, 1990.

[13] E. Brynjolfsson, and L.Hitt, "Paradox Lost? Firm-Level Evidence on the Returns on Information Systems," *Management Science* 42(4): pp. 541-558, 1996.

Why Invest?[14]

In measuring productivity, the input and output numbers are obtained by counting—be it hours worked, number of circuit boards used, or the number of checks processed. These standard measures work well if a firm is trying to reduce cost to produce the same product. However, in many cases, managers want to invest for other purposes, for example, to improve service or product quality. In fact, the latter two reasons were found to rank consistently above cost reduction as the investment motive.

ATMs are an example of how conventional measurements can mislead. ATMs, being more convenient, reduced the number of checks written. Yet, for banks, the number of checks cleared was used as a surrogate for measuring productivity. Thus, ATMs could be seen to increase cost (for the machines) while at the same time decreasing output. Thus, when you can count the investment cost but find it difficult to assess benefits, particularly benefits that occur after a time lag, IT can look like a poor investment.

Firm-level data allows measuring some of the productivity intangibles associated with computers. When consumers will pay more for convenience and/or quality, then a firm's income will reflect the increase in intangibles. High-quality firms force low-quality firms to lower price to be competitive. The net effect can be that while the computer-using firms gain revenue, the industry as a whole can remain flat. Thus, industry data does not necessarily reflect the productivity gains being achieved. Firm-level studies consistently found that a dollar of IT capital results in a substantial increase in revenue each year. Of course, the value that IT brings to a company can vary substantially from firm to firm.

Organizational Change

It is unfair to make the simplistic statement that the entire long-term gain in productivity is the result only of the computer. The gain comes from integrating technology with organizational change that takes advantage of the technology. Generally, for every dollar invested in IT, several dollars need to be invested in organizational change to achieve the rise in productivity and value.

Peter Drucker,[15] the renowned management guru, argued as early as 1988 that technology-rich firms would change to a flatter form from hierarchical organizations. In such firms highly skilled knowledge workers would be more involved in making decisions. We are also seeing self-directed work systems, flexible production, and business process redesign. These organizational changes are only possible because of information technology and low cost communications. Are both high IT use and high decentralization needed to achieve the productivity gain? In an analysis of the relations between them,[16] it was found that high productivity and high decentralization are indeed correlated.

---

[14] E. Brynjolfsson and L. Hitt, 1996, op cit.

[15] P. F. Drucker, "The Coming of the New Organizations," *Harvard Business Review* 66(1): pp. 45-53, 1988.

[16] E. Brynjolfsson and L. Hitt, 1996, op. cit.

Some Practical Problems

Although the data show that computerization can lead to productivity gains, several practical problems need to be overcome. Examples abound of such problems. Here are two of them from a manufacturing context:

1. When a new system is installed, workers (often unconsciously) wind up resisting the change. They are not trying to sabotage the change, but they simply use their old habits. In conventional assembly line manufacturing, the main objective is to keep the machines running and to create long intervals between changes. When a flexible or a "cell" manufacturing system is introduced, the old habits make people try to use the new machines just like the old ones, thereby negating the hoped-for gain.

2. Although managers want to empower workers to make decisions, many are afraid to do so. They want to talk about last night's ball game, not improving quality control.

The lesson here is that simply introducing computerization is not enough. The cost of the equipment was the smaller part of the investment in the new manufacturing system. The bigger part was changing the organization and its work habits. Investment in the organizational costs needs to be included if the productivity gains are to be achieved. The organizational investments and the technology investments need to be in alignment.

DOES INFORMATION TECHNOLOGY MATTER?

In the May 2003 issue of the *Harvard Business Review*, Nicholas Carr, then editor at large of the magazine, wrote a lead article entitled "IT Doesn't Matter," a polemic, in which he argued that the days when IT offered strategic advantage are long since gone and that managers therefore should undertake a different approach to IT. The article, obviously, became notorious among people who make their living in information systems but was hailed by many who had experienced the love–hate relationship with IS. Even 2 years after it appeared, the article still stirs raw emotion among IS people. Viewpoints range from "How Dare He!" to "Right On!" Many, even people in the supposedly cloistered halls of academe, are engaged in the debate. Most of them, of course, take the former view.

Our objective in this section is to discuss Carr's arguments and the arguments for and against Carr's position.

Carr's Argument[17]

"What makes a resource ... the basis for a sustained competitive advantage—is not ubiquity but scarcity. You only gain an edge over rivals by having or doing something that they can't have or do.... The core functions of IT ... have become available to all. Their very power and presence have begun to transform them from potentially strategic resources into commodit(ies). They are ... costs of doing business ... paid by all but provide distinction to none."

Starting with this premise, Carr concludes that there is no advantage to be had from IT. Therefore, he argues, firms should spend as little as possible for IT both in people and in treasure since the primary objective for commodities is to minimize their cost.

---

[17] N. Carr, "IT Doesn't Matter," *Harvard Business Review* 85(5): pp. 41-49, May 2003.

Carr argues that in recent years, particularly during the dot.com era, too much money was being invested in IT with little to show for it. Therefore, he argues, it is time to call a halt. Enough is enough.

Carr doesn't actually say that IT doesn't matter. While he acknowledges that IT is essential for business operations, he makes the case that IT should be managed as a commodity input, squeezing cost out of IT budgets while at the same time ensuring that IT platforms deliver the necessary reliability and security to avoid business disruptions.[18]

The Response to Carr

The most cogent response to Carr is by Michael Schrage,[19] codirector of the MIT Media Lab eMarkets Initiative and a columnist for *CIO* magazine. Schrage argues that free and easy access to a commodity does not determine its strategic economic value to the company. Rather, management matters. That is, how the commodity is managed that determines its impact. He says: "The idea that companies can divorce their resources—no matter how cheap, powerful and ubiquitous—from the act of managing them is patently absurd."

This Book's Position

This book takes the position that Schrage is right: IT is a management problem. Further, it recognizes that few firms below the Fortune 500 (and even some of those) can afford all the IT tools that are now available. They must select which applications to undertake and must assign sufficient managerial effort and energy to obtain the benefits that can be achieved. Unless managers understand how they are (or are not) involving their company when they make a decision about information technology, they run the risk of making the wrong decision.

Before proceeding to discuss some of the issues involved, we devote the next several pages to considering the arguments for and against Carr's position. [20]

The Arguments for Carr

Until the mid-1990s, IT was unique for companies because most computer applications were either proprietary or highly modified from the basic computer packages that were on the market. Thus, Merrill Lynch with its Money Market accounts, American Airlines with its SABRE seat reservation system and its customer loyalty program, and American Hospital Supply with its online ordering were able to gain competitive advantage. These systems were strategic because they gained competitive advantage by moving computing from back-office operations (e.g., payroll, accounting) into customer-centric applications. Unfortunately, because the advantage came from computer programs, their general features could be copied and copied quickly. The competitive advantage did not last long. Innovators, in effect, had to keep inventing so that they would not be overtaken.

The early computer packages were generic and not tweaked for specific industries. Today's programs are industry specific, most "right out of the box." That is, they are commodities unless they are customized to distinguish the firm from its competitors. However, customizing is not cheap. Rarely can the return on investment (ROI) be justified. Worse, the application vendors continually

---

[18] J. Hegel and J. S. Brown, "IT Does Matter," http://www.johnhagel.com/blog20030515.html.

[19] M. Schrage, "Why IT Really Does Matter," *CIO* August 1, 2003.

[20] The discussion that follows is based on L. DeJarnett, R. L. Laskey, and H. E. Trainor, "From the CIO Point of View: The 'IT Doesn't Matter' Debate," *Communications of AIS* 13, p. 26, April 2004.

modify their programs, which implies that customizing must be repeated each time the program is upgraded. That's not a winning combination.

Another support for the Carr argument comes from IT itself. Many IT organizations lack people with user experience and perspective. Their people tend to be technocentric with internal rather than company goals. They seem to speak a strange language. The result is that they do not communicate well, if at all, with the rest of the enterprise. Furthermore, most firms experience some IT failures: systems that don't work, are delivered late, are over budget, or all of these three. Although each failure may be explainable and understandable, people in the rest of the organization only remember the outcome, the times they were burned by an IT venture. The net effect is that many IT organizations lack credibility within their own firm.

Carr's rules for firms that follow his viewpoint are

1. Spend less.
2. Follow, don't lead.
3. Focus on the risks of IT, not the opportunities.

These dicta are hard to argue with. Companies that spend the most on IT do not necessarily do the best financially. Following rather than leading reduces risk. Vulnerabilities from technical glitches, outages, and security breaches are threats. These arguments make sense to a CEO or CFO.

Note that if a company gives up on IT as its strategic advantage, then it needs to find some other means of distinguishing itself in the marketplace, for example, patents, branding, or superb service.

The Arguments against Carr's Position

The Carr article triggered a series of letters to the *Harvard Business Review* to rebut Carr's position. Here are some excerpts[21]:

> *IT adds great first mover value: "With standards in place, the IT staff can finally concentrate on ... applications that reflect the firm's distinctive characteristics and allow it to share information easily with customers and suppliers." IT is not a commodity because, "Even the most tightly controlled generic application suite ... can deliver completely different results for look-alike firms."*

Paul Strassman, former CIO for the department of
Defense and for Xerox Corporation

> *While there are no innovative ways of using other infrastructure commodities like electricity, adding the human element to IT proves that more is going on here than meets Carr's eye. It's actually business practice innovation plus IT innovation that results in success: "The differentiation is not in IT itself but in the new practices it enables. IT does indeed matter," citing Wal-Mart and Dell as companies that used IT to help build and sustain strategic advantage.*
>
> *"It has never been true that IT matters in isolation. It only matters in the context of a concerted effort to innovate based on new possibilities and opportunities offered by the technology. Then it matters—and will continue to—a lot."*

John Seeley Brown, former Chief Scientist at Xerox and
John Hagel III, management consultant

---

[21] These comments are based on the letters to *Harvard Business Review* responding to the Carr article. They were organized by Line 56.com http://www.line56.com/articles/default.asp? NewsID=4650.

Carr asks why lead in IT when being first follower is easy, timely, and involves less risk? "The fast fol-lower is up against less risk but also has to recover lost ground," they noted, offering Charles Schwab versus Merrill Lynch, and Walgreens versus CVS as examples. American Airlines' SABRE reservation system, an IT innovation, is responsible for the very existence of "an otherwise doomed" organization.

Warren McFarlan and Richard L. Nolan, Harvard Business School professors

Carr's point that "simple possession of infrastructure technology" is in itself a misguided premise, because it is actually the integration of innovative processes with technology (as in the case of Wal-Mart and Dell) that leads to real IT benefits.

Marianne Broadbent, Mark McDonald, and Richard Hunter of Gartner Group

"Information systems can be embedded in a company's ... processes and combined inextricably with other capabilities and assets to produce superior performance."

Vladimir Zwass, professor Fairleigh-Dickinson University and editor of the
Journal of Management Information Systems

John Hegel III and John Seeley Brown (whose letter is cited above) also wrote:[22]

Extracting business value from IT requires innovations in business practices. *In many respects, we believe Carr attacks a red herring—few people would argue that IT alone provides any significant business value or strategic advantage.*

The economic impact from IT comes from incremental innovations, rather than "big bang" ini-tiatives. *A process of rapid incrementalism enhances learning potential and creates opportunities for further innovations.*

The strategic impact of IT investment comes from the cumulative effect of sustained initiatives to innovate business practices in the near-term. *The strategic differentiation emerges over time, based less on any one specific innovation in business practice and much more on the capability to innovate continually around the evolving capabilities of IT.*

TYPES OF INFORMATION SYSTEMS

Computer-based information systems are usually classified into three broad categories:

- Transaction processing systems
- Management information systems
- Decision support systems

Transaction Processing Systems

Transaction processing systems are the workhorses that create much of the productivity gains from computerization. In retail establishments, the day of the clerk laboriously entering every sale, pay-ment, and return by hand and ringing up the cash register are long gone. Rather, clerks scan a bar code and punch a keyboard or swipe a credit card, and see the transaction recorded on a screen. Sitting underneath this activity is a computer (often one bought long ago and now called a legacy) and its software that records the transaction and keeps track of simple quantities such as the total sales and returns by register.

---

[22] Published in John Hegel III's weblog: http://www.johnhagel.com/perspectives.html May 15, 2003.

Management Information Systems

Although transaction systems do well at keeping track of individual events as they occur and can create some totals, they do not give a picture to managers of how well or poorly a business is doing. That's the next step up. Here, for example, the information system aggregates the transactions in various ways: by department, by store, by line of business, by sales person, and more. The core of management information system is the standard and ad hoc reports it produces. These reports allow first-level, mid-level, and senior managers to keep track of where their organization stands.

In more formal terms, a management information system (MIS) provides previous, current, and forecast information needed for planning, organizing, and controlling business operations. Management information systems deal with structured problems; that is, problems which are repetitive and well understood.

Decision Support Systems

Decision support systems (DSS) deal with semistructured problems. Such problems arise when managers are faced with decisions where some but not all aspects of a procedure or task are known. To solve these problems and use the results for decision making requires judgment of the person using the system. Typically, such systems include models, data manipulation tools, and the ability to handle risk and uncertainty. Thus, for example, decision support systems can include the ability to do what-if analysis to look at the impact of changes in assumptions, goal seeking to find the value of the inputs needed to reach specified objectives (e.g., profit level, return on investment), and simulation capabilities to show the potential distribution of outcomes. Models may include standard financial models or more complex management science models.

A simple form of decision support system is a spreadsheet. It can be used for what-if analysis, for goal seeking, and, with add-in software, for simulation.

A sophisticated form is a group decision support system (GDSS). The idea is to use the computer to support groups of people involved in a decision. Although the early efforts in GDSSs were designed to help people in a conference, the present technology focuses on Web-based systems, such as Lotus Notes and Domino from IBM and NetMeeting from Microsoft , that help people dispersed in time and space.

Knowledge-Based and Other Systems

In recent years, a number of large-scale specialized computer-based systems were developed that don't fit neatly into the three categories of transaction systems, MIS, and DSS. We will discuss a number of them in the following chapters of this book. As indicated in Chapter 1, these specialized systems include (in alphabetical order) business and competitive intelligence, customer relationship management (CRM), data mining, enterprise requirements planning (ERP), knowledge management, and supply chain management.

INTERORGANIZATIONAL COMPUTING

Interorganizational computing is the last step in an evolution of business computing:

1960s	Stand-alone applications for a single business or SBU
1970s	Online and integrated applications that support multiple applications

| 1980s | Enterprisewide computing where data are a computer resource across multiple computer systems |
| 1990s forward | Leverage data and information technology across firms. |

As implied by the list, interorganizational computing refers to sharing computer information (and systems) between two or more firms. An example is the national networks for ATMs that allow you to use almost any bank's ATM machine to access your account at another bank. Sharing can also be the result of the greater interdependence of firms as they rely on one another as parts of the supply chain (Chapter 11).

Interorganizational computing does not imply the need for major new hardware and software. The technology that is used for enterprisewide computing is applied to allow access to people outside the organization. These systems also require communications access, but that is often handled through the World Wide Web. The systems need to know (e.g., by creating lists) which outside firms are to be given access to which data. Access is a matter of security (Chapter 15) about what is critical to the firm. For example, a firm may be willing to share information about anticipated demand to their supplier (so that supply can be adjusted to anticipated production) but not pricing and certainly not customer lists.

A common way to think about interorganizational systems is in terms of four questions[23]:

- *Why?* Is there a business purpose? Can you leverage the existing business or enter a new business?

- *Who?* Who participates (customers, dealers, suppliers, competitors)?

- *What?* What information capabilities are given to participants? Do these capabilities include entering, storing, and manipulating data? The specific capabilities depend on the way the firms cooperate.

- *How?* How do participants improve the way they work together?

In the "what" question, three ways of cooperating can be defined. The simplest is a boundary transaction where one firm enters an order or scans a catalog. More complex is where a firm's database is shared among participants, such as the FedEx tracking system for packages. The greatest complexity occurs when the firm helps its clients perform their internal functions, for example, maintaining inventory in a drugstore.

Interorganizational systems, working between separate legal entities, can introduce legal problems. For example, when does an e-mail become an order or an order cancellation?

Replacing Intermediation through Electronic Markets

Interorganizational systems started with electronic data interchange where two or more business partners exchanged orders according to a rigid format to gain operational efficiencies. These systems are now expanded to where a firm can scan the price and availability lists of its vendors to find the best vendor with whom to place an order.

Electronic markets reduce the need for intermediation, since they are themselves intermediaries. Whether it is Reuters for currency exchange or NASDAQ for brokering stocks, the communications link replaces the intermediary. Disintermediation is also the case in air travel, where the share of bookings by travel agents (the intermediaries) declined significantly as travel schedules and prices became available online and electronic tickets replaced physical tickets.

---

[23] Neumann, op. cit., p. 58.

KEY ISSUES

For over 25 years, periodic surveys sponsored by the Society for Information Management (SIM)[24] were made to determine the key issues in information systems. This section describes the most recent of these surveys, taken in 2003.

The results are based on 253 responses from SIM members and 48 from the Conference Board.[25]

The top 10 managerial concerns are listed in Table 2 and then described individually.

Table 2   TOP 10 MANAGERIAL CONCERNS ABOUT IT

1. IT and business alignment	6. Measuring performance of IT organizations
2. IT and strategic planning	7. Creating an IT architecture
3. Security and privacy	8. Avoiding complexity
4. The supply of IT professionals	9. Speed and agility
5. Measuring the value of IT investments	10. IT governance

Source: J. Luftman and E. R. McLean, "Key Issues for IT Executives," *MISQ Executive* 3(2): p. 91, June 2004, copyright by the University of Minnesota. Used by permission.

1.   *IT and Business Alignment.*

Alignment of the IT organization, discussed earlier in this chapter, implies that IT is applied appropriately and in a timely way. Thus, IT should be in harmony with business strategies. Re-alignment may be needed when corporate strategy changes.

2.   *IT Strategic Planning.*

Strategic planning differs from strategic use of IT (Chapter 1). It is closely related to IT and business alignment.

3.   *Security and Privacy.*

The vulnerability of IT to terrorists, hackers, viruses, and other ills as well as the loss of privacy and the threat of identity theft are included here. Security and privacy (Chapter 15) also relate to homeland security.

4.   *The Supply of IT Professionals.*

Despite the recession of the early 2000s and the offshoring of jobs (Chapter 9) that led to extensive layoffs, firms believe that attracting, developing, and retaining IT professionals is a serious problem. The fewer people studying IT in the universities and the shortage of people who can manage the new global sources are particularly worrying.

5.   *Measuring the Value of IT Investments.*

As discussed earlier in this chapter, there is a division of opinion, based on interpreting the IT productivity statistics and represented by articles such as Carr's, on whether IT makes a difference

---

[24] The Society for Information Management (SIM), located in Chicago, Illinois, is an international professional association of about 3000 senior people in information systems, most of who are IS executives and Chief Information Officers. Established in 1968, SIM is a community of thought leaders who share experiences and intellectual capital, and who explore future IT direction. The data in this survey is presented in J. Luftman and E. R. McLean, "Key Issues for IT Executives," *MIS Quarterly Executive* 3(2): June 2004, on which this discussion is based.

[25] http://www.conference-board.org.

in the firm's bottom line. Part of the problem is that it is difficult to measure the contribution of particular IT projects or of IT as a whole to the business. Simply saying that a firm would close down without its IT capabilities is not enough.

6. *Measuring the Performance of IT Organizations.*

Just as it is difficult to measure the economic impacts of IT at both the national and firm level, it is difficult to determine how well a particular IT organization is doing. Is the IT organization developing applications cost-effectively? Is it doing a good job compared to IT organizations in similar firms? Only a few firms try to use quantitative measurements to measure performance.

7. *Creating an Information Architecture.*

Architecture is usually thought of in terms of the plans and aesthetics of a building. In IT, "architecture" describes how the firm's infrastructure (its processors, its PCs, its networks, its software, and other components) works together. Over time, the architecture of a firm becomes more complex and the need to integrate the pieces (Chapter 10) becomes greater. Some equipment and software become legacies in that they come from an earlier era and must work with later acquisitions. Integration is a difficult task and never seems finished. Outsourcing (Chapter 9) becomes an appealing alternative if integration becomes too difficult to do well.

8. *Reducing Complexity.*

Complexity is linked to architecture. If a firm streamlines its information architecture by creating common IT platforms and standard configurations, it reduces complexity. Complexity is also an issue with respect to the IT hardware, software, and services that a firm buys. Vendors continually offer upgrades and additional features, many of which do not serve a business purpose but which incur training and conversion costs.

9. *Speed and Agility.*

As the business pace quickens, the time available for activities and changes moves from years to months or weeks. IT must be able to deal with this time compression if the firm is to lead rather than follow. IT, like other parts of the business, is moving into a "sense and respond" mode and must attain as much if not more speed and agility than other functions.

10. *IT Governance.*

Governance refers to how IT is organized and run. Some firms use an IT steering committee, consisting of executives from the other functions and the Chief Information Officer, to provide policy and governance oversight. The steering committee also sets priorities for the order in which projects should be accomplished when the number of desirable projects exceeds the funds and manpower available. In this approach, the CIO doesn't become the one who determines whose job gets done next. Others argue that no other function in a business has a steering committee (e.g., a marketing steering committee? an accounting steering committee?) and that therefore IT should not be singled out.

Although issues moved up and down over the years, most of them were in the top 10 on many of the previous lists. Therefore it is reasonable to expect that the current issues will still be there in the years ahead. Note that, over time, the emphasis shifted from the top five concerns, including two or three technology issues, to the 2003 survey where the top five issues were all business related.

Table 3 shows the issues ranked from 11 to 20.

Some of the issues in Table 3 such as managing outsourcing relationships (15), Sarbanes–Oxley (17), and societal impacts (20) can well be expected to become more important in the future.

Table 3   ISSUES RANKED 11 TO 20

11. Business process reengineering	16. Leveraging the legacy investment
12. Introducing rapid business solutions	17. Sarbanes–Oxley Act of 2002
13. The evolving role of the CIO	18. Globalization
14. IT asset management	19. Impact of offshore outsourcing on IT careers
15. Managing outsourcing relationships	20. Societal implications of IT

Source: J. Luftman and E. R. McLean, "Key Issues for IT Executives," *MISQ Executive* 3(2): p. 91, June 2004, copyright by the University of Minnesota. Used by permission.

Application and Technology Developments

In addition to looking at the managerial concerns, this survey also ranked application and technology developments. The 13 areas identified are listed in Table 4.

Unlike the key issues for management described above, where many issues reappeared year after year, only infrastructure development (which appeared in 1994 as issue 1) reappeared in 2003. The reason is that all the other technologies are effectively new since 1994.[26]

The top application, business intelligence (Chapter 8), combines many other applications and technologies, including data warehousing and data mining (Chapter 5), CRM (Chapter 6), and knowledge management (Chapter 7) so that firms can leverage information about their own business and their competitors and make improved decisions. Business intelligence, in particular, makes use of large data bases to help managers assess the firm's performance better and improve its operational productivity.

On the other hand, e-business strategies (Chapter 3), which was first or near first in many recent surveys, slipped to sixth, indicating that we are beginning to understand e-business better and are able to make it just another way of delivering products.

Table 4   RANKING OF APPLICATION AND TECHNOLOGY DEVELOPMENTS

1. Business intelligence	8. Customer relationship management (CRM)
2. Infrastructure development	9. Enterprise resource planning (ERP)
3. Enterprise application integration	10. Employee portals
4. Web services	11. Mobile and wireless applications
5. Knowledge management	12. Supply chain management
6. E-business strategies	13. Supplier portals
7. Customer portals[27]	

Source: J. Luftman and E. R. McLean, "Key Issues for IT Executives," *MISQ Executive* 3(2): p. 96, June 2004, copyright by the University of Minnesota. Used by permission.

---

[26] Although there were precursors and early versions in 1994 for some of the technologies and applications (such as ERP) listed in Table 3, they all rose to prominence in the years since then.

[27] Portals, discussed briefly in Chapter 1, refer to gateways to websites, which may be public (e.g., Yahoo or Google) or private (e.g., to a corporate website). A customer portal, for example, is designed to lead prospective buyers through the various wares offered by vendors such as Dell or an auction house such as eBay. Employee portals are available only to people who work in a firm. They can include, for example, human relations information (e.g., work rules or forms to be filled out), parts lists, or company private knowledge bases.

ANSWERS TO MANAGERIAL QUESTIONS

When does an information system become strategic?

An information system becomes strategic when it helps a firm increase its return on investment above the normal level in an industry. Strategic advantage tends to be transient because the functions and outputs of strategic information systems can be copied.

How can I evaluate the strategic ability of the information systems I have?

Most strategic systems were developed for other purposes. They became strategic when they were modified to perform functions that had not been done before and management understood that the new product or service would change the terms of competition in their industry.

What are some examples of strategic use?

Airline reservation systems, online customer ordering systems, Merrill Lynch's Cash Management account, and Otis Elevator's maintenance system.

Is creating strategic advantage easy?

No, definitely not. It requires vision, strong implementation, dealing with risks, and more.

Why should I worry about business–IT alignment?

Business–IT alignment measures how well the objectives and actions of the information systems group coordinate with and support the objectives of the firm as a whole. If they are not aligned, the firm is wasting resources.

What are interorganizational systems and what can I do with them?

In simplest terms, interorganizational systems allow sharing computer information (and systems) between two or more firms.

What are the economics of information technology?

The large, continuing investment by firms in information technology is designed to improve productivity in the office and the factory. Whether the productivity gains pay for the investment was long a subject of dispute. As we moved into the twenty-first century, it became clear from data at both the national and the firm level that the desired productivity gains are being achieved and that they can be expected to continue into the future.

However, just spending money on IT is not enough. IT changes the way people work. Thus, it is necessary to introduce organizational changes to take advantage of the technology. Simply making a new system act like an old system is not sufficient.

Investments in information technology are also designed to improve customer service and product quality, which turn out also to increase productivity.

Does information technology matter?

Critics of IT argue that information technology no longer distinguishes firms from one another. That is, since everyone can buy and use the same equipment and software, IT is a commodity. Therefore, IT costs should be minimized. The counterargument to this view is that firms that are clever in the way they use IT can, in fact, outcompete others in their industry. IT advocates argue that free and easy access to a commodity does not determine its strategic economic value to a company. Rather, management matters. That is, how the commodity is managed determines its impact. Schrage, for example, says, "The idea that companies can divorce their resources—no matter how cheap, powerful, and ubiquitous—from the act of managing them is patently absurd."

What kinds of information systems are there?

Information systems are characterized by what they do. They range from transaction processing systems (TPS) that keep track of events as they occur, to management information systems (MIS) that aggregate events and provide the data managers need to keep the business running, to decision support systems that combine data and models to help solve semistructured problems. In addition, specialized systems are used for such tasks as enterprise requirements planning, managing knowledge, business and competitive intelligence, customer relationship management, and supply chain management.

What are the key IT issues in the years ahead?

The three top management issues are

- Business–IT alignment
- IT strategic planning
- Security and privacy

The three top application and technology developments are

- Business intelligence
- Infrastructure development
- Enterprise application integration

Complete lists are provided in the Key Issues section of this chapter.

PROBLEMS

1. STRATEGIC INFORMATION SYSTEMS

    Consider your own industry (or one with which you are familiar). Describe the strategic advantages that have been gained by your firm and by your competitors through information technology. Indicate which of these are still competitive advantages and which have become strategic necessities. Indicate the time periods for both advantages and necessities. In addition to listing the changes that occurred, pick one and describe its history in detail.

2. DOES IT MATTER?

    Examine the original Carr article in *Harvard Business Review*, the responses to the article, if possible Carr's book on *IT Doesn't Matter*, and the *Communications of AIS* article (http://cais.isworld.org/contents.asp Volume 13, Article 26, April 2004). Consider Carr's main arguments and discuss why you agree or disagree with each of them. Give examples from your own firm if possible.

3. BUSINESS–IT ALIGNMENT

    Consider a firm where business and IT are finally aligned. Suppose something occurs in the business (e.g., a change in profitability, a new technology by a competitor, a new CEO with a different approach) that causes the firm to change direction or change its way of doing business. At this point, the work on alignment has to be done over to face the new realities. Describe some of the things that can be done by IT (and/or the business) to realign. Use specific examples of situations and responses. Consider the costs and benefits involved.

4. INFORMATION ECONOMICS

    The key argument made for investment in information systems is that IT increases productivity. Such arguments are relatively straightforward when transaction processing systems are considered. However, it is not as clear that they apply when other types of information systems, such as decision support systems are involved. Present arguments (pro or con) on why the other types of systems considered in this chapter lead to productivity improvements for the firm.

5. WEB-BASED SYSTEMS

    The 1990s were the era of client-server hardware systems. The idea was that rather than doing all the computing at centrally located mainframes, the computer at a worker's desk would perform the calculations needed to create the interface and other functions. A countertrend was the thin client, where all computing was done centrally and the terminals are given little or no computer capability. A third way, an evolution in the twenty-first century, is the use of web-based (e.g., Internet) computing where users need only use the browser on their machines. Discuss the advantages and disadvantages of the three ways of organizing computing.

Chapter 3

Electronic Commerce

MANAGERIAL QUESTIONS

What is e-commerce?

What benefits can I expect?

How much is it going to cost?

What are the risks?

What are electronic markets?

What do I need to do to become involved as a pure dot-com?

What do I need to do to take my brick-and-mortar business into e-commerce?

INTRODUCTION

The more things change, the more they remain the same.

Old French Proverb

E-commerce may well fit this proverb. Commerce is certainly not new. E-commerce, that is, the use of communications and electronics to conduct commerce, is also not new. Think of some examples:

- People wired money to their children at school almost since the telegraph became commercial.
- Large firms figured out they could save money by using electronic data interchange, a system for placing orders and exchanging messages that can be traced back to the 1948 Berlin Airlift.

E-commerce, from one point of view, simply adds one more channel for communicating among business partners and between business and consumers.

This view is not the popular one. The "Electronic Superhighway'" and e-commerce were hailed (hyped?) only a few years ago as a new be-all and end-all that would change business forever.

In the heady days of dot-coms, many firms combined e-commerce with unusual business models to deal with consumers, for example:

- Offer the product at no cost to the consumer and gain revenue from selling advertisements. Many information providers tried this approach. Google is an example where this approach was successful.

- Offer products and services only over the Internet, thereby reducing the costs associated with "brick and mortar" for stores and offices. Amazon.com is the classic Internet-only store.

- Let consumers offer merchandise and let other consumers bid on it. That is, run a massive auction house such as eBay designed for everyone rather than just the rich.

- Be a personal shopper (e.g., Priceline.com) who scours the Internet to find the best price for an item such as an airline ticket.

- Use the Internet as a catalog that creates demand.

Looking at these business models it is clear that they, too, were around a long time. Auction houses, brokers, Penny Savers in the mail, mail-order houses, telephone marketing, and 800-numbers advertised on TV are precursors of e-commerce business models.

What is new is the use of electronic communications, in particular the Internet. Since the Internet allows you to conduct business with individuals in their homes or offices rather than having the individual come to your premises or your salesperson visiting them, the business models just described become much more attractive. Furthermore, the Internet allows business to be conducted 24 hours a day, seven days a week (known as 24/7, for short).

The Internet, of course, is the key information technology that makes e-commerce possible. Most business is conducted via the World Wide Web, a collection of hardware, software, and communications that allows people to work together any time and any place. The Internet goes back to developments in the late 1960s for managing government crises.[1] However, it did not become available for commercial use until the mid-1990s. In the years since then, it moved from being a hobby for technocrats to being a useful communications tool.

To see the pervasiveness of the Internet, consider the range of things people do using the Internet (Table 1).

Table 1 WHAT PEOPLE DO ON THE INTERNET

What people do	Examples
Communicate	E-mail, chat rooms, videos, voice
Work	Telecommute, cooperative work
Find, learn	Surf, use databases
Do business	Electronic data interchange, place orders, exchanges
Shop	Catalogs, advertisements
Invest	Stock market trades, investment advice, money management
Play	Games, video on demand, casinos

[1] Murray Turoff and his associates at the Institute for Defense Analysis developed the initial system. Turoff is now a professor at the New Jersey Institute of Technology (NJIT).

SIDEBAR 1	*Timeline of the Steps Along the E-commerce Highway*

1970s	Electronic funds transfer between banks (now ranges to debit cards and income tax payments)	Late 1980s	Chat rooms, newsgroups
		1990s	Groupware and cooperative work
		1995	World Wide Web
1980s	Electronic interchange for business to business transactions	Coming	Internet 2

WHAT IS INVOLVED IN E-COMMERCE?

E-commerce involves carrying out all or part of a business transaction using electronic means. The transaction can be

- *B2B*. Business to business, where the seller and buyer are both firms (e.g., Intel and its business customers and suppliers).
- *B2C*. Business to consumer, where the buyer is the end user of the product (e.g., Amazon.com).
- *C2C*. Consumer to consumer, where consumers both sell and buy (e.g., eBay).
- *C2B*. Consumers indicate a need for a product or service and vendors compete for the business (e.g., Priceline.com).
- *G2C*. Government provides information or services to citizens using the Internet.
- *Intrabusiness*. Electronic transactions among different parts of a business. Sales to employees are a special case.
- *M-commerce*. The use of cell phones and other wireless devices for e-commerce. This category is really a subset of each of the previous cases in that it deals with *how* communication takes place rather than who the participants are.

The use of the Internet is a different way of conducting business. Although the public thinks about the Internet as a freeway for e-commerce, it is not free. (It is, however, often much, much cheaper at the margin than other communications means once the infrastructure is in place.)

The potential for revenue from e-commerce can be quite large. For example, when Intel opened its Web-ordering connection, it started doing $1 million in business from the first day. Toshiba reduced its cost per order to $10.

As will be shown in this chapter, to realize the potential of e-commerce, firms must be willing to change the way they do business. That is, they must change processes, speed of operation, hours during which they do business, and more.

SOME E-COMMERCE STATISTICS

Before proceeding to the nuts and bolts of e-commerce, we present statistics that indicate both the size of e-commerce as an industry and the potential clients that can be reached. What is evident is that e-commerce is taking place much more at the B2B level than at the B2C level.

Retail

The Economics and Statistics Administration of the U.S. Census Bureau routinely reports U.S. e-commerce retail sales as well as total U.S. retail sales. Table 2 shows the data for the second quarter of 2001 through the second quarter of 2004, every even quarter. These data are not corrected for seasonalities, shopping days, or other normalizations usually performed on such data.

These figures indicate that:

- on a relative basis, the percentage of retail sales that are e-commerce is terribly tiny in the annual three and a half trillion retail market (~900 billion/quarter) and

- on an absolute basis, $65 billion annually is a very large niche market.

Note that these numbers do not include online travel sales, financial brokers, and ticket sales. That would make the absolute numbers larger but would not change the share of the retail total significantly.

Business to Business (B2B)

Although the conventional thinking is that e-commerce is retail because of what is published in the newspapers, the statistics show that the major market is, in fact, business to business. In 2002, for example,[2] e-commerce accounted for 11.8% of merchant wholesaler shipments. However, 85% of these sales were via EDI.

TECHNOLOGY

The underlying, pervasive technology is the use of communications networks. These networks take three forms:

- *Internet*. A public, worldwide network that is now universal. It links businesses, governments, and education.

- *Intranets*. Private Internets for a firm. An Intranet may be within a single location (such as a corporate headquarters) or may connect multiple locations.

- *Extranets*. A private Internet that connects multiple firms.

Table 2   TOTAL RETAIL AND E-COMMERCE RETAIL SALES ($ BILLIONS), SECOND QUARTER 2001 THROUGH SECOND QUARTER 2004

Year	2001	2001	2002	2002	2003	2003	2004	2004
Quarter	2	4	2	4	2	4	2	4
E-commerce Retail	7.8	10.8	10.4	14.0	12.5	17.5	15.6	18.4
Total retail	803	850	814	859	852	912	919	948
% of total	1.0	1.3	1.2	1.6	1.5	1.9	1.7	2.0

Source: http://www.census.gov/mrts/www/current.html. Last consulted 8-25-04.

---

[2] The latest data available in 2004 as given in http://www.census.gov/eos/www/historyical/2002ht.pdf.

Connection to the various nets requires hardware and software (e.g., servers) that typically is in operation 24/7.

Standards are being established on digital characters, sounds, pictures, multimedia, and motion video. Technology is converging in terms of both content and transmission. All business functions, except production, distribution, and delivery, can be digital.[3] Even in the exceptions, network and digital techniques are being used more and more. For example, when a package is sent, it is tracked digitally by courier services such as FedEx and United Parcel Service along its entire route until it is delivered.

BENEFITS AND COSTS

Benefits

Existing firms undertake e-commerce to achieve increased efficiency or increased effectiveness.

- Efficiency includes lowering operating costs and increasing operations speed.

  Efficiencies include more accurate transactions with suppliers and customers, information sharing, centralized customer service (e.g., call centers), increased integration of back-office operations (Chapter 4 on ERP), a single-digital format for receiving and transmitting information, and lower inventories.

- Effectiveness includes increasing quality, reaching large numbers of customers (at reduced cost/customer), improving customer satisfaction, and improving organizational decisions. Electronic commerce allows communicating and coordinating with many more customers and also lets small firms compete with big ones for niche markets. The larger number of transactions also provides more data about the customer base.

Start-up firms undertake e-commerce because they see it as a quick way to accomplish one or more of the following benefits as well as those listed in the previous paragraph:

- Become national and/or international.
- Reach a niche target audience.
- Avoid the overhead and inventory costs associated with creating retail outlets.
- Provide information or services to people already connected to the Internet.
- Obtain venture capital (although that is becoming rarer).
- Use their existing Internet skills and have fun doing something they see as cool.

Consumers can also benefit from e-commerce. For example, they do not have to leave the house and go store-to-store to do price comparisons. They can gain additional choices because they can find more sellers, shop anytime that is convenient to them (24/7), obtain more detail on products, participate in auctions, and obtain products that are customized to them.

Costs

Establishing an e-commerce presence can involve large costs. For example, Gartner Group was quoted as saying that the website for a major firm can cost on the order of a million dollars. Numbers in the public press run from $150,000 on up. Sidebar 2 shows where the money goes.

---

[3] For some digital products, such as software or pictures, the entire process can be digital.

SIDEBAR 2   *Costs of Going into E-business*

Initial Costs

- Site development (includes site design). Involves using in-house IT or outside consultants and Web designers.
- Hardware, software.
- Integrating with legacy systems.
- Project management.
- Staff (dedicated staff and consultants).
- Initial training requirements.
- Internet access, hosting (if outsourced), domain registration fees.
- Initial marketing (traditional marketing methods, banner ads, registering with search engines, printing literature, public relations).
- Transaction costs.
- Translations (if seeking international presence).

Source: www.ecomm2001.com/resources/tools/38.doc

Operational Costs

- Site maintenance and development (in-house IT or outside consultants).
- Upgrading and adding capacity.
- Ongoing staff training.
- Internet access including domain registration fees.
- Hosting (if outsourced).
- Electricity and telecommunications.
- Security.
- Ongoing marketing (banner ads, e-mail, traditional marketing activities).
- Fulfillment, distribution, and delivery.
- Transaction accounting.
- Handling foreign inquiries (languages, currencies, value added tax (VAT), duty).

SIDEBAR 3   *Intangible Costs*

- Danger of alienating existing customers, agents, distributors, suppliers.
- Ability to ramp up or shut down activities as conditions dictate.

- Failure to achieve forecast traffic and/or revenue.
- Cost of not investing in e-commerce.

The costs in Sidebar 2 are tangible. However, intangible costs associated with risk also need to be considered (Sidebar 3).

Intangible costs translate into real costs if the events in Sidebar 3 (and others not thought of beforehand) occur. The implication is that analysis of benefit-cost ratios, return on investment, or whatever form of payback analysis the firm uses for investments should be undertaken before beginning. The costs are large, the risks are great, and perhaps most important, the existing business model will need to adapt to a changing environment.

BUSINESS TO CONSUMER (B2C)

In business-to-consumer e-commerce, merchants offer products that consumers can buy directly from them. Among the most popular products for B2C are

- Computers and computer-based items
- Books, CDs, DVDs, movies, videos, magazines
- Clothing, toys, food

Popular services sold online include

- Travel reservations
- Stocks and bonds
- Electronic banking
- Insurance
- Job matching

This list of services does not include services offered for free, such as real estate listings and catalogs, which provide information intended to entice people into buying goods conventionally. In general, the products sold directly tend to be commodities (highly standardized, of known quality, and easy to ship) or information products rather than products which are customized to the individual.

As the Internet spread and more and more people used it from their homes, the possibilities for B2C e-commerce expanded. On the business side, B2C e-commerce was a new channel through which to reach clients that had not been accessible before. On the consumer side, many people appreciated the safety and convenience of being able to shop from home rather than having to venture out into the night.

Infrastructure

To make B2C sales happen, companies need an infrastructure that connects them with their customers and often connects within their firm and with other firms. Table 3 shows a set of infrastructure connections that a large firm would maintain. Some, such as banks and suppliers, may be over highly secured lines to ensure privacy and security of data flow.

Table 3 INFRASTRUCTURE CONNECTIONS FOR E-COMMERCE

Internet	Extranets	Intranets	Internet or extranet
Public	Industry association	Headquarters	Large customers
Small customers	Banks	Manufacturing	Contractors and subcontractors
Small vendors	Business partners	Retail stores	Sales and other mobile employees
Travel agency	Suppliers	Employees	
Public agencies	Internet		

Electronic Retail Business Model

The Process

The Internet shows the customer a retailer's storefront. Much like a supermarket, the storefront allows the customer to browse the merchandise and put specific items in their virtual "cart" as they go through the inventory. When done, the customer passes through a virtual "checkout counter" where they are presented a bill and offer their credit card number to complete the purchase. The retailer collects the money from the credit card company and then sends the goods via ground or air package services such as FedEx or United Parcel Service.

The Consumer's Problems

All this sounds easy. It is not. Here are some of the problems. The prime reasons that customers don't shop online is that they are concerned about the security and privacy of their information (see Chapter 15) and/or they perceive no benefits from ordering online. For example, many shoppers put items into their shopping carts they want to buy but abort the purchase before completing the transaction. It's a form of buyer's remorse. Barriers that lead consumers to this behavior include lack of trust in the payment method and complicated ordering processes. Although credit card payment is relatively easy, those who don't want to put that information on the Internet have to be billed. That delays transfer of the goods further since, unless credit is established, payment is required up front.

The customer may want to return a purchase and exchange it or receive credit for it. They may report that the wrong goods were shipped or that the goods arrived damaged. If the product is moderately difficult to operate (e.g., a scanner or a digital camera), they may need technical support. In short, the consumer suffers all the trials and tribulations of a conventional store and of a mail-order house. Furthermore, in the digital world, return processes are often more complex.[4,5]

The Retailer's Problems

At the retailer end, the system for delivering goods must be superb if the customer is to be satisfied. Employees must be able to pick an order from a warehouse rapidly, package it, and get it out the door. The back office must keep track of the sale and the progress of the delivery. Inventory control and demand forecasting are vital. A "help desk" should be available to respond to inquiries and complaints. Returns must be attended to. For example, firms in the online grocery business find it difficult to sustain the quality of service for perishables (e.g., fruit).

The important point is that, although many of these considerations also apply to other forms of retailing, they are accentuated in e-commerce. Eliminating the "bricks" (i.e., the physical storefront) saves cost, but the more sophisticated order fulfillment and return processes that are put in place can eat up most of the savings.

---

[4] Returns are part of the reverse supply chain, discussed in Chapter 11.

[5] For an example of the problems in returning merchandise, see Steven Alter, "Shopping.com: When E-Commerce Isn't a Bargain", *Communications of AIS*, 2 (Article 22): November 1999. http://cais.isworld.org/articles/2-22/default.asp? View=html&x=39&y=16.

Information Transactions

Firms do find that providing information about what they sell and about specials helps to attract customers, even when they do not carry out transactions on the Web. A presence on the Web is considered an indicator of a substantial company (whether it is or not). Large sums are spent to create elegant websites.[6] In many cases, these websites are an advertising medium for the firm that creates leads rather than a viable sales outlet.

Advertising

In the first flush of B2C operations, advertising was hailed as the way to make sites profitable. That is, enough advertising would be bought so that content could be provided without charge. Firms were conscious of the ethos that the Internet had been and therefore should continue to be a free good. This dream did not prove sustainable when times were good, and disappeared in the recessionary times after the turn of the century.

Nonetheless, there are advertising aspects of B2C.

- The ability to provide a presence 24/7. No matter what time of day a customer is interested in a firm, they can find out about the firm and, importantly, can link to the advertiser to begin the process of ordering.
- The cost is independent of where the customer is located (but does depend on the audience reached by this advertising medium).
- Advertising is part of customer relationship management (Chapter 6) when using the Internet.
- Clever ads involving multimedia, sound, and ease of navigation can be created [but at an up-front fixed cost for creation and relying on the sophistication of the user's equipment (Sidebar 4)].
- Ads can easily be updated and the response to different ads can be measured.

SIDEBAR 4   *Selecting the Level of Technology for Your Internet Site*

The Internet is a different medium because it requires the advertiser to make assumptions about the quality of the user's technology. In telephone, television, and movies, for example, the provider controls the technology. In telephone or television, the consumer does need to buy the receiver, but these tend to be standard. For movies, the consumer walks into the theater and the technology is there. For B2C commerce on the Internet, however, the business depends on the consumer's technology.

It is mostly a matter of bandwidth. Messages sent to consumers can include text, pictures, sound, and video. Within each of these categories, the degree of complexity (and hence bandwidth required) can vary.

The more complex the message, the more bandwidth it requires. On the Internet, consumers expect messages to pop up quickly and are turned off by messages that take a long time to display. If the consumer's connection is slow (e.g., a 28.8 K modem or a slowdown in the cable connection), they will not wait.

Other factors can also enter. For example, if you want the user to hear music or a message, they must have audio capabilities. If you want to send them a video clip, they need video display capabilities.

The bottom line is that in setting up a website for B2C, the firm must decide what technology it requires the audience to have to receive its messages.

---

[6] A badly designed website turns customers off. Stinting here can make customers go to a competitor's site.

Two approaches are used: pull and push. In pull, the advertiser tries to lure the customer to visit their site. In push, typically using e-mail, the advertiser sends the customer information and order forms for specific products. For example, a firm offering a seminar extolling the virtue of their product sends e-mails containing advertising about the seminar and a registration form to people on a mailing list.

A particular advertising problem, detested by most people, is spam. Spam is unsolicited advertising sent to thousands upon thousands of e-mail addresses. Most companies derive ill will from spam activities. Filtering systems that detect and dispose of spam are prevalent.[7]

Impact on Retail Distribution

Retailers act as intermediaries between manufacturers and customers. Where manufacturers offer direct purchase (i.e., provide more than a catalog and a list of dealers), some disintermediation takes place. Retailers generally assume they are being cut out completely, although that is not usually the case. However, some large retailers bar manufacturers from selling their goods over the Internet.

On the other hand, some reintermediation also occurs. The B2C firm provides new services for which it charges or finds sources of revenue. The big search engines (such as Google or Excite), online market makers, and comparison shoppers are examples.

Dell Computers is an example of a firm that started out by working only with a direct channel in which the customer had to contact Dell either on the Internet or the phone. Over time, Dell began selling goods through computer stores and college bookstores as well. Although only a small part of their volume, these channels make Dell visible to people who might otherwise not know about the firm.

Manufacturer's strategies for using the Internet include

1. *Catalog only*. This strategy avoids channel conflicts between the manufacturer and the dealer. The policy may be instigated by the manufacturer to keep peace with their dealers or by the distributor.

2. *Coexistence*. Offer specialized or custom-made goods over the Internet but let the dealers sell the product and provide service. For example, you can create the specifications for your Jaguar convertible on the Internet, but you wind up working with the local dealer to get it delivered.

3. *Regional*. Sell over the Internet directly only in some countries, not worldwide.

Retailers. If they carry sufficient clout, retailers can also affect how B2C commerce is carried out. For example, Home Depot told manufacturers who supply goods to them that they should not sell B2C on the Internet if they wanted to keep this major chain's business.

B2C in Service Industries

Where the service is digital, B2C makes sense. The largest service application is in banking and online brokerages. Their major contact with consumers involves changing records on who owns what. Thus, a bank increases or decreases your balance and transfers the amount to someone else's account. It can handle transactions like bill paying or account status without a human intermediary. For the bank, a major expense is salary for tellers and the real estate required for making physical transactions. Although electronic transactions eliminate errors by tellers and in transcribing information, they are offset somewhat by input errors that customers make.

Other information transactions, such as real estate listings or ticket purchases for airlines or theaters are also suited for the Internet.

---

[7] Spam is discussed further in Chapter 15.

Physical transactions can also be digitized. For example, toll roads[8] now use smart cards that carry the driver's balance to allow entry to the road. The amount of the toll (which can change with the time of day) is deducted from the smart card. Filling stations, such as the Mobil/Exxon chain, offer simpler cards that verify creditworthiness and record the gas sale for later billing.

Cybermalls and Metamalls

Be aware that storefronts, as we just described, are only one form of B2C. Two others are cybermalls and metamalls. These arrangements use a single URL to lead to a collection of electronic retailers. A metamall is a one-stop shopping center that provides entrance to many cybermalls. Although popular initially, these multiple sources are disappearing. The major retailers prefer that people come to their storefront directly. Thus, these alternative malls contain mostly firms you never heard of. You might think of them as the pushcarts you see in the aisles at conventional malls. Affiliating with these malls also leads to being dependent on the outcomes of all the other merchants there. A consumer with a bad experience with any one merchant is unlikely to come again to look at anyone else at the same address.

BUSINESS TO BUSINESS (B2B)

A restructuring of the very basis for conducting business

J. Senn [2000][9]

Business-to-business e-commerce (B2B) refers to transactions between businesses over the Internet. We use the term business to include not only for-profit firms but also not-for-profits and government since the basic mechanisms are essentially the same.

The B2B marketplace is believed to be much larger than that for B2C. In 2002 (the latest date for which Census Bureau data were published in 2004), B2B business accounted for 92.7% of all e-commerce, compared to 7.3% for B2C. To put it into perspective, e-commerce represented 0.2% of B2B transactions in 1997, 2.1% in 2000, and 16.2% in 2002.[10] Table 4 lists the industries, which lead in B2B e-commerce.

B2B is still growing. It takes several forms:

- Electronic data interchange
- Interorganizational systems
- Electronic markets

Table 4 INDUSTRIES LEADING IN B2B E-COMMERCE

Agriculture	Food	Petrochemicals
Chemicals	Motor vehicles	Shipping and warehousing
Computing electronics	Paper and office products	Utilities

---

[8] You may not think of a toll road as a form of electronic commerce. Yet the smart cards combined with RFID (see Chapter 11) use electronic means to make a sale.

[9] J. Senn "Business to Business E-Commerce," *Information Systems Management,* pp. 23-32, Spring 2000. This section on B2B commerce is based on the Senn article.

[10] Source: U. S. Census Bureau, Economics and Statistics Administration E-Stats http://www.census.gov/eos/www/ebusiness614.htm   April 15, 2004. Consulted August 25, 2004.

STRUCTURE OF THE E-MARKETPLACE

Electronic Data Interchange (EDI)[11]

B2B e-commerce can be traced back to electronic funds transfer (EFT) used by banks and electronic data interchange. EDI provides direct computer-to-computer interchange of data. The two parties agree on the format in which the data is to be transmitted so that both understand what was being transacted. These methods of doing business usually involved private connections, often provided by third parties. They tended to be expensive and hence used mostly by large firms. Over time, some large firms, such as General Motors (GM), decided they wanted their suppliers to interact with them through EDI since it was more economical for the large firm to do so. Most small firms complied because they knew that if they did not, they would lose their prime customer. The capital expense was usually borne by the smaller firm. Firms dealing with several large customers requiring EDI found that each firm used its own standards. As a result, they maintained multiple technologies, one for each customer. Two standards evolved, one for the United States (ANSI X.12) and the other for Europe and the rest of the world (EDIFACT).

Figure 1 shows the interconnections in an EDI network. The specific information sent among the four elements in Figure 1 is shown in Table 5.

Although somewhat clumsy, EDI did the job. More than that, it persuaded firms that they could move data accurately between computers and, perhaps more important, eliminate the errors that resulted from previous systems that required manual data entry at both ends of the transaction.

Moving to the Internet

Moving to the Internet for B2B e-commerce is not new either. For example, Boeing set up a PARTS site in 1996. Within a year they were handling 50% of their parts ordered and service inquiries through this site. Moreover, they grew their parts business by 20% per month without adding staff. Being the large customer that they were, Boeing was able to tell its suppliers they had 1 year to go to the Web or lose their status.

Some believe that B2B on the Web is restructuring the basis for conducting business. Certainly it is speeding up the connections among suppliers, manufacturers, and distributors along the value chain. It is possible even for small firms to build their business model around e-commerce. In part these changes in how business is done are the result of the much smaller number of transactions that are involved in B2B, which is wholesale, rather than B2C, which is retail.

Interorganizational Systems

EDI is only one form of interorganizational system. Others include

- Electronic funds transfer (EFT), which is a form of EDI in which money is exchanged between parties through a bank.
- Electronic business forms (such as travel expenses, purchase orders, contracts duly signed electronically) that are routed within or between organizations.
- Integrated messaging that provides e-mail and often EDI and forms.
- Shared databases that allow outside firms access to internal computers. Such databases are used, for example, to let contractors know about current inventory and can trigger automatic shipments.

---

[11] This section is based on J. A. Senn, "Business to Business E-Commerce," *Information Systems Management,* pp. 23-32, Spring 2000.

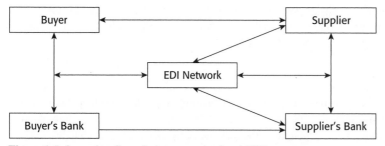

Figure 1 Information flows in interorganizational EDI systems.

Source: Adapted from J. A. Senn, "The E-Commerce Revolution," *Information Systems Management,* p. 24, Boca Raton, FL: Taylor and Francis Group, LLC, Spring 2000. Used with permission.

Table 5   INFORMATION FLOWS IN INTERORGANIZATIONAL SYSTEMS

From participant	To participant	Information transferred
Buyer	Supplier	Request for quote
Supplier	Buyer	Purchase order (P.O.)
		P.O. change
		Receiving notice
		Billing
Buyer	Buyer's bank	Payment authorization
Buyer's bank	Buyer	Payment remittance notice
Buyer's bank	Supplier's bank	Payment remittance notice
		Electronic funds transfer
Supplier's bank	Supplier	Deposit notice
		Payment remittance notice
EDI network	Buyer	Response to request for quote
		Purchase order acknowledgment
		Status response
		Shipping notice
		Invoice
EDI network	Supplier	Request for quote

Private Networks and Value Added Internet

For an interorganizational system to make economic sense requires that the trading partners anticipate engaging in transactions over a period of time. Either a private network or a value added public network could be used. Both sides may need to use middleware to make certain that the data formats are understood.

Interorganizational systems go back approximately 20 years. They are well established with each participating organization knowing (by contractual or other agreement) its responsibilities for what data to send, what data it can retrieve from a partner's computer if it is allowed access, and what data it can expect in return.

Large companies, such as Wal-Mart, Home Depot, Circuit City, General Motors, and DaimlerChrysler maintain their relationships with their suppliers along their supply chain (see Chapter 11) through interorganizational systems.

Electronic Markets

If two firms do not meet the basic requirement of ongoing, repetitive business associated with interorganizational systems, they may be better off using electronic markets. Electronic markets are ordinary markets that do not require people to meet at a specific place. They exchange

- information,
- products,
- services, and
- payments.

In a sense, these markets are like NASDAQ, which does not have a trading floor such as that used by the New York Stock Exchange. Transactions are performed by people sitting at screens, not shouting at one another. Electronic markets can be a danger as well. Electronic markets are particularly risky to buyers and sellers because of the speed at which transactions take place. Unless strong controls are in place, the market maker can manipulate the situation to maximize their revenue or their brokerage fees without the other parties involved even knowing that they were victimized. Look, for example, at what happened to energy prices in California as the electricity market went electronic.[12] Two major electrical power companies almost went bankrupt, the state suffered blackouts, and electricity prices escalated because an artificial shortage was created.

Figure 2 shows the relations among the components of an electronic market. The electronic market differs from an interorganizational system in that two new players are introduced

- The electronic market itself, which acts as a transaction handler.
- The transaction handler's bank.

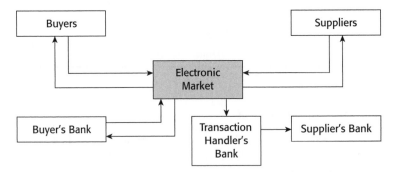

Figure 2 Electronic market.

Source: Adapted from J. A. Senn, "The E-Commerce Revolution," *Information Systems Management,* p. 26, Boca Raton, FL: Taylor and Francis Group, LLC, Spring 2000. Used with permission.

---

[12] Enron and other electronic market makers manipulated prices by making sales to themselves and/or by moving electricity (on paper) out of California and then selling it back to California at a higher price. It was a classic scam. The net effect was the loss of $60 billion in stock market value, bankruptcy for Enron and for Arthur Andersen (Enron's auditing firm), and jail time for many of its senior executives.

Table 6 INFORMATION FLOWS IN AN ELECTRONIC MARKET

From participant	To participant	Information transferred
Buyers	Electronic market	Request for quote Purchase request Payment authorization and payment
Electronic market	Supplier	Purchase request Purchase order (P.O.) Purchase change requests
Supplier	Electronic market	Response to P.O. Shipping notice Billing
Electronic market	Buyer	Purchase acknowledgment Shipping notice Payment acknowledgment
Electronic market	Supplier's bank via transaction handler's bank	Payment remittance notice Electronic funds transfer
Electronic market	Buyers bank	Payment authorization request
Buyer's bank	Electronic market	Payment approval Electronic funds transfer
Network	Buyer, seller, electronic market	Carries messages among participants

Table 6 lists the transaction flows in the electronic market.

Electronic markets are really virtual markets. The buyers, sellers, and the market may all be in different locations, and the people involved may not know one another personally. The connection between buyer and seller may be one time only rather than continuing. The physical connection uses a publicly accessible network such as the Internet rather than a private network.

The business benefits for an electronic market are

- **Extended Reach**. The seller can make sales to any potential buyer, no matter where they are. Unlike interorganizational systems, they do not require previous arrangements.
- **Bypassing Traditional Channels**. Electronic markets add another distribution channel.
- **Augmenting Traditional Markets**. Electronic markets are an extension of catalog and direct sales that bypass other intermediaries.
- **Improved Service**. With 24/7 operations, the electronic marketplace can make service a strategic advantage.

Given the benefits, how well have electronic markets fared? The answer is that while a few survived, most fail. The truth of the matter is that the marketplaces are not profitable because they do not attract sufficient customers. Most buyers and sellers do not yet turn naturally to electronic markets for specific needs or for obtaining spot market resources. In late 2002, the major survivors were firms created by industries. However, these firms were having a difficult time. An example was Covisint, (the auto industry's online marketplace whose sponsors included DaimlerChrysler, Ford

Motor, GM, Nissan, Renault). But even Covisint could not survive the recession. It expired in February 2004 when it sold its remaining assets to Compuware even though it claimed 135,000 customers in 96 countries.[13] Global Exchange,[14] on the other hand, continues to operate.[15]

CONSUMER TO CONSUMER (C2C): THE CASE OF EBAY[16]

Consumer-to-consumer (C2C) e-commerce is a small, special category that involves consumers selling to one another through an intermediary. It is typified by eBay, the auction house. The basic idea of eBay is to connect consumers with one another, as the firm puts it, to help practically anyone trade practically anything. Of course eBay acts as the broker.

The statistics of eBay's growth from the first quarter of 1997 to the second quarter of 2004 (Table 7) are remarkable.

On an average day, on eBay

- Someone buys a Corvette every 3 hours.
- A diamond ring is purchased every 6 minutes.
- A digital camera sells every 90 seconds.
- People buy 10 CDs and 5 videos every minute.
- Someone purchases a PC every 30 seconds.

eBay is an example of the information systems problems that are encountered with e-commerce success. The challenge is not only to keep track of every transaction [that's done by an ERP System (Chapter 4)] but also to organize the complex information generated for management reporting and for analysis [i.e., create appropriate business intelligence (Chapter 8)]. The capabilities of the website and of their ERP system are not appropriate for business intelligence. Complex analyses when done on the ERP system, for example, hurt performance that means lost transactions. The ERP system does not have the tools needed by users to perform the needed ad hoc reporting from the original data. Therefore, eBay decided on a data warehouse (Chapter 5) as a critical business enabler. Their requirements are stringent: 99.5% availability and consistent response across geographies and times of day. Furthermore, they wanted to be able to scale seamlessly to 10 times their current data volume so that they could accommodate growth and integrate new data sources such as partners and subsidiaries.

Table 7   EBAY GROWTH STATISTICS 1997–2004

	First quarter 1997	Second quarter 2000	Second quarter 2004
No. of customers	100,000	34 million	114 million
No. of transactions	400,000	98 million	Not available
Gross sales	Millions	$2.2 billion ($9 billion when annualized)	$8.0 billion ($32 billion annualized)

[13] Source: http://www.internetnews.com/ec-news/article.php/3309311.

[14] General Electric originally created Global Exchange. In 2002, it sold the business to Francisco Partners, a technology buyout fund, for $800 million. Global Exchange became an independent firm.

[15] See http://ww.gxs.com. Last consulted February 27, 2005.

[16] The information about eBay, other than the 2004 data in Table 7, is based on a presentation made at the Data Warehousing Institute in 2001 by the firm's Chief Information Officer.

CONSUMER TO GOVERNMENT (C2G): THE CASE OF WIRELESS AND 911

Federal, state, and local governments, like industry, turn to e-commerce ideas to connect to their customers. In the case of government, much of the traffic is information (e.g., census data, congressional hearings, regulatory rulings) or filling out forms or e-mail with people's representatives. Government, it turns out, is one of the early users of mobile wireless for e-commerce.

Wireless is still in a rudimentary state. It is, however, the next big Internet application as phones become Internet-enabled. A large fraction of the population uses cell phones to communicate. A particularly interesting application is the use of voice cell phones and 911. Studies[17] done in Minnesota, for example, show that people use 911 whenever they observe a traffic accident, particularly after a pileup of cars during snowstorms. The 911 system became overwhelmed with cell phone calls because everyone takes on the Good Samaritan role. The same phenomenon is observed in Los Angeles. The Department of Motor Vehicles maintains a very high-tech video system as a means of spotting the locations of traffic jams on the freeways. Yet, they find that with cell phones, more than 80% of the traffic jams are reported by motorists using 911 before the people monitoring the many screens observe them.

E-COMMERCE STRATEGIES

The trade press and the academic analyses are filled with advice on what is the best strategy for e-commerce. Unfortunately, the advice is scattered and often one author contradicts another. The following discussion is based on *Computerworld*[18] and includes a conceptual model from Stanford University.

Existing intermediaries believe they are being displaced. Even large retailers perceive e-commerce as a threat. For example, Home Depot and others warned suppliers not to sell direct because they would be in competition with the retailer. New intermediaries are indeed appearing, using the interactivity of the Internet. For example, Monster.com uses the Internet's two-way interaction capability to link job seekers and recruiters. eBay, described above, uses the Internet's real-time capabilities to create dynamic pricing, which allows price to fluctuate with supply and demand.

Electronic businesses include both conventional firms who do e-commerce in addition to their regular business, such as Barnes & Noble, and pure dot-com companies who are stand-alone electronic. Amazon.com, who started as an online bookseller and then moved into many other businesses as well, is a classic example of the latter.

Pure dot.com ventures include

- Those whose product is digital (such as software or news) and can be delivered directly over the Internet.
- Those that provide a complete service such as creating and delivering a website or running an auction or being a travel agent.
- Those that offer a new concept and sustain it, such as Amazon.com when it opened.

For B2C, an E-commerce firm should provide the three "C's": community, content, and commerce.

- Community (which is more difficult for conventional firms) involves using the Internet for person-to-person communications such as message boards and chat rooms.
- Content refers to providing information such as schedules, products, prices, news stories, and stock quotes.

---

[17] I am indebted to my colleague, Thomas A. Horan, of Claremont Graduate University for this example.
[18] J. Emigh, "E-Commerce Strategies," *Computerworld,* August 16, 1999.

- Commerce, in which people pay money over the Internet to purchase physical goods, information, or services posted or advertised online.

The Stanford model, developed by Haim Mendelsohn, argues that in going into a new e-commerce business you start with making decisions about four dimensions:

- The type of market (B2B, B2C, C2C)
- The type of product (physical, information, services)
- The selling environment (bricks-and-mortar, electronic, or both)
- The geography of the market (local, domestic, international)

You also need to consider how you will defend the business once you are in it. All businesses face the risk that a competitor will come in and match or improve on what they offer. There are defenses, however:

- Require a large investment that acts as a barrier to entry.
- Keep innovating more quickly than your competitors can respond.

Table 8[19] shows examples of the business strategies of specific firms. Some are pure dot-coms (e.g., Amazon.com, eBay), while others offer both e-commerce and physical locations. In each case, the table, using Mendelsohn's four dimensions, analyzes various markets, showing the firms in it, their products, environment, and geography.

Table 8   EXAMPLES OF BUSINESS STRATEGIES FOR THE FOUR DIMENSIONS OF THE MENDELSOHN MODEL

Type of e-commerce	Firms	Primary products	Environments	Geography
B2B	Cisco.com	Hardware	Brick-and-mortar	International
	Fidelity.com	Financial	Web	International
	Intel	Chips	Brick-and-mortar	International
B2C	Amazon.com	Books	Web	International
	Barnes & Noble.com	Books	Brick-and-mortar, Web	International
	eBay	Auctions	Web	International
	CVS.com	Drugstore	Brick-and-mortar, Web	National
	Drugstore.com	Drugstore	Brick-and-mortar, Web	National
	ClockworkPizza.com	Food	Brick-and-mortar, Web	Regional
	Fidelity.com	Financial	Web	International
	Wall Street Journal	News and Data	Brick-and-mortar, Web	International
C2C	eBay.com	Auction	Web	International
G2C	U.S. government	Data	Brick-and-mortar, Web	National
	State governments	Data	Brick-and-mortar, Web	State

Source: *Computerworld*, August 16, 1999.

---

[19] Based in part on *Computerworld*, August 16, 1999.

CONCLUSIONS

E-commerce can be looked at from four complementary perspectives:

1. *Communications*. Deliver information, products, services, and payments via computer networks

2. *Business Process*. Automate transactions and work flows

3. *Service*. Reduce service costs while improving quality and increasing speed of delivery

4. *Online*. Buying and selling products and information on the Internet

Most firms will use multiple perspectives. The particular ones you choose depend on the business of the firm.

The proverbial "bloom is off the rose" applies to e-commerce. In the mid- and late-1990s it was the "next big thing." Having a webmaster and a website was thought sufficient for instant fame and fortune. However, reality quickly set in. E-commerce is now just one more channel for communicating and selling to the customer. It does allow you to contact new customers and for new customers to find you. But full-blown e-commerce is not for every industry. In business-to-consumer e-commerce, for example, businesses that deliver information (i.e., news) or digital content (i.e., software) are well suited to this channel. Others, such as those selling high-touch items, (e.g., groceries, mattresses, automobiles) still require letting the customer touch and feel the goods.

ANSWERS TO MANAGERIAL QUESTIONS

What is e-commerce?

E-commerce is the use of electronic means to carry out all or part of a business transaction.

What kinds of e-commerce are there?

E-commerce is divided according to the parties involved. The parties are businesses, consumers, and government. An acronym is used to indicate who the parties are. Thus, for example, B2B refers to business-to-business e-commerce. In this chapter we discussed B2C, B2B, C2C, and G2C. Other combinations are possible.

What is B2B?

B2B refers to the use of communications to conduct transactions between businesses. It includes an older form, electronic data interchange, and the use of the Internet. At the most automated levels, everything from orders to bill payment is automated, with only the physical shipment of goods from seller to buyer being manual.

What is B2C?

B2C refers to the use of the Internet to help conduct transactions between businesses and consumers. The applications range from simple catalogs, to placing orders, to payment, typically via credit card.

What benefits can I expect?

At the simplest level, e-commerce is another channel of distribution and communication among firms and between firms and customers. It offers new markets that, for many firms, could not be reached before. As we understand more about how to use this channel, e-commerce can be expected to transform the way business is conducted.

How much is it going to cost?

A lot more than you or the people who sell you the idea of e-commerce think it will. In addition to the costs of buying and setting up the equipment, you usually need to provide 24/7 order taking and hire help desk people. You need to reorganize your back office so it can deal with e-commerce orders and your warehouse so it can pick and ship electronic orders. You need to set up your systems so that they can grow as your volume increases. You will have additional personnel expenses. In B2C, you need an advertising budget that uses both conventional and e-commerce media to tell people you are in the e-commerce business. You need to convince your marketing and sales people that sales will improve and that they will not suffer from reduced commissions. And that's for starters. A detailed, complete cost–benefit analysis is recommended. Although you can reduce the capital expenditures by outsourcing (Chapter 9) many of these functions, outsourcing can be more expensive in the long term.

What are the risks?

Like any new business venture (if you are starting a pure dot-com) or an extension of your existing distribution channels, the risk of failure must be considered. The history of dot-com start-ups and ventures into e-commerce is not comforting. They failed as much, if not more, than conventional business ventures. If you are funded by venture capitalists, remember that they expect not only equity but also actual returns. Although they do expect some failures in e-commerce, they are likely to force you out and take your business if you do not perform.

A good business plan is a prerequisite. However, unless you can meet or exceed the plan's estimates, you are likely to be treated as a failure.

What are electronic markets?

Electronic markets are a class of intermediaries that connect buyer and seller. The market maker can be anywhere. E-markets exist mostly in the B2B domain. After a huge, initial wave of electronic markets, a shake-out considerably reduced the number of firms making e-markets.

What do I need to do to become involved as a pure dot-com?

If you are thinking of starting a stand-alone dot-com, be aware of the risks involved and the failure rates. Have enough capital (preferably someone else's) that you can meet your start-up costs and can last 2 or more years without turning a profit. Be sure you either have or hire the people who have the needed skills in e-commerce and can make it happen. Also be sure to retain them because turnover is high. You can outsource some functions but at a price. Recognize that you will be running a complex business that may be subject to low barriers to entry. If successful, you can expect both start-ups and existing large firms to compete in your market space.

What do I need to do to take my brick-and-mortar business into e-commerce?

Your advantage is an ongoing operation with established products and clients. To expand into e-commerce, you will be saved some start-up costs and can initially use existing people and infrastructure. However, you still need a combination of new people with e-commerce skills and you will need to do some outsourcing. Although you will gain some cost savings from doing transactions electronically, these savings are usually not enough to pay for your investment, much less obtain a return on it. You must be able to gain new customers (e.g., by extending your reach and range) to make it worthwhile. If you are a B2C enterprise, you may move into e-commerce as the number of potential customers with PCs and related equipment rises. In some cases you may be forced to enter into e-commerce as a defensive move if a new e-commerce entrant starts capturing a part of your existing market share.

PROBLEMS

1. DEBATE

   A debate is to take place on the question:

   Resolved: E-business fundamentally changes the way business is conducted

   If your last name begins with the letters A through K, you are assigned to the affirmative on this question; if it begins with L through Z you are assigned to the negative view (i.e., no fundamental change due to e-commerce). Prepare up to eight PowerPoint charts plus supporting documentation for the side of the argument to which you are assigned.

2. ELECTRONIC MARKETS

   In this chapter we describe electronic markets and indicate that with few exceptions they did not succeed over the long term. Is this conclusion correct or incorrect? Give your reasoning. If it is correct, explain with case examples why they failed and your views based on your findings on what would be needed to make them succeed.

3. BRICKS AND CLICKS

Most businesses of any size (and even some tiny ones) now have a presence on the Internet. Some are pure bricks; that is, although they have a website, you must go to the physical location to deal with them; a few, such as Amazon.com and eBay, are pure clicks, transacting their business entirely on the Internet; but most do business both ways. Suppose you are faced with the decision of which approach to take (or alternatively, went through the experience of making that decision). Discuss the factors that go into this decision and explain how those factors would affect your firm. Come to a bottom line decision as to which way to go.

4. MENDELSOHN E-COMMERCE STRATEGY MODEL

The Mendelsohn model described under e-Commerce Strategies and illustrated in Table 8 argues that there are four dimensions in selecting an e-commerce strategy: type of market, type of product, selling environment, and geography. Consider your own firm (or a firm described in a case study if your firm is not engaged in e-commerce). Explain where the firm stands on each of these four dimensions, whether there were other factors for the firm in selecting its e-commerce strategy, and whether, given hindsight, you should have done it differently.

Chapter 4

Enterprise Requirements Planning

MANAGERIAL QUESTIONS

What is ERP?
How will it help my business?
What are its costs?
What are the risks?
What is ERP II and when can I expect it?

INTRODUCTION

Enterprise resource planning, usually abbreviated ERP, is a term that today covers a very large number of computer-based applications that are integrated into a single package. It is reputed to be (and actually is) a very expensive, complex, difficult to implement set of software that, at least in theory, runs the entire back office of the business. Its focus is on the firm's transactions, both with customers and internally, within the business.

ERP is the descendant of a relatively simple concept that came from the manufacturing world, material requirements planning, or MRP. MRP, which goes back to the 1970s, is based on the idea that the firms should manage the production scheduling and inventories for all their products together, not just inventory on a per product basis. The next step was to incorporate the allocation of resources and the costs associated with production. The result was MRP II. Extension to the enterprise as a whole, that is, ERP, was the next natural step.

The vision of a single integrated information system to run the back office had to overcome the way people organized computing by departmental silos. In the 1970s that was all that they could do technically. The results were "islands of automation." When new applications were added, manual interfaces needed to be created. Thus, for example, it was difficult to combine data from sales and manufacturing or to track an order from the time it arrived until payment was received. Another part of the problem was that the data were "dirty," that is, it contained duplicates and errors.

The net result was that firms wound up with a large number of separate systems whose cumulative maintenance costs exceeded the cost of the systems when new. ERP was the response. With ERP, multiple applications could share one database. Furthermore, a single transaction could flow through the ERP system without manual intervention and could automatically update financial and inventory data.

Implementation of ERP faced another barrier: large companies preferred to develop their own systems rather than buy applications packages. They had to become convinced that the packages could be bought and maintained for less than it would cost them to develop the capabilities in-house. Three other factors helped ERP:

1. The development of client-server architecture. In client-server arrangements, the main software is kept on a central computer (server) that provides data to each user. The users (clients) use PCs and are able to do both local computing and to request computing to be done on the server. The client-server arrangement also provided real-time access to data and a graphical user interface, that is, it could provide diagrams and charts in color that are much easier to understand than columns of figures.

2. The Y2K problem. As the year 2000 approached, firms became aware that they faced serious disruptions unless they either found (and then changed) all the places where they used two digits to represent a year in their programs[1] or they replaced the software they had. For many firms, much of their existing software was quite old. Faced with maintaining old, slow software or replacing it with Y2K-compliant ERP systems, many firms took the plunge and bought the new systems.

3. Most companies did not integrate their systems (see Chapter 10 on system integration) so they could work together. They wound up with custom-built systems that were stand-alone silos that could not communicate with one another. In most companies, integrating systems so they could communicate with one another was prohibitive in both cost and difficulty. ERP offered an opportunity to start over and do the job right.

The initial systems came from vendors with a particular point of view. Four of the initial large vendors were SAP, Oracle, PeopleSoft (acquired by Oracle in 2004), and Baan (now Invensys). SAP started with financial modules, PeopleSoft with personnel modules, and Baan with materials requirements planning. These companies and others that followed rapidly found that the marketplace wanted all the applications in one place, rather than needing to integrate their separate offerings. Thus, over time, each firm (and new entrants) started offering what their competitors offered.

HOW SAP WORKS

In this section we discuss SAP[2] and its main products R/2 and R/3. We choose to discuss SAP because it is the largest of the ERP firms, with 44,500 installations serving 10 million users at 17,500 organizations in 120 countries across the globe.[3] Furthermore, its competitors take similar approaches and offer similar modules. Over time, it became possible to mix and match modules, that is, to create a system that consisted of modules from several vendors. Therefore, many of the SAP installations include modules from other vendors and vice versa.

The history of SAP goes back to 1972 when a group of IBM employees in Germany developed the concept of providing integrated software to run the transactions of large firms. When IBM rejected the idea, they left and founded SAP.

---

[1] For example, if the firm wanted to determine the length of a loan, if they stored 1998 as 98 and 2008 as 08, they would compute the loan length as 08 - 99 = -91; that is, the loan lasted a negative number of years.

[2] SAP is an acronym for Systemanalyse und Programmentwicklung (German for Systems Analysis and Program Development). The full name is no longer used.

[3] Based on SAP's claims on its website http://www.sap.com/company/history.aspx. Last consulted 8-28-04.

SAP's R/2 and R/3 products differ principally in the hardware arrangements (i.e., "architecture") on which they operate. R/2 is designed for large mainframes with dumb terminals,[4] whereas R/3 is designed for client-server arrangements in which individual users are given PCs. Most systems today are R/3's. A new version, called mySAP.com, began to be marketed in recent years. This version is designed for the Internet, for e-commerce, and for collaboration with other firms.

SAP claims it supports all aspects of normal company operations with each of its three versions. SAP's core modules perform the following basic functions:

- Finance
- Sales and distribution
- Manufacturing
- Human resources

In addition, SAP offers modules for

- Enterprise portals
- Supply chain management
- Customer relationship management
- Product life cycle management
- Supplier relationship management
- Business intelligence
- Mobile business
- Hosted solutions

SAP also offers packages designed for specific industries, for small- and medium-sized businesses, and for data warehousing.

In observing the evolution of SAP's and its competitor's offerings, it is clear that each vendor tries to extend out from beyond where they started. In the case of SAP, they started in manufacturing and finance. SAP added modules to compete with Seibel, then the largest firm in sales and distribution software, and with PeopleSoft, that started out with a human resource module. Once the basic modules were in place, SAP expanded into supply chain management and into its other major offerings. Each module is designed to capture additional information systems business from firms that use several of its core modules.

Each of the modules that a firm buys connects with all of the other modules so that data do not have to be entered or stored repeatedly. The ERP system works in approximately real time, which means that the data retrieved is current.

SAP R/3 is a top-down system. That is, it assumes the firm is organized hierarchically. It is controlled by a set of thousands of tables that manage the hierarchy. These tables are set in such a way that the system reflects how the firm's processes will work. Each of the modules can access hundreds of business processes. Each of the processes is based on whatever SAP considers "best practice." The idea is that if a process changes, the tables are reset to reflect the change. Although this concept sounds ideal, in practice it is very difficult to change how SAP works once it is in place. Some claim that SAP is like concrete: flexible and easy to change when you install it but that it

---

[4] A dumb terminal is a display connected to a computer mainframe that can do no computing of its own. In a client-server architecture, the server stores the database being used and computing is divided between the server and the PC machines connected to it.

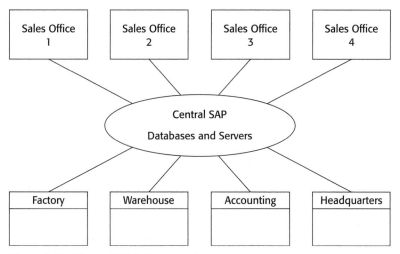

Figure 1 Handling a SAP R/3 sales order.

Based on E. Turban, E. McLean, and J. Wetherbe, *Information Technology for Management,* 2nd ed., update edition, 2001, p. 124. Used by permission, John Wiley & Sons.

hardens over time and becomes impossible to change without great expense. Thus, although the tables allow operating in a seemingly infinite number of ways, this flexibility is true only if the firm is organized in the same top-down way as SAP. Thus, for example, SAP (as do many other ERP systems) does poorly with project industries (e.g., aerospace), industries that involve product dimensions (e.g., clothing), or continuous processes (e.g., food, paper, chemicals).

Figure 1 shows how SAP works for a simple sales order. The order originates in one of the firm's sales offices and is sent to the SAP central database, which is located on SAP's servers. It then proceeds through the system:

- The factory receives the sales order and begins production.

- At the same time, the warehouse is notified and makes sure there is space to store the product as it is built. It also arranges for shipping.

- Accounting receives updated information on both sales and on each step of production. It also undertakes the billing process.

- Headquarters can obtain current data on sales, inventory, and production.

CULTURAL PROBLEMS OF IMPLEMENTATION[5]

In implementing ERP, as for many other large software systems, cultural factors must be taken into account if the system is to be used across countries or by a multiethnic workforce. Almost all ERP systems are designed in North America or Western Europe and embody the designer's cultural assumptions. However, these assumptions are not necessarily valid everywhere.

Consider best practices. ERP systems incorporate specific processes that are considered best practices in their home countries. Because of the cost to customize the ERP system to fit a company's

[5] This section is based on R. Davison, "Cultural Complications of ERP," *Communications of ACM 45*(7): pp. 109–110, July 2002.

particular way of doing business and the repeated expense of customizing each time the ERP is upgraded, these built-in processes are usually adopted. For example these processes assume that ERP will function in an online environment that is open and where standard reports are available to everyone. Yet, in Southeast Asia, information is treated as an individual rather than an organizational resource, with individuals being informed only if they have a specific need to know. The culture is highly bureaucratic, with forms for every purpose and reports that are user-specific, something which ERP does not provide. Reengineering information processes to make them open is difficult because reengineering implies (undesired) organizational change.

Another simple example is the use of numbers. ERP systems generate identification (ID) numbers for system entries. Yet in the Chinese language, the symbol for 4 is also the symbol for death and the symbol for 8 is used for wealth; one is to be avoided and the other is sought.

ERP assumes that with use of the system, employees will be empowered, able to do knowledge work rather than rote tasks. The assumption in North America is that people want responsibility for their own activities and want to make their own decisions. This assumption is not the case in high power distance cultures[6] such as Hong Kong or Singapore, where entry-level employees want to be told what to do and promotion to decision-making levels is based on seniority.

You can't simply promote or retrain. You need to shift values as well. You have two choices:

1. Try to find software that matches your culture. Recognize that the best you can do is find an ERP package that matches in some, not all, dimensions.

2. If you can't find a package that matches your culture or you choose one that is out of step with your firm, then even though ERP systems are difficult to change, it is easier to modify the system than to change the culture.

ERP VENDORS

The principal ERP vendors are shown in Table 1. They break down into vendors who offer enterprise systems for large firms and for what is called "mid-market."

Oracle competes with SAP for large installations. Oracle's PeopleSoft is in the education market aggressively because it was able to modify the personnel modules (its strength) to handle the people record keeping which is intensive in education. J.D. Edwards, acquired by PeopleSoft, concentrates on the middle-sized firm. Geac Computer, which is not well known in the United States, is a Canadian firm that moved in recent years to concentrate on business performance management (see Chapter 8). Many of the smaller companies base their ERP systems on Microsoft products.

COSTS[7]

The costs of ERP can cover a wide range. In an analysis of large-scale systems, Meta Group quoted an average cost of $15 million for large firms. That boiled down to over $53,000 per frequent user. This total included hardware, software, internal staff, and consultants plus 2 years of postimplementation support. Time to implement ranged from 6 months for small installations to several years.

---

[6] G. Hofstede, *Culture's Consequences: Comparing Values, Behaviors, Institutions, and Organizations across Nations,* 2nd ed. London: Sage, 2001.

[7] Cost data are based on reports in *CIO* magazine. Large system costs were obtained by Meta Group and quoted by *CIO* in its October 15, 1999 issue. Mid-size costs were reported November 15, 2001.

Table 1 ERP VENDORS

Firm
SAP
Oracle
PeopleSoft (acquired by Oracle)
J.D. Edwards (acquired by PeopleSoft)
Geac Computer (Canada)
Lawson Software
Microsoft (Great Plains)
QAD
SSA
Siebel
IBM
Epicor
Syspro

Notes:

J.D. Edwards was acquired by PeopleSoft who continued to service existing J.D. Edwards products. PeopleSoft (including J.D. Edwards) was then acquired by Oracle.

SSA acquired Baan software and rebranded it. Baan at one time was third/fourth in ERP sales.

Table 2 AVERAGE COST TO INSTALL ERP

Expenditure	Amount (millions)	Percentage
Hardware	1.46	13.8
Software	1.86	17.5
Internal staff	2.46	23.2
Professional services	4.82	45.5

Source: *CIO*, October 15, 1999.

In a separate estimate of cost prior to and including installation, *CIO* magazine[8] estimated an average cost of $10.8 million, with the breakdown shown in Table 2. Note the large fraction of the cost for professional services, that is, consultants.

For two mid-sized firms ($200 to $500 million revenues), costs to buy the system and install it were quoted by *CIO* magazine as $150,000 and $200,000, with implementation completed in 9 weeks. These firms used a technique called rapid ERP that is being offered by the large vendors. The cost numbers assume a bare-bones installation in which the firm purchasing the system adopts all of the "best practices" built into the system and attempts almost no customization of the ERP system to its processes. Rather, the firm must change its processes to fit the system because customization involves large additional costs. This approach is not for the trepid. The advantage is that the contract specifies both a price and a time line. Because time is money in these contracts, explicit

---

[8] October 15, 1999.

and accurate project planning is paramount to avoid additional charges. As it is, the firm will incur additional costs in retraining, in change management, and in integrating existing legacy systems, none of which are included in the systems price. Even in well-planned transitions, some system customization will be required. Note that these small cost numbers include only the money paid to the ERP vendor; they do not include the costs in the firm for IT, for training, and, most important, for changing processes to be compatible with the ERP system.

BENEFITS

The anticipated benefits of ERP include

- Shorter cycle time—that is the time from receipt of order to delivery
- Increased productivity
- Lower IT costs
- Better cash management
- Reduced personnel

Done right, ERP makes some processes transparent. For example, if the shipping dock does not check the packing slip, the order does not exist. The customer is not billed and accounts payable doesn't know that money is owed. With ERP that problem can be resolved.

Table 3 shows the results of a survey about achieving these benefits. The numbers indicate the percentage of respondents who expected a particular benefit and the percentage who actually achieved the benefit.

The results shown in Table 3 are mixed, in that some benefits occurred more frequently than expected, while others less frequently.

THE MARKUS AND TANIS VIEW OF THE ERP EXPERIENCE[9]

M. Lynne Markus and Cornelis Tanis described the ERP experience that firms go through. They focus on five characteristics:

- Integration
- Packages

Table 3   EXPECTED AND ACTUAL BENEFITS

Benefit	Expected (%)	Actual (%)
Shorter cycle time	19	31
Improved productivity	24	31
Lower IT costs	24	11
Better cash management	24	13
Personnel reduction	43	33

[9] Source: M L. Markus and C. Tanis, "The Enterprise System Experience—From Adoption to Success." Chapter 10 in R. W. Zmud (Ed.), *Framing the Domain of IT Management,* pp. 173-208, Cincinnati, OH: Pinnaflex Education Resources, 2000.

- Best practices
- Some assembly required
- Evolving

Integration

The promise of ERP is that all information flows through the company seamlessly by "configuring" the system to reflect the organization. Modules are chosen and software parameters are set. However, it is possible to configure the system so that the benefits are not achieved! For example, if a firm adopts only a part of ERP (such as the financial or the human resources modules) or if the firm allows SBUs to configure their system differently, most of the benefit is lost.

Packages

ERP systems, like word processors or spreadsheets, are bought as software packages rather than developed in-house. The firm is immediately faced with either accepting how the package works or customizing the package to fit the way the company worked in the past. Neither choice is ideal. If the package's rules are followed, the firm usually must change the way it performs work. This approach changes business processes, which usually results in massive employee resistance to change. It can also result in forcing the firm to standardize its business practices to that of its industry and thereby lose strategic differentiation. In addition, this choice affects the information systems group by obsolescing some in-house IS skills and changing the IS life cycle. On the other hand, if the firm chooses to customize the ERP package, it incurs large modification costs, costs that are incurred over and over for each new version as the package is upgraded. And upgrading is a routine event in the life of ERP systems.

Best Practices

The vendors want to support as many different types of firms as possible. As a result, enterprise systems contain built-in processes that are generic. The vendors, of course, claim that their processes are best practices, although it is never clear how that status was obtained. If the company follows these best practices it must, of necessity, do some business process reengineering (BPR). Unfortunately, BPR does not come for free. For example, Baan (now Invensys) required a firm to have an "integrated product team" that included contract management, project accounting, project management, and estimating. These functions were previously separate functions in aerospace. Even if a firm wanted to adopt Baan's best practice, it had first to reengineer its process. The implications of the best practice approach are

1. ERP can force substantial changes in organizational structure, job design, work sequencing, training, and more.
2. It adds considerably to the expense and the risk of implementing ERP.

Some Assembly Required

Although ERP systems claim to be integrated, this claim is overstated. For one thing, although the software is integrated, complete integration requires compatible computing platforms (e.g., hardware, operating systems, database management software, and telecommunications). For most firms, it is difficult to integrate ERP software with all of this hardware. The software also requires interfaces with the company's legacy systems and with other packages. The firm's IS group must make these connections, usually after the ERP system is installed, and incurs costs that are often not budgeted for.

REASONS FOR ADOPTING OR NOT ADOPTING ERP

The reasons for adopting or rejecting ERP depend on what the company is trying to achieve and on whether ERP capabilities are believed compatible with the company and its operations.

Adopting ERP

ERP creates a single company way of doing things. As a result, it solves both business and technical problems. The business problems solved include

- Presenting one face to the customer.
- Knowing what is "available to promise."
- Eliminating or reducing the number of applications doing the same thing (which can be used to reduce operational errors).
- Filling orders for merged businesses.

The technical problems solved include

- Handling transaction growth.
- Reducing mainframe operating costs.
- Solving maintenance problems with legacy systems.
- Providing modern transaction capabilities.

Not Adopting ERP

The prime reason for not adopting ERP is a perception that the features and functions of commercial ERP systems do not fit what the firm needs. The difficulties in some industries, such as food, paper, clothing, and aerospace were cited earlier in this chapter. Often companies will adopt only parts of an ERP system or modify it (at great expense) to increase its "feature-function" fit.

ERP's assumed top-down organizational structure is not compatible with a decentralized decision-making style. Company growth patterns and desire for strategic flexibility are other reasons for rejection. Some companies use alternative approaches for increasing systems integration such as the use of a data warehouse (Chapter 5) or middleware.[10]

Other reasons for not adopting ERP include

- *Cost.* As shown in the section on costs earlier in this chapter, spending over $50,000 per frequent user and multiple millions of dollars on the system as a whole can be a major deterrent. Escalating cost without closure on delivering the ERP system is often the reason why ERP projects are dropped in midcourse. Some companies, to avoid the high costs of an ERP system, undertook to integrate their transaction data in an "operational data store," a form of data warehousing discussed in the next chapter.

---

[10] Middleware describes software that acts as an intermediary between different components in a transactional process. The classic example of where middleware is needed is the separation that exists between the client's user and the database in a client-server system.

- *Competitive Advantage*. Some companies believe they lose competitive advantage when they adopt ERP because their back office no longer distinguishes them. Closer investigation often shows that these companies were unwilling to change culture or to bear the pain of implementation.

- *Resistance to Change/Lack of Management Commitment*. Like all large IS systems implementations, ERP requires change and can only occur if management is committed to the project. If change management and/or commitment are not present, an ERP system does not make sense.

- *Company Culture*. ERP systems vendors come out of the European and American cultures. Firms that operate outside these cultures (see Cultural Problems of Implementation, page 61) or whose company cultures are not imbedded in a particular ERP package are best advised to avoid implementation.

THE ERP TEAM[11]

"After a company turns on its ERP software, the only people who understand how the business works are on the ERP implementation team." That is, the team learns both the business and the software. Team members know more about sales than the people in the sales department and more about manufacturing than the people in the manufacturing department.

A firm that adopts ERP should recognize that the team it puts in charge of creating the system is really reinventing the way the company works. Thus, when the initial project is completed, it is advantageous to keep them together rather than dispersing them back to the organizations from which they came. Furthermore, firms often experience a drop in performance for 3 to 9 months after implementation because of the need to fix glitches. As a result, firms need to keep people, resources, and money flowing for the project to meet postimplementation demands.

SUCCESS CASE STUDY: Nestlé[12]

Nestlé SA is a Swiss-based conglomerate in the food business. Founded in 1867, it is a worldwide firm with sales over $60 billion, $8 billion of which is in the United States. In June 2000, Nestlé signed a $200 million ERP contract plus $80 million for consulting. This contract was in addition to the $200 million that Nestlé USA would have spent on its ERP project. This figure includes the entire project from its inception in 1997 to its final rollout in 2003. This section explores the Nestlé USA implementation.

Nestlé USA was formed in 1991 by combining independent brands, such as Carnation and Stouffer's, which were owned by Nestlé. By 2002, Nestlé USA consisted of seven autonomous divisions, making their own decisions and reporting to Glendale, California rather than to Switzerland. The objective of the ERP installation was to create common processes, systems, and organization structures.

The need for coordination was highlighted by the 29 different prices brands paid for a common ingredient, vanilla, to the same vendor. The various computer systems didn't even have a common name for vanilla, so no one knew (except perhaps the vendor) what was going on. In the spring of 1997, a new CIO was appointed, the problems were pinpointed, and an ERP effort began. The situation was chaotic. The process involved massive reengineering, unhappy employees, and points along the way where the participants believed that the project would never end. These experiences are, of course, endemic to ERP implementations.

---

[11] Source: *CIO,* October 15, 1999.

[12] This section is based on B. Worthen, "Nestlé's ERP Odyssey" *CIO,* May 15, 2002.

The company had

- Nine different general ledgers.
- Twenty-eight points of customer entry.
- Multiple purchasing systems.
- No data on their volume of business with individual vendors since factories were autonomous.

Their key idea was that the project (named Business Excellence through System Technology, abbreviated BEST) was about change in business processes. ERP was the vehicle for that change.

A team of 50 executives and 10 senior IT professionals was formed to implement the vision. The team was to devise best practices that would be standard for every division. A separate team looked at all the data items in the divisions and standardized them. By March 1999, decisions were made to use SAP's purchasing, financial, sales and distribution, accounts payable, and accounts receivable modules as the ERP system. However, because SAP's supply chain software was new and not yet proven, Manugistics[13] software was chosen to reduce risk for the supply chain applications.

Four of the modules were to be ready by December 31, 1999, to cope with Y2K problems. Although Nestlé made the deadline, all was not smooth. Users, who had not been represented on the stakeholder teams, resisted the changes. They liked their existing processes, didn't understand the new processes, found the software complex (particularly for the supply chain), and didn't know how to use the new system. Furthermore, the team made a fundamental technical mistake. They did not integrate the modules with one another. Thus, a change in one subsystem (e.g., offering a customer a discount) did not show up in the one to which it connected (e.g., recognizing the discount in accounts payable). Thus, while replacing divisional silos, the implementation created new silos between processes.

The situation was out of hand by July 2000. A reevaluation led to changing the SAP supply chain module, which had matured in the 2 years since it was rejected.[14] The reevaluation also led to the conclusion that it had been wrong to set a date and to try to meet it rather than to set business goals, define the desired end state, and let the date be determined by how long it would take to meet the end state. Nestlé also understood that the relationships between the project team and the end user community needed to be mended so that users would know what changes were being made, why, and how. It took until the following April to define the end state and 2 more years to complete the system.

Although the cost of the system and the time spent are at the high end for ERP applications, the results more than cover the cost. Demand forecasts are more reliable, forecasts can be made down to the distribution level, inventory levels are reduced, and the supply chain is improved. Nestlé management claims it saved $325 million from its ERP.

CASE STUDIES OF FAILURE: FoxMeyer and Hershey[15]

The history of ERP, particularly early implementations, is studded with total and partial failures. They include a well-known list of firms such as appliance manufacturer Whirlpool, trash processor Allied Waste Industries, fabric maker W.L. Gore and Associates, and distributor W.W. Grainger. But perhaps the poster children for the downside of ERP failures are FoxMeyer Drugs, a pharmaceutical distributor, and Hershey Foods, best known for its chocolate kisses.

In this subsection we consider the last two cases, both of which received extensive coverage in the press.

---

[13] At the time, Manugistics was an SAP partner.

[14] The change increased the cost by 5%.

[15] This section is based in part on C. Steadman, "Failed ERP Gamble Haunts Hershey" Computerworld November 1, 1999; A. Osterland, "Blaming ERP" CFO.com, January 1, 2000; and J. E. Scott, "The FoxMeyer Drugs' Bankruptcy: Was It a Failure of ERP?" Proceedings of The Association for Information Systems Fifth Americas Conference on Information Systems, Milwaukee, WI, August 1999.

FoxMeyer Drugs

The extent of an ERP failure can be catastrophic to a company. FoxMeyer Drugs, a $5 billion company, then the fourth largest wholesale distributor of drugs and beauty aids based in Dallas, collapsed in 1996 after attempting an R/3 installation. Its bankruptcy trustees wound up suing SAP, its ERP vendor, and Andersen Consulting, its systems integrator for $500 million each.

FoxMeyer expected high growth in drug sales because of the aging population. They were operating in a market with extreme price competition, which meant eroding margins. In the early 1990s they decided their strategy should be to manage inventory efficiently, reduce operating expenses, strengthen marketing, and increase services. Their Unisys computer systems were reaching the end of their life and the vendor was discontinuing support. Given that customers sent orders electronically, that they engaged in hundreds of thousands of transactions, and needed to maintain detailed records for government compliance, ERP was deemed the appropriate solution. They selected three vendors: SAP to provide R/3, Andersen Consulting to perform integration, and Pinnacle Automation to provide a warehouse automation system. The initial total contract value was $15 million and the expected time for the system to be up was 18 months, both unrealistic goals.

The work started in 1993 with a planning effort. The plan, unfortunately, was not matched by the implementation. With two vendors (SAP for ERP software and Pinnacle for warehouse automation) FoxMeyer experienced coordination problems. They needed to change their system requirements after testing was underway. As a result, they were late and over budget. Although SAP was deemed to be implemented properly, the system did not work. The drug company was plagued by late orders, incorrect shipments, and lost shipments. In August 1996, they filed for Chapter 15 bankruptcy and were later taken over by McKesson.[16]

Analysis of the bankruptcy indicates that the problem was much more a management problem than a software problem. Although the SAP software generally worked as it was supposed to, the management choices made created many of the difficulties encountered. FoxMeyer closed three warehouses. That resulted in disgruntled workers who damaged inventory and were not able to cope with the new system. A total of $34 million worth of inventory was lost. Second, the new system initially could only process 100,000 orders per night compared to 420,000 orders with the previous system. The situation was made worse by signing a contract to supply a new customer with a high volume of transactions. FoxMeyer management assumed the ERP system could handle the increased load but it couldn't. Third, FoxMeyer did not have the necessary skills in house. They relied on their consultant to implement R/3 and to integrate it with the automated warehouse software. The consultant is alleged to have provided inexperienced people and to suffer from high turnover. FoxMeyer management did not feel it knew enough to cope with the consultants and the vendors. The project spun out of control and project costs eventually went over $100 million.

Hershey Foods

For Hershey Foods Corporation, like for most candy manufacturers, the most important part of its revenue comes in three seasonal sales periods: Halloween, Christmas, and Valentine's Day. In 1999, when a new ERP system was running late, they missed the Halloween and Christmas seasons. They issued two profit warnings in the 2 months before Christmas and their stock decreased by over 25% from their year's high at a time when the overall market was booming.

Hershey invested $112 million into ERP and related software. Not only were the ERP systems to be installed, but a CRM system (Chapter 6) and a logistics package were to be installed at the same time. The new system was supposed to replace a large number of legacy systems that the company was running. The plan was straightforward but risky. Installation, estimated to take 4 years, was scheduled for 30 months and was to be completed in July, just before Hershey's heavy shipping season. Rather than a parallel operation to begin with, a full cutover was to be made to the new system.

---

[16] As reported in The Business Journal On-Line (http://www.business-journal.com/lateJuly02/PharMorBleeding.html), the co-CEOs of FoxMeyer took over a drugstore chain, PharMor, shortly before declaring bankruptcy of FoxMeyer and also drove PharMor into its second bankruptcy from which it did not emerge. As was the case with other firms, the co-CEOs enriched themselves in the process.

Unfortunately, order processing and shipping were not ready on time. The company was still fixing problems in September. Because details of what went wrong were not available from the company, the following discussion is based on a variety of press reports and opinions.

1. Hershey tried to do too much at the same time. Going live with an ERP system is difficult enough, but trying to get three systems on line at the same time introduces daunting complexity even for the best companies.

2. Trying to cut 18 months off the normal schedule exacerbates the problem. Admittedly, Hershey was trying to beat the December 31, 1999, deadline for fixing Y2K problems. However, complex systems are best put in with a more leisurely and more flexible schedule. The schedule can most charitably be described as a bad gamble.

3. Hershey tried to go live at the peak of its shipping season. Conventional wisdom advocates selecting quiet times because, even with good implementations, it takes several weeks to find all the problems.

4. Employee training was inadequate and employee resistance to change was not dealt with fully.

Although the immediate results were dire, Hershey was able to fix its ERP troubles over time as it gained experience. In August 2002, it reported[17] that its original system was working and that they had upgraded to the SAP Internet version (mySAP.com). The firm claimed that 95% of its revenue and business transactions were being processed on the system and that 30 business processes were enhanced.

SIDEBAR 1 *Lessons Learned*

The cases indicate some of the lessons learned over the last decade of ERP implementations.

1. ERP is about changing processes and the way the business is run. Software can be made to work. Managing the resultant change is much more difficult.

2. Good general management and project management are needed. The following management practices apply not only to ERP but to most large projects that firms undertake.

- Include the people whose lives will be changed in the planning process. It will make change management easier.

- Determine the business goals and make those the objective rather than setting a time deadline for implementation. The implementation process can't be hurried.

- Avoid customizing ERP as much as possible. Customization results in recurring costs each time an upgrade occurs.

- Integrate the modules with one another and with the remaining legacy systems. The point of ERP is to have an "all-in-one" system. All the pieces must be able to understand one another and operate off the same database.

- Because additional costs are likely to be incurred, update the budget periodically to minimize surprises.

- Although it is getting easier, mixing and matching ERP modules from different vendors is still a difficult task.

- Don't stint on the training budget. ERP usually requires a mindset change on the part of employees, and that can't be done in a short training session.

- Manage your ERP consultants just as you manage your own employees. Be sure that the consultants leave enough knowledge behind when they leave so your own employees can take the job over (see Chapter 7).

3. If you can stay the course, the benefits can far exceed the costs.

---

[17] T. R. Weiss, "Hershey Stays the Course with mySAP.com Upgrade." *Computerworld IT Reports.* http://www/computerworld. com August 30, 2002.

THE FUTURE: ERP II

ERP was designed as an infrastructure to improve networking in the virtual communities that large organizations really are. Conventional ERP, as described in this chapter, has been available for nearly 20 years. The market for new ERP installations is shrinking and the business went through a series of shakeouts of weaker firms. It is starting to be considered "old hat" by some. As a result, ERP is slowly being transformed into ERP II. The new system, as it is envisioned by the Gartner Group,[18] expands existing ERP by adding knowledge sharing with clients and suppliers, Internet use, virtual supply chain models, customer relationship management (Chapter 6), and e-commerce models (Chapter 3). Thus, not only must additional complex technology be incorporated into ERP, but the organization must become more customer-oriented than in the past.

The present ERP systems focus on transparency of transactions, effectiveness, efficiency, and business processes. They are not designed for collaboration outside the firm in such areas as supply chain management. The objective of ERP II is a system that includes interorganizational as well as intraorganizational data. That is, ERP II systems are being touted as providing front-office as well as their present back-office[19] capabilities. In terms of products, Gartner Group expects that ERP vendors will build sector-specific capabilities that are integrated into their packages. The vision is that the systems will be able to reduce the latency that is built into them at present, that is, the ability to deliver to a customer in, say, an hour, rather than 3 days.

With ERP II, it is claimed, firms will be able to manage information to create long-term relationships both inside and outside the firm. The firm's supply chain process is integrated with their supplier's supply chain (Chapter 11). In that way, the information systems extend to the retailer's shelves and allow direct customer feedback. In addition to promoting customer loyalty by keeping the customer fully informed, ERP II uses the idea of knowledge management (Chapter 7) that knowledge sharing leads to increasing, not diminishing returns.

To make all this work requires major changes at the technology, process, and people levels. In terms of technology, the rigidity of ERP is replaced by open sourcing in which modules are components that can be connected much more easily than at present with third-party software modules such as for supply chain or customer relationship management. The hope is to introduce additional technologies that used to be considered leading edge such as voice, portals, and intelligent agents. The fundamental problem that needs to be resolved is integrating modules from multiple sources.

ERP usually results in changes in business processes. However, change is hard for organizations and is often rejected. As a result, ERP II, like ERP, will need to overcome resistance to change and lead people to think and work together.

FINAL THOUGHTS

For many firms, ERP is the single largest information technology investment they will make. The investment includes cash, resources, and reengineering processes. It will inevitably change the way the company does business. It can be a risky, "bet your company" investment that is not for the faint of heart. The good news is that most companies survive installing an ERP system and become easier to operate. Although ERP rarely, if ever, provides competitive advantage, for many firms and industries it is a competitive necessity.

---

[18] The Gartner Group of Stamford, Connecticut, is a firm that monitors the information systems business. This section is based on two reports of their findings: M. Mohamed, "Points of the Triangle," *Intelligent Enterprise,* September 3, 2002; and A. Harrington, "Gartner Touts EDRP II Vision," http//www.vunet.com/print/1115981.

[19] The term front office generally refers to customer-facing operations, such as sales, whereas back office refers to internal processes such as billing and payroll.

ANSWERS TO MANAGERIAL QUESTIONS

What is ERP?

Enterprise resource planning (ERP) is a collection of software modules that integrate with one another for running the firm's back-end transaction data processing. It focuses on both customer and internal transactions. Its promise, not fully achieved as yet, is that information flows through the organization seamlessly.

Its advantage over "islands of automation" is that multiple applications work with the same database, thereby resulting in a "single truth." The initial, basic SAP modules supported finance, sales and distribution, manufacturing, and human resources. Over time, additional modules were offered that support more specialized functions such as supply chain management and customer relationship management.

Will I need to change my business processes?

ERP incorporates processes that are judged by software vendors such as SAP to be best practices. As a result, firms must change many of their existing processes to be compatible with the ERP system or must customize the software to fit their processes. Both approaches are quite expensive.

How will it help my business?

The principal benefits claimed for ERP are

- Shorter cycle time for manufacturing
- Increased productivity
- Better data input for decision making
- Integrated financial information
- Reduced inventory
- Reduced personnel
- Lower IT costs
- Better coordination within the firm
- Integrated customer order information
- Standardized (and self-service) human resource (HR) information

With most large and many medium-sized firms now using ERP, the software itself rarely provides competitive advantage. It is a competitive necessity. What it does is allow firms to reengineer processes that can lead to competitive advantage.

What are its costs?

The expenditures for ERP can vary over a large range. Two case examples involved expenditures of over $200 million. Some smaller installations run well under $200,000. Why the disparity?

The out of pocket cost depends on such factors as

- The size of the firm and the size of the installation. The more modules that are adopted, the greater the cost.
- The extent of customization. The larger the amount of customization, the greater the cost since customization is labor intensive.
- The extent to which consultants are used.
- The skills of the internal IT shop.

The last two factors are interrelated. If ERP skills exist in-house, fewer consultants are needed and vice versa. The peak of the demand for ERP skills occurred in the late 1990s, as Y2K approached. The number and availability of people with ERP skills became better in balance as more people were trained.

Total cost of ownership for a full-time user in a large firm is estimated to be over $50,000. Hidden costs include training, the learning curve to get people up to speed on the new system after training, converting data to ERP-usable form, implementation costs beyond project completion, and the lag between installation and realizing ROI.

How long will it take?

Like cost, time from decision to operation can vary widely. For small systems and organizations using "fast-track" implementation, times as short as a few months have been observed. For large firms installing full-blown systems, 4 years is not uncommon.

What are the risks?

As with any large software project, the risks are large. Some systems were abandoned or replaced. Some companies, such as FoxMeyer (see case above), go bankrupt. Installing an ERP system is difficult. Most firms tend to underestimate the difficulty and (big mistake!) accept the vendors' promises. As a result, they overrun both budget and schedule. The good news is that many systems eventually are completed and meet their technical specifications.

The most serious risks are managerial. ERP changes business processes. Therefore, it changes the way people work. Most people, of course, don't like to learn new ways of doing things on the job. Many fear unemployment. Therefore, a deliberate effort must be made to reduce resistance to change and to integrate ERP into the firm. The resistance-to-change problem is larger for ERP than most of the other systems discussed in this book because ERP, properly implemented, affects every department in the firm.

Care must be taken in selecting the right package. If a package does not allow processes that are inherent in a business, such as continuous flow rather than discrete manufacturing, or tracking inventory you don't own outright, then adopting it is high-risk because workarounds may be unsatisfactory. Similarly, if the package assumes a top-down organizational structure and the firm is distributed, the package is not appropriate.

Most firms depend on a large contingent of outside consultants. Although the consultant firm may have many skilled people, if it assigns junior people with little experience in either ERP or your industry, serious problems can result. If knowledge is not transferred from the consultancy to in-house technical and operating people, the system may not be sustainable.

What is ERP II and when can I expect it?

ERP II is the anticipated direction in which ERP is heading. It includes knowledge sharing with clients and suppliers, Internet use, virtual supply chains, integrating CRM, and e-commerce. It moves ERP to being an interorganizational, customer-oriented system rather than being confined to the interior of the firm. ERP II was still a promise, not a reality in 2005.

PROBLEMS

1. HOW ERP WORKS

   Near the beginning of this chapter, we describe how ERP works. Pick one of the existing ERP offerings from a major vendor (e.g., SAP, Oracle, Microsoft for small and medium enterprises) and prepare a much more detailed description of the functions that ERP offers.

2. PERSONNEL FOR INSTALLING AND RUNNING ERP

   If your present or past company installed an ERP system while you were with the company, describe the team that put it together, their individual functions, how the members of the team changed over time, and the people assigned to run the system currently. Consider the improvements (if any) that could be made either by including or removing members of the team. If you don't have experience with an ERP installation, find one or more case studies that deal with the people aspects of the problem.

3. ERP FAILURES

   Two cases of ERP failure are described in this chapter. Find and summarize at least two other failures and why they occurred. Also, find a success story and compare the differences between success and failure.

4. ERP PLANNING

   The P in ERP refers to planning. Explain how ERP systems are being used in planning at the tactical and at the strategic level. Give examples.

Chapter 5

Data Warehousing

MANAGERIAL QUESTIONS

What is a data warehouse?
Why build one?
What are the differences among a data warehouse, a data mart, an operational data store, and a
real-time data warehouse?
How expensive is it?
What can you use it for?

INTRODUCTION

Starting in the late 1960s, computer-based systems started to be used for what was then called decision support. It was recognized that management information systems (Chapter 2) were designed to help with operational problems by providing reports and other aggregated information drawn from transaction processing systems. Decisions are different. Managers require an integrated view of the organization over time and they require aggregations of information from multiple sources. The general model[1] describes decision support systems as consisting of three components: a database, a model base, and an interface. The data are the input. The model base consists of (usually mathematical) models used to evaluate the data, and the interface is what the user sees on the computer screen. While the model base and the interface were well developed, databases tended to be ad hoc mostly because data were not being aggregated or stored from a decision viewpoint.[2]

Data warehouses proved to be a solution to the data problems faced by software developers to deal with ever-larger and more complex databases needed for decision making.

---

[1] First developed in R. H. Sprague and E. D. Carlson, *Building Effective Decision Support Systems,* Englewood Cliffs, NJ: Prentice-Hall, 1982.

[2] Decision support systems also underwent changes over the years. As it became clear that managers faced great difficulties in trying to deal with mathematical models, simplified versions of decision support were developed that were known as executive information systems. In recent years, as described in Chapter 8, the primary focus of these systems is on business intelligence.

Database developers long understood that their software was required for both operational processing and analytic processing.[3] However, the principal developments were directed to the ever-larger transactional databases that are the lifeblood of operating a business. This process occurred even though operational and analytic data are separate, with different requirements and different user communities within a firm.

However, by the late 1980s, when these differences were understood, new databases, the data warehouses, were created specifically for decision and analysis use. Today, the major data warehouse applications are

- Online analytic processing for business intelligence (Chapter 8)
- Data mining (later in this chapter)
- Customer relationship management (Chapter 6)
- Supply chain management (Chapter 11)

As is clear from this list, the data warehouse is central to a number of present-day applications.

The management role of the data warehouse needs to be stressed. The data warehouse is physically separated from operational systems and operational databases. Except for data warehouses sold by ERP manufacturers, they are separated from back-office, online operations. As will be seen in this chapter, data warehouses contain both aggregated and detailed data for management that are separate from the databases used for online transaction processing (OLTP). Furthermore, the data in the warehouse are "clean." That is, there is a "single version of the truth" since the value in the warehouse is the official value for the firm. The concept of a single version of the truth is the key idea in data warehousing.

Definition of a Data Warehouse

Inmon's definition of a data warehouse[4] is now standard. It states that:

A data warehouse is a
- *subject-oriented*
- *integrated*
- *time-variant*
- *nonvolatile*

collection of data in support of management decision processes.

We discuss each of these characteristics in the next section.

CHARACTERISTICS OF A DATA WAREHOUSE

The characteristics of the data warehouse are summarized in Table 1, and the characteristics of the data in the warehouse are listed in Table 2.

We now discuss each of the characteristics of the data warehouse given in Table 1.

---

[3] Operational processing, as we saw in Chapter 4 on ERP, deals with recording events such as transactions as they occur. Analytic processing refers to analyzing the data collected for management decision making.

[4] See W. H. Inmon, *Building the Data Warehouse,* New York: John Wiley & Sons, 1990.

Table 1   SUMMARY OF DATA WAREHOUSE CHARACTERISTICS

Subject orientation	Data are organized by how users refer to it.
Data integration	Data are organized around a common identifier, consistent names, and the same values throughout. Inconsistencies are removed.
Time	Data show history, not current status.
Nonvolatile	Data do not change over time.

Table 2   CHARACTERISTICS OF DATA IN THE WAREHOUSE

Summarized	In addition to operational data where needed, data summaries used for decision making are also stored.
Larger database	Time series implies much more data are included.
Not normalized[5]	Data can be redundant.
Metadata	Includes data about how the data are organized and what it means.
Sources of input data	Data come from operational systems.

Source: W. H. Inmon, *Building the Data Warehouse,* New York: John Wiley & Sons, 1990.

Subject Orientation

Applications are typically designed around the functions and processes of the enterprise, whereas the data in the warehouse are oriented around the subjects and data that drive the enterprise. Table 3 shows an example of how these two approaches differ for a bank. Operational data relate to immediate needs and are based on current business rules. It typically follows the organizational structure of the firm. Data warehouse data span time and hence allow more complex relationships.

Table 3   COMPARISON OF APPLICATIONS AND SUBJECT ORIENTATION FOR A BANK

Operational data	Data warehouse
• Loans	• Customer
• Savings	• Vendor
• Bank card	• Product
• Trust	• Activity
Application orientation	Subject orientation

---

[5] Data normalization makes sure that an individual data point appears once and only once in a database. It is followed strictly in the theory of relational databases but is not required conceptually in data warehouses. However, some data warehouse designs, such as those by Teradata, do normalize their data.

Data Integration

Legacy systems serve as the major input to the data warehouse. However, legacy systems were developed at different times by different people. As shown in Figure 1, they generally refer to the same quantity in different ways and may show different values. To get to the single version of the truth, the data warehouse contains rules to integrate the data from multiple sources.

The figure shows that legacy systems refer to the same data in many ways. When the data are transferred to the data warehouse, they are integrated so that:

- Data are referred to in only one way. That is, they are given a common identifier, such as "balance."

- Data are the same format and in the same units as the attributes that are measured.

That is, the data are stored in the data warehouse in a single, globally acceptable fashion even though the sources from which it comes may differ. That is, data are organized around a common identifier. The result is that the user focuses only on the data, not their credibility or consistency.

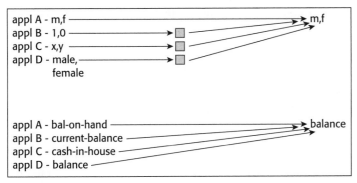

Figure 1 Data integration.
Source: W. H. Inmon, *Building the Data Warehouse*, p. 31, New York: John Wiley & Sons, 1990.

Countless hours are wasted in conference rooms while people argue about whose data are correct. Part of the argument can come from variations in the definitions of data elements among legacy systems. For example, in one airplane company, now defunct through merger, salespeople defined a sale by the time of a customer handshake. The finance people recognized the sale only when the down payment was received, and the legal people when the contract was signed. The data warehouse, by using a single, agreed-on definition solves this problem.

Time

The data warehouse and operational systems view time differently. As shown in Table 4, in an operational environment, the data are accurate[6] when the user accesses the file, whereas in the data warehouse, data are accurate only at the moment they are loaded. Warehouses are typically loaded with new data only once or a few times a day. So, although accurate at some moments in time, warehouse data are not necessarily accurate "right now."

This difference results from the way the two systems work and their purposes. The operational system is designed to be able to respond to a query about a customer on the telephone who, say, is asking for credit. The warehouse is used for planning and analysis where an average of a 6 or 12 hour lag does not affect the decision.

Since much of the data in the warehouse are used to understand how conditions change over time, the key used for data retrieval always contains the unit of time (e.g., a specific day or week). Warehouse data cannot be updated except to correct an error.

Nonvolatile Data

The data warehouse turns out to be technically simpler than the conventional database. Figure 2 compares the way the two systems operate.

Table 4   TIME IN THE DATA WAREHOUSE AND IN OPERATIONAL SYSTEMS

Characteristic	Data warehouse	Operational system
Time	Snapshot of data at time of loading	Current value
Time horizon	As long as 5 to 10 years	60–90 days
Search key	Always contains an element of time	May or may not include time as an element
Updating	Cannot be updated by users	Always updated whenever a change occurs

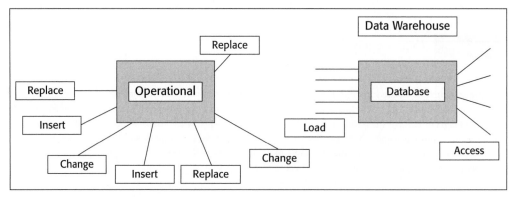

Figure 2 Relative complexity of data warehouse and operational environments.
Source: W. H. Inmon, *Building the Data Warehouse,* p. 32, New York: John Wiley & Sons, 1990.

---

[6] Assumes that the data entry is performed without error and immediately. In many situations, such as when recording payments for insurance policies made by mail, there is a delay between the time the check is written by the consumer and the time the data are recorded.

In an operational environment, updates (such as insert data, delete, change) are done on a record-by-record basis as changes occur. In a data warehouse, new data are added only at the regular time for loading. Furthermore, since users cannot make changes in the data (nonvolatility in Table 4) and new data are added (i.e., loaded) periodically rather than as changes, the contents of the data warehouse are much more stable than that of a database where changes are made as they occur.

There is little or no redundancy between the operational and data warehouse environments.[7] Data are filtered and transformed as they pass from the legacy system to the warehouse. This process, called ETL (for extraction, transformation, and load), is designed to get to a single version of the truth and to make sure that only data needed for applications is stored in the warehouse.

Nonvolatility also makes it possible to create and store summary data in the warehouse. Because analysts use some standard summary reports over and over, it is easier to compute frequently consulted summaries ahead of time rather than each time they are requested.

STRUCTURE OF THE DATA WAREHOUSE

The data warehouse contains not only the current detail data that were transferred from the legacy systems but also lightly summarized data, highly summarized data, and old detail data (Figure 3). Metadata, discussed further below, may also be stored in the data warehouse.

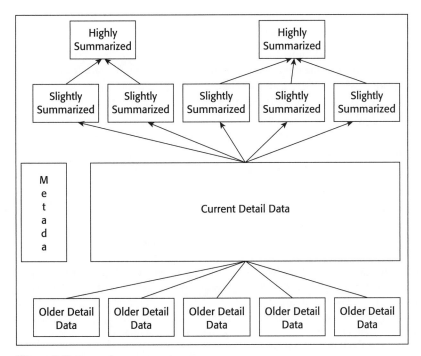

Figure 3 Data warehouse structure.
Source: W. H. Inmon, *Building the Data Warehouse,* p. 34, New York: John Wiley & Sons, 1990.

---

[7] Later in this chapter, we discuss the operational data store (ODS), a data warehouse used for operational decision making. It is updated much more frequently (e.g., 10 minutes, hourly) than the conventional data warehouse or data mart.

The current detail data reflect the most recent happenings, usually stored on disk. Detail data are voluminous and are stored at the lowest level of "granularity" (Sidebar 2).

Two or more degrees of summarization are used to preposition data for analysts and for executives. To establish what the summaries contain, decisions must be made on the unit of time for summarization (e.g., weekly data, daily data) and on the attributes to be summarized. In general, lightly summarized data are used at the analyst level, whereas senior managers use highly summarized data (which are compact and easily accessible).The choice of summarization level involves trade-offs because:

- The more highly summarized the data, the more the data are accessed and used.
- The more highly summarized the data, the quicker they are to retrieve.
- The more highly summarized the data, the less detail is available for understanding them.

To keep storage requirements within reason, older data are moved to a lower cost mass storage medium for which data retrieval is much slower. An aging process within the warehouse is used to decide when to move data to mass storage.

Metadata

Finally, the warehouse contains metadata.

Definition: Metadata are data about data.

Metadata contain three types of information:

1.   What the user needs to know to be able to access the data in the warehouse. Metadata for the user include a directory of the data in the warehouse and where they are located, definitions of the data items stored, what reports are available, the sources of the data, when they were last updated, and more. This information answers the user's questions about what is stored in the warehouse and where to find it.

2.   A guide to how data were mapped from operational form to warehouse form. This guide is provided to the IT personnel, such as the warehouse administrators, so they know what transformations occurred as data were moved from the legacy systems to the warehouse.

SIDEBAR 2   *Granularity*

Granularity is shorthand for the level of detail provided by a data point in the data warehouse. The more detail provided, the higher the level of granularity. The highest level is, of course, transaction data such as are required for performing data mining or for CRM. For decision support and planning, the level of granularity can be much lower. The choice of granularity is an important trade-off because:

- The higher the level of granularity, the more data must be stored.

- The higher the level of granularity, the greater the level of detail available in answering queries.
- The higher the level of granularity, the more computing needs to be done, even for questions that do not use that level of granularity.

   Example: A gasoline company that records every motorist's stop made at its stations can use the transaction data from the cardholder's credit transactions to understand the detailed buying patterns of its customers. The company that wants only total sales by station does not need that level of granularity.

3.   The rules used for summarization, and the contents, keys, and indexes associated with the data. Like the mapping data in item 2, this information is principally designed for the data warehouse administrator.

Metadata keep track of changes made converting, filtering, and summarizing data, as well as changes made in the warehouse over time. For example, data added, data no longer collected, and format changes.

Metadata, being fairly static information, may be kept in a variety of places:

- in the data warehouse,
- in one or more of the data warehouse tools used to improve operations, or
- in simple spreadsheets.

FLOW OF DATA

As shown in Figure 4, data flow involves three tiers:

Data loading software extracts the data from the legacy systems and external sources and copies the data into the warehouse according to the metadata rules. As part of the process, the data are cleansed to remove duplicates, errors, and inconsistencies. Once the data are in the warehouse, they are ready to be analyzed and to create reports.

WHY A SEPARATE WAREHOUSE?

A fundamental tenet of data warehouses is that their data are separate from operational data. The reasons for this separation are

Performance. Requests for data for analysis are not uniform. At some times, for example, when a proposal is being written or a new product is being considered, huge amounts of data are required. At other times, the demand is small. The demand peaks create havoc with conventional online transaction systems because they slow them down considerably, keeping customers waiting.

Data Access. Analysis requires data from multiple sources. These sources are captured and integrated by the warehouse.

Data Formats. The need for summary data and time-based data implies that data formats must be uniform.

Data Quality. The cleansing process (extraction and transformation) is required to create a single version of the truth.

Figure 4 Data flow in the data warehouse.

OTHER FORMS OF DATA WAREHOUSES

Data marts are small versions of data warehouses. They have all the characteristics of an enterprise data warehouse, but are much smaller in size. They are typically stand-alone units used by departments or SBU's that often support only a specific subject area. Data marts are much less expensive than a full data warehouse. For small- or medium-sized businesses, they can serve as their only data warehouse.

In addition to data marts, several other forms of data warehouses are in use.

- Operational data store
- Real-time warehouse
- Prototype warehouse
- Exploration warehouse

Operational Data Store

An operational data store (ODS) is a data warehouse used for transaction data. The idea is that, since some decisions need to be made in near real time and these decisions need many of the characteristics of a warehouse such as clean data, a form of data warehouse for operational use should be created. Table 5, which compares the ODS to the data warehouse, shows that an ODS is subject-oriented and integrated like the warehouse. However, the data are volatile and contain current or near-current information but not historical data.

When data move from legacy systems to the ODS, they are re-created in the same form as in the warehouse (Figure 5). Thus, the ODS converts data, selects among sources, may contain simple summaries of the current situation for management use, and alters the key structures and the physical structure of the data as well as its internal representation. Loading data into a data warehouse from an ODS is easier than loading from individual legacy systems, since most of the work on the data is already performed. However, like other operational systems, the ODS, despite its data warehouse characteristics, should not be combined with a warehouse.

Table 5 COMPARISON OF ODS AND DATA WAREHOUSE

Operational data store	Data warehouse
Subject-oriented	Subject-oriented
Integrated	Integrated
Can be updated	Cannot be updated
Current and near-current data	Historical data plus detail data
Contains some data that is never included in the warehouse	Contains much more data than the ODS
Serves clerks, day-to-day decision makers	Serves analysts and middle and upper managers for long-term decisions
Full function, update record environment	Simpler load-access technology
Typical update cycle: 2 to 4 hours	Typical update cycle: 24 hours

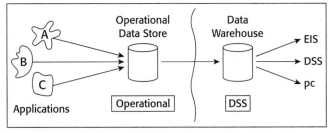

Figure 5 Architecture of the operational data store.

Source: W. H. Inmon and R. D. Hackathorn, *Using the Data Warehouse,* p. 30, New York: John Wiley & Sons, 1984. Used by permission.

One of the characteristics of the ODS is the much shorter time between successive loading of data. They are still batch loaded but the batch cycle is 2 to 4 hours rather than the typical 24 hours for a data warehouse. For a very busy organization, the ODS can require a large amount of storage rapidly. As a result, many organizational data stores use a variety of techniques for aggregating data.

Real-Time Data Warehouse

As the data warehouse and ODS concepts became commonplace, organizations started finding new ways of using the warehouse. One example is the real-time data warehouse, which is used to support ongoing analysis and action. A form of operational data store, real-time data warehouses are closely tied to operational systems. They hold detailed, current data and try to use even shorter times between successive loadings than operational data stores. Users can query the real-time data warehouse.

With a real-time data warehouse, an enterprise can respond to customer interactions and changing business conditions in real time. For example, it enables a credit card company to detect and stop fraud as it happens, a transportation company to reroute its vehicles, or an online retailer to communicate special offers based on a customer's Web surfing behavior. The real-time data warehouse thus is an integral part of both short-term, tactical, and long-term, strategic decisions. It becomes an integral part of business activity monitoring (BAM) discussed in Chapter 8 on business intelligence.

Prototype and Exploration Data Warehouses[8]

As data warehouses became important to enterprises, it became difficult to explore new approaches to warehouse design or to use the warehouse for operations that require a large amount of unstructured number crunching for analysis.

1. The prototype data warehouse is used to provide prototyping and iterative development capabilities. It reduces the time to complete a design to weeks or months, rather than years. It also allows database designers and administrators to adapt to new requirements and insights "on the fly."

---

[8] Source: B. Inmon, "The Exploration Warehouse," *DM Review,* June 1998.

2.   The exploration data warehouse is used for unstructured processing in a DSS environment. Because the processing may be quite ad hoc, it is preferable to do the analysis away from the primary data warehouse for the enterprise. Exploration warehouses are temporary and transient, designed to help with solving a particular problem. They may last for a few hours or a few weeks; they are never permanent.

The relations between the data warehouse and the prototype and exploration warehouses are shown in Figure 6.

When used for processing data that already exists, the exploration data warehouse is fed directly and only from the enterprise's data warehouse. When the data are to be refreshed, the exploration warehouse is simply reloaded in its entirety from the data warehouse to obtain the latest, freshest data. Because the prototype warehouse is used to ask "what-if" questions in design, it is fed by legacy systems and, where appropriate, by external data sources.

APPLICATION: ONLINE ANALYTIC PROCESSING

History

In the early 1990s, E. F. Codd introduced online analytic processing, usually referred to as OLAP. Codd was known and revered for introducing the concept of storing data in two-dimensional tables (referred to as relational databases). His relational concept drove the database market for two decades. But by the early 1990s, most firms had a relational database and the market consisted primarily of upgrading existing systems. The relational database was particularly applicable to online transaction processing (OLTP). As a result, while the original concepts called for using databases for both transaction processing and for analysis, the database vendors generally neglected the analysis needs of the business.

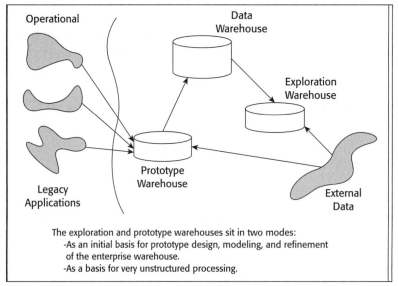

Figure 6 The prototype and exploration warehouses.

Source: B. Inmon, "The Exploration Warehouse," *DM Review*, June 1998. Reprinted with permission from Source Media/DM Review.

Multidimensional databases (MDDB) store data as an *n*-dimensional cube (Figure 7). This arrangement allows creating data views defined by such quantities as product, region, sales, actual expenses, budget, and time. These databases are optimized for speed and ease of query response. They are also more intuitive to use. However, they are limited by the size of the database they can handle (e.g., <100 gigabytes) and the number of dimensions (<20).

Relational databases (RDB) store data as two-dimensional tables. While somewhat slower than MDDB for OLAP, these databases are able to handle almost unlimited database sizes and dimensions. They

also have the advantage that most firms have:

- A large inventory of legacy relational databases
- Existing software licenses for relational databases
- Skilled programmers and database administrators for relational databases.

That is, firms are more familiar with relational databases (such as shown in Figure 8) and therefore more likely to adopt them for OLAP.

These two approaches were given the name MOLAP (multidimensional OLAP) and ROLAP (relational OLAP). Although both are available in the marketplace, ROLAP seems to be dominant at this point.

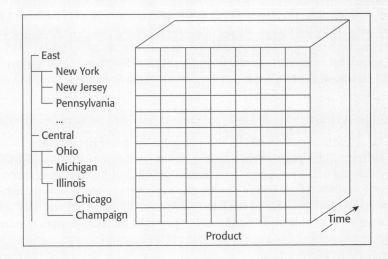

Figure 7 A data cube.

Type	Market	Quarter	Units sold
HiDefinitionTV	NYC	1	650
HiDefinitionTV	NYC	2	850
HiDefinitionTV	CHICAGO	1	600
HiDefinitionTV	CHICAGO	2	500
PC Portable	NYC	1	1200
PC Portable	NYC	2	1500
PC Portable	CHICAGO	1	900
PC Portable	CHICAGO	2	800

Figure 8 Relational database.

Table 6   WHEN TO USE OLAP

Data are used for analysis, not for individual transactions.

The analysis is based on aggregated data, not data as they come into the enterprise.

Analysis involves complex calculations on aggregations of transaction level data.

The data are almost all numbers, not words or pictures.

The data are being examined across many dimensions or involve multiple consolidations.

Codd came to the conclusion that relational databases for online transaction processing had reached their maximum capabilities in the views of the data they provided users. As constituted, they were inadequate for supporting decision making because decision making involved asking questions of the data that had not been asked before. A Standard Query Language (SQL) had been developed for relational databases that did allow users to ask questions, but massive computing could often be required to answer relatively simple SQL queries. Worse, users couldn't tell in advance whether a large or a small effort would be needed. Since transaction systems were generally working in real time dealing with company customers who demanded quick responses, delays introduced by answering SQL queries were unacceptable. He also realized, as decision support people had known for a long time, that operational data by themselves are not adequate for answering managerial questions. He therefore recommended the use of a multidimensional view and organization of the data. (See Sidebar 3 for the differences between relational and multidimensional databases.) Codd's conversion to the decision support viewpoint gave legitimacy to the data warehouse concept.

Description

The basic idea of OLAP is that managers should be able to manipulate enterprise data models across many dimensions to understand changes as they occur in their business. In many respects, the OLAP concept is no different than the decision support and executive information systems that existed previously. The main change was that OLAP systems, rather than needing to create their own databases, could use the data warehouse as the source of data. In practice, OLAP systems focus on the data directly rather than on the sophisticated models and analysis provided by decision support systems.

When to Use

Table 6 shows the circumstances under which OLAP should be used. OLAP is discussed further in Chapter 8.

APPLICATION: DATA MINING

Data mining is also referred to as "knowledge data discovery" (KDD). The two terms, although related, refer to slightly different situations. Data mining is about finding answers about a business directly from data in the data warehouse that an executive or an analyst had not thought to ask. It is designed to find information that SQL queries and reports don't reveal effectively. KDD seeks to find patterns in data and to infer rules.[9]

---

[9] To a certain extent, the choice of terms depends on the author. Business analysts tend to use data mining for both cases, whereas university professors who study data mining tend to use the more academic term KDD. In this section, we use data mining throughout.

The important point here is that the conventional approach to dealing with data is to create a hypothesis and then do what the statisticians call hypothesis testing. Data mining, however, argues that the analyst may not know which questions to ask because he or she cannot even conceive of the relationship. Data mining serves as an analytic way of finding relationships. Once a potential relationship is found, it becomes a hypothesis that can be tested for correctness with standard statistical techniques.

KDD applies techniques, many from artificial intelligence and statistics, to find new information. KDD techniques include

- Statistical analysis of data
- Neural networks
- Expert systems
- Fuzzy logic
- Intelligent agents
- Multidimensional analysis
- Data visualization
- Decision trees

The software associated with these approaches is called *siftware*. The following are some of the successes achieved with data mining:

Australian Vacations. People who buy scuba gear are likely to take Australian vacations.

Financial Sector. Data mining is used in fraud detection and consumer loan analysis. For example, it triggers the phone call you receive from your credit card companies when you (or someone who stole your credit card information) make an unusual purchase or a purchase in a place you don't generally frequent.

Diapers and Beer. This story, which may be apocryphal, claims that men who buy diapers in a supermarket on Friday night also buy beer.

Data mining can be bottom-up (explore raw facts to find connections) or top-down (search for hypotheses to test). The process is iterative, with the data mining analyst asking questions after each new output. The analyst must be careful not to overfit the data; that is, find relationships which are not in the data.

Data mining deals with looking for five types of relationships:

1. *Associations*. Things done together like buying grocery items.
2. *Sequences*. Events that follow each other over time, such as buying a house and then a refrigerator.
3. *Classifications*. Recognizing patterns that lead to rules.
4. *Clusters*. Defining groups that go together.
5. *Forecasting*. Extrapolating time series to predict future situations.

APPLICATION: CUSTOMER RELATIONSHIP MANAGEMENT

Customer relationship management, discussed in more detail in Chapter 6, refers to the idea that customers are unique and that marketing to them should be done on a one-to-one basis. To do so, you need accurate data about the customer: what they like, what they spend money on in your line of business, and more. The concept, which is controversial, argues that the day of mass merchandising by newspaper and television ads is nearing its end and firms should revert to the model of the old-time grocer who knew each of his customers and treated people as individuals.

While the concept of one-to-one marketing was simple in the late 1800s when towns and neighborhoods were small and merchants knew each customer personally, it becomes much more difficult for large firms dealing with hundreds of thousands of customers. That is where the data warehouse comes in. By keeping data on each transaction (which implies low granularity and very large amounts of data in the warehouse), it is possible to develop a picture of individual purchasing habits over time. The data warehouse serves as the source of clean data on the customer (remember ETL discussed earlier) and a single place where all the customer's transactions are available. However, because a warehouse dedicated to CRM is usually much larger than one for supporting decision making, it is more expensive to create and to operate.

The benefits of the warehouse data for CRM include

- Better segmenting of customers.
- Increased cross-selling capabilities.
- Increased customer loyalty and hence retention. (It is argued that acquiring a customer is five or more times as expensive as keeping a customer.)
- Improved target marketing.

As with all collections of customer data, other issues, such as privacy of the data, must be dealt with. As described in Chapter 6, the data warehouse is only one element of CRM.

APPLICATION: BUSINESS INTELLIGENCE

At its simplest level, business intelligence (BI), discussed in Chapter 8, refers to the types of granular information that line-of-business managers seek as they analyze

- Sales trends
- Customer buying habits
- Other key performance metrics about the organization and its competitors
- Potential products, mergers and acquisitions, potential customers
- "What-if" analyses

The tools used include

- Simple querying and reporting
- Online analytic processing
- Statistical analysis
- Forecasting
- Data mining
- Geographic information systems

Most of these tools are associated with the data warehouse, which serves as part of the infrastructure for business intelligence. The data warehouse is particularly attractive for business intelligence use because BI requires clean data.

STRATEGIC USE[10]

The data warehouse can be a strategic asset to the firm. Figure 9 shows the Porter–Millar value chain[11] and the types of industries that have used the data warehouse to gain advantage along the chain.

The chain indicates where value is added in bringing products to customers. Of the elements of the value chain, data warehousing is most used in marketing where it is applied to analyze trends, buying patterns, and sales promotions, as well as for CRM. However, applications occur in all four areas of the value chain. For example, in product development:

Banking	Customer service
Credit card	New services for a fee
Insurance	Risk management
Telecom.	New service promotions

Analysis of a sample of firms leads to the strategic grid (similar to the famous 2 x 2 grid developed by the Boston Consulting Group) shown in Figure 10. Here the two dimensions are the strategic impact of the data warehouse system and the intensity of the transaction data.

The four quadrants of the grid correspond to the following situations:

Opportunity. In this quadrant, the firm is generating lots of transaction data and information systems are vital to its success. Information supports relations to customers. The data warehouse can be used to develop new information services. Example: banking.

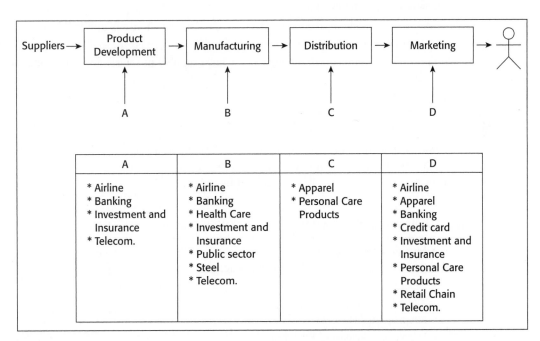

Figure 9 Strategic uses of the data warehouse along the Porter–Millar value chain.

---

[10] This section is based on Y. T. Park, "Strategic Uses of the Data Warehouse," *Journal of Data Warehousing* 2(1): January 1997.

[11] M. E. Porter and V. E. Millar, "How Information Gives You Competitive Advantage," *Harvard Business Review,* July 1985.

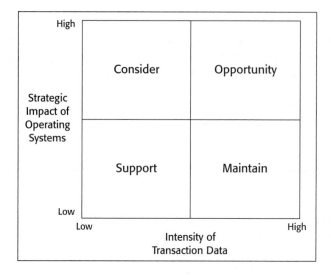

Figure 10 Strategic impact and intensity of transaction data for data warehouses.

Consider. This quadrant involves low data intensity but high strategic impact. Information systems play a strategic role in organizational success. Firms in this quadrant may not need a data warehouse now, but can use a data mart to gain insights into the business. Examples: apparel or personal care.

Support. In this quadrant, the value added by the data warehouse is minimal because the number of transactions is small and not strategic. Example: steel.

Maintain. Firms in this quadrant engage in a large number of transactions but make low strategic use of IT. Example: food.

MANAGING THE DATA WAREHOUSE

This section is concerned with managing the data warehouse once it is built. The warehouse is a major facility for the organization and care must be taken to keep it in control. Table 7 shows the range of managerial issues. We discuss three of them here.

Table 7 DATA WAREHOUSE MANAGEMENT CONSIDERATIONS

- Monitoring activity
- Determining what data are kept in the warehouse
- Security
- The data model
- Keeping metadata up to date
- Degree of redundancy of the data
- Team roles and responsibilities
- Staffing
- End-user roles and responsibilities

Monitoring Activity

Over time, the contents of the data warehouse grow, but the amount of data in the warehouse actually used decreases as a percentage of the data stored. The following is a typical pattern:

Year	Size (gigabytes)	Usage
1	20	~100%
2	60	90%
3	120	70%
4	300	50%

Unless you actively delete unused data, the growth in contents requires continually adding storage and computing power to the warehouse. You will therefore need to monitor usage to determine what is not being used and could either be deleted or moved to less expensive storage media.[12] However, the data about usage by itself are not enough. Some data may be important but used infrequently (e.g., only during tax season or for occasional site location analyses). Monitoring also helps identify who is using the warehouse, who is experiencing long response times, the mix of activities (large, small queries), and other performance parameters. A decision must also be made on how much to monitor, because the monitoring itself uses up storage.

Staffing

A large data warehouse may require considerable staff to keep it going. The following categories of people are needed.

- *Database designers* work to keep the data warehouse efficient as changes occur. They are also metadata managers and hence must know both the business and the technology.

- *Database archeologists* know the legacy system inside and out. They are important because more than half the total upkeep involves finding data, figuring out what they mean, and cleansing them before they are loaded into the warehouse.

- *Systems programmers* make sure that data move smoothly between the legacy system and the warehouse.

- *Trainers*, who are required more when the warehouse first opens, but are needed on a continuing basis as the warehouse changes and as new people become involved.

- *The data warehouse administrator* is the project team leader who coordinates the warehouse efforts. Like the database designers, the administrator must be a two-culture person, conversant in both the business and the technology. The administrator is responsible for maintaining support of the warehouse in the organization and for mediating between the user community and the information systems department.

---

[12] The time required to retrieve data depends in part on the retrieval speed of the medium on which it is stored. In current technology, disk drives are usually the fastest, with DVDs, CD-ROMs, and magnetic tape trailing behind. Usually, the faster the retrieval speed, the greater the cost for storing the same amount of data.

Users

Data warehouse users fall into four categories:

- *Report viewers* who receive structured reports at regularly scheduled times.
- *Data tourists* who want guidance as they explore the data. Tourists occasionally wander off on their own and become surfers.
- *Information surfers* who want to look at any data at any time. Typically these heavy users learn SQL and other tools so that they can surf on their own.
- *Information planners and data warehouse staff* who visit the warehouse daily, doing a variety of tasks to improve and maintain the warehouse.

WHY WAREHOUSE PROJECTS CAN FAIL[13]

Early in the history of data warehouses, failures were fairly common. While this situation is becoming much rarer as the skill and sophistication of both IT organizations and vendors increase, failures are still sometimes encountered. Failures are, of course, costly to both the organization and the people involved. What is a failure is a matter of definition. In many cases, a working warehouse is produced but doesn't live up to expectations.

Table 8 lists the sources of failure in three studies.

What is striking about the three lists in Table 8 is that a large number of people were to blame for the failures that occurred. The problems came from management and users as well as from the IT organization.

Table 8   REASONS WAREHOUSE PROJECTS FAIL – THREE SOURCES

Watson and Haley	Stackoviak	Love[14]
Poor data quality	Failure to involve everyone in process	Diffusion of leadership
Not enough money	Failure to understand why warehouse exists	No relation between business and IT benefits
Poor objectives	Incorrect assumptions	No senior management input
Technical limits	Unrealistic time frames and scope	Poor use of data
Misunderstanding legacy data	Poorly managed expectations	Inappropriate systems development
Lack of user support	Short-term rather than long-term view	Lack of control
Missed deadlines	Failure to learn from experience of others	Lack of up-front MIS involvement
Lack of training, expertise		
Poorly managed expectations		

---

[13] This section is based on H. J. Watson et al., *Journal of Data Warehousing,* Spring 1999.

[14] Love's results are based on a single case.

Typical of the failures is a large retailer. The story went like this: The project was initiated by IT and sold to management. It was agreed to use existing hardware and software. IT rapidly found that the project would take longer than planned, the hardware was inadequate for the volume of data, the software could not handle the job, and the software vendor dropped the product. Upper management naturally became disillusioned and terminated the project. The retailer then restarted the project as a subject area data mart using new hardware and software. The idea was to replicate the data mart until a 2 terabyte data warehouse was achieved. The work proceeded as an R&D project, not as a major IT project because of the lead time to complete, the small amount of money involved, and the short-term focus of top management.

In looking at the eight cases they studied, Watson et al. found that in five of the eight cases, the project was being revived, often in the smaller form of a data mart. If there was a business need, the firms tried again but used a different approach and a new internal sponsor. Overall, the failures were more organizational than technical. After the initial failure, the data mart approach was taken to lower risk.

DATA WAREHOUSING COSTS

Being designed for the enterprise so that they can provide everyone with a common data set, data warehouses are large and invariably increase in size with time. Typical storage sizes run from 50 gigabytes to several terabytes. Among the firms with multi-Terabyte warehouses are American Express, BankAmerica, Nations Bank, J.C. Penney, and Wal-Mart.

Estimates of the total size of the industry vary considerably and cannot be compared directly because individual estimates differ in what they include, and firms that do such analyses do not make their inputs public.

For individual warehouses, typical costs are estimated as:

Warehouse size	Cost ($)	Time to implement
1 terabyte	3 million	2 years
500 gigabytes	<1 million	90 days

For terabyte-size warehouses, consulting costs are estimated at $1 million of the $3 million cost. At the upper end, costs of $30 million are reported. Note that these costs are for building the warehouse and turning it on, and do not include costs of operating and maintaining the warehouse over time.

Factors affecting initial cost include:

Categories of data to be warehoused	Summary data to be generated	Construction schedule
Historical time period to be stored	End-user sophistication	In-house vs. vendor development
Granularity	Amount of competitor data to be stored	Centralization vs. decentralization

Operating expenses include

Warehouse maintenance	Maintaining metadata	Meeting requests for data	Archiving
Warehouse updating	Validation of warehouse data	Monitoring activity	Security

THE DATA WAREHOUSING INDUSTRY[15]

The drivers for the growth of the data warehousing industry include

- The increasing need to transform business data into useful information.
- The need for better demand prediction and inventory control.
- Applications such as CRM, data mining, and business intelligence.

Expenditures are growing in customer-oriented industries through the use of CRM.

The data warehousing industry includes firms that sell central hardware (platforms, memory), software, professional services such as consulting, and user hardware (desktops, peripherals).

A large number of database vendors sell data warehousing and data mart software. They include such large firms as IBM, Microsoft, NCR, Oracle, SAP, and Sybase. In addition, consultants and a large number of firms that specialize in OLAP and business intelligence (e.g., Cognos, Hummingbird, Hyperion, MicroStrategy, and SAS) also resell warehouses.

The product categories include

Integrated solutions	Data marts	ETL
Data cleansing	Virtual data warehouses	MOLAP/ROLAP tools
Data replication	Operational data stores	Query and reporting
Repositories	RDB management systems, MDDB management systems	Data mining

BENEFITS AND PROBLEMS

In a survey by the Meta Group of adopters of data warehousing, the following benefits were anticipated:

Better data for decisions	42%	Competitive advantage	38%	Enterprise view of data	20%
Faster decisions	42%	Decreased cost	24%	Increased revenues	14%

These gains were not for free. Among the problems encountered were

Inadequate planning	Hardware limits	Insufficient funding	Shrinking budgets
Poor estimates of organizational, political, cultural effects	Lack of coordination among data marts	Providing desired user access	Systems integration

Technical difficulties included data quality, managing expectations by users and management, transforming legacy data, analyzing business rules, and business data modeling.

ANSWERS TO MANAGERIAL QUESTIONS

What is a data warehouse?

Data warehousing refers to databases that unify a firm's data resources so that they present a single version of the truth for management. These databases are used as inputs for a variety of managerial tasks.

Why build one?

Data are the lifeblood of an organization, whether it is learning what is selling, what items a specific customer has in stock, or planning for the future. With the increasing proliferation of data sources, the data warehouse provides a single, central place where the single version of the truth can be found.

---

[15] Source: Meta Group.

What are the differences among a data warehouse, a data mart, an operational data store, and a real-time data warehouse?

The term data warehouse refers to a full-fledged enterprisewide database that is subject-oriented, integrated, time variant, and nonvolatile. A data mart is a small data warehouse designed for a work group or a strategic business unit. In some organizations, portions of the data warehouse are downloaded to data marts to create a hierarchical data system. An operational data store carries the concept of data warehouse to the operational level, where data are volatile. A real-time data warehouse is used to support near-real-time decision making.

How expensive is it?

Enterprisewide data warehouses can run to 2 to 5 million dollars in initial cost and incur annual maintenance costs. Data mart costs are in the $100,000 or less range for initial cost.

What can you use it for?

Applications include online analytic processing, business intelligence, data mining, customer relationship management, and supply chain management. These applications are discussed in the chapters that follow.

PROBLEMS

1. DATA WAREHOUSE AND YOUR FIRM

   If your company has a data warehouse or (one or more) data marts, describe its size, organization, and what the technology is used for in your firm.

   If you do not work for a firm with a data warehouse or data mart, discuss what applications could use a warehouse and what size and type of warehouse(s) would make sense. If your answer is none, explain why none.

2. DATA WAREHOUSE AND ERP

   A data warehouse is one way of creating a single truth about transaction and management data. With the interrelations that exist in ERP systems (Chapter 4), an argument can be made that an ERP system is also a source of a single truth. Yet most large firms operate both kinds of systems. Explain why you believe this dual approach is correct or incorrect.

3. METADATA

   Metadata, that is, data about the data in the warehouse, are considered essential. Yet, many people believe that metadata are poorly understood and badly implemented. Think about what different classes of users need to be able to navigate their way to find data and to be able to know what questions can be answered by the warehouse. Discuss, from the user's point of view, what metadata should be supplied for casual users, regular users, and power users.

Chapter 6

Customer Relationship Management[1]

MANAGERIAL QUESTIONS

What are the goals of customer relationship management (CRM)?

What is new about customer relationship management? Haven't we been doing CRM since the company was founded?

Is CRM a marketing strategy by itself?

How difficult is it to implement?

Do I need a consultant?

How much is it going to cost me?

Show should I implement? By stages or all at once?

How long before I see a return?

INTRODUCTION

Over a century ago, in small-town America, before the advent of the supermarket, the mall, and the automobile, people went to their neighborhood general store to purchase goods. The proprietor and the small staff recognized the customer by name and knew the customer's preferences and wants. The customer, in turn, remained loyal to the store and made repeated purchases. This idyllic customer relationship disappeared as the nation grew, the population moved from small farm communities to large urban areas, the consumer became mobile, and supermarkets and department stores were established to achieve economies of scale through mass marketing.

Although prices were lowered and goods became more uniform in quality, the relationship between the customer and the merchant became nameless and faceless. The personal relationship between merchant and customer was a thing of the past. As a result, customers grew fickle, moving to the supplier who provided the desired object at lowest cost or with the most features.

The last several years saw the rise of customer relationship management (abbreviated CRM) as an important business approach. CRM seeks to attract, maintain, and enhance the ways in which the firm interacts with customers so that revenue and profits increase. The improvements in the customer relationship are to be achieved by improving customer service and better meeting customer needs and preferences.

---

[1] This chapter is based on P. Gray and J. Byun, Customer Relationship Management http://www.crito.uci.edu/publications/pdf/crm.pdf originally published as a working paper by the Center for Research, Information, Technology and Organizations (CRITO) at the University of California at Irvine. Used by permission.

Operationally, the CRM concept itself is relatively simple. Rather than market to a mass of people or firms, market to each customer individually. In this one-on-one approach, information about a customer (e.g., previous purchases, needs, and wants) is used to frame offers that are more likely to be accepted. Advances in information technology make this approach possible.

Remember that CRM stands for customer relationship *management, not* customer relationship *marketing.* Management is a broader concept than marketing because it covers marketing management, manufacturing management, human resource management, service management, sales management, and research and development management. Thus, CRM requires organizational and business level approaches—which are customer centric—to doing business rather than a simple marketing strategy.

CRM involves all of the corporate functions (marketing, manufacturing, customer services, field sales, and field service) required to contact customers directly or indirectly. The term "touch points" is used in CRM to refer to the many ways in which customers and firms interact. Touch points include call centers, salespersons, distributors, stores, branch offices, Web, or e-mail.

The following is a formal definition of CRM[2]:

> *Any application or initiative designed to help an organization optimize interactions with customers, suppliers, or prospects via one or more touch points for the purpose of acquiring, retaining, or cross-selling customers.*

To achieve CRM in practice, companies focus on three aspects:

1. Individual CRM applications that result in business value.

2. A technology infrastructure to support both present and future CRM applications.

3. Using CRM, transforming the organization, made possible through CRM.

These three aspects are increasingly complex.

HISTORY OF THE CRM MARKET

Before 1993, CRM included two major markets.[3]

- Sales force automation (SFA)
- Customer services (CS)

Sales force automation was initially designed to support salespeople in managing their touch points and to provide them with event calendars about their customers. SFA's meaning expanded to include managing opportunities; that is, supporting sales methodologies and interconnection with other functions of the company such as production. Sidebar 1 indicates the range of sales force automation capabilities currently available.

Whereas sales force automation is a before-sales activity, customer service (CS) is an after-sales activity. The goal of Customer Service is to resolve internal and external customer problems quickly and effectively. By providing fast and accurate answers to customers, a company can save cost and increase customer loyalty and revenue. As shown in Sidebar 2, customer services include call center management, field service management, and help desk management.

---

[2] D. L. Goodhue, B. H. Wixom, and H. J. Watson, "Realizing Business Benefits through CRM: Hitting the Right Target in the Right Way," *MISQ Executive* 1(2): June 2002.

[3] "Financial Times," *Financial Times Surveys Edition,* June 7, 2000.

Today, CRM includes all customer-facing applications, including

- Sales force automation (SFA),
- Customer service (CS),
- Sales and marketing management (SMM), and
- Contact and activity management.[4]

SIDEBAR 1   *Sales Force Automation Capabilities*

- *Contact Management*. Maintain customer information and contact histories for existing and prospective customers. May include points in the sales cycle and in the customer's replenishment cycle.
- *Activity Management*. Provide calendar and scheduling for individual sales people
- *Communication Management*. Communicate via e-mail and fax.
- *Forecasting*. Assist with future sales goals, targets, and projections.
- *Opportunity Management*. Manage leads and potential leads for new customers.

- *Order Management*. Obtain online quotes and transform inquiries into orders.
- *Document Management*. Develop and retrieve standard and customizable management reports and presentation documents.
- *Sales Analysis*. Analyze sales data.
- *Product Configuration*. Assemble alternate product specifications and pricing.
- *Marketing Encyclopedia*. Provide updated information about products, prices, promotions, as well as soft information about individuals (e.g., their influence on buying decisions) and information about competitors.

Source: http://www.benchmarkingreports.com/salesandmarketing/sm115_sfa_profiles.asp

---

SIDEBAR 2   *Customer Services Capabilities*

- Call center management
- Provide automated, end-to-end call routing and tracking.
- Capture customer feedback information for performance measurement, quality control, and product development.
- Field service management
- Allocate, schedule, and dispatch the right people, with the right parts, at the right time.

- Log materials, expenses, and time associated with service orders.
- View customer history.
- Search for proven solutions.
- Help desk management
- Solve the customer's problem by searching the existing knowledge base.
- Initiate, modify, and track problem reports.
- Provide updates, patches, and new versions for previously sold merchandise.

Sources: http://www.clarify.com/products/suite/service/
         http://www.peoplesoft.com/en/us/products/applications/crm/product_content.html

---

[4] Emerging Market Technologies, 2000, CRM defined http://www.emtpitcrew.com/free/definition.html.

THE CRM APPROACH

Traditional marketing strategies focused on the four Ps (price, product, promotion, and place) to increase market share. The main concern was to increase the volume of transactions between seller and buyer.[5] Volume of transactions was considered a good measure of the performance of marketing strategies and tactics.

CRM is a business strategy that goes beyond increasing transaction volume. Its objectives are to increase profitability, revenue, and customer satisfaction. To achieve CRM, a companywide set of tools, technologies, and procedures promote the relationship with the customer to increase sales.[6] Thus, CRM is primarily a strategic business and process issue rather than a technical issue.

Figure 1 shows that the three components of customer, relationship, and management must be considered together.

CRM tries to achieve a "single integrated view of customers" and a customer-centric approach.[7]

BASIC ASSUMPTIONS OF CRM

In this section we discuss the basic assumptions of the CRM approach. For each assumption, we also present counterarguments and/or limitations.

1. *Customers Act According to Habit*. A basic idea of CRM is that the future behavior of customers is determined by, or similar to, their previous behavior. In other words, the people will continue to behave as they did yesterday and a month ago. This assumption is partially right and partially wrong. As time goes by, behavior patterns change. Therefore, the important thing is the prediction model of future behavior. By predicting future behavior, a company can better serve its customers' changing demands and preferences.

2. *Current Customer Information Is Always Correct*. It is important to maintain the quality of customer demographic and behavioral information. The right decision about a customer requires correct data and information. Can we believe or trust the customer data in the database or in the data warehouse? The customer database comes from a variety of sources and is obtained by different input methods. Considerable attention (and expense) is required for cleansing the data periodically to make it useful for CRM. The firm must update as customer information changes. For example,

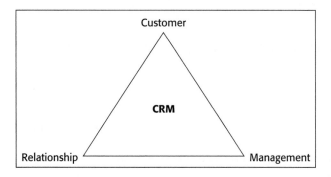

Figure 1 Components of CRM.
Source: P. Gray and J. Byun, *Customer Relationship Management*, Figure 1, Irvine, CA: CRITO, March 2001, http://www.crito.uci.edu/publications/pdf/crm.pdf, with permission.

[5] G. A. Wyner, "Customer Relationship Measurement," *Marketing Research* 11(2): pp. 39-41, Summer, 1999.

[6] Sweeney Group, What Is CRM? 2000, http://www.sweeneygroup.com/ crm.htm.

[7] G. A. Wyner, "Customer Relationship Measurement," *Marketing Research,* 11(2): pp. 39-41, Summer, 1999.

people move; income levels change; marriages, births, and deaths occur. Admittedly, the correct decision is sometimes made accidentally from incorrect data; however, that is a rare event.

3. *Consumers Want Individual, Differentiated Treatment, Services, and Products.* CRM assumes that the customer always wants individualized products and services. However, this assumption cannot always be satisfied because a company cannot always deliver all of the required products and services. Furthermore, instead of individualization, customer-buying decisions for products and services often follow fashion or trends. Technology developments are also important in the decision process. Therefore, some argue the importance of providing the right products and services at the right time or moment rather than just providing individualized products and services.

4. *Customers with the Greatest Profitability Should Receive the Best Service.* The customers that are most valued are those that are most profitable. To hold on to these customers, the CRM philosophy calls for them to receive exceptional service. For example, Harrah's Entertainment, which operates casinos in Las Vegas and throughout the country, follows this approach. By using its data warehouse as the data source, Harrah's keeps track of all its customers. It offers the best of these customers a variety of free services, upgrades, and personal attention that other customers do not receive.

Customer

The customer is the primary source of the company's present profit and future growth. However, a good customer, who provides more profit with less resource, is always scarce because customers are knowledgeable and the competition is fierce. Distinguishing who is the real customer can be difficult because the buying decision is frequently a collaborative activity among participants of the decision-making process.[8] Information technologies can provide the abilities to distinguish and manage customers. CRM can be thought of as a marketing approach that is based on customer information.[9]

Relationship

The relationship between a company and its customers involves continual bidirectional communication and interaction. The relationship can be short-term or long-term, continuous or discrete, and repeating or onetime. Relationship can be attitudinal or behavioral. Even when customer attitudes toward the company and its products are positive, their buying behavior can be highly situational.[10] For example, the buying pattern for airline tickets can depend on whether a person buys the ticket for their family vacation or a business trip. CRM involves managing this relationship so it is profitable and mutually beneficial. Customer lifetime value (CLV), discussed in Sidebar 3, is a tool for measuring this relationship.

Management

CRM is an activity that goes beyond the marketing department. It involves continuous corporate change in culture and processes. The customer information collected is transformed into corporate knowledge that leads to activities that take advantage of the information and of market opportunities. CRM requires a comprehensive change in the organization and its people.

---

[8] G. A. Wyner, 1999, op. cit.

[9] G. A. Wyner, 1999, op. cit.

[10] G. A. Wyner, 1999, op. cit.

SIDEBAR 3	*Customer Lifetime Value*

A fundamental concept of customer relationship management is the lifetime value of a new customer. The basic idea is that customers should be judged on their profitability to the firm over the total time (dubbed "lifetime") they make purchases. Profitability is usually based on net value, that is, the markups over cost less the cost of acquiring and keeping the customer. Fixed costs are not considered because it is assumed that these costs will be incurred with or without the particular customer.

This sidebar presents a very simple, very crude, way of doing the calculations for a single customer. It is based on the average customer and does not consider time value of money or the effects of marketing actions such as loyalty programs and referral programs. In addition it is also possible to model such factors as the total number of customers and the increasing percentage retained from year to year.

The simplest approach to lifetime value begins by computing the average net revenue from a customer by multiplying four quantities together:

Avg. revenue = Avg. sale × No. of purchases/year ×
    Stay of customer × Avg. profit %

and then subtracting the cost to acquire and the cost to retain × number of purchases. For example,

Average sale	$2,000
Cost to acquire	$500
Number purchases/year	2
Cost to retain/purchase	$20
Average length of customer stay (years)	3
Number of purchases	6
Average profit margin	24%

Then, the net lifetime value of the customer is

$$2000 \times 2 \times 3 \times 0.24 - 500 - 20 \times 6 = 2260$$

Three strategies can be followed to increase the value of the customer:

1. Increase average size of sale (tie-ins, package multiple items).
2. Increase number of sales to customer (find other customer needs and satisfy them).
3. Increase profit margin (reduce overhead cost, reduce cost of goods, and raise price if market will stand it).

The computer, of course, can play a role in all of these.

The same methods apply to an existing customer. When considering their future value from now on. However, there is no acquisition cost for an existing customer.

Specific software is available to support the management process. It supports such processes as:

- E-commerce ordering
- Self-service applications
- Catalog management
- Bill presentation
- Marketing programs
- Analysis applications
- Field service

All of these techniques, processes, and procedures are designed to promote and facilitate the firm's sales and marketing.

The foregoing can be made more succinct:

CRM aligns business processes with customer strategies to build customer loyalty and increase prof-its over time.[11]

Note that this short definition does not imply software or technology, although most firms involved in CRM use both.

DRIVERS FOR CRM APPLICATIONS

Having defined the three components of CRM, we are ready to turn to the factors that drive CRM applications in the firm. Competition for customers is intense. From a purely economic point of view, firms learned that it is less costly to retain a customer than to find a new one. The oft-quoted statistics[12] go something like this:

- By Pareto's principle, it is assumed that 20% of a company's customers generate 80% of its profits.[13]

- In industrial sales, it takes an average of 8 to 10 physical calls in person to sell a new customer, 2 to 3 calls to sell an existing customer.

- It is 5 to 10 times more expensive to acquire a new customer than obtain repeat business from an existing customer. For example, according to the Boston Consulting Group,[14] the costs to market to existing Web customers is $6.80 compared to $34 to acquire new Web customers.

- A typical dissatisfied customer tells 8 to 10 people about his or her experience.

- A 5% increase in retaining existing customers translates into 25% or more increase in profitability.

In the past, the prime approach to attracting new customers was through media and mail advertising about what the firm has to offer. This advertising approach is scattershot, reaching many people including current customers and people who would never become customers. For example, the typical response rate from a general mailing is about 2%. Thus, mailing a million copies of an advertisement yields only 20,000 responses on average.

Another driver is the change introduced by electronic commerce (Chapter 3). Rather than the customer dealing with a salesperson either in a brick and mortar location or on the phone, in electronic commerce the customer is in front of their computer screen at home or in the office. Thus, firms do not have the luxury of someone with sales skills to convince the customer. Whereas it normally takes effort for the customer to move to a competitor's physical location or dial another 800-number, in electronic commerce firms face an environment in which competitors are only a few clicks away.

---

[11] D. K. Rigby, F. Reichheld, and P. Schefter, "Avoid the Four Perils of CRM," *Harvard Business Review* 80(2): pp. 101-109, February 2002.

[12] Although often repeated, sources for many of these numbers could not be found. They may be the equivalent of an urban legend.

[13] Some even claim that 20% of a firm's customers contribute 110% of its profits whereas the rest of the customers, in aggregate, cause losses.

[14] C. Hildebrand, "One to a Customer; Customer Relationship Management," *CIO Enterprise Magazine,* October 15, 1999, www2.cio.com/archieve/printer.cfm?URL=enterprise/ 101599_customer_print.cfm.

REVENUE AND COST GOALS

Major revenue and cost goals of CRM include

- Increase revenue growth through customer satisfaction.
- Reduce costs of sales and distribution.
- Minimize customer support costs.

The following examples illustrate tactics to achieve these goals:

1. To increase revenue growth
   - Increase share of wallet[15] by cross-selling.
2. To increase customer satisfaction
   - Make the customer's experience so pleasant that the customer returns to you for the next purchase.
3. To reduce cost of sales and distribution
   - Target advertising to customers to increase the probability that an offer is accepted.
   - Use Web applications to decrease the number of direct sales people and distribution channels needed.
   - Manage customer relationships rather than manage products (a change in marketing).
4. To minimize customer support costs
   - Make information available to customer service representatives so they can answer any query.
   - Automate the call center so that representatives are given direct access to customer history and preferences and therefore can cross-sell (see Goal 1).

PRINCIPLES OF CRM

The overall processes and applications of CRM are based on the following basic principles.

- ***Treat Customers Individually***. Remember customers and treat them individually. CRM is based on a philosophy of personalization. Personalization means the "Content and services to the customer should be designed based on customer preferences and behavior."[16] Personalization creates convenience to the customer and increases the cost of changing vendors.

- ***Acquire and Retain Customer Loyalty through Personal Relationships***. Once personalization takes place, a company needs to sustain relationships with the customer. Continuous contacts with the customer—especially when designed to meet customer preferences—can create customer loyalty.

- ***Select "Good" Customers Instead of "Bad" Customers Based on Lifetime Value***. Find and keep the customers who generate the most profits. Through differentiation, a company

---

[15] Share of wallet is shorthand for saying that the customers spend more of their available budget with your firm than they otherwise would.

[16] P. Hagen, H. Manning, and R. Souza, "Smart Personalization," *The Forrester Report,* July 1999.

can allocate its limited resources to obtain better returns. The best customers deserve the most customer care; the worst customers should be dropped. Customers on which the firm loses money (e.g., through high sales or other transaction costs) should certainly be dropped.[17]

In summary, personalization, loyalty, and customer value are the main principles of CRM implementation.

TECHNOLOGY AND SERVICE

Table 1 shows the principal functions CRM packages provide. Recognize that all vendors do not provide all services. Strategies for implementation range from buying integrated packages that provide almost all the CRM functionality (e.g., integrated packages from Oracle, Siebel, or SAP)[18] to mixing and matching capabilities in modules from a number of vendors.

Customer service and support, marketing automation, and Web and field sales areas are the most important parts of the CRM packages.

INFORMATION TECHNOLOGIES FOR CRM

Key Tasks

"I know who you are, I remember you. I get you to talk to me. And then, because I know something about you my competitors don't know, I can do something for you my competitors can't do—not for any price." [19]

CRM differs from the previous method of database marketing in that the database marketing technique simply tried to sell more products to the customer for less cost.[20] The database marketing approach is highly company centric in that it starts with the company's products. Unfortunately, customers were not kept loyal by the discount programs and the onetime promotions that were used in this approach. Customer loyalty is, indeed, quite difficult to obtain or buy. The CRM approach is customer centric. This approach focuses on the long-term relationship with the customers by providing the customer benefits and values from their point of view rather than based on what the company wants to sell.

Table 1 PRINCIPAL FUNCTIONS OF CRM PACKAGES

Product management	Field services	Customer service	Analysis
Web sales	Partner collaborations	Customer support	Brand management
Field sales	Marketing automation	ERP	

[17] Some argue that dropping customers is counterproductive because some of these customers—and you can't tell which ones—may turn out to be good customers in the future.

[18] These firms differ somewhat in the modules they provide in their packages. They also come from different backgrounds, which affects their offering. Oracle started in databases, PeopleSoft in human resources, Siebel in sales force automation, and SAP in manufacturing. All provide ERP packages.

[19] F. Newell, *loyalty.com; Customer Relationship Management in the New Era of Internet Marketing,* New York: McGraw-Hill, 2000.

[20] M. Seiler and P. Gray, *Database Marketing,* Center for Research in Information, Technologies, and Organizations, University of California at Irvine.

Four basic tasks[21] are required to achieve CRM's goals of increasing the benefit to the customer and adding to the customer's value:

1. ***Customer Identification***. To provide value to the customer, the company must know or identify the customer through marketing channels, transactions, and interactions over time.

2. ***Customer Differentiation***. Each customer's lifetime value is different from the company's point of view (Sidebar 3) and each customer imposes unique demands and requirements on the company.

3. ***Customer Interaction***. Customer demands change over time. From a CRM perspective, the customer's long-term profitability and relationship to the company is important. Therefore, the company keeps learning about the customer.

4. ***Customization/Personalization***. "Treat each customer uniquely" is the motto of the entire CRM process. Through the personalization process, a company can increase customer loyalty. Jeff Bezos, CEO of Amazon.com, said, "Our vision is that if we have 20 million customers, then we should have 20 million stores."[22] The automation of personalization is being made feasible by information technologies.

IT Factors of CRM

Traditional (mass) marketing doesn't need to use information technologies extensively because there is no need to distinguish, differentiate, interact with, and customize for individual customer needs. Although *Computing* magazine argues that IT's role in CRM is small,[23] each of the four key CRM tasks depends heavily on information technologies and systems. Table 2 shows this relationship for the marketing processes, for the goals, for traditional mass marketing, for CRM, and for the information technologies used in CRM.

Table 2   IT FACTORS IN CRM

Process	Identification	Differentiation	Interaction	Customization
Goal	• Identify individual customer	• Evaluate customer value and needs	• Build a continuing relationship	• Fulfill customer needs • Generate profit
Traditional mass marketing	• Not done	• Clustering	• Call center	• Sales • Services
CRM	• Customer profiling	• Individual level analysis	• Call center management • Auto response system	• Sales automation • Marketing process automation
Information technologies	• Cookies • Website personalization	• Data mining • Organizational learning	• Web application • Wireless communication	• ERP • E-commerce

Source: P. Gray and J. Byun, *Customer Relationship Management* Table 4, Irvine, CA: CRITO, March 2004, http://www.crito.uci.edu/publications/pdf/crm.pdf, with permission.

---

[21] D. Peppers, M. Rogers, and B. Dorf, "Is Your Company Ready for One-to-One Marketing?" *Harvard Business Review,* January-February 1999.

[22] M. Wheatley, "Jeff Bezos Takes Everything Personally," *CIO,* August, 2000, http://www.cio.com/archieve/080100_bezos.html.

[23] "Computing" IT 'Playing Only a Minor Role in CRM' 2000, http://www.vnunet.com/News/1105945.

CONSULTANTS

Like any other major software development/deployment project, consulting plays an important role in the CRM project. Three different types of consulting companies work in the CRM industry.

- *General Consulting Companies*. Traditional business-consulting companies such as McKinsey & Company, Bearing Point (formerly KPMG), and PricewaterhouseCoopers provide consulting services for CRM integration. This work focuses more on organizational and marketing management integration than technical implementation of CRM software.
- *CRM-Specific Software Vendors*. The consulting arms of software vendors such as Siebel Systems and Onyx Software Corporation, are dedicated to CRM. These companies focus more on technical integration than conceptual or managerial consulting services.
- *Back-End Software Vendor*. SAP AG, Oracle, IBM Global Services Consulting, SAS Institute Inc., and Microsoft also sell CRM consulting services. However, these companies primarily sell their own back-end applications such as ERP systems, database management systems, and statistical analysis systems.

RETURN ON INVESTMENT OF IMPLEMENTATION

Cost and Time

A 2000 report on a Capgemini and IDC survey found that the average total investment in CRM of 300 U.S. and Europe companies was $3.1 million. More than 69% of the companies surveyed spent less than $5 million, and more than 13% of the companies spent over $10 million.[24]

As shown in Tables 3 and 4, based on Gartner Group data, the implementation cost of CRM depends on the industry, project size, and application requirements.

According to Gartner Group, the average implementation cost of CRM can be between $15,000 and $35,000 per user in a 3 year project.[25]

Table 3   ANNUAL CRM EXPENSES (IN $MILLION)

Health care products	3.4
Manufacturer	5–8
Publisher	6–8
Consumer goods manufacturer	6.3
Office supplies manufacturer	8–10

Source: J. Golterman, 2000, *op. cit.*, as quoted in P. Gray and J. Byun, *Customer Relationship Management*, Table 5, Irvine, CA: Crito, March 2001, http://www.crito.uci.edu/publications/pdf/crm.pdf, with permission.

---

[24] J. Sterne, *Customer Service on the Internet,* New York, NY: John Wiley & Sons, 2000. Note that these numbers are now several years old. However, they are indicative of the large amounts that firms spend on CRM.

[25] J. Golterman, "How Will Companies Measure and Justify Spending for a CRM Solution?" Gartner Interactive, 2000, http://gartner11.gartnerweb.com/public/static/crm/crm_qa.html.

Table 4   COST ALLOCATIONS

Services	38%
Software	28%
Hardware	23%
Telecommunication	11%

Source: J. Golterman, 2000, *op. cit.*, as quoted in P. Gray and J. Byun, *Customer Relationship Management*, Table 6, Irvine, CA: CRITO, March 2001, http://www.crito.uci.edu/publications/pdf/crm.pdf, with permission.

The initial cost of a CRM implementation depends strongly on the number of subsystems (Table 1), the size of the firm, and the time to implement. For large international firms, 24 to 36 months are not unusual.

With the economic turndown of 2001, firms became more selective, buying only specific applications. This attitude persists into the middle of the decade. Often firms would take a sequential approach rather than a scary big bang that required nearly "bet-the-company" kinds of expenditures. Companies are looking at increments of $500 thousand to $3 million. In a December 2001 survey of 199 respondents, *CIO* magazine found 64% were looking to implement CRM incrementally through small pilot projects and 49% were hoping to implement in less than 12 months. Some firms were turning to outsourcers, Web services, and application service providers (ASPs; see Chapter 9) who, in effect, rent the software to the user company. In one deal, a bank rented sales force automation software for 134 users at $65/user/month, an expenditure of $104,000.00/year.

Benefits

The principal benefits of CRM are to:

- Improve the organization's ability to retain and acquire customers.
- Maximize the lifetime value of each customer (share of wallet).
- Improve service without increasing cost of service.[26]

Some of these benefits can be measured and others cannot.

CRM Processes

CRM is composed of four continuous processes.

- Identification
- Differentiation
- Interaction
- Customization

Each process provides distinctive benefits to the organization. To obtain all of these benefits, sales, marketing, and service functions need to work together. The benefits are shown in Table 5.

---

[26] CMG, 2000, http://www.cmgplc.com/UK/Products+and+Services/Business+Solutions/RM/The+Business+Benefits.htm.

Table 5   BENEFITS OF CRM PROJECT

	Identification	Differentiation	Interaction	Customization
Source of benefits	Clean data about customer Single customer view	Understanding the customer	Customer satisfaction and loyalty	Customer satisfaction and loyalty
Benefits	Help sales force cross-selling	Cost-effective marketing campaign Reduce direct mailing cost	Cost-effective customer service	Lower cost of acquisition and retention of customer Maximize share of wallet

Source: P. Gray and J. Byun, *Customer Relationship Management,* Table 7, Irvine, CA: CRITO, March 2001, http://www.crito.uci.edu/publications/pdf/crm.pdf, with permission.

Based on a survey of more than 500 executives in six industries (communications, chemicals, pharmaceuticals, electronics/high-tech, forest products, and retail), a 10% improvement of overall CRM capabilities was estimated to add up to $35 million benefits for a $1 billion business unit.[27]

More than 57% of CEOs in another survey with 191 respondents believe that the major objective of CRM is customer satisfaction and retention. Another 17% said it is designed to increase cross-selling and up-selling.[28]

ROI of CRM Project

It is difficult to predetermine the return on investment (ROI) of CRM[29] since CRM does not bring any direct monetary benefits until after implementation. Rather, CRM requires a large amount of initial investment in hardware, software, and training without immediate cost saving or revenue improvement. The benefits of CRM need to be measured on a long-term basis. CRM is designed to build long-term relationships with customers and to generate long-term benefits through increased customer satisfaction and retention.[30]

A survey of 300 companies conducted at a CRM conference concluded that CRM is not a cheap, easy, or fast solution. More than two-thirds of CRM projects end in failure. However, the successful third can obtain up to a 75% ROI.[31]

---

[27] D. Renner, Focusing on Customer Equity—The Unrealized Asset, 2000, http://www.crmproject.com/crm/toc/keynote.html.

[28] M. Seminerio, e-CRM: The Right Way, 2000, http://www.zdnet.com/enterprise/stories/main/0,10228,2605385,00.html.

[29] C. Trepper, "Customer Care Goes End-to-End," *InformationWeek* May 15, 2000.

[30] Cyber Marketing Services, The Great Debate Justifying Your Investment in Customer Relationship Management Solutions, 2000, http://www.crmxchange.com/sessions/debates/july99-transcript.html.

[31] E. Mooney, "CRM Is Costly; Not Managing It Even More Costly," *Radio Communication Report,* April 17, 2000.

CRM ISSUES

Customer Privacy

Customer privacy is an important issue in CRM. CRM deals with large amounts of customer data through various touch points and communication channels. The personalization process in CRM requires identification of each individual customer and collections of demographic and behavioral data. Yet, it is the very information that most customers consider personal and private.

The individual firm is thus caught in an ethical dilemma. It wants to collect as much information as possible about each customer to further its sales, yet in doing so it treads on and beyond the bounds of personal privacy.

Privacy issues are not simple. Customer concerns, legal regulations, and public policies are overwhelming around the world. While it still is unclear and undetermined what extent of customer privacy should be protected and what data should not be used, four basic rules might be considered.[32]

- The customer should be notified when their personal information is collected and will be used for specific purposes.
- The customer should be able to decline to be tracked.
- The customer should be allowed to access their information and correct it.
- Customer data should be protected from unauthorized usage.

Some companies provide a customer consent form to ask the customer to agree to information collection and usage. Providing personalized service to customers is a way to satisfy customers who provided their personal information. All of these efforts are designed to build trust between the company and its customers.

TECHNICAL IMMATURITY

The concept, technologies, and understanding of CRM are still in their early adopter stage. Many of the CRM technologies are immature and the typical implementation costs and time are sufficiently big to frustrate potential users.

Although software and hardware vendors sell themselves as complete CRM solution providers, few technologies and implementation protocols are standardized in the market. Even the scope and extent of what CRM includes differ from vendor to vendor; each follows different implementation requirements to achieve the customer's expectations.

CRM is one of the busiest industries in which frequent mergers and acquisitions occur. Many small companies merge together to compete with large vendors. Large companies such as PeopleSoft acquired small vendors to enter this hot CRM market.[33] Due to these frequent mergers and acquisitions, stable technical support from the market becomes rare. Vendors publish new versions—such as more integrated software—as frequently as they can and expect firms to pay for the upgrade.

---

[32] J. Sterne, 2000, op. cit.

[33] And, as indicated earlier in this book, PeopleSoft itself was merged into Oracle.

Often the technical immaturities or unstable conditions of a firm's CRM software are combined with unclear requirements of the firm's customers and lead to project failure. These technical immaturities may be overcome over time, but the process seems to be long and painful. An implication is that software vendors need to practice CRM with the firms to which they sell.

CRM MYTHS

Sidebar 4 describes some of the myths associated with CRM.

Figure 2 shows the relations between CRM and the customer.

SIDEBAR 4   *Common Myths of CRM*

Myth 1: An Excellent CRM System Guarantees Marketing Success

CRM is not a strategy but a tool to help and modify the marketing strategies of a company. Before it achieves a viable CRM system, a company needs the right value propositions and strategies to implement the customer-centric philosophy of the CRM. CRM requires more commitment and loyalty by the company to the customer rather than by the customer to the company. Without competitive products and services, a company cannot obtain the benefits of CRM.

Myth 2: To Use CRM, a Company Must Be Organized by Customer Segments Rather than Products

Organizational restructuring is an expensive, time-consuming, and painful process for a company and the people in the company. Without appropriate coordination with other functions in a company, restructuring is not as effective as expected. For example, channel strategies should be combined with CRM capabilities so a customer does not receive different offers from the same company through different channels.

Myth 3: Successful CRM Requires a Large Centralized Database with Complete Customer Data

Conventional wisdom is that the larger, more centralized the CRM database, the better the CRM system. Many successful financial companies maintain databases at the product level. By using a smaller database, a company can simplify the system design and maintenance and the customer ownership. Common

standards of hardware and software are more important than large databases.

Myth 4: CRM Requires the Most Advanced and Sophisticated Analytical Techniques

Like the large database myth, the complex analysis myth assumes that the more technology the better. Clean data turn out to be more important and effective than ever-more sophisticated analytical tools. When incomplete, inaccurate, and outdated customer information is used, the result is the classic garbage in, garbage out. Future-oriented and hypothesis-based analysis and anticipation are more effective than complex analysis.

Myth 5: CRM Is a Turnkey Project

Database, infrastructure, and supporting business processes are required to start CRM programs. However, it is not necessary to set up everything together. Rather CRM is a test, run, test process. An iterative and incremental approach is cheaper and more effective than a turnkey-based approach. Lessons from mistakes are important to educate employees about how to use CRM.

This discussion of common myths of CRM implies that CRM is not a perfect single solution to the business problems. CRM is part of a complex set of business strategies and processes to serve the customer.

This sidebar is based on Adolf, R., S. Grant-Thompson, W. Harrington, and M. Singer (1997). "What Leading Banks Are Learning about Big Databases and Marketing," *The McKinsey Quarterly,* No. 3, pp. 187–192.

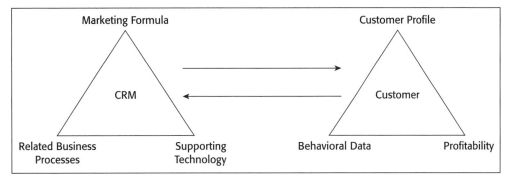

Figure 2 Relation between CRM and the customer.

Source: P. Gray and J. Byun, *Customer Relationship Management*, Figure 3, Irvine, CA: CRITO, March 2001, http://www.crito.uci.edu/publications/pdf/crm.pdf, with permission.

THE IMPORTANCE OF CHANNELS

The role of channels is referred to in Sidebar 4 and several other places in this chapter. Channels are the different avenues available for selling a product. It is considered important that CRM be used to provide integration and optimization across all channels.

VENDORS

A few years ago, technology vendors had their own specialties. For example, Siebel specialized in sales force automation, Remedy in help desk systems, Davox in call center systems, eGain in e-mail management, and BroadVision in front-end applications. Each branched out into CRM and tried to cover the entire area. Today there are no specific vendor boundaries. All vendors are trying to expand their products over the entire CRM area. For example, Siebel claims it can do everything, Davox moved into customer contact management, and BroadVision is trying to integrate backward with ERP.[34]

Most CRM vendors came from two different origins.

- ***Back-End Application***. Traditional ERP vendors (SAP AG, Oracle, and Invensys plc (formerly Baan) acquire, build, and partner their CRM application for ERP functionality.

- ***Front-End Application***. Some companies started with front-end solutions such as personal information management system (PIMS). Siebel, BroadVision, and Remedy are in this category.

Starting in late 1998, with the fast development of e-business, many of the larger firms acquired or merged with mid-sized companies to allow them to offer full service across the entire CRM spectrum. Table 6 lists some of the major categories and vendors. The table shows some of the mergers that took place. By the time you read this book, additional firms may have disappeared.

---

[34] B. McKenna, CRM: Know the Dangers, 2000, http://www.vnunet.com/Analysis/1109017.

Table 6   MAJOR CRM VENDORS

Category	Vendor company
Enterprisewide back-end office	SAP AG
	Oracle
Front-end office	Siebel Systems
	Saratoga Systems
	Vantive Corporation (a division of PeopleSoft, which later merged with Oracle)
	Clarify (a division of Amdocs)
	Onyx Software Corporation
Web-based front-end solution	Firstwave
	UpShot (a division of Siebel)
	Rubric
Adhere to Microsoft standards	Remedy Corporation (A division of BMC Software)
	Onyx Software Corporation
Midsize firm	SalesLogix
	Sales Automation Group
Contact management	Symantec Corporation
	Maximizer Software (Canadian)

Source: P. Gray and J. Byun, *Customer Relationship Management,* Table 2, Irvine, CA: CRITO, March 2001, http://www.crito.uci.edu/publications/pdf/crm.pdf, with permission.

MANAGEMENT RISKS

A CRM disaster is entirely possible. Gartner Group, for example, claims that 55% of all CRM projects don't produce expected results. A Bain & Company survey rated CRM one of the three least satisfying of 25 computer tools. This reaction and backlash to CRM started gathering steam in 2002. So why does CRM fail so often, given the benefits that successful systems provide? The answer lies, as it does for most system failures, in a mix of management and technical problems.

Many managers assume that CRM is a software tool that will manage customer relationships for them. Nothing could be further from the truth. CRM is a collection of strategies and processes, supported by software, that help improve customer loyalty and, over time, profitability. Implementing CRM requires that executives understand what it is they are buying and what it can help them do. Unfortunately, too many of them don't understand what they are approving nor do they have a sense of how much it will cost or how long it will take.

Rigby, Reicheld, and Schefter, writing in *Harvard Business Review,*[35] argue that managers make the following four mistakes:

1. They implement CRM software before they create a customer strategy.

2. They implement CRM software before they change the organization to match the software. (This error is also made in ERP; see Chapter 4.)

---

[35] Rigby, Reichld, and Schefter, *Harvard Business Review,* 2002.

3. They assume that more CRM technology is better.

4. They stalk, rather than woo, customers.

Furthermore,

- CRM systems are hard to implement
- Sales and marketing teams, being people-oriented rather than technology-oriented, are often loath to adopt the new technology.
- Vendor sales people (and internal advocates) overpromise and underperform and CRM is a high-risk situation.

There is a silver lining. Two previous high-ticket technologies, ERP systems and data warehouses, also experienced major implementation failures early in their history. However, over time, as vendors and firms climbed up the learning curve, failures became rarer. CRM systems are going through the same phenomenon. They are improving over time. The risk of failure is decreasing but it is nowhere near zero.

CASE STUDIES

The four cases presented in this section illustrate how individual firms in different industries (booksellers, PC vendors, auto manufacturers, and banks) apply the principles described in this chapter.

Amazon.COM

When you try to buy something from Amazon.com, you can see the following statement; "Customers who bought this item also bought these items." If you have any previous purchasing experience with Amazon.com, the company will support a "Welcome to Recommendations" Web page.

The personalized Web pages, vast selection of products, and low prices lead customer loyalty and long-term relationship of Amazon.com. More than 20 million people purchased at Amazon.com. The percentage of returning customers is about 15% to 25%, compared with 3% to 5% for other e-business retailers.

Amazon.com assembles large amounts of information on individual customer buying habits and personal information. Based on a customer's previous purchases and Web-surfing information, Amazon.com recommends books, CDs, and other products. Sometimes a customer buys additional products because of this information.

Through its 1-Click system, which stores personal information such as credit card number and shipping address, Amazon.com simplifies the customer buying process.

Like the corner merchant of old, Jeff Bezos, the founder of Amazon.com, believes the Internet store of the future should be able to guess what the customer wants to buy before the customer knows. He wants to make the Amazon.com website that smart and that personal.[36]

Dell

Since 1983, Dell Computers operated on two simple business ideas: sell computers directly to individual customers and manufacture computers based on the customer's order. The individual customer can make his/her system unique and obtain it directly from the company.

If the system incurs a problem, the user can contact the Dell website directly and receive personalized services by using the customer system service tag number, which is on the side of the computer. These personalized services also provide related information and make software downloads available. In addition, a call center provides technical assistance at multiple levels. If the first-level technician cannot resolve the problem, the customer is routed to a more skilled contact.

---

[36] F. Newell, 2000, op. cit.

Dell is organized by customer segment, such as education, government, small business, large business, and home, instead of by product lines. Dell developed *Premier Dell.com* that covers entire processes of computer ownership: purchasing, asset management, and product support. Premier pages support online purchasing, standard management, price quotations, and order management.

Volkswagen

Volkswagen AG is the largest automobile maker in Europe. More than 36 million vehicles carry their logo. Like other automobile manufacturers, the company is well-informed about its customers and heavily depends on this information. However, they lose contact with the car owner after the first change of ownership (after an average 3.7 years). As a result, the company's information about many of its customers is not current.[37]

In 1988, the company started its Customers Come First marketing strategy. Under this strategy, all of the decision-making processes are based on the voice of the customer. The company carefully monitored their response to advertisements, customer expectations, and customer satisfaction. Customer forums and focus group are used to hear the customer voice.

Volkswagen developed services such as a service guarantee, the emergency plan, the mobility guarantee, the customer club, and a toll-free service phone number. All advertising media are designed toward two-way communication. This approach allows the company to obtain useful information such as lifestyle, demographic, and behavioral data.

The company maintains a central database to provide club card, bonus point programs, club shops, and the Volkswagen magazine. Every contact point with a customer gives the company more information about the customer, so the company can constantly improve the quality and value of the customer database.

Wells Fargo

Banking differs from other industries because the average relationship between customer and bank lasts much longer. For example, in the auto industry, the relationship between the customer and the company is becoming weaker over time. You don't need to contact the car dealer or manufacturer once a week or a month. You can change your oil or maintain your car with a service station rather than a dealer. However, once you open your account in a specific bank, your relationship or dependence on the bank increases. You may write checks more frequently, use direct deposit, transfer money, pay bills, and withdraw money. The bank contacts you regularly by sending you your monthly statement. You can obtain credit card or investment opportunities from the bank.

Wells Fargo transforms these relationships into opportunities. It was the first bank that started 24-hour phone banking service and opened branches in local supermarkets and Starbucks coffee shops. It always tried to provide more touch points to its customers and a one-stop shopping environment.

Since 1993, Wells Fargo tried to integrate all of its back-end customer information into its customer relationship system. Previously, customer information was managed by several different back-end systems. Software was organized by account number, with each back-end system using its own numbering system. Customer service agents found it difficult to integrate customer information when they received a request to transfer funds from one account to another. They had to log on to several different systems to obtain the information and do the transactions requested. In the new system, the service agent can access all required information by using the customer's social security number instead of the account numbers. These changes increase convenience for both customers and service agents.

Wells Fargo provides Internet banking. It built a website as a new touch point in 1995 and provided advanced technologies to its customer. By using online banking, customers can manage their account anytime and anywhere. Online banking also reduces the operating cost of the bank's branches.

In the future, by providing more power to individuals to manage their account and money, Wells Fargo expects to increase customer loyalty and obtain long-term mutual benefits with its customers.[38]

---

[37] K. Chojnacki, "Relationship Marketing at Volkswagen," in T. Hennig-Thurau and U. Hansen (Eds.), *Relationship Marketing,* pp. 49-58, Springer-Verlag, Berlin and Heidelberg, 2000.

[38] P. Seybold and R. Marshak, *Customer.com* New York: NY Times Books, 2000.

CONCLUSIONS

The present is an era of company loyalty to the customer in order to obtain customer loyalty to the company. Consumers are more knowledgeable than ever before. Therefore companies must be faster, more agile, and more creative than a few years ago.

Because the Internet allows information to be obtained almost instantaneously, firms can establish a personalized customer experience through online help, purchase referrals, quicker turnaround on customer problems, and quicker feedback about customer suggestions, concerns, and questions.

CRM is very hard to implement throughout a company. The IT department needs extensive infrastructure and resources to implement CRM databases successfully. Departments must be involved in creating the systems and their people must be trained. Executives must understand that CRM is an end-user project, not just an IT project, and must be willing to support the CRM implementation process forever because CRM never ends.

ANSWERS TO MANAGERIAL QUESTIONS

What are the goals of customer relationship management?

The goals of customer relationship management are to attract, maintain, and enhance the ways in which the firm interacts with customers so that revenue and profits increase.

What is new about customer relationship management? Haven't we been doing CRM since the company was founded?

Firms have, indeed, been involved in customer relationship management from the day they were founded. What is new is a shift in approach from mass advertising to one-to-one marketing, the ability to find out which customers are profitable, and concentrating on retaining existing customers. Although not mandatory, CRM usually involves a major new computer application that must be integrated with the capabilities of the firm.

Is CRM a marketing strategy by itself?

Buying CRM software is not a marketing strategy by itself. The software won't substitute for a customer strategy and for old-fashioned hard work.

How difficult is it to implement?

Quite. CRM is a major IT initiative and is still on the low end of the learning curve, as evidenced by a high failure rate. CRM also requires melding IT's technology culture with marketing and sales' people culture.

Do I need a consultant?

CRM systems are outside the skill set of both existing marketing departments and existing IT departments. They require a shift in thinking by both. Consultants are often necessary and can help, but firms must make sure that they transfer knowledge from the consultants to their own staff.

How much is it going to cost me?

Lots. A full-blown CRM system can easily be a multimillion dollar investment for a large firm.

How should I implement? By stages or all at once?

The conventional wisdom is that, to reduce risk, CRM systems should be rolled out a module at a time rather than trying for a big bang.

How long before I see a return?

Like most IT initiatives, a large fraction of the investment is up-front. Providing you do the necessary training and you overcome the resistance to change, returns should start coming in soon after the initial rollout.

PROBLEMS

1. CRM VERSUS DATABASE MARKETING

Before CRM, many people argued that the problems of finding new customers could be solved by what was called "database marketing." That is, new customers could be found by sending mass mailings to (usually) purchased databases. Compare and contrast CRM and database marketing. Also consider the differences and similarities of database marketing and "spam" on the Internet.

2. DRIVERS

The Section, Drivers for CRM Applications, lists a large number of reasons for CRM, many of which may be urban legends. Find experimental data (not just assertions by marketing people) that supports or counters the arguments given for at least three of the assertions made. Be sure to include references to your sources.

3. PRIVACY AND CRM

Describe privacy regulations in the European Union, in a South American country, in a Mid-East country, and in an Asian country. (You should be able to find the data on the Internet.) Compare the regulations with those in the United States. Also discuss the "safe harbor" provisions for data transfer for CRM between the United States and the European Union.

Chapter 7

Knowledge Management

MANAGERIAL QUESTIONS

How much knowledge does a firm have?

Why manage knowledge?

What types of knowledge are there?

How do you gather knowledge?

How do you transfer knowledge?

How do you update knowledge?

Do you need a separate department for knowledge?

What technologies are available?

How much should you invest?

INTRODUCTION

Why is knowledge important? Thomas H. Davenport and Lawrence Prusak give the answer[1]:

"In a global economy, knowledge may be a company's greatest advantage."

In many cases, it may be your company's only advantage. That is, your firm knows how to do things that other firms don't. Some experts go even further. They argue that if you don't pay attention to knowledge, you will be overtaken by your competitors who do, and you will go out of business. This is a strong statement, but it's most likely true.

At a more micro level, when someone leaves your organization either voluntarily or is fired, all the knowledge in their head goes with them. You lose not just an employee but also a knowledge asset. There is something going on here and managers need to know about it. In fact, starting in the early 1990s, a whole business discipline of "knowledge management" (KM) arose and technologies followed.

---

[1] T. H. Davenport and L. Prusak, *Working Knowledge,* Cambridge, MA: Harvard Business Press, 1998.

To proceed, we need to define three terms: knowledge, knowledge management, and knowledge management systems:

- *Knowledge* refers to ideas that lead to action. It is distinguished from data (individual facts like the details of a transaction) and information (data put into context; see Sidebar 1). Knowledge may be
  - explicit (you can write it down as in a procedure manual or a report) or
  - tacit (in the heads of people but difficult to explain or write down).
- *Knowledge management* is the organizational process for acquiring, organizing, and communicating both tacit and explicit knowledge so that people may use it to be more effective and productive.
- *Knowledge management systems* are information systems designed to facilitate
  - creating,
  - organizing,
  - gathering, and
  - disseminating

  an organization's *knowledge* rather than its *information* or its *data*.

Knowledge management is a general concept of importance to business. Knowledge management systems are specific implementations designed to improve an organization's knowledge position.

Claims

The claims for knowledge management are quite strong. Specifically, it is believed that organizations will

- be more flexible,
- respond more quickly to changing markets,
- be more innovative, and
- improve their decision making and productivity.

That's a lot, and much of it still remains to be proven.

Role of Information Technology

Information technology does NOT, by itself, create knowledge, or guarantee that knowledge will be generated, or promote knowledge sharing in a culture that does not favor knowledge sharing. It is possible to create a knowledge management system (such as that for the London taxicabs described in Sidebar 3 later in this chapter) that does not use computers at all.

| SIDEBAR 1 | *Data, Information, Knowledge* |

Data refers to individual items that are kept in a database. Typically numeric, in business data, center on transaction information. For example, Gray's account shows that he bought six pairs of socks on June 23 for $25.83 on credit. This transaction may create additional data such as the total amount owed by Gray. However, such transaction data are usually not sufficient for making decisions.

Information, Peter Drucker tells us, is "data endowed with relevance and purpose."* Others say that information is data that makes a difference. Information in some way adds value to data by, for example, adding insight, abstraction, or improved understanding. Whereas Gray buying six pairs of socks is data, the number of pairs of socks sold each month during the past year in a store's men's department is information.

Information becomes *knowledge* when data and information are integrated into ideas. This integration may be explicit or tacit. Knowledge is information about which you can take action.

The progression from data to information to knowledge is the conventional way of thinking about knowledge. However, an alternative approach is to realize that you need knowledge to decide which data to obtain. It is also true that, over time, knowledge is downgraded to information and information is downgraded to data. For example, in the late 1800s, electricity was the province of knowledge. Then it became information and now it is ordinary data.

*P. F. Drucker, *The New Realities,* p.189, New York: Harper and Row, 1989.

PRINCIPLES OF KNOWLEDGE MANAGEMENT

It is always heartening to know that a discipline contains some fundamental principles. In the case of knowledge management, Davenport and Prusak defined the principles.[2] The following are four of them.

1. Knowledge originates and resides in people's heads. It is often aided and abetted by what people learned from what is stored on the computer, but not necessarily so.

2. Knowledge becomes useful to firms when it is shared among employees. Sharing is a key part of the knowledge management idea. However, sharing knowledge requires trust among people.

3. Sharing is counterculture in that we are told, from kindergarten on, not to copy. Knowledge sharing therefore requires a culture change. At Capgemini (formerly Ernst and Young), for example, a significant fraction of the annual review process involves measuring how well people share. Thus, many companies need to learn how to share knowledge internally.

4. With technology, we have new ways of dealing with knowledge. Scanning systems, document management systems, and group support systems are examples. Note that, with perhaps the exception of document management systems, the technologies are generic in that they can be used for many applications.

[2] T. H. Davenport and L. Prusak, 1998, op. cit.

KNOWLEDGE STRATEGIES

This section considers the impact of knowledge on the firm.[3] The view is that of the consulting firm McKinsey & Company.[4] Specifically, McKinsey believes that knowledge is a different asset than physical assets. Knowledge has four characteristics that do not seem obvious at first:

1. Knowledge offers extraordinary leverage and increasing rather than decreasing returns over time.

2. Knowledge is subject to fragmentation and leakage. Therefore, it must be refreshed over time if the knowledge advantage is to be maintained.

3. The value of investing in knowledge is uncertain.

4. The value of knowledge generated through an alliance is uncertain for each partner.

These characteristics make investing in knowledge a tricky business.

Leverage

The economics of knowledge differ from those of manufacturing and distribution. The fixed cost is in creating the knowledge. But, once created, initial development costs can be spread across rising volumes rather than being depreciated. Furthermore, network effects[5] emerge as more people use the knowledge. The users benefit both from the knowledge itself and from its increased value. As knowledge grows, users add to it, adapt their work to it, and enrich the knowledge base, thereby also increasing the value.

Fragmentation, Leakage, Refreshment

Although the value of knowledge for a firm increases over time, two countervailing phenomena are also present. Knowledge becomes more complex over time and divides into subspecialties. As knowledge on a particular subject increases, the person who was a specialist finds that what they know is the irreducible minimum required to work in a field. Some knowledge increases in value as it becomes the industry standard. Other knowledge, however, decays in value. For example, patents and copyrights expire and trade secrets become well-known. The implication is that knowledge is not static. A successful company continually refreshes its knowledge to keep its competitive advantage.

Uncertain Value

When investing in knowledge (which implies a fixed cost), it is difficult to estimate what the value of the outcome will be. Sometimes the results far exceed expectations whereas at other times the results fall far short. Even refreshing knowledge is not certain. Although advances in knowledge

---

[3] As indicated in the section on consultants (see Sidebar 4 later in this chapter), consulting firms divide into those who use a repository strategy for their consultants to allow them to use many juniors, and those who use senior consultants. McKinsey, discussed here, falls into the latter group.

[4] This section is based on "Best Practices and Beyond: Knowledge Strategies," *McKinsey Quarterly* 1, pp. 19–25, 1998.

[5] "Network effects" refers to the idea that value increases as the number of people connected increases. Thus, the value of a single telephone is zero. As the number of people who have telephones and can communicate with one another increases, the value of the system grows faster than the number of people connected.

build on one another, the sequence of gains may stop or slow down for known or unknown reasons. For example, Moore's law that states that the number of transistors on a chip doubles every 18 months to 2 years has been remarkably consistent over a long time period. Yet, no one knows whether or when these gains will stop.

Uncertainty in Value Sharing

Although knowledge investments can create large values, when partners engage in the development it is not certain who will receive the major benefit. The partners can be separate firms in an alliance or different strategic business units in a firm. The reasons for this uncertainty are

- knowledge is imbedded in people's minds,
- knowledge is a difficult asset to trade,
- the knowledge generated may be worth a different amount to each partner.

Since knowledge is in peoples' heads, it is more difficult than plants or equipment to be owned or managed. People typically know more than what they are able to say and tend to hold on to it unless there is value to them of sharing the knowledge. Even when the knowledge is explicit, it may be hard to determine who owns jointly developed knowledge. Since the outcome is unknown, it is difficult to determine in advance who owns what at the end of the process. Furthermore, the value generated by the partners may differ even if they have equal rights. For example, the value of particular knowledge to one firm may be to confirm that what they are doing is correct, while to its partner it opens a new vista for product development.

Implications

Because the traditional models of value in specific industries are not the same as the value of knowledge, knowledge requires a different strategy. The traditional models don't tell managers how value is created. For partnerships and alliances, they don't forecast how value will be created or who will capture most of it.

TACIT VERSUS EXPLICIT KNOWLEDGE

As indicated at the beginning of this chapter, we can divide knowledge into explicit knowledge and tacit knowledge. Individuals and organizations possess both kinds. The two types of knowledge operate in a stereo effect,[6] are combined holistically, and are almost inseparable. They must be managed together, but each in its own way.

Explicit knowledge is knowledge that can be written down and made available to everyone. That is, it is codified. It includes books, documents, e-mail, forms, and procedure manuals. In an organization, explicit knowledge can be stored in and retrieved from the computer. Some consulting firms, for example, maintain a "knowledge repository" to which individual consultants contribute and from which all consultants can retrieve knowledge they need for a particular client.

---

[6] The stereo concept is due to Omar El Sawy of the University of Southern California. He originally enunciated it in O. El Sawy, "Knowledge Management Around Business Processes," Presentation to the SIM Academic Workshop on Knowledge Management in Practice.

SIDEBAR 2 *Examples of Capturing Tacit Knowledge*

At General Electric (GE), a senior employee was about to retire. GE ran a lucrative diesel locomotive repair business in upstate New York. The employee was expert in diagnosing what was wrong with a newly arrived engine. He would read its gauges and listen to the noises it made to determine what repairs were needed. When he was about to retire, the managers realized that none of his knowledge was written down and that he could not sit down and explain what he knew. They therefore assigned a "knowledge engineer" from their artificial intelligence group to follow him around as he worked, write down what he recommended, and ask him to explain why he made a particular recommendation. Although this procedure did not cover all contingencies, it made a significant portion of the retiree's knowledge explicit.

A firm, Tacit.com, provides software to scan e-mails and to create "yellow pages" (http://www.tacit.com/). That is, its software uses the e-mail to create lists of people who have expertise. The software is interactive. It examines e-mail dynamically to answer the query supplied by the inquirer. The idea is that people will write things in their e-mail that is really tacit knowledge.

Tacit knowledge is the accumulated expertise of individual members of the firm. Tacit knowledge, being internal to the user, is almost impossible to put into a document or a computer database. You may not be able to separate its rules from how people act. For example, how does a scientist decide which topics to research? Although tacit knowledge is usually hard to express in a structured or explicit way, some methods are available to elicit it (see Sidebar 2).

The Hungarian philosopher, Polanyi, who offered three theses, made the tacit–explicit distinction:

1. True discovery cannot be accounted for by rules or algorithms.

2. Knowledge is public but is to a great extent personal. It therefore also contains emotions.

3. Explicit knowledge is either based on tacit knowledge or rooted in tacit knowledge.

The conclusion reached is that knowledge is an activity best described as the process of knowing. Furthermore, acquiring knowledge is action oriented. For example, a doctor's diagnostic skill comes as much from doing as from knowing.

If knowledge is essentially tacit, how can it be transferred among members of an organization? The means are direct and indirect. Direct transfer involves imitation (do as she does), identifying (recognizing a situation and letting other people know what is going on), and learning by doing (the school of hard knocks). Apprenticeships, where the senior person identifies what needs to be done and the apprentice then tries to do it, are representative of this kind of transfer. Indirect transfer comes through information and then putting the information to work. An example is the London Taxi cab case discussed in Sidebar 3.

SIDEBAR 3 *London Taxicabs**

The licensing process for driving a taxicab in London, England, is an example of a knowledge management system that does not use a computer. Driving a cab in London is a highly desired occupation. For many it is a step up the social and economic ladder. The process was first put in place in 1851 in the days of the horse-drawn hansom cab.

Taxi drivers, in addition to being old enough, of good moral character, physically fit, and able to drive competently and safely, must demonstrate their knowledge of London streets and addresses. The mission statement is straightforward and very British:

You are required to know any place within the Metropolis to which a member of the public may wish to go.

This definition includes 25,000 streets within 6 miles of the Charing Cross railway station. Candidates are handed a "blue book" of typical runs. They then make a series of sixteen 15 minute appearances before examiners over 2 years at which they are asked to give the shortest route between specified points, including traffic restrictions and left/right turns. The questions deal with routes not in the blue book.

In addition to going all over London by bicycle or car, candidates usually attend a training school that helps them master the intricacies of the city. As one training school puts it:

"You need to get a mental visual picture of the journey so that when you do a callover practice or attempt to answer the Examiner's question you should have in your mind's eye flashes of the streets along the way. A recall is just like a piece of film."

In the language of knowledge management, the candidate must convert the explicit knowledge of street maps into tacit knowledge that connects places in his head. The driver internalizes the knowledge.

The process is highly successful without technology. The objectives are clearly defined and the procedures are enforced rigorously. Creating and sharing knowledge is the critical success factor.

Note that the learning environment is formal rather than competitive as in business. There is a set of stakeholders (public, police, examiners, training schools) that, together with the candidates, form a knowledge organization.

*This sidebar is based on Knowledge Management: London Taxi Cabs Case Study by W. Skok, Proceedings of SIGCPR '99, New York: Association for Computing Machinery, 1999.

A HIERARCHY OF KNOWLEDGE

Knowledge comes at three levels:

- *Skills*. Being able to follow rules, such as typing or reading house plans.
- *Know How*. Skill plus being able to act in unforeseen circumstances, such as a carpenter knowing how to deal with circumstances not included in the house plans. Know how involves applying skills to solving problems.
- *Expertise*. Know how plus creating new knowledge that influences a domain of knowledge. The people with expertise are the gurus and researchers who lead a field.

Generating Knowledge

Knowledge will be generated in an organization, whether there is a conscious effort on the part of the firm to create knowledge or not. People meet in the hall or over the proverbial coffeepot. They discuss ideas, leading to new ideas. People do R&D. They write memos. All these activities create new knowledge in an organization. All of this activity is not systematic and it rarely generates the knowledge needed by a firm at a particular time. It is possible, however, for firms to make a specific effort to generate the knowledge they need.

Modes of generating knowledge include[7]

- Acquisition
- Dedicated resources
- Fusion
- Adaptation
- Knowledge networking

Before considering each of these methods, consider the factors that are common to knowledge generation.

The first factor is to provide adequate space and time for people to meet and exchange ideas. Space not only includes libraries and laboratories, but also places where knowledge workers can meet one another. The space can be physical (e.g., a cafeteria with connections for plugging portables into the network) or electronic (e-mail, chat groups, video conferences). A scarcer resource for most firms is providing the time needed for these informal meetings. The second factor is management's recognition that generating knowledge is important for the firm's success and that the process can be nurtured. For example, reading a book is real work, not a way of goofing off.

Knowledge Acquisition

Knowledge is acquired both internally (see dedicated resources below) and externally. It can be bought by hiring people with a given expertise, through acquiring another firm, or by renting knowledge.

Acquiring Another Firm

As shown below and in Sidebar 4 below, buying another firm may not always be successful.

---

[7] These modes are described in detail by T. H. Davenport and L. Prusak, 1998, op. cit.

SIDEBAR 4   *Examples of Acquisitions to Obtain Knowledge*

IBM purchased Lotus for $3.25 billion to obtain Lotus Notes and it bought ROLM to gain entry into telecommunications. Lotus was judged a success but ROLM was a failure.

AT&T bought NCR but the purchase did not give AT&T the entry to the computer business as hoped. NCR was later spun off.

AOL bought Time-Warner for its content knowledge. Time-Warner wound up as the major partner. The AOL name was scrapped.

Microsoft bought Visio rather than building a graphics program of its own. The acquisition achieved its goal.

The major problem in acquisition is that company cultures may clash. For example, IBM's purchase of Lotus, a Boston area firm, worked. However, IBM's New York suit and tie culture clashed with ROLM's laid-back California culture, and was spun off to Siemens. Lotus' knowledge transferred to IBM and became a significant part of their business, but ROLM's did not.

It is also important to recognize that knowledge may not survive the upheaval of a purchase if talented people leave and if the new environment creates barriers to exchanging knowledge. The latter is in part due to the acquiring company treating its acquisition as a conquest and existing employees of the acquired company not wanting to be told by newcomers how to do things.

Rental

Renting knowledge implies paying for use of a knowledge source. Rental may be ongoing or it may be temporary to solve a particular problem. Small firms may hire an R&D organization to perform ongoing work for them. For example, Tencor (now part of KLA-Tencor) for years contracted with SRI International to do basic research for them.

For specific problems, a consultant or a consulting firm may be brought in for their expertise. The source rented is typically hired based on the reputation of their people, their past success and experience, and an estimate of their future potential. Hiring a consultant is speculative, since success cannot be guaranteed. Sidebar 5 discusses the role of consultants. Much of this sidebar applies not only to knowledge management but also to many of the other IT applications discussed in this book.

Dedicated Resources

In addition to providing space where individuals and teams meet, organizations dedicate resources to generating knowledge. Typical examples are

- An R&D department.
- An analysis unit for business intelligence (Chapter 8) that scans the environment for new developments and for competitive knowledge.
- Training units to improve worker knowledge.
- A company library.

Some companies find that their culture makes it difficult to transfer knowledge generated by units that generate the knowledge. For example, the Xerox Palo Alto Research Center (Xerox PARC) developed many computer-based innovations (including the now ubiquitous mouse and icon metaphor) but the company could not commercialize many of them. One way around this dilemma is to move people from R&D to operational groups, although many R&D people don't want to make such a transfer.

SIDEBAR 5   *The Role of Consultants*

Implanting knowledge management into a firm usually involves a major effort. Although existing staff may provide some of the needed skills (e.g., the firm may employ company librarians who keep track of books and documents), hardly any firms possess the full range of skills. As indicated in the section on Chief Knowledge Officers (CKO) below, the firm should appoint an insider who is respected to head the knowledge effort. However, since the firm usually doesn't have the additional staff needed, consultants are usually brought in.

The direction that the consultants take is a matter of style.[8] Two pure strategies can be defined.

1. *Knowledge Repository*. This strategy, followed by Capgemini (Ernst & Young) and Accenture, is to create a knowledge repository in the consultant firm's computer. The repository contains a record of previous engagements, recorded by teams as they work on and complete projects. It also contains an "after action" report that summarizes the lessons learned. When a new job is obtained, the team assigned to it consults the repository and tries to find the input it needs to solve the client's problem.

From the consultant's point of view, the advantage is that reuse of old knowledge brings new and young consultants up to speed and allows the firm to assign only one or a few senior consultants to the job. Customers dislike this approach because they feel that they receive a cookie cutter copy of what other

firms received rather than a unique solution that fits them and gives them competitive advantage. The cost savings to the clients may be small because a large number of junior consultants are assigned, running up the bill.

2. *Senior Consultant Approach*. This strategy, followed by firms such as McKinsey & Company, assigns high fee senior consultants to the project. These consultants do refer to a repository in the computer to bring them up to date on the client and on what was done before, but pride themselves on offering unique answers to their clients.

Consultant's Knowledge Sharing

For most firms, it is important that consultants transfer their knowledge to them so that they can deal with the same problem by themselves in the future. Others may simply want to solve a particular problem and don't insist on knowledge transfer.

Even though consultants are temporary, some knowledge will stay after they leave. Some firms demand transfer in the consulting contract, and some consultants offer training as part of their service. A firm needs to know what it wants if it is to have a good chance of getting it. Unfortunately, most firms do not ask questions to encourage knowledge transfer by their consultants. Most consultants will not volunteer, hoping to resell the same knowledge in the future.

Fusion

Fusion refers to forming a team of people with different perspectives to find a joint answer to a problem. To quote Leonard-Barton (1995)[9], "innovation occurs at the boundary between mind-sets." The idea is that, since they have no solution in common, individuals in such a team must devise a new answer. Team members must commit time and effort to share knowledge and language about the problem. These teams require nurturing so they share knowledge, devise a common language, and generate light, not heat. From a knowledge point of view, the team needs to know that it will be rewarded for generating knowledge. Metrics must be in place to measure their success.

---

[8] This discussion is based in part on the article by M. Hansen, N. Noriah, and T. Tierney, "What's Your Strategy for Managing Knowledge?," *Harvard Business Review,* pp. 106-116, March-April 1999.

[9] D. Leonard-Barton, *Wellsprings of Knowledge,* Boston: Harvard Business School Press, 1995.

Adaptation

Business history is littered with companies that failed to adapt to changing circumstances and changing competition. Examples in the computer business include Digital Equipment Corporation (DEC), Wang Laboratories, and Compaq Computer Corporation. K-Mart and the U.S. auto companies of the 1980s are other examples. These companies were successful at what they did, and did not see the need to change. By the time crisis hit, they were no longer able to change. Their motto was "WE ARE (name of company)" and they assumed that was sufficient for success. They did not understand that the world around them was changing.

The adaptation strategy involves creating a sense of urgency, of crisis before the crisis exists, in the hope that this approach will help the firm avert a real crisis.[10] Davenport and Prusak argue that companies fail to adapt because their "core rigidities" don't allow them to change rapidly. The way around this rigidity is to provide new knowledge and skills to employees and to broaden their outlook by changing people's jobs frequently. In addition, and this is easier said than done, adaptation involves hiring people who are open to change.

Networks

People working and talking together inevitably share knowledge and, over time, create it. Individual workers belong to several social networks. As they communicate in these networks, knowledge starts flowing through the organization. It is this intersection of networks that raises innovative thinking. Networks, however, involve large elements of chance because they depend on who communicates with whom.

TRANSFERRING KNOWLEDGE

"Hire smart people and let them talk to one another." Davenport and Prusak[11]
"What we don't know, we explain to one another." J. Robert Oppenheimer[12]

Unfortunately, in most organizations, people are too busy to exchange ideas on a regular basis. So, knowledge transfer (and sharing) is random. Most of the time, people talk to those who are physically close to them, to obtain a "good enough" answer. As a result, they are not assured that they are talking to the best person or even the right person when they try to find knowledge. This approach is not as irrational as it sounds because transaction costs are associated with trying to find the best person, and that person may not be reachable. The larger the organization, of course, the less likely the best person will be contacted (even if that person works for the firm).

Ways of transferring knowledge include

- *Mentoring relations* between senior and junior people.
- *Document management systems* (discussed later in this chapter) that make document retrieval easier.
- *Yellow pages* listing people ready to share their knowledge.
- *Videoconferencing systems,* such as used by BP[13] to connect people at different locations.
- *Debriefing* people who retire.

---

[10] Such a policy also runs the risk of creating a Chicken Little "the sky is falling" effect.

[11] T. H. Davenport and L. Prusak, 1998, op. cit.

[12] J. Robert Oppenheimer in a television interview with Edward E. Murrow in the 1950s, explaining how people work at the Institute for Advanced Study at Princeton University.

[13] BP used to be known as British Petroleum.

To achieve transfer, just making knowledge available is not enough. All of these methods require the intended recipient to absorb the knowledge. Furthermore, even if they absorb the knowledge, it is of no value unless behavior changes. Barriers to absorption include not trusting the source, pride, stubbornness, lack of time, and perceived risk. In short, although knowing is required for doing, knowing does not necessarily result in doing.

The conventional approach to knowledge transfer is improved access, electronic communication, and document repositories. However, human factors are as important, if not more so. People need to pay attention to new knowledge and they need both discussion and documents.

How firms approach knowledge management depends on the size of the organization. The conventional wisdom is that the maximum size organization where everyone knows everyone is 200 to 300 people. In such organizations, people know who knows about what and whom to contact when they have a problem. For larger organizations, it is often the case that knowledge needed by one individual is known by someone else in the organization. However, the two people don't have contact and the knowledge seeker doesn't even know that the capability exists within the firm. The mere existence of knowledge in a large organization therefore is of little benefit.

The usual solution to this situation is to create an index, referred to as yellow pages, of who knows what. Analogous to the phone directory organized by subject matter, yellow pages are an application of technology to institutionalize knowledge transfer. An example is the pharmaceutical firm Eli Lilly and Company. They institutionalize their yellow pages on their intranet to serve two purposes: to circulate resumes so people can locate expertise and to aid in succession planning.

The application is imperfect, but better than not doing anything. The following problems can be encountered

1. People may be unwilling to reveal their expertise. They want to avoid being bothered by others when they already have more than 40 hours of their own work per week that needs to be done. They don't want to spend the time to bring people up to speed[14] if sharing results in little reward. Furthermore, some are paranoid about being replaced if they share their unique knowledge. The rewards and culture of sharing must be institutionalized together with the creation of yellow pages.

2. Who is knowledgeable changes over time. Some people leave or retire. Others who may be knowledgeable now lose their expertise as knowledge fragments and decays over time. Yellow pages are dynamic, not static documents. Both the organization and the content of topics must be kept up to date.

PERSONNEL ISSUES

When something is everyone's job (and knowledge management is certainly that) it becomes no one's job. Therefore, large companies involved in knowledge management establish a small bureaucracy, often headed by a "Chief Knowledge Officer." The consensus is that this individual should report high in the organization (to a VP or the Chief Operating Officer or the CEO), operate through a small staff, and create and implement a knowledge policy as his or her chief duty.

---

[14] This goal is not always possible. For example, a person who is an electronics specialist may not be able to communicate meaningfully with an aerodynamicist.

For simplicity, we use the term "Chief Knowledge Officer" or CKO in this section. Other titles for the same function include Director for Knowledge Transfer (Buckman Laboratories), Director of Intellectual Assets (Dow Chemical), Director of Intellectual Capital (Skandia), Chief Learning Officer, and many more. The title on the door does make a difference, since people behave according to what they are called. For example, a Chief Learning Officer focuses on training whereas a Chief of Intellectual Capital tries to convert existing knowledge (such as patents) to revenue.

CKOs are basically advocates for organizational knowledge and learning. Typically they are appointed from within the organization, have a long history in the firm, and are generally respected. They are selected because they are seen as "knowledgeable" people in the organization. Their skills cover the technical, human, and financial aspects of the firm. Such people are rare, but most organizations have a few of them.

The CKO may be in a senior, stand-alone position, or combined with the information systems function or the HR function. If combined, the signal is clear that knowledge is not a priority for the organization. CKOs are most likely to be appointed in knowledge-based businesses such as advertising, computers, consulting, engineering and science, and insurance.

In a firm, knowledge activities occur at four levels:

- Senior knowledge executives such as the CKO
- Knowledge staff who run knowledge projects
- People who work with knowledge such as librarians, editors, integrators
- Operators who manage the knowledge in their own job

To be successful, the CKO must make KM pay off economically for the firm. To do so, he or she needs to create a knowledge culture and create an infrastructure. The infrastructure is not only technical but also includes the networks and relations for generating and transferring knowledge. Doing so is a difficult task and varies depending on the nature of the organization and the style of the CKO. There is no single model that will work everywhere.

KM AS AN INDUSTRY

Few current data on knowledge management expenditures are available. One indicator is the amount spent by the U.S. government. The federal market for knowledge management solutions is estimated to grow from $850 million in fiscal 2004 to about $1.1 billion in fiscal 2009,[15] a 29% increase in spending, according to the report released September 2004.

A survey by *Knowledge Management* magazine[16] found that companies do understand the value of deploying knowledge management and that they put high priority on the success of the deployments. For example, executive managers led 40% of the projects. The CKO, if a firm had one, often served as a full-time member of the senior management group. IT and many management groups were also involved.

---

[15] J. Hasson, "Input Predicts Growth in Knowledge Management," *Federal Computer Weekly,* September 22, 2004, http://www.fcw.com/fcw/articles/2004/0920/web-km-09-22-04.asp.

[16] Dyer, Greg, and Brian McDonough, "The State of KM," *Knowledge Management* (4):5, pp. 31–36, May 1, 2001.

The survey also found that:

- Companies realize that knowledge management is not an overnight phenomenon but a shift in business strategy and process.
- Planning was needed and involved users.
- The organization's culture had to support trust and collaboration.
- Firms moved from a single project to using knowledge as a strategic initiative.
- Consultants were usually a key part of the deployment.

Knowledge management was adopted usually for one of the following reasons:

- to retain talent,
- to improve customer service,
- to increase revenue and profits,
- to support e-business initiatives, and
- to shorten the product development cycle.

The bottom line of this particular study was that "Despite, or perhaps because of, the state of the economy, the KM market will grow impressively."

TECHNOLOGY[17]

Most of the technology in use for disseminating knowledge, ranging from the telephone to the World Wide Web, e-mail, groupware, knowledge repositories, intelligent agents, and information portals, was originally developed for other purposes and adapted for knowledge use. Perhaps the only unique technology is the document management systems (discussed on p. 131) that some vendors tout as being all of knowledge management, but which are, in reality, only a small part of knowledge management.

The knowledge repository is a database that contains explicit knowledge for use by individuals and groups. Although the repository may be physically located in the data warehouse (see Chapter 5), its objectives and contents are different. For example, the repository may contain the company's procedures manuals, its records of previous projects, the yellow pages, and cross-references to more detailed sources both inside and outside the company. An individual using the repository may combine what he/she finds there with his or her own tacit and/or explicit knowledge before disseminating it. For capturing or transferring knowledge, they may use paper (e.g., document, memorandum, manual) or digital technology. Although in this section we assume that the knowledge repository is digital and that the retrieval and dissemination methods are compatible with a digital knowledge repository, they need not be as was illustrated by the London taxicab study in Sidebar 3.

Table 1 shows some of the technologies, their uses, and examples (in parenthesis).

---

[17] This section is based on P. Gray and S. Terahni, "Technologies for Disseminating Knowledge," in C. Holsapple (Ed.) *Handbook of Knowledge Management: Knowledge Directions* 2 (Chapter 37), pp. 109-128, Berlin: Springer-Verlag, 2003.

Table 1 KNOWLEDGE DISSEMINATION TECHNOLOGIES

Technology	Uses and examples
World Wide Web	For connecting individuals to a repository (search engines, URLs)
Online access	For real-time sharing (*Net Meeting,* Online chat rooms)
E-mail	One-to-one and one-to-many dissemination; computer conferences (*Outlook, Eudora*)
Groupware	For topic-based discussions and collaboration. (*Lotus Notes*); team room software (*Groupsystems*)
Wireless technology	For stand-alone connecting electronic devices (laptops, PDAs, cell phones, WAP devices)
Videoconferencing, teleconferencing	For connecting ad-hoc groups (Microsoft *NetMeeting, WebEx, Sharepoint*)
Document management systems	To access reports, purchase orders, and other corporate documents (*Documentum*). Use of XML.
Intelligent agents	To find knowledge on the Internet or in a knowledge repository
Geographic information systems	To display knowledge in two and multiple dimensions
Information portals	To point to the location of knowledge

Document Management

Document management is the principal technology specifically devised for managing knowledge. Electronic document management systems (EDMS) are computer applications that manage the sharing of documents across multiple users and networked environments. The systems are used to optimize and reorganize workflow, reduce document handling costs, improve customer support, and assist in internal decision making (Chapter 8, Business Intelligence). Document management systems provide

- A single access point
- Configuration management
- Ownership
- Interface with office automation tools (word processing, e-mail)
- Security
- History of documents

Most EDMS are now Web-based because:

- A browser is easier to use since people are browser experienced (i.e., no learning is required).
- The World Wide Web allows remote (off-site) access.
- Web-based documents are easier to maintain than those on distributed client-server systems.
- The Web is essentially independent of hardware and supports different types of hardware.
- The Web is scalable as the number of documents increases.

SIDEBAR 6	*What Are Documents?*

A document is a collection of information created for transferring and preserving knowledge. Documents include

- correspondence,
- reports,
- meeting minutes,
- drawings,
- forms,
- purchase orders,
- memos,
- manuals, and
- procedures.

A document may be simple (text, voice, video), images (drawings, diagrams, pictures), or compound (information pulled together from different sources but pieces remaining in original location, such as hypertext). Some exchange is possible between documents (as in copy and paste in Microsoft Word) but no universal platform-independent file format exists.

Documents are usually paper, but may be stored in any medium (e.g., magnetic disk, microfilm, tape, CD-ROM, DVD). Despite the extensive development of other media, paper is still the overwhelmingly used method of storage for most firms.

The activities associated with a document are

1. Creating or recording
2. Manipulating
3. Storing
4. Retrieving
5. Communicating
6. Deleting

Document management must still resolve a number of issues. First is the stability of the storage medium. Over time, a firm's hardware and software changes and it is no longer possible to read old formats. (Think of 8-track tape.) Furthermore, the media themselves have limits. For example, CD-ROMs are designed for a 10-year life. Another important issue is legality. Can you substitute signatures and other requirements that only paper can satisfy? How long do you have to retain a document?

CASE STUDIES

The trade magazines, such as *CIO, Data Management Review, KMWorld,* and *Intelligent Enterprise,*[18] are filled with case reports. Cases can be found in many places on the World Wide Web. In this section, we briefly discuss three cases that illustrate specific points about knowledge management. URLs, where available, show additional sources for each case.

Retaining Intellectual Capital at Northrop Grumman

URL: http://www.cio.com/archive/090101/thanks_content.html

In the late 1990s, the Air Combat Systems division at Northrop Grumman cut its workforce. They faced a major loss of expertise and the tacit knowledge accumulated by laid-off engineers, most of whom had over 20 years experience.

Their first step in knowledge management was to create a database with 100 knowledge categories or cells (e.g., armaments, software engineering) and to identify 200 subject matter experts in each cell. Workers can search these yellow pages for areas of expertise by name, program group, or skill.

---

[18] The URLs for these magazines are: *CIO:* www.cio.com, *DM Review:* www.dmreview.com, *KMWorld:* www.kmworld.com, *Intelligent Enterprise:* www.intelligententerprise.com.

In 1999, Northrop Grumman reduced the workforce by another 25%. They then instituted a "knowledge audit" to learn about the employee's cultural attitudes about sharing knowledge. The response rate was 70%. The results showed that workers valued expertise and experience; viewed others as knowledge sharers, not hoarders; and understood that tacit knowledge was the source for best practices and lessons learned. However, they also found

- no central repository in the firm,

- that engineers spent at least 8 hours/week looking for information (annual cost to the firm of ~$150 million), and

- little reuse of knowledge.

In short, workers were willing to share knowledge but did not have the proper means or technology to do so.

To remedy the situation, the firm created

- "communities of practice" responsible for sharing knowledge across boundaries,

- a Web-based tracking system for knowledge and lessons learned,

- "portals" for information access and input, knowledge capture, and collaboration.

Having accomplished the goal of retaining knowledge, they turned to increasing innovation and customer responsiveness.

Hiding Knowledge

The title of the article says it all: "On Factory Floors, Top Workers Hide Know-How from Managers." The story describes a classic manufacturing plant in Grand Rapids, Michigan, that does metal cutting for industrial pumps. A significant fraction of older employees keep their tacit knowledge to themselves because they fear that if their secrets are known, the plant will move offshore or entry-level workers will replace them. For years, workers would make adjustments in how they worked to increase their productivity. However, as digital controls replaced mechanical controls on the machines, the information systems became able to tell exactly what steps were followed. Many workers who previously introduced changes in settings to speed the process no longer did so. Again, they feared for their own jobs.

The article discusses other aspects of employees' tacit knowledge that affected productivity. For example, workers can tell the difference between Teflon and neoprene o-rings just by their feel, without looking at them. None of this knowledge is written down, but it makes a difference in the work output.

Sustaining Knowledge Management[19]

Buckman Laboratories became the poster child of knowledge management when it unveiled its "K'Netix" knowledge sharing system in 1992. Here was a major mid-sized old-line company selling chemicals to businesses using knowledge to gain competitive advantage. K'Netix was a knowledge repository to be used by its 1300 employees (particularly its salespeople) in 70 nations. It was put in just as the company was changing its business model from a product focus to a customer intimacy focus. K'Netix is basically an intranet that allows this firm's employees (and now customers) access to knowledge ranging from engineering and product data to technical discussion groups. It is particularly useful for a sales force dealing with a large number of products used across many industries.

In the over 10 years since its initial inception, the company adapted and refined its knowledge system. For example, it established a learning center that could be used both by its own salespeople and its customers in 1997. It changed its mission statement in 1998 and installed a new technology infrastructure in 1999. An "after-action report" concept was introduced in 2001 to create a consistent experience for customers. The system is now fully Web-oriented rather than the dial-up approaches used when it was started.

---

[19] Source: *Wall Street Journal*, July 1, 2002, p. 1.

Buckman centers its customer engagements on knowledge and learning. The system aims to answer questions within 24 hours. The company prides itself on the system's ability to coordinate efforts and to break down the walls of isolation among its various silos. Buckman illustrates the need for continually improving and fine-tuning a company's knowledge efforts to meet changing business conditions.

WHEN KNOWLEDGE MANAGEMENT MAKES SENSE

Thomas A. Stewart, who began writing about intellectual capital and knowledge management in the mid-1990s, wrote an article provocatively entitled "The Case Against Knowledge Management."[20] When reading it, however, you find that it really talks about the situations in which knowledge management makes sense and those in which it doesn't. We summarize that advice here.

The key point is that simply creating large repositories containing white papers and other explicit knowledge is not successful by itself. Many ignore general repositories, and others who use them initially will use them rarely unless information important to them is included. The repository is basically a supply-side device and knowledge is demand-side driven. People want answers to their specific problems and they want them without having to do extensive searches. They do the rational thing by looking first to people who are physically close to them or whom they know personally. They seek people's tacit knowledge to help them, not just the explicit knowledge in the repository. The implications are

1. Define the specific knowledge that each work group needs. Don't try to give everything to everyone. In the insurance business, for example, the underwriters need different knowledge than the actuaries.

Yes, each company has knowledge about itself that everyone in the group needs to be familiar with and which should be generally available. The rest depends on each group's needs. Some will need magazine subscriptions to keep current; others will need to retrieve from databases. You can usually find out what is needed from the work group and from its customers. The principle is to manage knowledge within the context where it is created.

2. Some groups reuse knowledge and hence try to standardize knowledge, whereas others customize. Standardization is usually the case in repetitive operations such as manufacturing; innovators such as the "creatives" in advertising and marketing prefer customization.

Reuse is appropriate for well-understood, routine tasks. Techniques include codification, automation, and libraries that allow people to obtain, say, the files and designer notes on every model produced over the last 10 years. For innovators, the questions are unstructured and the problems are usually new. They want to be able to talk to smart people and to find the right experts for a team. They need to know not only what worked, but also which approaches failed previously and why.

The bottom line is that knowledge should be managed so that it matches the way value is created. Knowledge management systems cannot be generic. They need to be tailored to the organization in which they are used.

---

[20] This section is based on "The Case Against Knowledge Management" by Thomas A. Stuart, *Business 2.0* January 7, 2002, http://www.business2.com/articles/mag/0,1640,36747,FF.html.

ANSWERS TO MANAGERIAL QUESTIONS

How much knowledge does a firm have?

A firm contains a huge amount of knowledge. This knowledge includes its products, its processes, its procedures, its patents and its trade secrets, its customers, its competitors, what is in the heads of the firm's staff, and more. It is a significant asset.

Why manage knowledge?

As with any asset, knowledge should be managed to increase its value to the firm.

What types of knowledge are there?

Knowledge can be either explicit (written down, teachable, easily transferable) or tacit (in the heads of the firm's people).

How do you gather knowledge?

We described five ways of gathering knowledge:

Acquisition. Gaining knowledge from consultants, new hires, mergers and acquisitions

Dedicated Resources. Things such as R&D laboratories, libraries, training

Fusion. Forming teams from different units with complementary skills but no preconceived notion of how to solve the specific problem at hand.

Adaptation. Creating a sense of urgency that the world is changing and that the firm must change with it.

Knowledge Networking. Encouraging people to interact with one another to exchange knowledge.

How do you transfer knowledge to others?

You can transfer knowledge within the organization by such activities as:

- Mentoring relations between senior and junior people.
- Document management systems that make document retrieval easier.
- Yellow pages listing people ready to share their knowledge.
- Videoconferencing systems to connect people at different locations.
- Debriefing people who retire.

How do you update knowledge?

Knowledge changes over time. Some existing knowledge becomes information or merely data over time. New knowledge appears. An important part of knowledge management is keeping the firm's knowledge at the forefront of its business. To do so requires continually updating knowledge repositories by removing old knowledge, updating existing knowledge, and adding new knowledge. Furthermore, because a large portion of knowledge is tacit and in people's heads, it is necessary to hire people skilled in new areas of knowledge and to retrain existing people to keep up with (preferably stay ahead of) the continual changes in the firm. Updating knowledge is an important role for a Chief Knowledge Officer.

Do you need a separate department for knowledge?

A separate department is not necessary but is highly desirable. Such an organization, often of only a few people, clearly signals the importance of knowledge to the firm. It makes encouraging knowledge generation, transfer, and use the responsibility of specific people rather than diffusing it among everyone. In the latter case, it becomes no one's responsibility.

What technologies are available?

Knowledge management mainly uses software created for other purposes. Document management systems for retrieving tacit knowledge from e-mail are two of the few systems developed specifically for KM.

How much should you invest?

To keep costs within bounds, the conventional wisdom is to start with a pilot program. Clearly, when you fully cost out even a small, full-time staff of two or three people, you start off with a quarter of a million dollars a year. When you consider the amount of work on knowledge put in by the firm as a whole, the cost quickly escalates. The problem of determining return on investment in knowledge is made more difficult by the problems of estimating the benefits that will be obtained. However, failing to invest in knowledge can make many of the other initiatives discussed in this book fail.

PROBLEMS

1. TACIT KNOWLEDGE

    Give six examples of tacit knowledge in personal or business life beyond the examples given in this chapter.

2. ROLE OF KNOWLEDGE IN THE DECISION PROCESS

    Describe a situation in your experience (or those of people you work with) where knowledge was a key issue in decision making.

3. SOCIAL NETWORKS

    One of the ways people find knowledge is by tapping into their company and professional social network; that is, talking with people they know to obtain knowledge needed in their work. Write a short paper about what social networks are and describe their role in knowledge management.

4. CASES

    There are many cases of knowledge management successes and failures reported in the information systems press. Find three such cases. Summarize them and turn in your summary together with the URL or other location where the case is described.

Chapter **8**

Business Intelligence

MANAGERIAL QUESTIONS

Is business intelligence (BI) an oxymoron? A shorthand for cloak-and-dagger spying on competitors and government? An important, legitimate activity?

What types of business intelligence are there?

What is new about today's business intelligence systems compared to previous systems?

Who uses BI?

How do you gather and transfer BI?

Do you need a separate organizational unit for BI?

What technologies are available?

What are the developments in BI?

INTRODUCTION

Business intelligence (BI) systems are sophisticated analytical tools that attempt to present complex corporate and competitive information in a manner that allows decision makers to decide quickly and appropriately. While the term Business Intelligence is relatively new,[1] computer-based business intelligence systems have been in existence, in one guise or another, for close to 40 years.[2] BI-type functionality was available previously to varying degrees in financial planning systems (4GLs), executive information systems (EIS), decision support systems (DSS), data mining (Chapter 5), and OLAP (Chapter 5 and later this chapter). With each new iteration, capabilities increased as enterprises grew ever more sophisticated in their computational and analytical needs and as computer hardware and software matured. In this chapter we explore the capabilities of state-of-the-art business intelligence systems, their benefits to adopters, the structure of the BI supplier industry, and present practical advice for those considering implementing BI in their enterprise.

DEFINITION

Business intelligence systems combine data gathering, data storage, and knowledge management with analytical tools to present complex corporate and competitive information to planners and decision makers. The objective is to improve the timeliness and quality of the input to the decision process.

---

[1] The term was coined by Howard J. Dresner of the Gartner Group around 1989. It became fashionable in the late 1990s.

[2] For a history of business intelligence, see http://dssresources.com/history/dsshistory.html.

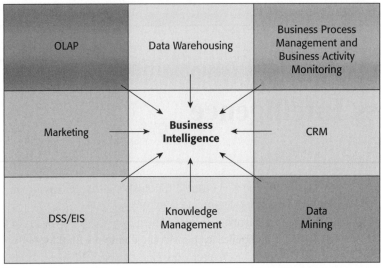

Figure 1 Relation of business intelligence to other software packages.

Source: Dyer, Greg, and Brian McDonough (2001). "The State of KM." *Knowledge Management* 4(5), 31–36, May 2001.

RELATION TO OTHER SOFTWARE

Figure 1 shows the relationship between business intelligence and other software.

The important point about this diagram is that many of the software applications described in this book provide the input for business intelligence. The data warehouse is the central repository (Chapter 5). OLAP, data mining, CRM (Chapter 6), and database marketing are applications of the data warehouse. Knowledge management (Chapter 7) helps in sorting through the data and the information obtained from these systems. Business process management and its subset business activity monitoring are discussed at the end of this chapter. DSS and EIS, which focus on decision making, are the precursors of business intelligence. The overall objective of these systems is to create the business intelligence environment needed by the firm at managerial levels.

WHAT CAN BI DO?

Business intelligence provides access to the mountains of data that a firm keeps in its data warehouse and in its legacy systems. Its aim is to convert the data into useful information and, through human analysis, into knowledge. Among the many tasks that business intelligence performs are

- Examine the opportunities for
  - proposed products,
  - mergers and acquisitions (Sidebar 1),
  - acquiring new customers, and
  - locating sites for new branches (Sidebar 2).

- Create forecasts based on historical data, on current performance, and on estimates of the direction in which the future will go.[3]

- Monitor key performance indicators (KPIs) for the firm and its competitors so that managers can see where the firm stands in its industry and its market (Sidebar 3).

- Do "what-if" analysis to examine the impacts of changes and of alternative scenarios.

- Ad hoc access to data to answer specific, nonroutine questions.

These examples cover both reporting done on a regular, repetitive schedule (e.g., monthly reports on sales by region, department, or strategic business unit) and special investigations aimed to solve specific problems. The latter includes studies done in response to a crisis or an opportunity (e.g., a contract proposal).

SIDEBAR 1   *Example of Using Business Intelligence for an Acquisition*

An example of using BI is the acquisition of Execucomm of Austin, Texas, by Comshare of Ann Arbor, Michigan, several years ago. These firms were arch competitors in developing and selling fourth generation financial planning languages, which were standard business intelligence products at the time. The then-president of Comshare, Crandall by name, used a service that monitored newspaper articles about specific competitors. One day his screen showed an article that reported an interview in the Austin newspaper with Execucomm's chairman, Anderson, in which Anderson unburdened himself. Anderson discussed the miserable relation between his company and its owner, a firm in an adjacent state, which, he said, did not understand what Execucomm did, having assumed that it was acquiring a way into the computer business. Reading the interview, Crandall recognized that Execucomm could be bought, probably relatively cheaply. The acquisition would eliminate a major competitor, broaden Comshare's product line, and perhaps most important, move a cadre of very smart people into Comshare. Acting on this intelligence information, Comshare bought Execucomm.

Although the business intelligence led to the acquisition, the end result was negative. Comshare rapidly stripped the Austin operation, moved key personnel to Ann Arbor, and a couple of years later took Execucomm's premier product off the market in favor of its own.

SIDEBAR 2   *Example of Strategic Insights*

The Dallas Teacher's Credit Union (DTCU) wanted to expand. It asked two questions of its BI system:

1. Who are our most profitable customers?
2. How far will they drive to reach our outlets?

Once they found the answer to these two questions, they were able to select branch sites that were within the buying radius of the preferred customers.
(This firm is described further later in this chapter.)

---

[3] The techniques of Futures Research, such as the Delphi method and cross-impact analysis, are two of many ways of making such estimates. The Delphi method is discussed in the Wikipedia at http://en.wikipedia.org/wiki/Delphi_method. Cross-impact is explained, for example, in O. Helmer, "Cross Impact Gaming," *Futures* (4)2: pp. 149–167, 1972. Olaf Helmer was one of the originators of the method.

SIDEBAR 3   *Market Forecasting*

Most grocery chains sell their bar code scanner data to companies such as Information Resources Inc. (IRI) who, in turn, aggregate the data and sell the summaries to grocery wholesalers and vendors. Individual firms want to find out how well their (and their competitors') special offers, such as a 20-cents-off coupon, worked in the marketplace. By examining how well an offer worked previously, how well it worked in the current situation, and forecasting the future effects of the promotion, firms can decide whether to continue the offer or change it. If it is a competitor's offer, the forecast is used to decide whether to match or exceed the competitor. Thus, the forecasts based on the data are converted into policy at the tactical level.

Hierarchy of Uses

A survey by the Gartner[4] Group of the strategic uses of business intelligence found they were ranked by firms in the following order:

1. Corporate performance management.

2. Optimizing customer relations, monitoring business activity, and traditional decision support.

3. Packaged stand-alone BI applications for specific operations or strategies.

4. Management reporting of business intelligence.

The implication of this ranking is that simply reporting your own and your competitors' performance, which is the primary strength of many existing BI software packages, is not enough.

BI TECHNOLOGY

Figure 2 shows a typical advanced technology configuration for BI systems that is representative for a large installation and which centers around the use of World Wide Web technology for distributing the BI output.

As shown in the figure, the input data comes from a variety of systems into the data warehouse. The specific data needed for BI is downloaded to a data mart used by planners and executives. Outputs result from both routine push of data by the BI analysts to a network of managers and from responses to inquiries from Web users and from OLAP analysts.

The outputs can take several forms:

- Exception reports that are sent whenever parameters are outside prespecified bounds.
- Routine reports.
- Responses to requests for specific reports of interest to a BI user.
- Creation of custom data cubes (see below) based on specific requests from analysts.
- Alerts that conditions exist or will exist that require action.

The specific application technologies used for business intelligence are shown in Figure 3.

---

[4] *Intelligent Enterprise,* p. 11, January 14, 2001.

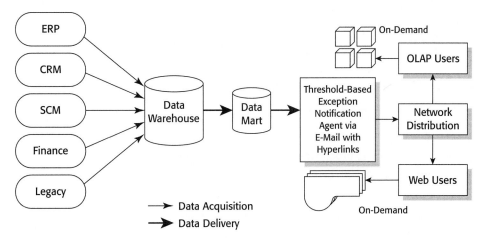

Figure 2 Business intelligence architecture.

Source: R. Skriletz, "New Directions for Business Intelligence," *DM Review*, April 2002. Reprinted with permission from Source Media/DM Review.

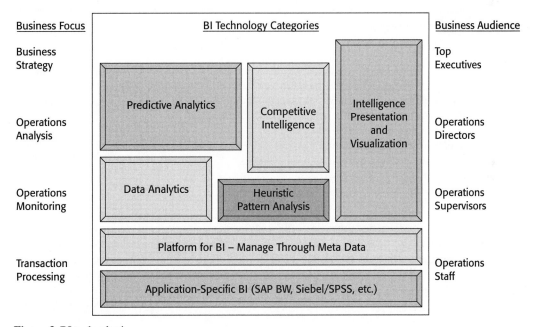

Figure 3 BI technologies.

Source: R. Skriletz, "New Directions for Business Intelligence," *DM Review*, April 2002. Reprinted with permission from Source Media/DM Review.

The left side of Figure 3 shows the business focus of the technologies and the right side the levels of people in the organization who are the consumers of the intelligence. At the bottom of the hierarchy is transaction processing based on application-specific data in the warehouse or in ERP or sales systems. The next level involves processing the data so that it is useful to first-level managers.

Here *analytics*[5] *and pattern analysis* are performed and data are presented in visual form. At the top level, predictions, compilations of competitive analyses, and summary presentations for executives are created.

Tools

Many of the tools for business intelligence are used for other applications as well. They include

- simple querying and reporting,
- online analytic processing (OLAP) (see next subsection),
- statistical analyses and data mining,
- forecasting, and
- geographic information systems and visualization.

Of these tools, the only ones not discussed previously are geographic information systems (GIS) and visualization. These two systems, described in Sidebars 4 and 5,[6] help executives gain a visual understanding of the business situation.

SIDEBAR 4 *Geographic Information Systems (GIS)*[7]

In the narrow sense, a geographic information systems (GIS) is a software package that links databases and electronic maps. At a more general level, the term GIS refers to the capability for analyzing spatial phenomena. These systems are an important business intelligence tool for exploiting the increasing amount of two (and more)-dimensional data available in a form that can be understood by analysts and managers.

In addition to collecting, storing, and retrieving spatial location data, GIS are used to

- display selected environments both visually and numerically,
- identify locations which meet specified criteria (e.g., for new stores),
- explore relations among data sets,
- assess alternatives, and
- aid in decision making.

In practice, a GIS consists of a series of layers.[8] Each layer presents a particular feature, which can be superimposed accurately on top of another. Some examples:

- A marketing group overlays customer locations, school locations, distribution centers, and existing retailers selling their own and/or their competitors' products.
- A telecommunications company selects the number and location of switching centers and routers in a communication network. The system displays such quantities as traffic, costs, and transmission times. Users can redefine the network on the screen, can create multiple views, see the effect of what-if changes and new data because the system recomputes for each change, takes constraints into account, and finds where the proposed solution fails to meet criteria.

---

[5] Analytics refers to sophisticated data analysis. Like data mining and statistical analysis, analytics is based on extensive computing using models. It applies existing patterns and key performance indicators (KPIs) to both industry and company metrics.

[6] Sidebar 5 is based on D. Tegarden, "Business Information Visualization," *Communications of AIS* 1(4): January 1999.

[7] For more about geographic information systems, see J. B. Pick, "Geographic Information Systems: A Tutorial and Introduction," *Communications of AIS* 14(16): September 2004.

[8] The use of layers is like that used in CAD/CAM for engineering design.

In addition, the extraction, translation, and loading (ETL) tools of data warehousing (Chapter 5) are important for business intelligence. They help standardize the data so they can be analyzed with accuracy and provide a single truth. When operational data are used, as from an operational data store (ODS), the objective is to use data dynamically, that is data that reflects the situation at the moment.

SIDEBAR 5 *Visualization*

With the flood of data available from information systems, business intelligence analysts and decision makers need to extract the relevant information in a way that people can understand. For example, on a representative day, the New York Stock Exchange may process over a billion transactions. Business decision makers face the task of sorting through the jungle of data created. Visualization technologies allow the use of human visual-spatial abilities to solve the abstract problems found in business. Representing data suitably in a visual manner improves the efficiency and effectiveness of the analyst. This sidebar introduces visualization technology and describes its potential for use in business intelligence. Virtual reality and visualization technologies already are deployed in finance, litigation, marketing, manufacturing, training, and organizational modeling. In short, visualization technology improves the effectiveness of business intelligence.

Visualization is the process of presenting data as visual images. The underlying data could, for example, be abstractions, such as profit, sales, or cost. If the data is abstract, then a visual analog must be created. A typical visual analog is a pie chart or line graph.

The purpose of visualization is *not* to replace quantitative analysis, but instead to allow the quantitative analysis to be focused.[9] Visualization allows

- exploiting the human visual system to extract information from data,
- providing an overview of complex data sets,
- identifying structures, patterns, trends, anomalies, and relationships in data, and
- assisting in identifying the areas of "interest."

In other words, visualization allows BI analysts to use their natural visual-spatial abilities to determine where further exploration should be done. Visualization, when used appropriately, can help find the information in the data.

Table 1 lists typical problems that are solved using visualization technology.

Table 1 REPRESENTATIVE BUSINESS APPLICATIONS OF VISUALIZATION

Financial risk management	Industrial process control
Operations planning	Capital markets management
Marketing analysis	Network monitoring
Fraud/surveillance analysis	Derivatives trading
Budget planning	Portfolio management
Economic analysis	Customer/product analysis
Operations management	Fleet/shipping administration

Source: D. Tegarden, "Business Information Visualization," *Communications of AIS* 1(4): Table 3, p. 21, January 1999. Used by permission.

(continued)

---

[9] G. Grinstein and M. Ward, "Introduction to Data Visualization," *IEEE Visualization Tutorial,* 1997.

SIDEBAR 5	*Visualization (continued)*

Figure 4 is a very simple example of visualization, a "Kiviat Diagram."[10] Such diagrams have been used for many years in computer performance evaluation. A Kiviat diagram allows showing the relations among multiple variables. Each value of each variable is shown on its own axis. For example, if we have five variables, the Kiviat diagram would have five distinct axes (radii). The points are then connected. The pattern that is formed is the information visualization for a particular case. To compare cases, you compare their patterns.[11]

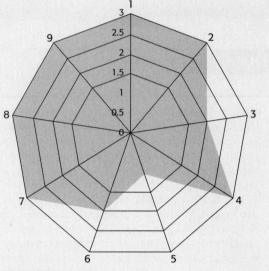

Figure 4 Kiviat diagram.

Dissemination

The key dissemination method for business technology is Internet technology, whether it is an intranet within the firm or an extranet connected to suppliers and/or clients. The idea is to reach everyone who needs specific intelligence data rather than just a few at corporate headquarters.

OLAP

OLAP, which stands for Online analytic processing (Chapter 5), is the analytic portion of decision support systems and is incorporated into business intelligence.[12] Codd originally conceived it[13] as he considered the use of the data warehouse to support array-oriented[14] applications such as financial forecasting and market analyses where the objective is improved return on investment or increased market share.

---

[10] K. Kolence and P. Kiviat, "Software Unit Profiles and Kiviat Figures," *Performance Evaluation Review* 2(3): pp. 2-12, September 1973.

[11] These diagrams are also known as radar charts, star graphs, spider graphs, and star glyphs.

[12] OLAP includes data analytics and predictive analytics in Figure 3 on BI Technologies.

[13] E. F. Codd, S. B. Codd, and C. T. Salley, Providing On-Line Analytic Processing to User Analysts, Sunnyvale, CA: E.F. Codd and Associates, 1993.

[14] In two dimensions, an array is a matrix or a spreadsheet. In three dimensions it is a cube where each dimension represents a variable such as name, cost, or price. The concept of array can be used in as many dimensions as you have in your problem.

Table 2 shows how OLAP differs from conventional online transaction processing (OLTP). OLTP traces the steps followed by individual orders and transactions, whereas OLAP looks at the big picture from a management point of view.

Codd defined four types of processing done by analysts (Table 3).

Don't be scared by the big words in Table 3. We'll explain each of them.

Categorical (from category) refers to static analyses of standard relational databases of what occurred in the past. The data is viewed in the form it is stored.

Exegetical analysis expands categorical analysis to perform queries on the existing data. Typically, the queries involve drilldown. That is, the user points to a particular number on the screen and asks to see the components that were used to obtain the number. For example, if the screen shows total revenue, the query asks to break that total down into the revenues by business units or by region. For multidimensional data, if the breakdown is not stored, the views must be created "on the fly."

Contemplative analysis refers to simple what-if questions in which a single quantity is varied (e.g., what-if the market price for computer chips goes up by 10%?). The result of such a question can change in the values of one or many variables (e.g., unit sales increase but profits go down).

Formulaic analysis extends contemplative analysis to changes in several quantities simultaneously. Formulaic analyses are difficult and not yet commercially common.

The principal analyses performed with OLAP are

- "Slice and dice" to create *data cubes*
- Drill down

Table 2 COMPARISON OF OLAP WITH OLTP

Characteristics	OLAP	OLTP
Operations	Analyze	Update
Screen format	User-defined	Unchanging
Data transactions	Large number	Few
Level of detail	Aggregate	Detail
Time	Historical, current, projected	Current only
Orientation	Attributes	Records

Source: P. Gray and H. J. Watson, *Decision Support in the Data Warehouse,* Upper Saddle River, NJ: Prentice-Hall PTR, 1997.

Table 3 TYPES OF OLAP ANALYSES

Categorical	Static, historical view of data limited by the design of the database
Exegetical	Drill down to see what happened
Contemplative	What-if changes for a single variable
Formulaic	What-if for changes in multiple variables

Source: P. Gray and H. J. Watson, *Decision Support in the Data Warehouse,* Upper Saddle River, NJ: Prentice-Hall PTR, 1997.

Data Cubes

In *slice and dice,* users can view data from many perspectives. Specifically, in slice and dice the user can extract portions of the aggregated data and examine them in accordance with the detailed dimensions of interest (Figure 5). For example, if the data show the total revenue from sock sales nationally, the user can find out about:

- The revenue by type of sock or location.
- The revenue by location (New York, Chicago, Dallas, and San Francisco).
- Combinations, such as revenue by type of sock, by city, and time (e.g., in New York and Dallas last week vs. this week).

Data cubes are discussed in more detail in Sidebar 3 in Chapter 5. An Example is shown in Figure 5.

a

Location	Sales
New York	$440
Chicago	$380
Dallas	$325
San Francisco	$245

b

Black Socks	Sales
New York	$170
	$110
	$125
	$70

Brown Socks	Sales
New York	$100
	$130
	$15
	$40

Blue Socks	Sales
New York	$120
	$40
	$160
	$95

Sweat Socks	Sales
New York	$50
Chicago	$100
Dallas	$25
San Francisco	$40

c

San Francisco	Sales
Black	$70
	$40
	$95
	$40

Dallas	Sales
Black	$25
	$160
	$15
	$125

Chicago	Sales
Black	$100
	$130
	$40
	$110

New York	Sales
Black	$170
Brown	$100
Blue	$120
Sweat socks	$50

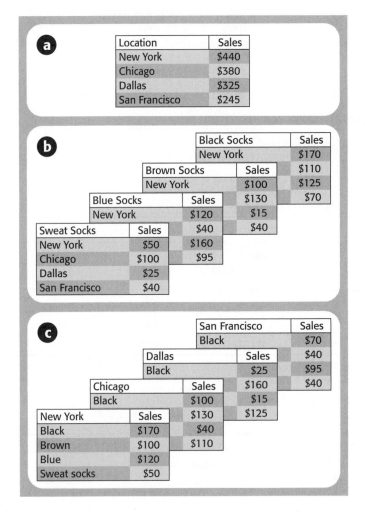

Figure 5a Two dimensions: location vs. sales.
Figure 5b Analysis by sock type.
Figure 5c Analysis by location.

Drilldown

As described in exegetical analysis, in *drilldown,* the user navigates through the data to obtain more detail that will help explain "why." Drilldown typically is used when a total is significantly larger or smaller than expected. For example, if cereal brands are selling particularly well in Washington, drilldown helps the user determine which brands are contributing to the observed increase. It is also possible to *drill up* (i.e., consolidate data) and *drill across* (obtain data at the same level for another quantity, such as milk or cookies).

The inverse of drilldown is "roll up." The idea comes from financial consolidations. Data from several sources at the same level, such as divisional profits or PC costs or sales in a geographic region, are combined into a single number. For example, starting with the Level 3 data in the drill-down example, roll up would lead to the level 2 data and then to the 510,000 units sold in the Washington metro area.

OTHER DATA SOURCES

Although much of the data for analysis comes from the data warehouse, many other data and information sources also contribute. For example:

- text available in news reports and documents,
- diagrams and photographs, and
- government data such as census figures

are all used in business intelligence. The outputs of analysis, such as a spreadsheet, may be fed directly to a particular application as well as being saved. Thus, the routine data gathering that is part of running the warehouse is not sufficient, by itself, to provide all the data inputs needed in BI.

SIDEBAR 6   *Drilldown Example*

Managers are examining the much better than average sales of cereal brands in their Washington, D.C., metro area grocery stores. The total looks good and drilling down one level shows little difference among the three sales divisions. But going down one level further shows that one brand (Circles) is a slow mover in two areas. Their problems: How to deal with differences in regional demand? What to do about Circles?

Week of August 29

Level 1	Washington Metro 510,000			
Level 2	Virginia 160,000	D.C. 170,000	Maryland 170,000	Three-Region Total 510,000
Level 3	Circles 20,000 Wheat 40,000 Sugared 50,000 Spheres 50,000	Circles 10,000 Wheat 20,000 Sugared 90,000 Spheres 40,000	Circles 60,000 Wheat 40,000 Sugared 10,000 Spheres 80,000	Circles 90,000 Wheat 100,000 Sugared 150,000 Spheres 170,000

Data indicate number of units sold during week.

EXAMPLE: COMPETITIVE INTELLIGENCE

The notion of competitive intelligence as "spy vs. spy," fed by such examples as France allegedly stealing U.S. industrial secrets, is far from the real situation. That doesn't mean that companies don't try to find out as much as possible about their current and their potential competitors. However, the people involved in it [15] claim that they do so in a legal and ethical manner. Competitive Intelligence is defined by the Society for Competitive intelligence professionals as [16] "A systematic and ethical program for gathering, analyzing, and managing external information that can affect your company's plans, decisions, and operations." Thus, it is the process of monitoring the competitive environment. The objective is to enable senior managers to make informed decisions about marketing, R&D, investments, and business strategies.

The competitive intelligence cycle [17] includes

1. Determine the intelligence needs of decision makers.
2. Collect information to meet these needs.
3. Analyze the data and recommend actions.
4. Present results to the decision makers.
5. Use the response to the findings to refine collection.

The focus is on determining both the current activities and the likely intentions of other firms and of the government. Based on the early warning provided, managers are in a position to detect market changes and to reposition the firm if necessary.

The raw data collected (facts, statistics) are organized and then analyzed to find patterns, trends, and relationships. The tools used include

- Simulations of alternative scenarios to test what-if conditions.
- Data mining of information about both competitors and the firm.
- Assessing competitor technologies by tracking (and extrapolating from) patent filings.
- Attending trade shows and conferences.
- Scanning publicly available data such as public records, the Internet, press releases, and mass media (think about Comshare's acquisition of Execucomm discussed earlier in this chapter).
- Talking with customers, suppliers, partners, and industry experts.

---

[15] The major U.S. professional group is the Society for Competitive Intelligence Professionals, headquartered in Alexandria, Virginia. Their URL is: http://www.scip.org. Much of the information presented on Competitive Intelligence is based on this website.

[16] http://www.scip.org/ci/.

[17] Based on S. H. Miller, Competitive Intelligence, an Overview, http://www.scip.org/library/overview.pdf.

Much of the data-gathering work is terribly dull and routine. To get done it has to be someone's (or some group's) responsibility. Yet it is the basis for evaluating each competitor's situation, determining how competitors are countering your firm's strategy, and alerting senior management about fresh competition from unexpected sources and alternate technologies.

Table 4 shows the results of a survey[18] of the use and effectiveness of competitive intelligence analysis techniques.

Specific software packages used include data mining, text retrieval and classification, patent searching, Web page tracking, and Internet monitoring. However, the consensus in the field is that software specifically designed for competitive intelligence lags that for conventional business intelligence.

Good data on annual spending on competitive intelligence are not available. Surveys in the late 1990s indicate some companies spend $100,000 while others spend $500,000 and a few over $1 million. However, the amounts were self-determined so it is not possible to know what expenditures were included.

Finally, since all systems are competitive, some companies practice counterintelligence. That is, they recognize that since they conduct competitive intelligence against other firms, they themselves could be targets. They try to safeguard their data from others by using a variety of security techniques. The extent of their success is not known.

Table 4 COMPETITIVE INTELLIGENCE ANALYSIS TOOLS

Tool	Percent using	Tool	Effectiveness percentage
Competitor profiles	88.9	SWOT analysis	63.1
Financial analysis	72.1	Competitor profiles	52.4
SWOT[19] analysis	55.2	Financial analysis	45.5
Scenarios	53.8	Win/loss analysis	31.4
Win/loss analysis	40.4	Gaming	21.9
Gaming	27.5	Scenarios	19.2
Conjoint analysis	25.5	Conjoint analysis	15.8
Simulation	25.0	Simulation	15.4

Source: T. Powell and C. Allgaier, "Enhancing Sales and Marketing Effectiveness through Competitive Intelligence," *Competitive Intelligence Review* 9(4): pp. 29–41, 1998, used by permission of the Society for Competitive Intelligence, www.scip.org.

[18] T. Powell and C. Allgaier, "Enhancing Sales and Marketing Effectiveness through Competitive Intelligence," Competitive Intelligence Review 9(4): pp. 29–41, 1998, as reported by SCIP at its website: http://www.scip.org/ci/analysis.asp

[19] SWOT is an abbreviation for analysis of strengths, weaknesses, opportunities, and threats.

EXAMPLE: *Financial Analytics*

Financial analytics are an example of business intelligence computations. Here, the analyst wants to see the changes in the balance sheet on a month-by-month basis to assess trends and directions of growth or decline. The analyst also wants to determine the potential effects of changes in the environment (such as changes in interest rates or currency exchange rates) on the balance sheet. Changes in payables (e.g., to whom and how much is owed) and receivables (including the length of the receivable cycle) indicate the health of both individual units and the firm as a whole.

For the income statement, the analysis revolves around changes in the origins of revenue and operating expenses. The company wants to know such things as which parts of the enterprise are producing financial resources and which are consuming them, and the variances between actuals and budgets. When anomalies (better or worse than expected values) occur, the analyst drills down to see which specific unit or product is the source of the anomaly.

POTENTIAL AND SHORTCOMINGS

In investing in a BI system, some firms take an integrated approach and gain BI's full potential. Others take a fragmented approach to implementation and, as a result, fail to obtain the capabilities offered by the software. Those are the conclusions of a report of the Hackett Group.[20] Hackett Group first divided the companies they surveyed that adopt BI technologies into two categories: world class and average. The results shown in Table 5 indicate the differences in the percentages of companies in each category.

The companies that Hackett Group calls world-class integrated BI techniques within their firms, while the average companies are implementing on a piecemeal basis, often leaving department or line of business managers to select specific BI tools to meet their local needs. As a result, the analyses by these companies are not consistent across the firm as a whole, and considerable effort is expended trying to decide which answer is correct. Another major difference is the relative percentage of time spent gathering data and analyzing it. In world-class firms, it is 50–50, whereas average firms spend 80% in gathering and 20% in analysis. Finally, world-class firms allocate 20% of their staff to decision support activities, while average firms allocate only 11%.

Table 5   PERCENTAGE OF COMPANIES INVESTING IN BI

BI capabilities	World-class companies (%)	Average companies (%)
Consolidation engines	72	25
OLAP	57	25
Analytical applications	57	25
Performance management	57	20

Source: T. Hoblitzell, "CEO Perspectives: Disconnects in Today's BI Systems," *DM Review,* p. 56, July 2002, reprinted with permission from Source Media/DM Review.

---

[20] This discussion is based on data developed by Hackett Best Practices. It is reported in T. Hoblitzell, "CEO Perspectives: Disconnects in Today's BI Systems," *DM Review,* p. 56, July 2002.

Although sophisticated BI tools exist, most of the analyses being performed in average companies deal with financial data captured in accounting and ERP applications. Much of the analysis winds up being done by hand and presented in paper reports. In Hackett's average companies, only a third of senior executives take advantage of computerized decision support tools.

RETURN ON INVESTMENT

Computing return on investment for business intelligence is a difficult problem. Like most information systems, BI up-front costs are high and can be estimated fairly accurately because they involve purchases as well as labor. Upkeep costs can also be forecast. Unfortunately, although reductions in costs from efficiencies[21] can be forecast, these savings are often only a small portion of the payoff. Cost reductions are usually insufficient by themselves to pay for BI systems.

Costs

Most firms do some form of business intelligence, although only a few have complete BI systems. To simplify the discussion, consider a firm starting from scratch. Putting a BI system in place includes

Hardware Costs. These costs depend on what is already installed. If a data warehouse is in use, then the principal hardware needed is a data mart specifically for BI and, perhaps, a capacity upgrade for the data warehouse. However, other hardware may be required such as additional storage, and more powerful servers and user PCs. In addition, an intranet (and extranet) is needed to transmit data to the user community. Most firms have these networks in place; however, they may need to be enlarged to handle the additional load imposed by BI.

Software Costs. For a sophisticated firm, the tools outlined in the section, BI Technology, at the beginning of this chapter (see, e.g., Figure 2) would be available. Typical BI packages for a single function that sits on this technology can cost $60,000 base price.

Subscriptions. Although firms generate considerable data of their own, most also pay for subscriptions to various data services so that they can compare their operations to those of competitors and so that they can scan the economic and regulatory environment. For example, if selling to the retail industry, firms buy product scanner data to find out how their products and their competitor products respond to special offers, new introductions, and other day-to-day changes in the marketplace (see Sidebar 3).

Implementation Costs. Once the hardware and software are acquired, a large onetime expense is implementation, including training. Training, however, is an ongoing cost as new people are brought into using the system and as the system is upgraded. In addition, software maintenance contracts typically run 15% of the purchase costs per year.

Personnel Costs. Personnel assigned to perform BI and for IT support need to be fully costed, taking into account salary, general and administrative costs (G&A), space, personal computing equipment, and other infrastructure for people. A sophisticated cost analysis also takes into account the time spent reading output by the consumers of BI, that is, the people to whom the reports are addressed.

---

[21] For example, time saved in creating and distributing reports, operating efficiencies, and the ability to retain customers.

Benefits. Improvements in pricing, in understanding competitive efforts, and similar incremental gains can often be identified. For example,[22] Alliant Exchange in Deerfield, Illinois, was able to identify tangible return on investment from closer analysis of purchasing and rebates from suppliers. It is clear that managers will have a much better picture of their operations and their opportunities. Where BI software is installed for large numbers of operational people (see the section, BI Everywhere, near the end of this chapter), the users contribute benefits from the way they use the intelligence. For large, one-shot returns on investment, the hope is that a good BI system will lead to a big bang that changes the firm at some time in the future. However, it is not possible to forecast big bangs because they are fortuitous and infrequent.

BUILDING A BUSINESS INTELLIGENCE SYSTEM

The process of building a business intelligence system is similar to that for building any large information system.

- Project plans and schedules must be developed.
- User requirements must be determined and evaluated. This task is difficult because users often do not know what they want nor what can and cannot be done.
- Software and hardware must be selected.
- The system must be given an adequate budget.
- Users must be trained.
- System operations must be monitored and modifications made as the firm's business changes.

Overriding all these specific steps is the need for a corporate sponsor who believes in the project, who is at a high enough level in the firm, controls sufficient budget, and with clout to ensure the project's completion, implementation, and operation.

Although a few firms still build their own systems or subsystems, most firms wind up buying one or more packages. As was shown in Figure 3, a complete system involves a large number of components, which must be integrated with one another seamlessly. This issue is one of systems integration discussed in Chapter 10. Despite the claims of the software vendors, most packages are far from comprehensive and are not plug and play. Most firms, therefore, hire outside consultants to achieve systems integration.[23]

Consulting firms vary in size (i.e., the number of consultants), skill sets, and the software packages with which they are familiar. The consultants can be hired from local software value added resellers, the Big 4 accounting firms, research organizations, and BI boutiques. The role of the consultant is to handle the complexities of BI systems that are beyond the capabilities of the people in the firm, particularly in the IT shop. BI packages differ in their capabilities, strengths, and weaknesses. Some consultants specialize strictly in assisting the firm in evaluating and selecting software packages. Other services consultants provide include

- Developing the BI architecture
- System selection

---

[22] http://www.informationweek.com/story/IWK20020315S0062 March 13, 2002.

[23] Dan Pilone, "The Strategic Outsiders," *Intelligent Enterprise,* pp. 58–59, April 16, 2002.

- Project management
- Implementation
- Program and policy formation
- Training
- Ongoing operations

Be warned, however, that consultants are not cheap and that some do not possess all the competence they claim. For the long haul, care must be taken that the consultant's knowledge is transferred to your firm (see Chapter 7, Knowledge Management). Otherwise, you will continue to be dependent on them.

THE BUSINESS INTELLIGENCE INDUSTRY

Datamonitor[24] developed the following industrywide figures for vendor revenue for 2001 through 2005 in billions of dollars:

Year	2001	2002	2003	2004	2005
$ Billions	2+	3	4	6	8

The Datamonitor estimate agrees with IDC's[25] estimate that analytics for business intelligence were approaching a $3 billion/year industry in 2002.[26] However, although these estimates are several years old, a more recent (2005) estimate of the size of the BI market is an IDC estimate that analytics revenues are approximately $8 billion in 2005 and will exceed $11 billion in 2008. This amount will be split between core analytic tools that perform simple tasks such as computing statistics on existing data and creating data cubes (see above), and predictive analytics which are more advanced mathematically.[27]

Whether these estimates for business intelligence applications can be realized is still a matter of dispute. To achieve them, companies will need to change culture and allow sharing of intelligence information. The business intelligence packages have to be integrated with other software. Integration is a continuing problem because of the complexity of the tools and complexity of other applications with which they interact, such as data warehousing, data mining, and CRM. In addition, continual mergers and acquisitions among BI vendors exacerbate the integration problem, as software that meshes today may not do so tomorrow.

The market is highly fragmented, with no one vendor or group of vendors controlling the whole industry. The vendors include manufacturers of specific point solutions, prepackaged BI solutions, consultants, and integrators, ancillary software, and support providers.

The following is a sampling of vendors (in alphabetical order)[28]

- Analytica
- Business Objects (includes Crystal Decision, which specializes in reporting)

---

[24] As reported in *Information Week,* March 4, 2002.

[25] IDC is one of several firms that monitors the computer industry and provides estimates of industry revenues.

[26] *DM Review,* 2002.

[27] Source: http://ie.bizintelligencepipeline.com.

[28] A more complete list of vendors and products can be found at http://www.intelligententerprise.com/011004/pdfs/415feat1_guide_table.pdf.

- Cognos
- Group 1 Software (a division of Pitney Bowes)
- Hummingbird
- Hyperion
- IBM
- Information Builders
- Microsoft
- MicroStrategy
- Oracle
- ProClarity
- SAS

Many of these vendors are also leading participants in other technologies such as data warehousing, data mining, and CRM, discussed in other chapters in this book. Often, the smaller firms act as resellers of major components such as data warehouses. The firms are generally well established. As customer requirements grew, these vendors increased the capabilities of their software packages. The total annual revenue of the smaller firms generally falls in the $50 million to $125 million range.[29]

The recent trends in the industry are toward consolidation. That is evident both from the reports in the trade press and from the declining number of vendors exhibiting at trade shows. The survivors are trying to cover the entire business intelligence space by offering "enterprise business intelligence suites" including complete reporting capability. Firms are also moving into related markets in business activity monitoring (BAM) and business performance measurement (BPM) (see below).

CASE STUDIES

Dallas Teacher's Credit Union[30]

The Dallas Teacher's Credit Union (DTCU) is a local Dallas credit union serving customers in the Dallas Metroplex. From 2001 to 2004, they grew their membership from 147,000 to 165,000 and their net assets from $765 million to over a billion. The credit union started its business intelligence system in 2000 as a marketing project: they wanted to find the top 10% of their profitable customers.

To analyze these profitable customers, DTCU examined internal information on the products the customers were using, which branches they patronized, and how they did business with the credit union. DTCU then supplemented this internal information with external demographic information about their members.

Some of the key insights that came from the analysis were

- who were their most profitable customers,
- the customers' key characteristics, and
- the customers' banking habits.

---

[29] Based on estimates of OLAP sales in the OLAP Report http://www.olapreport.com/Market.htm.

[30] http://www.banktech.com/story/technologyLeaders/BNK20010713S0015.

http://www.unicacorp.com/documents/case_studies/credit_union.pdf.

http://www.esri.com/library/fliers/pdfs/avba-credituniontx.pdf.

They found, contrary to preexisting beliefs by bank personnel, that one of the most important factors to profitable customers was drive time. From this insight, and from the demographic information about the type of people who banked with them and where they lived, DTCU was able to decide where new branches should be located, which ones needed expansion, and which branches to downsize or close.

DTCU also uses its BI system to craft effective marketing campaigns. They use their database to segment customers. Based on past historical data, their BI software determines which customer segment is most likely to respond to a particular marketing initiative. The result is higher response rates (increasing from 1% to 8%), lower customer acquisition costs, and more efficient cross-selling than in the past.

Through the use of another BI component, the DTCU realized that by changing its charter, it could serve many other types of people in addition to their original teacher customer base. By analyzing the characteristics of their credit union, versus the demographic information of their communities, they saw that their potential customer base increased from 250,000 to 2.2 million. The state of Texas approved the charter change and the renamed Credit Union of Texas is now one of the top 100 credit unions in the nation.

Nygard[31]

Nygard, a Canadian firm, is North America's fourth largest women's apparel manufacturer. Their garments are sold in over 200 retail stores they own, by major retailers (such as Nordstrom, Sears, Dillard's, and Kohl) and approximately 900 other smaller retailers. They also sell over their website.

Nygard collects sales data from its many partners and uses business intelligence systems to make sense of the mountains of data for a variety of users within the firm. Designers and marketers use the data to identify trends for next season's designs. Merchandisers are able to see what products are in the stores. Turning all that data into information-rich reports used to take weeks; now it takes 10 minutes.

By analyzing what is selling, and what isn't, Nygard is better able to design products with the key features that consumers want. Nygard is also able to use the BI systems to identify regional and store-level peculiarities, such as fashion, material, or color preferences. This information allows Nygard and the stores to improve their inventory so that it meets the requirements of their customers.

In fashion, timeliness is a key concern and a sales season for a fashion line can be as short as 5 weeks. By collecting and comparing the data from a wide variety of stores, Nygard is better able to identify and exploit irregularities in sales. By analyzing why certain products or stores sell effectively, Nygard is able to replicate conditions and determine the causes of shortcomings. For example, a product may not be displayed properly or stores may be too cramped.

While Nygard's system was designed for internal use, the BI system also pays off for Nygard's retailers and customers. By understanding the needs of the end customers (i.e., consumers) and the practices of their retailers better, Nygard helps its partners to be more effective. Merchandise designs are more in line with customer requirements, store inventory levels are appropriate, and information can be provided to retailers to assist them in effectively selling product.

EMERGING IDEAS IN BUSINESS INTELLIGENCE

BI Everywhere[32]

In the past, business intelligence was a project for staff groups who only reported their findings to the highest levels in the organization. That is rapidly changing. While the definitive work on business intelligence in most companies is still being done at staff level, the results and the raw data are

---

[31] J. Shoesmith, "Knowledge Seekers," *Ivey Business Journal,* May 2002.

http://www.microstrategy.com/news/pr_systems/press_release.asp?ctry+167&id+396.

http://www.consumergoods.com/issue/oct_nygard.htm Consumer Goods Technology, October 2000.

[32] For a more complete discussion of intelligence everywhere see E. Schwartz, "Intelligence Everywhere," *InfoWorld* p. 12, August 23, 2004.

being shared with ever larger numbers of managers throughout the firm. This democratization of business and competitive intelligence (sometimes called pervasive BI or BI for the masses) is the direct result of improvements in computing and storage capabilities at the desktop. In some firms, by using profiles about the specific information used by individual managers, BI reports are being customized to individual needs. Thus financials go to finance and product and production information to manufacturing. The underlying concept is that business intelligence is only used if it meets the needs of the individual users.

Democratizing business intelligence is one response to the needs of reporting requirements under such legislation as the Sarbanes–Oxley Act and HIPAA (see Chapter 15). These requirements make it necessary for everyone's data in the firm to be transparent.

A BI everywhere approach changes the nature of the computing support required. Rather than providing software that is used by only a few, the software must now be "scalable" to hundreds or even thousands of people. These growth levels are not gradual. One company reported growth for financial reports from 200 users to thousands within 9 months.

Business Process Management and Business Activity Monitoring

Business process management (BPM) and business activity monitoring (BAM) are new developments in the last several years. Although the terms are sometimes used interchangeably, BAM is really a subset of BPM, which is the broader concept.

"BPM is a collection of software, business processes, and measures of business success (metrics, key performance indicators) that, when combined, enable an organization to understand, act on, and influence its business performance."[33] It can be applied to both small and large firms.

BPM builds on existing technologies and concepts discussed in this book including

Key performance indicators (KPIs)	Dashboards	Planning	Extract, transfer, and load
Scorecards	OLAP	Consolidation	Report and query tools

It uses a data mart (Chapter 5) specifically allocated to it. This data mart gathers information from multiple data sources including the data warehouse and other data marts. The BPM software, combined with the organization's business process and measures of effectiveness (KPIs), is designed to deliver accurate and timely information for decision making.

BAM[34] systems report business activity process outputs and key performance indicators to managers in (near) real time. In particular, firms that turn out huge numbers of items from their factory or ship a large number of items obtained from suppliers need business activity monitoring.

Typical BAM applications include comparing available inventory and shipping times to incoming orders, using inventory policy settings to reorder an item when the number in stock goes below a specified amount, monitoring key performance indicators for key accounts so that managers are alerted when performance is moving outside allowed quality bounds, warning banks about money laundering, and warning hospital administrators when emergency room cases exceed preset limits.

---

[33] BPM is discussed in a series of articles in *DM Review* by C. Schiff, starting in September 2003 and continuing monthly during the next year. The first article is C. Schiff, "Maximize Business Performance: BPM is Coming—and It's Not Just Hype," *DM Review,* September 2003.

[34] For a more detailed discussion of Business Activity Monitoring, see:L. Erlanger, "Monitoring Your Business in Real Time" *Infoworld* 26(30): July 26, 2004.

What is the difference between BPM and BAM? BPM and BAM are related, but are not the same. BPM includes dashboards and scorecards. Scorecards include the use of dashboards, but add a methodology that links the scorecards to corporate strategy. BAM is thus a subset of the dashboard approach to BPM because it monitors current activities (thus requiring real-time data warehousing and enterprise application integration). BAM is equivalent to process control in a manufacturing firm (and used as such in the Western Digital case discussed next). Note that not all BPM measures are real time. Hence, BAM is the real-time part of BPM.

CASE STUDY OF BAM

The case of Western Digital[35] illustrates the way BAM works. Western Digital Corporation,[36] located in Lake Forest, California, produces of the order of 10,000 hard disks[37] per day in their offshore factories in Malaysia and Thailand. The cost of even an hour's downtime in production is significant.

To perform business activity monitoring they built a "vigilant" information system[38] that includes both sensing and responding capabilities. The system includes an underlying layer of business intelligence applications that analyzes data from numerous sources, and a number of management dashboards that automate the alerting process and provide the means for responding.

The term dashboard comes from the automobile and the airplane where the driver or pilot is presented with a display that describes the current health of the system such as its speed and its gasoline supply. In a factory dashboard, such as Western Digital's, the displays show the current state of each element of the factory floor. Based on past experience, warning levels (equivalent to being outside quality control limits) are used to alert engineering and manufacturing personnel that a problem is likely to occur. People are alerted electronically by cell phone and by e-mail. Virtual teams are formed to respond both at the overseas plant and the U.S.-based headquarters.

General Conclusions on BAM

To make BAM work required both the revamping of business processes and the sensible use of dashboards so that the right people are alerted and have the means to respond correctly and quickly. For Western Digital, the real-time management dashboards became the nerve center for managing the enterprise.

In BAM, it is desirable to set up an OODA (observe, orient, decide, act; see Sidebar, pg. 158) loop (Sidebar 7) for learning because the faster the loop, the quicker (and hence less costly) the response. However, the response need not be instantaneous. The time latency of each OODA loop needs to be matched to the organization's needs and capabilities. Indiscriminately chasing zero latency does not pay off.

---

[35] The Western Digital case is described in detail in R. Houghton, O. A. El Sawy, P. Gray, C. Donegan, and A. Josh, "Vigilant Information Systems for Managing Enterprises in Dynamic Supply Chains: Real-Time Dashboards at Western Digital," *MISQ Executive* 3(1): March 2004.

[36] http://www.wdc.com.

[37] The hard disks are used in storage in PCs and other digital equipment.

[38] The term vigilant information system was first enunciated by J. Walls, G. Widemeyer, and O. El Sawy "Building an Information System Design Theory for Vigilant EIS," *Information Systems Research,* pp. 53-69, May 1992. The idea is to build an information system that keeps watch on current conditions and informs managers (or acts in prescribed ways) when action is required.

The concept of OODA loops (shown in Figure 6) was originated by U.S. Air Force Colonel John Boyd and later converted to business use.[39] Boyd wanted to understand how fighter pilots won air combat engagements (dogfights) against other pilots despite aircraft with inferior maneuverability. Boyd found that winning pilots were able to compress the whole cycle of activities that happens in a dogfight and complete them quicker than their adversaries. Boyd's OODA loop of activities included

- *Observation* (seeing situation and adversary),
- *Orientation* (sizing up vulnerabilities and opportunities),
- *Decision* (deciding which combat maneuver to take), and
- *Action* (executing the maneuver).

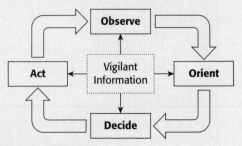

Figure 6 OODA loops.

Source: Houghton, El Sawy, Gray, Donegan, and Joshi, "Vigilant Information Systems for Managing Enterprises in Dynamic Supply Chains: Real-time Dashboards at Western Digital," *MISQ Executive* 3(1): June 2004, copyright by the University of Minnesota. Used by permission.

Thus, to pursue a BAM strategy requires providing the building blocks for "sense-and-respond" in a real-time enterprise through a vigilant information system and real-time management dashboards. Of course, just as with all of the initiatives described in this book, implementation requires a management initiative (not a technology initiative) because it requires active, collaborative engagement from all top management to instill the needed organizational transformation.

ANSWERS TO MANAGERIAL QUESTIONS

Is business intelligence an oxymoron? A shorthand for cloak-and-dagger spying on competitors and government? An important, legitimate activity?

Despite its name, business intelligence is about trying to understand your own position, your customers, and your competitors. It is neither ethical nor legal to spy on competitors. However, it is legitimate to use publicly available data. Competitor intelligence is an important part of a firm's planning and operational decision making.

What types of business intelligence are there?

The main uses of BI were explained in its definition at the beginning of the chapter: Business intelligence systems present complex corporate and competitive information to planners and decision makers. The objective is to improve the timeliness and quality of the input to the decision process.

What is new about today's business intelligence systems compared to previous systems?

Business intelligence is a natural outgrowth of a series of previous systems designed to support decision making such as executive information systems[40] that makes use of the advances in information technology shown in Figure 1 of this chapter. The emergence of the data warehouse as a repository, the advances in data cleansing that lead to a single truth, the greater capabilities of hardware and software, all combine to create a richer business intelligence environment than was available previously.

---

[39] Boyd, J. Patterns of Conflict, unpublished manuscript, USAF, 1986. Also see Curts, R. and Campbell, D. "Avoiding Information Overload through the Understanding of OODA Loops," *Proceedings of the Command & Control Technology Research Symposium,* 2001.

[40] Haeckel, S. *Adaptive Enterprise: Creating and Leading Sense-and-Respond Organizations,* Harvard Business School Press, 1999.

Who uses BI?

Managers throughout the firm use business intelligence. At senior managerial levels, it is the input to both strategic and tactical decisions. At lower managerial levels, it helps individuals do their day-to-day job.

How do you gather and transfer BI?

Business intelligence is a form of knowledge. The techniques described in Chapter 7, Knowledge Management, for generating and transferring knowledge apply. Some knowledge is based in data purchased from third parties (e.g., scanner data in the wholesale grocery business) while other is created by analysis of internal and public data. Knowledge transfer often involves disseminating intelligence information to many people in the firm. For example, salespeople need to know market conditions, competitor offerings, and the firm's special offerings.

Do you need a separate organizational unit for BI?

Most medium and large firms assign people, often full-time, for planning and for monitoring both their own and their competitors' actions. These people are the ones who form the core groups for business intelligence initiatives. Whether they are centralized or scattered through SBUs is a matter of organizational style.

What technologies are available?

Most of the technologies needed for business intelligence serve multiple purposes. For example, the World Wide Web has been adopted for both knowledge generation and knowledge transfer. However, specialized software for doing analysis is the heart of business intelligence. This software is an outgrowth of the software used for decision support and executive information systems in the past.

What are the developments in BI?

BI is a quickly developing field of information systems. One of the current developments is the expansion of the number of users so that in many firms BI [and competitive intelligence] is available at most managers' desks. Another is the movement to real time intelligence through the use of dashboards for vigilant, rapid response.

PROBLEMS

1. BUSINESS INTELLIGENCE

    Select one of the inputs to business intelligence shown in Figure 1. Describe the various ways that the input is used in creating business intelligence reports.

2. COMPETITIVE INTELLIGENCE

    The following are examples of ethical situations involved in competitive intelligence. For each of these situations, give your opinion as to whether the action is (1) normal, (2) aggressive, (3) unethical, or (4) illegal. Explain the reasons for your opinion.

    a. Hotel documents left behind

    You learn that your competitor's board meeting is in the hotel across the street from you. You drop into the hotel after the meeting is over to see whether anyone left documents behind.

    b. Airplane

    While sitting on a 3-hour airplane flight, you overhear one passenger tell another about information that would be considered confidential in your own firm. They do not know you and they don't know you can overhear them.

    c. While attending an industry convention, you take off your badge that identifies your company and approach a competitor's booth. You tell the person at the booth that you are interested in their product.

    d. Same situation. However, instead of going to the competitor's booth you enter a private suite marked "Alpha company customers only."

3. BPM AND BAM

    Go to http://dmreview.com (and other sources if you choose) to search for "business process management" and "business activity monitoring." Prepare a three page paper comparing and contrasting these two ideas.

4. OODA LOOPS

    Discuss the merits and the shortcomings of OODA loops.

Chapter 9

Outsourcing and Its Variations: Letting Someone Else Do the Work

MANAGERIAL QUESTIONS

What is outsourcing?
What are its risks and its rewards?
If I outsource, what form of outsourcing should I use?
What is the information utility concept about?

INTRODUCTION

In this chapter we consider the various ways in which a firm can hire people who work for others to do the firm's information systems work. Contracting work, that is, outsourcing, to other firms is not a new idea. Firms have been doing it for a long time to reduce cost, gain additional capacity, or obtain human skills that they lack. All three of these objectives, if met, save money and hence make a firm more cost-competitive. What is new is that outsourcing has come full force to information systems in two ways:

- domestic outsourcing (onshore) and
- overseas outsourcing (offshore).

Overseas outsourcing of information systems work is a relatively new phenomenon that grabs newspaper headlines. High-paying jobs, particularly computer programming jobs in an industry once considered a near-exclusive First World capability, are being exported because workers in countries such as India or the Philippines possess the same skills and work for less.

From a societal point of view, overseas outsourcing is a classic example of the concept that a local good is not necessarily a general good. An individual firm that outsources overseas successfully to save money improves its competitive position by reducing its costs. If most firms outsource overseas, the competitive advantage becomes a competitive necessity. Worse, as was found in the first half of the current decade, new people do not enter the field. Enrollments in computer science and information systems drop, and the long-term information systems capabilities of the country decline quickly.

Origins of Outsourcing

The origins of outsourcing IT work can be traced back to the 1950s and 1960s, when firms would bring in contract programmers from organizations such as Volt Technical to cope with overloads. They would outsource routine operations such as payroll, which was a specialty of Automatic Data Processing (now ADP) founded in the early 1950s. However, outsourcing was considered a minor or peripheral part of IT. The heyday of outsourcing started in 1989, when Kodak, the film and camera firm, outsourced almost its entire IS operation to three different contractors. (The Kodak story is told near the end of this chapter.) Outsourcing continues full force into the present.

Outsourcing involves the contracting of some or all information systems tasks by one firm to another. As will be shown later in this chapter, the contract under which outsourcing is performed is the key to the process. The contract period can be as short as a few months for one specific job or call for long-term relationships lasting up to 10 years.

Outsourcing introduced new arrangements such as offshore software development and help desks, application service providers, Web services, consultants brought in to integrate systems, and the use of a computer utility. Outsourcing and each of these variations are discussed in this chapter.

In brief,

- Offshore outsourcers, principally in India, Ireland, the Philippines, and Eastern Europe, offer a skilled labor force at a much lower direct cost (but not necessarily lower total cost). Offshore outsourcing is one form of globalization, discussed in Chapter 10.

- Application service providers, a model whose time may have come and gone, are firms that provide the software and the computers needed to run an application based on data you provide.

- Web services are a form of application service provider that uses the World Wide Web for communications. The applications use a universal language[1] to send data and instructions to one another, with no translation required. Since they use the Internet, most of the connection and communications problems are eliminated.

- Systems integration refers to the task of taking multiple, disparate applications and making them work together by the use of software. Systems integration is an alternative to ERP. Systems integration, discussed in Chapter 10, is sometimes achieved by outsourcing portions of the IS operation.

- Computer utilities is a concept being advanced by IBM, Hewlett-Packard (HP), and Oracle. These vendors and others would deploy information technology as a utility, like service that can expand or contract quickly, depending on the needs of a business customer. The customer pays only for the services used.

Offshore Outsourcing[2]

We begin our detailed discussion with offshore outsourcing. With increasing labor costs and tight budgets in times of recession or a shortage of skills available within the United States in times of boom, some firms turn to offshore outsourcing. Countries such as India, the Philippines, and

---

[1] The computer language is called UML, an abbreviation for Universal Modeling Language.

[2] Based on N. Ramarapu, M. Parzinger, and A. A. Lado, "Issues in Foreign Outsourcing," *Information Systems Management* 14(2): pp. 27-31, Spring, 1997, and T. M. Rajkumar and R. V. S. Mani, "Offshore Software Development: The View from Indian Suppliers," *Information Systems Management* 18(2): pp. 63-73, 2001.

Eastern Europe, with good IT education systems, turn out a large supply of people with software skills who will work at much lower wages. In some countries, where English is spoken, even the language barrier is removed. The Year 2000 (Y2K) problem (see Chapter 4) served as a testing ground in which a relatively routine task was sent overseas and completed successfully.

The range of information systems services outsourced overseas is quite large. It includes

- Data entry and simple processing
- Systems integration
- Facilities management
- Help desk operations
- Contract programming
- Disaster recovery

For example, American Airlines physically flew the airline tickets it collected from fliers to Jamaica where the data was entered into the computer. A call to a help desk may contact a young lady in India who not only is knowledgeable but trained to speak with an American accent. Facilities management may involve an overseas data center. Disaster recovery may provide storage for backup and maintaining computing after an earthquake. The largest offshored activity is contract programming.

In contract programming, the software requirements and design are already known. The foreign vendor creates the code, usually to create a computer application. Typical jobs are accounting systems, ATM systems, or modernizing an existing system.

The drawbacks of offshore outsourcing also need to be addressed. They include

- *Cultural and Language Barriers*. These barriers have nothing to do with technical competence. They involve the differences between countries. Simple things, like

  - How far away should you stand from the person you're dealing with? In some countries people are on top of one another, in others they separate by a large distance.
  - Business customs including appropriate business gifts, honesty, bribery, data privacy, security, and confidentiality.
  - The meaning of words and sentences in English, not to mention what happens when slang is used or translation is required.
  - Spelling and pronunciation differences (I say tomato, you say tomahto).
  - The way people in the United States enter dates (e.g., 11-7-05 is November 7 in the United States but July 11 in much of the rest of the world).

The list goes on and on.

- *Legal Differences*. Different countries have different laws, tax structures, and intellectual property rights. Some countries control e-mail and travel by citizens and visitors. Normal contract terms can differ, as may the level of recourse to the courts on either side.
- *Communication and Technical Infrastructure*. Technical incompatibilities in voltage, in bandwidth, in communications equipment and standards, and in the equipment available for computing must be overcome. For example, most of the rest of the world uses a different frequency standard than the United States for cell phones.
- *Travel Costs and Time*. The more distant and difficult a country is to reach, the more it costs to get there and back in dollars, time, and wear and tear on the travelers. Of these, time is perhaps the most precious.

- *Time Differences*. The time differences increase the further away the offshore outsourcer is from the company. For example, if it is 5 P.M. in Los Angeles, it is 6:30 A.M. in India. Time differences increase the difficulty in communicating either by phone or rapid turn-around on e-mail.

- *Risks*. Risks include political changes, taxes, unexpected cost increases, after-sales support costs, and contracting difficulties, to name a few. A particularly important risk is data security. Sending data offshore implies that people outside the firm obtain your firm's data. Not only are there issues about data privacy,[3] moving data to outside firms implies your complete trust in their ability to handle issues of confidentiality and security.[4]

Given this litany of drawbacks, why go offshore? One reason is that with a large inventory of software and the pressures on capital budgets, a large fraction of the information systems work is maintenance—a task which is not a desired career goal for skilled staff, leads to turnover, and can involve highly paid people doing low level work. At the other extreme, it is the ability to obtain new software technologies in which your own staff is not skilled, and there is an opportunity to expand the workforce temporarily while undertaking a major project. Costs can often be reduced. For example,[5] in the insurance industry, in-house programming costs range from $85 to $100 per hour compared to $20 to $60 per hour in India. However, to gain these benefits from offshore outsourcing, sufficient management attention must be paid to the arrangement and to transaction costs (which can be high).[6] Outsourcing is not a magic bullet.

OUTSOURCING CONSIDERATIONS

Outsourcing involves contracting all or part of the work done by internal IT (and other) staff to outside firms. The contract typically is for a number of years or for the duration of a particular project. It specifies in detail what services are to be performed. Note that very few firms outsource all of their information technology work, in part because of the difficulty this would cause if the relation with the outsourcer is terminated and work is brought back into the house and in part for the need to keep staff to monitor the contractor for contract adherence and for quality control.

A Typical Domestic Large Outsourcing Project

When a firm begins outsourcing a major portion of its work to a domestic outsourcer, it typically lays off those in its existing workforce who are doing the work. The contractor, who is called the outsourcer, then hires many of these people. The contractor brings in a small cadre of its own people to manage the operation. If the data center or desktop equipment is outsourced, the outsourcer makes an up-front payment for the equipment. For a company that runs at a low profit or a loss, the result is a onetime infusion of cash that changes its balance sheet.

---

[3] Privacy laws in some European countries are more stringent than those in the United States, while in many developing countries data security and privacy are much laxer.

[4] The tale is told of a lady in Bangladesh who was doing data entry for credit card data who felt underpaid. She put credit card data online and threatened to put more unless she was given a raise.

[5] J. Gallagher, "Outsourcing Necessary for Survival," *Insurance & Technology Online,* November 6, 2002, http://www.insurancetech.com/story/news/IST20021106S0004.

[6] Discussions by the author with CIOs in Southern California indicate that the net savings from outsourcing to India for their firms were around 15%.

| SIDEBAR 1 | *Drucker on Outsourcing* |

Peter Drucker, the management guru, talked about outsourcing in a famous column in the *Wall Street Journal* entitled "Sell the Mail Room." His argument was that firms are in a specific business and should not try to perform functions which are outside their core competence. He used the mailroom as a metaphor. Companies are not in the business of delivering mail and packages to their employees. The function requires a certain amount of managerial time that could better be used elsewhere. Mail room employees receive benefits, such as health care and retirement. The mail room is not a firm's core competency and does not add strategic advantage. So, why not let a contractor specializing in providing this service take on the task?

The Size of the Outsourcing Market

Outsourcing is a huge market, and one that grew quite rapidly. For example, India estimates that its outsourcing market grew by 31% in 2003–2004 and that its top 20 outsourcing firms generated $6 billion in that time.[7]

IDC[8] (formerly International Data Corporation) estimates that U.S. companies spent $16.3 billion in 2003 for offshoring IT services and that this amount would increase to $46 billion by 2007. The estimates for the United Kingdom are approximately $1 billion for 2003. These figures sound large, but need to be put into context. Offshore outsourcing (not just to India) accounted for approximately 2% of the total IT services market in 2003 and is estimated to account for only 5% by 2006. These numbers are small compared to the business process outsourcing market estimated to be worth around $200 billion globally in 2004, according to the Gartner Group. On the other hand, the three largest Indian firms (Infosys, Tata Consultancy Services, and Wipro) all passed the symbolic $1 billion revenue mark in April 2003.

Outsourcing is not unique to IT. Overall, the U.S. market for all outsourcing was estimated by the Gartner Group at $176.8 billion in 2003 and to rise to $235 billion by 2007.[9]

Large U.S. firms are involved in the outsourcing market, such as IBM, EDS, CSC, as are consultancies such as Accenture.[10] Many of these firms are setting up offshore operations of their own to gain wage advantages.

Why Outsource?

Outsourcing can be undertaken for a number of reasons, some good, some so-so, and some bad. The theme that runs through many of these reasons is the firm's desire to save money. Here are a few of them:

1. To obtain competencies not available in-house.
2. To augment the existing staff to handle overloads or undertake projects which are larger than can be handled with available personnel or resources.

---

[7] Source: ZDNet, UK http://news.zdnet.co.uk/business/0,39020645,39160549,00.htm.

[8] Source: Silicon.Com, special report on offshoring, August 4, 2004, http://www.silicon.com/research/ specialreports/ offshoring/0,3800003026,39121230,00.htm.

[9] Source: Gartner Group, March 2004, http://www4.gartner.com/DisplayDocument?doc_cd=119969.

[10] Accenture is not truly a U.S. firm because it moved its headquarters to Bermuda.

3. To reduce the number of people requiring supervision and/or the number of people requiring benefits.

4. To train the existing staff on new technology while an outsourcer handles the existing infrastructure (usually a short-term contract of 1 or 2 years).

5. To gain access to new technology that the firm does not have and either can't afford or doesn't want to invest in.

6. To get rid of a dysfunctional IT staff, one that is poorly managed, costly, or technically inept.

7. To sell IT equipment to raise cash.

8. To match the competition and not be seen as being out of touch.

9. To gain credibility among peer firms (the "everyone does it" argument).

As with any contracting, the reasons for outsourcing should include both strategic and tactical considerations at both the IS department and the company level. Many of the foregoing reasons don't achieve that goal.

The Central Role of the Contract

As outsourcing started to become widespread, academics began studying the phenomenon. Starting with the work of Lacity and Hirschheim,[11] the central role of the contract became clear. Outsourcing is a legal arrangement in which the firm and the outsourcer agree on the terms of what is to be done, by whom, and at what price. Like a marriage, an outsourcing contract is a long-term arrangement, and divorces do occur. Unlike a marriage, the two parties are *not* partners. The profit motive is not shared between them. The firm is in the same position as a buyer on a used car lot. The vendor is typically more skilled at negotiating the contract than is the firm because the vendor negotiates outsourcing contracts continually while the firm does so once every several years. This asymmetric contract relation makes it imperative to hire one of the law firms who specialize in representing companies in outsourcing negotiations.

If a firm is to realize its expectations in an outsourcing deal, it must negotiate both wisely and sharply. Account managers at vendors are rewarded for the profit they create. The vendor would like to be able to contract for minimal services and charge separately for every service not included in the contract. One of the author's students, for example, reported on the situation at a major aerospace firm in Southern California. The outsourcing contract specified that if someone wanted to move a PC even from one desk to the next adjacent one, only the outsourcer could make the move and that a fee of $150 would be paid for each move.

Handshake agreements don't work. Verbal promises are just that; they are not enforceable. Remember that in a major outsourcing agreement, the firm may sell its assets, transfer its leases, and terminate its employees who then often work for the outsourcer. Even in not so extreme cases, the company is no longer in a position where it is capable of doing its own information systems work. On the other side, for example, the vendor's account manager who made the verbal promises is long since gone, selling another contract to another customer. The operational manager, with whom the company deals daily, only has the contract as a basis for action and will be held accountable for every service that, in the view of the vendor organization, is given away. The natural response is to work to rule.

---

[11] M. C. Lacity and R. Hirschheim, *Information Systems Outsourcing: Myths, Metaphors, and Realities,* New York: John Wiley & Sons, 1993. This book is fundamental. Its conclusions still hold. It is essential reading.

Lacity and Hirschheim's bottom line is

"The contract is the only mechanism that establishes a balance of power in the outsourcing relationship."[12]

Service Level Agreements

Most contracts are written in terms of a service level agreement. This agreement is usually based on people in the firm measuring the existing service during some baseline time period and writing that quantity into the contract. Such an agreement specifies how much or how fast a service will be performed. For example,

95% of all PC repairs shall be completed within 8 working hours of the request and the remaining 5% in 3 calendar days. A replacement machine with at least the same capabilities shall be provided for repairs requiring more than 4 hours. Furthermore, all such requests shall be time stamped and documented. The vendor agrees to pay a penalty of ....

Even though it is possible to be precise in these definitions, often the contracts are not tight enough. Vendors will try to gain advantage by manipulating measures in their favor. Even where reporting is required, the reports can be written to obfuscate. A vendor's report that 50 security breaches were investigated during the month tells the customer nothing about how many other breaches were encountered and not followed up, how many were actually resolved, or what the turnaround time was between finding the problem and solving it.

Issues in Contracting

Table 1, based on Lacity and Hirschheim, offers advice on some (not all) of the issues in negotiating the contract.

Managing the Outsourcer Once the Contract Is Signed

The conventional wisdom is not to outsource everything, although some firms do that. No matter the extent of outsourcing, the company needs to retain enough talent in-house to manage the outsourcing contracts and supervise the relations with the outsourcer. It needs to assess whether current capabilities (including those outsourced) meet the firm's IT needs. The people assigned to managing the outsourcing need skills in contract management, charge-back schemes, and the technology.

Outsourcing also involves people issues. You need to maintain close communication with both the user community (the people in your firm that use the computing resource) and the IT professionals. For IT professionals, particularly those to be displaced, outsourcing is a red flag that leads to anxiety about their future and must be dealt with. Remember that many of these IT professionals will become the outsourcer's employees and continue to work on your problems. If they feel badly treated, they can bring your systems down.

Users need to know what to expect and how it will affect them. They will need points of contact before implementation and a process for resolving issues. Everyone needs to feel that his or her problems were considered both during vendor selection and in the implementation.

---

[12] The italics are Lacity and Hirschheim's.

Table 1 ISSUES IN NEGOTIATING AN OUTSOURCING CONTRACT

Advice	Discussion
1. Don't sign the vendor's standard contract.	The vendor wrote it to protect them, not you.
2. Do not sign incomplete contracts.	If it isn't in writing, you will be charged extra for it later.
3. Hire specialists in outsourcing agreements.	This is money well spent. The vendor is more expert than you are, knows most of the tricks and gambits, and faces the same situations all the time. A technical specialist and a contract specialist are needed to protect you.
4. Measure everything during the baseline period.	Include everything that goes on, including time spent giving advice. If something is not included in the services to be performed, it is an extra cost. Include not only data processing, telecommunications, application development, and number of people, but also include some slack for those small items that take time.
5. Agree on service level measures and reports.	These measures and reports are the basis for the work that is done, the management information that is exchanged, and (if worst comes to worst) the resolution of disputes.
6. Provide for problem resolution and include penalties for nonperformance.	These straightforward ideas must be specified in advance.
7. Provide for growth.	A business inevitably grows and so does the amount of computing required. Limiting the services to current levels inevitably benefits the vendor. Given that price/performance ratios for computing improve over time, provisions should be built into the contract so that you, the customer, gain some of the benefits.
8. Include a termination clause.	Basic business sense. Usually some notice time is agreed on. However, be aware that changing from one vendor to another or bringing computing back in house cannot be done in a few months. It is wise to require the vendor to assist in the transition to the next arrangement.
9. Include a penalty clause for unauthorized data release.*	Since the Lacity–Hirschheim book was written, new government regulations restrict personal and other data that can be released publicly (e.g., HIPAA, Sarbanes–Oxley; see Chapter 15). Failure to comply carries heavy penalties. Since outsourcers often access such data in your files, some companies insist that the outsourcers pay heavy penalties if they deliberately or accidentally violate the regulations.

*This item refers to twenty-first century issues.

Like any contracting arrangement, outsourcing entails risks. Among them are

- Losing control of the management of the resource.
- Failing to manage the outsourcers. It is particularly important to maintain strong oversight on the vendor. The company needs to maintain a core of people who supervise the contract and are on top of the changes that inevitably occur as processes, hardware, and software change. If the firm doesn't supervise the contract, the vendors wind up going off on their own, following their own technical and commercial interests. If new needs arise and the capability is not available in-house, the firm is at the mercy of its outsourcer.

- Replacing skilled people by people with less skill. One of the most common problems is a form of bait and switch. When the contract is signed, the vendor assigns its best management team and usually hires most of the people who used to do the job.[13] Over time, however, things change. The vendor gains new contracts or requires help on existing contracts. Good managers are moved to fight the new fires and less competent people come in. The learning curve for the new people repeats the learning curve for the previous people. Furthermore, as the vendor learns about the skills of the people acquired, a form of triage is employed. The poorest people are let go (a good thing and an outcome an existing employer may not be able or willing to do). The middle capability people continue. The best people, however, often become part of the vendor's cadre of high-skilled people used to win the next job and are transferred out. Add to this the natural turnover among good people who are marketable, and the quality of the IS workforce can become less than it was before.

- Losing people with knowledge about the organization. As pointed out in the previous paragraph, the outsourcer may move some of the best people to other clients. The net effect is that the company loses the knowledge of the people who move.

- Changing employers changes people's loyalties. Consider a member of the IS group who finds a way to make an improvement. If they work for the company, the natural response is to use the suggestion box. If they work for the outsourcer, the response is to suggest an additional task to be offered as a contract service.

- Failure of the vendor to achieve the desired benefits. When a company outsources, it has a mental model of what it expects the vendor to accomplish. However, even if the contract terms are performed meticulously, performance can be insufficient to gain the expected benefits. The usual result is finger pointing in both directions.

- Failure of the vendor to provide the operational and strategic services contracted. A contract is an agreement about the future. Even with the best of intentions on both sides, the vendor:
  - may overpromise to win the job,
  - may find they underbid and the funds are insufficient to accomplish the task, and/or
  - may find that the work entailed is beyond their capabilities.

Controls

We already discussed the issue of the contract, but that is only a start. Once an agreement is reached on what is to be done, the firm must monitor what is actually being accomplished. Although most outsourcing contracts contain penalty clauses for nonperformance and underperformance, the point of outsourcing is to get work done, not to collect penalties.

Table 2 lists oversight areas that prudent control requires. Metrics can be established for each of these areas.

---

[13] A classic tale is what happened at Kodak when most of the Kodak IS people changed one day from being Kodak employees to being vendor employees. Among other things, the workplace was deathly still. The phones didn't ring because these employees no longer worked for Kodak and therefore their service was cut off. Similarly, no mail was delivered, again because they changed employers. Although these problems can (and were) fixed quickly, they are representative of the multiplicity of details involved in starting outsourcing. The Kodak case is discussed in more detail at the end of this chapter.

Table 2 OUTSOURCING OVERSIGHT AREAS

Finance and budget. Delivery of agreed on product within financial constraints.	Operational service levels, which includes availability and delivery of work products.
Customer satisfaction. Both satisfaction by your own people and by your clients who depend on the output.	Skills provided by outsourcer, with particular emphasis on monitoring vendor personnel change.
The quality of the product delivered.	The ability to deliver on time.

Source: Based on H. A. Rubin, "Using Metrics for Outsourcing Oversight," *Information Systems Management,* pp. 8–9, Boca Raton, FL: Taylor and Francis Group, LLC, Spring 1997, with permission.

Oversight is a form of quality control. However, by itself, it is not sufficient for a good outsourcing experience. Good management involves your own performance as well. For example, if the requirements are poorly defined, if your firm signs away its rights to gain relief from poor performance, or if the vendor you choose does not have the needed competences to do the job, no amount of oversight will help. Remember that if something is important to your firm, it needs to be documented as a requirement because if it is not documented, it will not be done. If requirements change, particularly if there is scope creep, the relationship with the vendor deteriorates and you wind up in litigation that does neither side any good.

It is important to reiterate that a key indicator of vendor relations is the personnel changes in who is assigned to your company's work by the vendor. The following are two indicators of problems:

- The vendor puts in its A team to get started but then pulls it when the next client comes along.
- The vendor takes the best people who used to work for you and, after a while, reassigns them to other clients. Here there is a major drain of corporate knowledge (Chapter 7). The replacements, even if good, must get up a steep learning curve.

Bottom Line on Outsourcing

IS managers are expected to deliver Cadillac service at Chevrolet prices. Outsourcing is considered one way to do so. Yet outsourcing is a project that depends as much on the ability to manage it correctly as it does on the economies of scale provided by the outsourcer. In many cases, an internal IS department may provide better economies of scale compared to the resources and the people the outsourcer actually deploys.

Rarely, if ever, does it make sense to outsource everything. Selective outsourcing, a tight contract, and effective controls once the contract is signed leads to an IS portfolio that can best be called "rightsourcing."

OUTSOURCING THE INFRASTRUCTURE: WEB HOSTING SERVICE PROVIDERS, WEB SERVICES, AND UTILITY COMPUTING[14]

Infrastructure is the hardware and the software needed to make applications run. As discussed in Chapter 14, on infrastructure, it involves buying and operating high cost equipment and programs. Usually, these high cost items require capital investment, money that is hard to obtain, particularly

---

[14] This section is based on D. T. Dewire, "Application Service Providers," *Information Systems Management* 17(4): pp. 14-19, 2000, and E. Rutherford, "ABCs of ASPs," *CIO,* June 2000.

in times of economic difficulty. Outsourcing firms see a market in providing the infrastructure and running the applications as a service. As we will see, they make their profit from economies of scale.

The Outsourcers

In the early years of the twenty-first century, IT outsourcing evolved in a number of ways:

- Web hosts
- Service providers
- Web services
- Utility computing

These four approaches are basically similar. In each case, the outsourcer does a particular job for many companies. The client reduces the size of its own infrastructure, pays an annual fee, and then pays only for the amount of service used.

Web Hosting

The simplest form is Web hosting[15]. If a firm does not want to run its own website or wants to outsource its e-business technology, it asks the outsourcer to provide a Web server. This Web server "hosts" many domain names and hence many companies. It is, in effect, a virtual host. Each domain name owner is provided with all the features that they would have if they operated a dedicated Web server in their own computer center. Because of the sharing, however, the outsourcer can use a much larger, much faster server and thereby improve the quality of the websites hosted. For the firm, their cost for this virtual server is less than the cost of a dedicated server, yet offering most of the benefits.

Service Providers (xSPs)

The term service provider was originally applied to Internet service providers (ISPs) who provided connection for individuals and firms to the Internet. The term started to expand in the late 1990s to a range of service providers (SPs) including application (ASP), business (BSP), infrastructure management (MSP), storage (SSP), and more. Known collectively as the xSP model, the most established is the ISP. If you think about it, AOL, Earthlink, your cable company's high-speed Internet service, or your phone company's DSL service, all provide a service for a monthly fee. They are a relatively straightforward operation. From a management point of view, the other xSPs are of greater interest because they represent major new forms of outsourcing. This section discusses ASPs, since they were the earliest of the xSPs and are the most studied. The term ASP fell into disfavor and much of what they do is now given the name "utility computing." Utility computing includes the ASP function but is slightly broader. The other forms of xSPs follow the same general principles.

---

[15] This definition of Web hosting is based on http://www.webhostinginspector.com/ industryterms.php?from=1.

ASP Definition

An application service provider is an outsourcer who:

- provides access to a commercial software application,
- runs it on their computer (i.e., hosts it) at their own facility, and
- manages the whole process.

Communication can be over the Internet or a private network.

Rationale

The ASP provides:

- the computer and
- the software.

The ASP runs your firm's problem or process on their computer using the specified software, processing the data that your firm supplies. Inside your firm, to your end users the application appears to be on their corporate local area network or in the data center. However, like voice mail, which is at the phone company's location, the application is at the ASP.

The basic financial arrangement with the ASP is that you rent the computer and the software from the ASP. If you need a particular application (say ERP, e-commerce, data mining, payroll) you do not have to develop or lease or buy the software or hardware associated with it, or install the software. Typically, you pay a monthly fixed fee plus a fee for the amount of the service you use.

The financial advantages of using an ASP include

1. little money required up front,
2. reduced capital investment,
3. faster times from the decision to use the software to it's running your applications,
4. reduced requirements for IT managerial time, and
5. no maintenance cost and no cost to convert from one version of the software to the next. The ASP (usually) runs the latest version of the software.

An important consideration is that the ASP provides the software and hardware but you perform the business process. For example, the outsourcer handles all aspects of claims if you are an insurer who fully outsources claim service (including the decision whether to pay). If you hire an ASP, the outsourcer does only the computing work and you still run your own claims processes.

Table 3 summarizes some of the reasons for going the ASP route.

From the ASP's point of view, the profit comes from economies of scale of using the same software license for many clients, from more cost-effective telecommunications, and from the steady stream of revenue.

For the software vendor, pricing becomes an issue. The ASP reduces the number of copies of the software that are sold and the maintenance fees that are collected from individual firms. How much should the ASP (who effectively aggregates the clients into a single package) be charged? On the other hand, the vendor needs to provide maintenance to fewer copies and to upgrade fewer copies as versions change.

Table 3   REASONS FOR USING AN ASP

To avoid making significant IT investments if the firm is a start-up or strapped for capital
To scale up an application during a growth phase or after a merger or acquisition
To deploy a new application (such as CRM) rapidly
To obtain IT capability rapidly when available personnel skills in an area are scarce
To gain an IT core competency.
To gain access to a high-end application that (if yours is a mid-sized or small firm) you can't afford buying on your own.

Source: Adapted from D. T. DeWire, "Application Service Providers, *Information Systems Management* Exhibit 2, p. 19, Boca Raton, FL: Taylor and Francis Group, LLC, Fall, 2000, with permission.

Categories of ASP's

Major software package vendors (e.g., SAP, Siebel, Oracle) can and do join the ranks of ASPs, renting rather than leasing the use of their software. They want to gain the revenue that otherwise goes to ASPs, who are middlemen. ASPs also include freestanding companies, major consulting firms, and outsourcing vendors who seek economies of scale. The categories of ASP firms are listed in Table 4.

Should You Hire an xSP?

Computerworld, on its Web page,[16] is of the opinion that xSPs deliver quick turnaround and payback for companies such as American Express and Towers Perrin. The premiums for retailers and other cyclical companies with spikes and dips in transaction volumes are not always as compelling. In short, use a fine pencil to find out what the benefits are for your own company.

Web Services

Web services is the next stage after the xSP. Rather than turning over the job of running the entire application to the outsourcer, you turn over only specific modules (parts) to an outside firm. The key is that you ship your request and you receive your results via the Internet.

Table 4   TYPES OF ASPs

Enterprise	Offers high-end applications that may have some customization for such applications as ERP, CRM, or supply chain management. Usually includes availability guarantee.
Business	ASPs that target mid-size and even small firms to provide simple, standard applications.
Specialist	Focus on a particular application.
Vertical	Focus on an industry such as banking.

Source: Adapted from D. T. DeWire, "Application Service Providers," *Information Systems Management,* pp. 16–17, Fall 2000, Boca Raton, FL: Taylor and Francis Group, LLC, with permission.

---

[16] http://www.computerworld.com/managementtopics/xsp/ Consulted 11-22-02.

DEFINITION AND IMPLICATION OF WEB SERVICES

A definition of Web services used by people in computer science is

"Web services are self-contained modular applications that provide a computation upon request."

What this seemingly complicated definition really means is that a Web service is a program that:

1. Sits somewhere out on the Internet or an intranet on a server.

2. Will be run when someone asks for it and gives it the data that it needs.

3. Returns the answer to the person (or computer) that asked for it.

The idea that makes Web services so powerful is that a Web service program can be run by many people at different organizations who are working on different applications.

If you took an introductory programming course in the past, then one way of thinking about a Web service program is that it is a subroutine. But, rather than being part of your own program, it stands alone and is shared among many people. The economic incentive is that you don't need to write or lease the program but merely rent it whenever you need it. In a sense it is like using a cell phone where you pay a fixed monthly fee for access to the network and then are billed for each minute of use.

Many services that a firm uses in its business operations have the characteristic of Web services. For example, if you need to ship an item from your warehouse to Laramie, Wyoming, you can use a number of service providers, including UPS, USPS, FedEx, and DHL. You are interested in the results of the service, not how the provider implements the service. However, you also want to make sure that nobody steals your goods en route.

The implications of this way of computing by using the Internet[17] cannot be underestimated. Potentially, Web services can make software applications universally interoperable. Every software application in the world could interact with every other software application in the world. This interaction is independent of geographical location, system hardware, operating system, and programming languages of the software application.

To illustrate the power of this approach, consider the seemingly simple problem of verifying a customer's shipping address. Any number of application programs can do this. If each of these programs provides this service publicly on request, that service becomes a commodity. As a commodity you can substitute services.

Carrying this idea of commodity services to the extreme, you can develop a complete information system based on the computational services provided by the Web services paradigm of computing. Such a system can be developed at least cost because it only involves selecting a series of other people's commodities and connecting them for your purpose. This method of development impacts the cost of maintaining the information system. You are not responsible for the process that provides the service but the service provider is, and hence is required to maintain the quality of that service and, for competitive reasons, must supply you with the latest version of the service.

---

[17] The same principles apply if you run a Web service in house. That is, lots of people access the same program to solve their own problems. You save replicating the program but you still have the cost of creating and maintaining it.

Given the advantages of Web services, you still need to consider the risks that are involved. They include

1. You are trading off initial expense for operating expense. If you use the service often enough, the savings from not making an initial investment and not paying maintenance on the program will be eaten up by the operating costs. It's like renting a house versus owning it.

2. Security is a major, major issue. If you use Web services, you must have complete trust in its security. Remember that you are shipping your data (such as customer data, prices, employee names, and much more) to third parties. You may not even know who is working on your data because the firms providing the Web services may outsource some of the work to others, both onshore and offshore, and not tell you. You are therefore giving your contractors access to your information assets, which are often the crown jewels of your firm. Web services are an attractive target for malicious hackers, industrial espionage, and fraud. The assurance of security of Web services is necessary for you to be willing to adopt this technology as a means of creating your information systems.

SIDEBAR 2 *How Web Services Works*

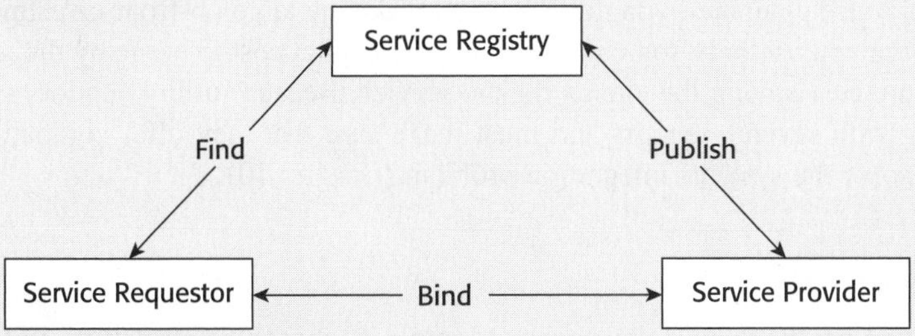

Figure 1 Web services.

The foundation of Web services is the request/response paradigm (Figure 1). This paradigm involves your requesting a specific service to a service provider. The service provider responds with either the service or a notification of why they cannot provide it at that time. An example is something most of us do all the time: using our Web browser to request a Web page from someone else's Web server. To accomplish this action involves three entities and three operations.

The *service requestor* is your application (e.g., the browser) that asks for a service (or a computation) from another application. If your requesting application does not know where this service is located, it sends a request to the *service registry* to find who provides the operation. (Think of asking Google.)

As the service requestor, you provide search criteria for the particular service you want found. The service registry returns information about the requested service and where to find that service. The service registry knows who can meet your request because the *service providers* "publish" the specifications of the services they provide and where (the Internet address) they are provided.

If the service provider's specifications match your requirements, you ship your work to the provider. The technical term used is that you "bind" your work to the provider. Once bound together, the service requestor and service provider can engage in the request/respond paradigm to complete a computation.

Running Computing as a Utility

In the long term, as the technology improves, outsourcing vendors dream of making information systems a utility. That is, much like plugging a lamp into the electricity grid or hooking a sink into the water supply, the local user plugs into an information technology utility that performs the computing functions requested. The analogy is, of course, much too broad. Electricity and water are single, standardized products that are the same for all firms. Computing differs from one firm to another and even within a firm; accounting, finance, marketing, and manufacturing as well as different divisions offering different products, each requires different computations.

Yet the dream continues. Where is it now? The cynics view is that utility computing is a form of xSP, that xSP is a form of ASP, which in turn is a form of time-sharing. What is basic to utility computing is metering. Just as the electricity bill depends on the amount of current used, the computing utility bills only for the services used. However, what is not clear is what is the total cost of computing when all the ancillary costs, such as the use of bandwidth and the use of storage, and the transaction costs are accounted for. Like all outsourcing, utility computing involves such issues as trust (Will they resell my data to someone else? Will they perform according to the contract?), security, and levels of service.

Why Do It?

The trade-off is that, while you are charged more to run a single case using utility computing than the marginal cost of your in-house computer, you don't have to make the large up-front investment in infrastructure for something you use only some of the time. The capital cost is borne by the xSP who spreads the infrastructure cost among the clients for the service. Because utility vendors specialize, you may be dealing with several vendors and must make sure that they offer compatible services. That is, you must solve the systems integration problem (Chapter 10).

Implementing the Utility Approach

Converting to a utility structure can be done in stages. For example,[18] Johnson Controls first shifted telecommunications to a utility basis. Then, in sequence, video conferencing, audio conferencing, multifunctional devices (such as printers and storage), and computing networks and services were outsourced to utilities. The concept is eventually to make computing a just-in-time operation.

To make this arrangement work, a company must plan capacity jointly with its utilities. If the firm requires increased capacity faster than the utility expands to provide it or, conversely, the firm fails to meet its load forecasts so that the utility is stuck with excess capacity, problems ensue. Another issue is globalization. Although the vendor providing the utility is expected to provide the same level of service, coordination, and skill everywhere, the reality of the situation is that performance globally often lags vendor performance in the United States.

Stages of Utility Computing

A Gartner Group's analysis posits that building a utility infrastructure goes through five stages.

1. Concentration
2. Consolidation

---

[18] The example is from Johnson Controls, a $22 billion revenue automotive parts and controls manufacturer. Reported in *Information Week,* August 16, 2004. http://www.informationweek.com/ showArticle.jhtml?articleID=28700229. The *Information Week* article also served as the basis for other parts of this subsection.

3. Virtualization
4. Automation
5. Extension

Firms move from one stage to the next, with each stage firmly established before going on to the next. In early 2005, most companies were in Stage 2 or Stage 3. That is, they were consolidating IT resources and starting to examine virtualization of vendor resources so that it doesn't matter where the computing is done.

Alternative Approaches

Firms do not necessarily move everything to utility services. An alternative approach is to create a base capability in-house and then use the utility to cope with spikes in demand.

Economics of Utilities

Does the utility approach pay off in cutting IT costs? Advocates claim that it does. Eliminating capital costs (money which is hard to obtain) allows a large company to move quickly into new applications. Furthermore, for existing applications, spare (and hence unused) servers and storage capacity to take care of peak loads is no longer needed. For smaller companies, utility computing means they no longer need to buy and manage IT systems, especially if their IT staff is small.

Risks of ASPs and Utilities

Hiring an ASP or buying into the utility concept assumes that the vendor

- will survive (not true for many start-ups; there have been spectacular failures),
- will provide the agreed on service levels, and
- most important, will maintain data security.

Since calculations are performed at the ASP's or utility's site, a firm must send data about its customers and its transactions over the Internet and be assured that the information will not be compromised.

Another risk arises because, in the usual arrangement, the vendor runs only one version of the software (usually the latest one). Thus, you must be willing to upgrade your processes to match the software whenever the software vendor and the utility upgrades, whether you want to or not. This decision becomes important when software changes require changes that you are not willing to institute in your business processes because the changes are not compatible with your customer base, the change management costs, and/or training requirements that you incur.

Fears of security breaches on the Internet and in the ASP's shop as well as doubts about vendor reliability and survival are major reasons given by companies for not using an ASP or a utility. The survival fear was increased when a major chip maker, Intel, shut down an ASP it owned (Pandesic) because it was not sufficiently profitable. A number of Pandesic's customers did not have backup computing capability because they gave up their internal computing capability. At the other extreme, if you miss a payment, for whatever reason, the outsourcer can cut you off from the service.

Like rent on your firm's building or an apartment, once you are locked into a vendor, your costs depend on the vendor's pricing changes. As Michael Schrage points out,[19] the history of utilities is not sanguine. Utilities, irrespective of field, combine and form monopolies. The result is regulation. The regulators invariably fall captive of the utilities they are supposed to oversee. Utilities favor cost recovery rather than value creation. For public policy reasons, utilities wind up with cross-subsidies; classic examples are energy companies and telephone utilities whose cross-subsidies prior to deregulation were far more sophisticated than their technologies. In short, accountants impacted a utility more than any engineer.

A few sensible precautions help in overcoming the risks:

- Review the vendor's financial statement and make contingency plans in case they fail.
- Ensure that your data don't end up in bankruptcy court if the vendor does fail.
- Obtain rights to the vendor's source code for the applications being used so that you can continue either at your own facilities or at another vendor.

As with all outsourcing, the contract is important. It should specify service levels (including uptime percentages) and other performance metrics, contain an escape clause that allows termination if service is poor, penalty clauses for failure to perform sufficient to motivate the vendor, and be set up to run for as short a term as possible, preferably less than 3 years.

The contract should also agree on a firm price as usage grows and should offer rebates if the vendor's hardware or software costs go down. That is, the vendor should pass some of their economies to you.

In summary, to make the pay-as-you-go utility computing concept work, vendors need to provide a reliable service at a good price. In addition to the cautions given in this subsection, all the principles of outsourcing, including the risks discussed at the beginning of this chapter, apply.

CASE STUDY: The Kodak Outsourcing Deal[20]

> "What IBM did for PC's, Kodak did for outsourcing. It authenticated the marketplace." Peter Bendor-Samuel[21]

Historically, computing was difficult and the tradition was to perform both application development and computing in-house. By the mid-1960s, a number of firms went into the business of creating software applications packages that saved firms the time and the risks associated with creating the applications in-house. They would also take standard computing operations and outsource them. For example, ADP (formerly Automated Data Processing) is a firm that has been in business over 50 years, starting in the punch card era. However, the outsourcing movement (for it is a movement) did not really take off until 1989 when Kodak, the photography company, in Rochester, New York, decided to outsource almost all its computer operations to three companies, the largest of which was IBM. Here is what happened. This deal was not the first. Earlier in 1989, for example, Enron (yes, the Enron of creative accounting) outsourced for $750 million dollars. However, that firm was then unknown whereas Kodak was an American icon.

---

[19] M. Schrage, "The Voodoo Economics Behind Utility Computing" *CIO,* May 15, 2001, http://www.cio.com/archive/051503/work.html.

[20] Based on a case study by CSC research: http://www.cscresearchservices.com/foundation/ library/105/RP08.asp. Technically, Kodak is Eastman Kodak Co. but refers to itself on the Web as www.kodak.com.

[21] As quoted in Tom Field, "10 Years that Shook IT," *CIO,* October 1, 1999.

Kodak's long-standing strategy was to focus on its core competencies, which are in producing film and cameras. Their policy was encapsulated in the idea of doing what they do best and divest everything else. In 1989, as the United States headed toward recession, Kodak found itself in an earnings decline as international competition heated up. A new vice president for information systems, Katherine Hudson, was recently appointed. She came to the job with a general management background and no experience in information technology. It was she who made the decision to outsource Kodak's data center operations, telecommunications services, and personal computer support. She chose three different vendors, two of whom [IBM and Digital Equipment Corporation (DEC)] had little or no previous experience managing outsourced IT services and the third a retail chain (BusinessLand) that would go bankrupt 18 months later.

Kodak in effect traded the costs of direct control and operation of activities associated with running their corporate data centers, networks, and PC support for the costs of coordinating those same activities.

The drivers for outsourcing were

a. An elite group of people in IS that was having problems managing its legacy systems and its infrastructure. The infrastructure was partially centralized and partially decentralized among business units. The IS culture also needed changing.

b. The need for new investment to build a new data center to consolidate five dispersed centers. It was argued that the large capital cost could better be used for other purposes.

c. A desire to cut IS costs and software investments while reengineering processes, improving services, and keeping pace with new technologies.

To meet these goals, Kodak entered into the following contracts:

a. A 10 year deal with IBM to consolidate its five data centers into one and run Kodak's mainframe network. This deal was the largest of the three.

b. A 5 year deal with DEC to run Kodak's voice networks and some of its data networks.

c. A 5 year deal with BusinessLand to run PC systems support.

About 700 employees in outsourced functions transferred to the vendors. Kodak did not outsource the work of its 500-plus people who worked on applications development. Kodak acted as its own prime contractor, and set up service and process metrics so that problems could be spotted early.

The relation with IBM proved to be a success. Services improved, costs went down, and Kodak no longer needed to manage its data centers. DEC and Businessland were a different story. Whereas both Kodak and IBM were both hierarchic and conservative, DEC was horizontal and entrepreneurial. The inevitable result was a culture clash. DEC also moved the people who had won the Kodak account elsewhere. Businessland was a disaster. Kodak replaced both DEC and the successor to Businessland when the contracts ended.

CASE STUDY: Pilot Network Services, a Cautionary Tale[22]

Outsourcing network security is at once a no-brainer and a high-risk operation. Most firms find that maintaining security on their networks is difficult, requiring people with expertise that is expensive and who turn over rapidly. As part of the dot.com growth of the 1990s, venture capital flowed to boutiques that specialized in the field. One was Pilot Network Services of Alameda, California. Pilot provided Internet access to corporations through high-speed lines. They scanned for computer viruses, managed the firewall, and ran their own intrusion-detection service to detect possible hacker attacks. They were in business for 6 years, with 200 clients and 200 employees in six data centers. In April 2001, they abruptly closed their doors, leaving clients such as the *Los Angeles Times*, RAND Corporation, The Gap, and PeopleSoft stranded. With no one watching their networks, Pilot customers were suddenly open to hackers and viruses. Worse, companies that routed office-to-office traffic through Pilot were at risk of losing secure virtual private network connections and remote access. Where Pilot had hosted entire Web networks for other companies, they became more vulnerable to a complete security loss.

---

[22] The Pilot debacle is reported in *Infoworld* (www.infoworld.com/articles/hn/xml/01/ 04/27/010427hnpilot.xml?0429mnne) and in *CIO* (http://www.cio.com/archive/ 080101/exposed.html).

Pilot Network Services is an extreme case of outsourcer failure. In the case of security services, companies that wanted to outsource were faced with the problem of selecting either a boutique with the specific skills they needed or a larger firm that was more generic and less skilled in the area. The boutiques paid their employees better and attracted the best talent. Those that chose Pilot Network Services opted for skill over financial security.

The victims of the Pilot bankruptcy used three different approaches to recover.

a. Bring the function in-house. This approach is expensive but, as one firm said, allowed them to sleep better at night.

b. Hire a general services firm and receive a lower level of service.

c. Find another boutique. This solution was simple, requiring only writing a monthly check, but highly risky. The combined capacity of all the boutiques turned out to be much larger than the size of the market. As a result, others also disappeared.

ANSWERS TO MANAGERIAL QUESTIONS

What is outsourcing?

Outsourcing involves contracting some (or all) information systems tasks by one firm to another. Outsourcing can involve hardware, software, and operations. Typical contract terms range from 3 to 5 years and even to 10 years.

What are its risks?

Outsourcing, like any information systems project, can fail. So can the outsourcer. These are the extreme risks. At a more mundane, but extremely important level, is the outsourcing contract. The risk is that the vendor (who writes contracts continually) will insert terms that are favorable to them and are detrimental to the firm that hires them in terms of level of service and/or cost. Another major risk is that the outsourcer shuffles personnel so that good people are sent elsewhere and inferior people replace them. If the contract is terminated or reaches the end of its life, the firm can bring the outsourced activity back in-house only at great expense. In effect, the outsourcer locks the firm in.

What are its rewards?

Outsourcing allows a firm to concentrate on its core competencies. It reduces the number of people on the payroll and the attendant personnel supervision and benefits required. Doing a job in-house poorly can be replaced by an outsourcer who does the job well. A dysfunctional IS group can be replaced by a corps of competent people. An outsourcer can provide new technologies, new software, and new processes that were not available previously and, because of their experience and capabilities, can do so much more quickly since they do not have to start at the bottom of the learning curve. For a firm in financial trouble, the onetime cash infusion from disposing of hardware can be significant.

If I outsource, what form of outsourcing should I use?

There is no single answer. It depends on your internal capabilities and even the corporate culture. In general, outsource those tasks at which you are not very good or which absorb resources that could better be used elsewhere. Make sure you keep enough capability in-house that the work can be pulled back if the outsourcer fails to perform. Except in rare cases, outsourcing the entire IS function should be avoided. Recognize that you will move from providing operational services to managing the outsourcer. Such management requires different skills than doing the job.

What are xSPs and should I hire them?

xSPs are service providers who perform specific functions. The most widely known of these is the ASP (application service provider) who runs applications for clients whenever they send data to be processed. Others provide business, infrastructure, data, and other services. Outsourcing to xSPs carries risks including security and failure of the xSP. An xSP can be an appropriate solution to specific problems (e.g., Table 1) but is not appropriate in all situations.

What is the information utility concept about?

The information utility concept is a long-term view of information systems in which computing is a centrally provided utility (like electric power) that does everything. In 2005 it was mostly in the concept stage.

PROBLEMS

1. OFFSHORE OUTSOURCING

   Using trade journals, newspapers, and other current sources, obtain estimates (preferably multiple) of:
   a. The number of information system jobs outsourced offshore by country and by specialty (e.g., programmers, project managers, call center operators).
   b. The number of jobs outsourced by category (or total) to all overseas outsourcers compared to the number of people employed in those jobs in the United States.
   c. The dollar value of the jobs outsourced.

2. COMPUTER SCIENCE/INFORMATION SYSTEMS STUDENTS

   a. Determine the number of overseas students and the number of U.S. students majoring in computer science and in information systems in U.S. universities. Examine undergraduate and graduate students separately.
   b. Plot the data over a 5 year or longer period.

3. WEB SERVICES

   Find case studies and/or Web pages of firms that provide Web hosting services. Describe what services they provide, their customer base, and other relevant information about the Web hosting business.

4. GRID COMPUTING

   Analyze grid computing in terms of outsourcing.

Chapter **10**

Working Together: Systems Integration, Interorganizational Systems, Alliances, and Globalization

MANAGERIAL QUESTIONS

What is systems integration and why is it important?

Don't ERP systems solve the integration problem?

What is involved in systems integration?

What are interorganizational systems?

What are their risks and rewards?

How do alliances work?

What are the criteria for entering or avoiding an alliance?

How can information technology help me in globalizing my business?

INTRODUCTION

Over time, computer systems become more interdependent both within the firm and with other firms. Internally, interdependence involves making seemingly disparate systems able to communicate with one another and work together so that, to the users, the boundaries between systems are seamless. The task of bringing everything together is known as *systems integration*.

We saw some of the interdependence between companies in the previous chapter on outsourcing, where we considered firms that contract part (or all) of their information technology to other firms that specialize in a given area. In this chapter we will look at other dimensions of interdependence among companies. Specifically we will look at three topics:

- Systems that involve more than one organization.
- Alliances between companies that require joint use of information technology.
- Globalization of company operations that lead to worldwide technology systems.

SYSTEMS INTEGRATION[1]

"It is the major opportunity and challenge for information technology."

Peter G. W. Keen[2]

Historically, companies built their own software to support their own business processes. Many of these processes, such as accounts receivable, payroll, billing, and inventory, were really quite standard for almost all business or businesses in a particular industry. There were, of course, small variations from one firm to another to take into account differences in hardware, software, and operating systems, in organizational structure, and in local or industry custom. Over time, vendors saw these standard processes as opportunities and began writing and selling software packages that could perform standard functions.

Unfortunately, most packages could not communicate with other packages, particularly those from other vendors. A Tower of Babel resulted, in part from firms encouraging decentralized business decision making. If the organization is decentralized, each unit makes its own technology decisions. For example, banks can wind up with different systems for checking, mortgages, trust departments, and lending. Such systems make it difficult to know the full extent of a customer's interaction with the bank. Similar problems need to be overcome in knowing about customers for CRM (Chapter 6), for satisfying orders and returns between a warehouse and the production floor, and in hundreds of other business processes.

Furthermore, firms adopting packages were faced with the problem of either:

- changing their business processes to conform to the packages, or
- keeping their business processes and customizing the packages (i.e., modifying the software).

Neither of these approaches is ideal because both involve considerable expenditure. Changing a business process to fit a software package can be expensive because it involves modifying what people do, including retraining costs, overcoming resistance to change, and often changing the interactions with customers. In the case of customization, since vendors upgrade the capabilities of their packages every year or two, the expense can be never ending. Not only must the package be customized when it is bought, each succeeding version must be customized. Vendors long ago learned that real money is to be made in customization.

The alternative to software customization and/or process changes is to provide systems integration. ERP systems, discussed in Chapter 4, are one attempt to do so. However, although ERP encompasses an increasing number of processes each year, some processes are not included. Hence, even with an ERP installation, firms must undertake systems integration if they are to make the whole enterprise seamless.

Definition

Systems integration involves connecting the separate components of computers, software, storage, and telecommunications so that they work together and share resources.

This definition implies that systems integration creates a coordinated organizationwide system that connects people and organizational units through hardware and software.

---

[1] This section is based in part on the chapter "Enterprise Application Integration" in *Making IT Happen: Critical Issues in IT Management,* by J. D. McKeen and H. A. Smith, Chichester, UK: Wiley, 2003.

[2] Peter G. W. Keen, *Every Manager's Guide to Information Technology.* Boston: Harvard Business School Press, 1995.

SIDEBAR 1   *History of Systems Integration*

Systems integration goes all the bay back to the 1950s and involved noncomputer as well as computer-based systems. The military required its various operational systems to work together but contracted for them individually. At the time it was called systems engineering.[3] Early practitioners were aerospace companies and not-for-profit research institutes. Over time, several large contractors, such as IBM and EDS, began specializing in the area. IBM, for example, created a Federal Systems Division. When military budgets started to contract in the 1980s and with it the military systems integration business, these specialty firms decided they should consult to business as well as to the government.

Objective

The objective of systems integration is to achieve seamless systems that deliver services to customers. Thus, to make manufacturing processes work together, manage supply chains, and create continuous work flows, information flows have to be integrated.

The Concept

From a business perspective, the idea is to make sharing information practical across various business processes even though the processes involve different hardware, software, and communication systems. It involves integrating information, processes, and people.

From a technical point of view, making different components of information technology work together requires

- compatibility among components,
- interoperability,[4] and
- standards.

Integrating the Enterprise

Integrated information systems play a cohesive role in creating a single set of business processes and functional applications to meet business needs. Creating such systems also requires consideration of external relations with suppliers, outsourcers, and customers.

To create integrated enterprises requires understanding:

- The configuration of business processes that are necessary to run the organization and their relationships with legacy systems and other functional applications.
- How IS can enable new organizational forms.
- The concept and major components of a typical enterprisewide conceptual database.
- The role of collaborative systems in developing more flexible, fast response organizations.

---

[3] The original book was H. H. Goode and R. E. Machol, *Systems Engineering,* New York: McGraw-Hill, 1957.

[4] Interoperability refers to the ability of software packages to work with one another, whether one vendor or multiple vendors produce them.

SIDEBAR 2   *Systems Integration Versus Systems Improvement*

Systems integration involves much more than simply improving existing systems.

In systems improvement:

- Systems are improved and redeployed without changing the organization.
- IT functions are leveraged to squeeze out additional technical functionality.
- Duplication may limit ultimate functionality.
- Little internal resistance to change occurs.

In systems integration:

- IT is leveraged for improving total organizational capability.
- Focus is on interdependence of organizational units.
- New systems are interconnected with legacy systems.
- Focus is on improving present rather than future functionality.
- High resistance to change usually occurs and must be dealt with.

Specific subjects include

- organizational needs for integration and flexibility,
- the role and content of an enterprise data model,
- generic business processes,
- business process reengineering,
- the integration of business, ERP functions/applications,
- collaborative systems and knowledge management.

That's quite a lot to know and understand. Most firms, particularly small- and medium-sized firms, do not have all that knowledge in-house. As a result, systems integration usually requires some assistance from outside consultants (see below).

Integrating the Technology

Once the decisions are made on what needs to be integrated in the enterprise, the task is to create the hardware and software technology environment that will accomplish the goals set. Tasks involve making intelligent choices about hardware platforms, integrated packages such as ERP, using middleware to connect disparate legacy systems, and Web-based approaches.

Integration of Data, Application, and Processes

Data. One of the initial problems in integration was that each application was designed with its own data structure (e.g., purchasing uses different product codes than does inventory). Then, in the 1990s, data warehousing (Chapter 5) ETL tools made it possible to move data between two or more databases and to integrate multiple databases into a single unified view. Today, data integration products can route and distribute data dynamically based on a set of preconfigured rules. At the data level, integration can now be done fairly routinely and elegantly.

Applications. Diverse applications need to be linked to accomplish specific business processes (e.g., selling a new automobile insurance policy involves credit checking, traffic records, billing,

SIDEBAR 3   *Middleware and Standards*

Why do we get so many disconnected applications that can't communicate with one another? It may seem like a failure in the marketplace, and in some ways it is. Organizations added one application at a time. Most were simple and stand-alone such as payroll. But as business sophistication grew and people started seeing more and more ways the computer could be used, new applications were devised. Because they were put into service one at a time, each application program became a legacy. Computer systems, in this regard, are like automobiles. Just as a car is classified as "used" the moment it is driven off the lot, a computer system is a legacy as soon as it is installed.

The following is a list of some of the applications areas:

Administration	Logistics and supply chains
Customer accounting	Manufacturing
Customer call centers	Marketing
Customer service	Materials management
Finance	Sales

Note that each area involves many programs and that even within a single area, the programs may not be compatible.

Although each program may be a technological marvel by itself, it can also create problems when its outputs serve as the inputs to other programs. The simple approach of copying the outputs manually from one program to another makes no sense. Not only is manual copying unreliable, it is costly and should, of course, be automated. Unfortunately, the output format of one program is usually incompatible with the input format of another. Even worse, if a program serves as input to several programs, each of them may (and most likely will) require different inputs.

The usual approach is to create "middleware". Middleware refers to programs that allow direct interactions among independently designed applications in a distributed computing environment. To make middleware work, "adapters" are used to connect application programs, databases, and middleware with one another.

Standards in programming techniques, computer languages, hardware, and software help in making integration easier and in reducing costs. Middleware itself imposes development standards to which applications must adhere if integration is to be realized.

The basic objective is to move from the massive communications needed for applications to talk to one another, shown in Figure 1, to the simpler arrangement shown in Figure 2.

Data warehouses (Chapter 5) are sometimes used in systems integration because they offer the hub for multiple data sources.

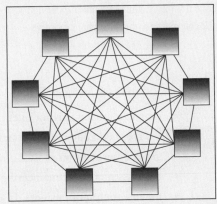

Figure 1 Communications among applications without integration.

Source: J. D. McKeen and H. A. Smith, "Enterprise Application Integration," *Communications of AIS* 8(31): Figure 2, p. 9, June 2002. Used by permission.

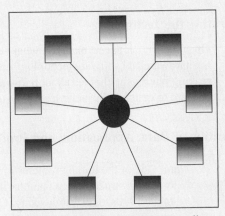

Figure 2 Communications among applications after integration.

Source: J. D. McKeen and H. A. Smith, "Enterprise Application Integration," *Communications of AIS* 8(31): Figure 3, p. 10, June 2003. Used by permission.

and more). Infrastructure software and application adapters now facilitate application-to-application (A2A) integration. Application-specific adapters are software that enable users to work with multiple applications based on different technologies. Intervendor connections (e.g., linking a SAP R/3 application to an Oracle application) are relatively straightforward with available adapters. Adapters facilitate integration by creating application independence and transparency. Another integration tool—called "screen scrapers"—allows sharing input data from an application with others; that is, they connect many custom or packaged applications.

Process. The next level of integration is to coordinate the flow of logic among the integrated applications. Process integration is referred to as "event-oriented" or "transaction-oriented" where transactions/events provide the linkage among various applications. This approach enables organizations to create common methods (e.g., transactions) and share those methods among many connected applications.

Recognizing a universal need, software vendors developed a set of workflow technology products to address process-level integration specifically. Application servers access the business logic exposed by adapters to be tied together into a cohesive, end-to-end transaction flow. They are focused on application development and are particularly good at supporting integration through the use of portals.[5]

SIDEBAR 4 *Data Integration, Enterprise Application Integration, and Enterprise Information Integration*

In industry, the following three integration terms emerged.

Data integration is the extraction, transformation, and loading (ETL) of data from multiple systems into a single data store to allow manipulation and evaluation (reporting). Data warehouses and data marts (Chapter 4) are typical data stores, and ETL[6] tools are the "data integration" components.

Enterprise application integration (EAI)[7] describes combining business processes, standards, software, and hardware to integrate two or more enterprise systems seamlessly so that they can operate as a single application. EAI can take place within a firm or between firms so they can work together, thereby allowing a single transaction to occur across multiple systems.

Enterprise information integration (EII)[8] describes integrating data from multiple systems into a unified, consistent, and accurate whole. EII is concerned with viewing and manipulating the data.

EAI is what is described principally in this section on systems integration. It came about as firms needed to make existing applications work with ERP systems (Chapter 4). The marketplace growth of EAI also helped with the increasing number of packaged applications, the growth of supply chain applications (Chapter 11), and Web applications.

In EII, data is aggregated, restructured, and relabeled (if necessary), and presented to the user. EII differs from ordinary data integration and from EAI as shown in Table 1.

In data integration, the view is that of the warehouse. Historical data is used for trend analyses presented to management decision makers. In application integration, current data is used to synchronize applications that are being run by the IT organization. In EII, the objective is to supply real-time data to improve end-user productivity.

(continued)

---

[5] For a discussion of portals, see Chapter 8.

[6] ETL is an acronym for data extraction, transformation, and loading.

[7] http://eai.ittoolbox.com/.

[8] The Integration Consortium, "Thoughts from the Integration Consortium: Enterprise Information Integration: A New Definition," *DM Review,* September 4, 2004.

SIDEBAR 4	*Data Integration, Enterprise Application Integration, and Enterprise Information Integration (continued)*

Table 1   COMPARISON OF DATA INTEGRATION, EAI, AND EII

	Data	Purpose	Audience
Data integration	Historical	Trend analysis	Decision makers
Application integration	Live data	Synchronization	IT organization
Information integration	Live	Productivity	End users

Source: J.T. Taylor, "Thoughts from the Integration Consortium: Enterprise Information Integration: A New Definition," *DM Review*, September 4, 2004. Reprinted with permission from Source Media/DM Review.

Aspects of Systems Integration

Islands of Automation

You can think of an island of automation as a particular function that is computerized but which either doesn't communicate with the inputs or outputs of other computerized functions, or one that requires manual operations at its inputs or outputs. Thus, for example, the situation where computer printouts must be hand entered into the next system is still true in many places. Such islands result in the fragmentation of applications and hinder the organizational units responsible for the application.

Although many islands of automation do meet the needs of specific operations, they do not really satisfy the company's needs. By integrating existing automation islands, past investments are preserved and new technologies and capabilities are accommodated. Although a number of techniques are available for connecting (i.e., integrating) the islands of automation, be aware that in practice, systems integration is not a simple task.

Enterprise Computing

Systems integration involves coordinating the organization's applications into an enterprisewide distributed network system. That is, enterprise systems are basically distributed information networks.

Vendors, of course, claim that their products integrate easily. In reality, a number of difficulties are encountered

- Different hardware and software often require bridges[9] and gateways (i.e., middleware) to connect with one another.
- Simply adding computers and operating systems doesn't get you integration. Cooperation, interoperability of applications, and information sharing are also needed.
- Integration makes network management and computer systems management more complex.
- It is difficult to handle multimedia across different systems because the available bandwidth is limited.

---

[9] If you've ever created a home network that connected the PCs in your house through, say, Windows XP, you will recall that the software created a bridge for you.

Lessons Learned from Experience[10]

Systems integration involves technical, organizational, and budgetary constraints. All three must be managed.

When starting the systems integration process, take small steps. Work with proven standards and technologies.

Do any needed reengineering first before undertaking systems integration. Don't try to get ahead of the reengineering process, because you will only have to redo the integration steps.

Avoid shortcuts and speedups to make deadlines. Problems magnify if you do. Systems integration can't be rushed.

As soon as a particular stage of an integration project is completed, software tools needed to execute it better and easier will become available on the market at an affordable price.

The Systems Integration Industry

For all but the largest IT organizations, the skills required are usually not available within the company. Systems integration is hard to do. Therefore, most systems integration is often done with the aid of consultants.

Systems integration contractors are referred to as "systemshouses." They include three types of firms.

- Stand-alone firms whose prime business is systems integration, such as EDS and Computer Sciences Corporation.
- Fortune 1000 firms such as IBM, Lockheed, and even some of the telephone operating companies.
- Consulting firms such as Accenture, Capgemini, and McKinsey & Company.

These firms blend the needed business, technical, and project management experience. They also deal with cultural and political barriers and with resistance to change. At least in theory, they are neutral and objective rather than having a specific agenda. They sell a service orientation, cost-effectiveness, and technical responsibility. Sidebar 5 lists the integrators' skills in more detail.

SIDEBAR 5 *Systems Integrator Skills*

- A coordinated set of methodologies, tools, techniques, and design approaches.
- Proficiency in functional system design, requirements definition.
- Ability to implement based on functional requirements.

- System engineering of components including middleware.
- Design, programming, quality assurance, operation of software.
- System assembly, installation, and test.
- Maintenance support for the integrated system.

---

[10] Lessons are based on "Information Strategies," *Computerworld,* 1993.

Having listed these capabilities, it is useful to look at the operational reality of systemshouses. The first thing to realize is that winning multiyear services and controlling accounts is their measure of success. They have to work at keeping customers because switching by their clients is relatively easy. They bill hardware and software at fixed prices but most charge for professional services on a time and materials basis. Only a few contracts are fixed price. If the integrator is part of a hardware or software company (such as IBM or HP), they try to lock in their own products.

Given these realities and the cost and time of educating the contractor, some firms undertake integration in-house or form a partnership with a systemshouse. In part, the go-it-alone option is followed if the chief information officer (CIO) is reluctant to give up control to a third party. CIOs (often with good reason) have little faith that the contractor will keep their objectives foremost. In the case of a partnership, the contract also needs to specify the terms of divorce if that should prove necessary. Integrating internally requires strong teams. If outside consultants are hired, the senior people in your firm must be able to lead them as well as the internal staff.

Finally, remember that hiring consultants is a form of outsourcing. As we discussed in Chapter 9, the contract you and the outsourcer sign is fundamental to success. However, even a good contract does not ensure success.

Management Strategy for Integration

The following near-term strategies for integration[11] are designed to help start integration, with results to be obtained within months rather than years. To be considered "near-term," the strategies can all be started immediately with the expectation of yielding results within months.

1. *Craft a Corporate Integration Strategy*. Integration does not/will not happen by itself. It requires a champion, typically (but not always) in the IT group who must gain the support of senior management in both IT and the firm as a whole. Once a decision to integrate is reached, an integration strategy must be crafted. This strategy should focus initially on applications that are strategic. It must make a business case for integration, including examining costs and benefits, and the business case must be sold to senior management who must buy in.

2. *Assemble a Tool Kit*. An integration tool kit is a set of programs that makes integration possible. No single vendor provides a complete package. Therefore, managers are put in the "general contractor" mode or must hire a consultant with experience to run the project. Among the features sought are

- The ability to integrate with internal systems and, in the case of interorganizational systems (see next subsection), with customer or supplier systems.
- The ability to make changes when (as often happens) business processes change.
- The ability to provide security, particularly important when integrating with other firms (see Chapter 15).
- Ease of use to reduce resistance to change.
- The ability to know when the integrated system is in trouble, since many applications can be affected by a single glitch.

---

[11] Based on J. D. McKeen and H. A. Smith, 2003, op. cit.

3. ***Deploy "Hub-and-Spoke" Design***. The hub-and-spoke design (which was shown in Figure 2):

- Doesn't connect anything directly to anything else.

- Leaves design applications separate and doesn't allow them to share databases directly.

- All knowledge of interconnections is removed from the source (and target) and placed within the hub.

Adopting hub-and-spoke architecture greatly reduces the complexity of integration by organizing all the communication, transformation, and process work flow within the hub where it can be managed. Individual applications can be replaced relatively easily since much of their logic, communication, and translation functions were removed.

4. ***Create an Integration Core Competency Team***. Because many of the functions normally contained within applications are now physically removed to the hub, application developers must change their mindset from that of "developer" to that of "integrator." An integration core competency team helps to create and maintain the hub. Application development teams use "hub" people for all interfaces. The hub people are also responsible for creating cross-platform projects. In essence, the hub people are the managers for these projects.

People with hub skills are still scarce, in part because they need process skills as well as programming skills and because IT organizations in the past did not commit significant staff to these roles. As the deployment of integrated systems spreads, this shortage is likely to disappear.

5. ***Reintegrate Legacy Applications***. When systems integration is undertaken, changes will inevitably need to be made in the legacy systems that remain: The user interface, the business rules followed, and the communications with other applications change. At the simplest level, the user interface is changed. However, more complex changes, ranging up to replacing the legacy system completely, may be required. Of course, the larger the change, the greater the cost and the time required accomplishing it.

6. ***Next Steps: the "Collaborative Enterprise."*** As is discussed in the next subsection, once integration is in place, it is possible for firms to link their systems directly with suppliers and trading partners. Such a collaborative enterprise is the next step. It requires the integration of application systems across firms, thus elevating the integration challenge to a new level. Even within organizations, where the firm controls all the technology, integration is a daunting task.

INTERORGANIZATIONAL SYSTEMS

Interorganizational information systems, as their name implies, span organizational boundaries. They are applications that take many forms. Here are some of them:

- Two firms use a common computer application which resides on either one or both firm's computers. For example, a firm and its contractors work on a joint project or in a supply chain relationship.

- Two or more divisions or departments of a company work together sharing computing operations and/or data sets.

- EDI, e-mail, and extranets connect multiple firms that work together.

We use the term EDI (electronic data interchange) in this discussion to refer to either the classic form using standards such as X.25 or EDIFACT (discussed in Chapter 3) or the use of the Internet to accomplish the goal of data transfer between buyers and sellers.

Readiness

When undertaking an interorganizational effort with another firm, it is important to consider both your own firm and your partner's. Are both of you experienced enough with handling transactions electronically that you can undertake the project? Very often, particularly for small firms, one or both of you are not.

To check whether you can both participate, run a pilot project. Make sure that your networking systems are compatible or, if not, you both have the right middleware (see the section on Systems Integration, p. 183) to be able to understand one another. You don't want to find out that your trading partner's system is incompatible with yours while your CEO or senior manager wants to know how soon the pilot will be completed and you can start full operations.

Control

Because interorganizational systems cross organizational lines, each partner loses some control. In particular,

- One partner can impose increased costs on the other because extra computing hardware, software, and people are required.
- Neither partner may be able to achieve all the benefits.

To understand the control issues, it is useful to think about two roles:

- Initiators
- Followers

Initiators are firms that want others to deal with them electronically. For example, they may be suppliers (e.g., American Hospital Supply, now part of Baxter International discussed in Sidebar 6) who offer an online service that allows their many regular customers to order from them, or they may be buyers (e.g., General Motors and other auto manufacturers) who insist that their much smaller parts suppliers communicate with them only through EDI. In both cases (pharmacies, auto parts suppliers) the smaller firms often have little choice but to participate.

When the customer mandates that a supplier use a particular EDI system if they want to continue on the preferred list, the supplier can't say no without losing the account. For suppliers in the auto industry, for example, who worked with several manufacturers, it meant running separate EDI systems for each customer, a costly but necessary expense to keep their customers.

By linking information systems with trading partners, an organization can check a supplier's inventory directly, check the status of in-process orders, preview pricing structures, choose delivery options, and interface ordering systems directly with a supplier's fulfillment systems. Because these systems connect organizations, they create value by enabling instant movement of data, products, and services, thus eliminating the "float" between an action (e.g., the placement of an order) and its realization (e.g., the processing of that order).

| SIDEBAR 6 | *American Hospital Supply and McKesson* |

Control also implies trying to lock in your partners and keep competitors out. For example, American Hospital Supply (AHS) wanted to reduce its field sales force and to speed up its ordering process. To accomplish these goals, they placed terminals (at AHS's expense) at their customers' locations and linked them directly to their own in-house ordering system. Having made the purchasing manager's work simpler, they then provided a free inventory management software package. The idea was that once AHS knew their customers inventory position for each of their products, they could trigger replenishments automatically as soon as they were needed. No need for the purchasing agent to remember to reorder. Once purchasing agents trusted this inventory management software, they started ordering more and more items from AHS, reducing

(and in some cases eliminating) AHS's competitors. Competitors found it hard to gain market share because hospital purchasing agents did not want to accept a second terminal that would clutter up their desktop and learn how to use another set of software for order-entry and managing inventory.

McKesson, with their Economost, a system designed for local drugstores, used the same strategy. McKesson, like AHS, provided inventory software that tied the druggist to ordering from them. McKesson happened to use the Apple as its platform because their system designer preferred that computer. Its competitors were tied in to Microsoft operating systems. Companies that wanted druggists to change from McKesson to them as the prime provider essentially had to give away a free computer with their software.

Such collaboration between enterprises involves significant technological challenges. Applications must be integrated between the firms. Even within organizations, where the firm controls the technology, integration is difficult. When moving beyond the corporate boundary, organizations have little control over their partner's technology. At present, interorganizational integration is difficult, expensive, and time-consuming.

Web Services

An alternate approach is to use Web services. As described in Chapter 9, Web services is based on the idea that organizations buy computing services from a third party (a form of outsourcing) with whom they communicate through the Web. In interorganizational terms, Web services are a form of just-in-time integration of applications. Collaborating enterprises send their data to a third party that owns a copy of the application and runs the data. The results are available to both organizations.[12] Web services, in effect, create a decentralized collaborative environment. Furthermore, it makes it possible for either side of the cooperation to drop out and be replaced without the change causing major havoc.

While Web services are still in their infancy, it is possible to forecast the transitions that would be required. Web services would change the enterprise from a self-contained set of applications into a collection of services, data flows, and interfaces shared by enterprises. Web services create a market economy for services, much like an electricity grid, where organizations draw from (or supply to) the grid.[13]

---

[12] We describe Web services in terms of two cooperating firms. However, the model is scalable to multiple firms.

[13] Source: John Hagel III and John Seeley Brown, "Your Next IT Strategy," *Harvard Business Review,* October 2001 (79), 105–113.

Who Benefits?

Just as is the case with joint ventures in knowledge management (Chapter 7), who benefits most from an interorganizational system is not always clear a priori. For example, a customer, such as General Motors, who streamlines their purchasing by demanding EDI may gain most of the benefits while their supplier is faced with additional costs to implement a particular EDI system to keep GM as a customer. Conversely, a supplier who adopts the technology may reduce the number of competitors and thereby increase their market share.

ALLIANCES

Alliances are formal agreements between businesses to achieve a particular aim. Usually the firms agree to cooperate on one or more projects or products. Unlike a joint venture, where each firm puts up equity, a separate corporate entity may be created to share risk. Alternatively, the firms simply agree to work with one another to meet their agreed-on aim.

The advantage of alliances over mergers and acquisitions is that they can be formed and dissolved quickly. They are particularly favored in industries where change is rapid, such as software, electronics, and the media. They are also used in creating new lines of business, entering new markets, and for developing new capabilities. Although inherently simple in concept and able to confer quick benefits on the partners, nearly half of all alliances fail.[14] Organizations need to determine whether the greatest value comes from an alliance rather than a merger or a joint venture.

In terms of information systems, alliances are a form of interorganizational system. Rather than being a buyer–supplier relationship, alliances involve two or more companies working together for a particular objective. Neither partner has an advantage over the other. Decisions must be made about which information systems are to be used and how information and knowledge is to be transferred among the members of an alliance.

An example of an alliance is the agreement among Nokia (the large Finnish mobile phone company), Symbian (a software developer specializing in operating systems for mobile phones), and Intel (the large chip manufacturer) in Fall 2004 to cooperate in developing technology for advanced mobile phones.[15]

Another example is PalmOne (handheld computers), which signed a licensing deal with Microsoft (previously a longtime foe) that will allow the next generation of PalmOne's Treo smart phones to work directly with Microsoft's Exchange e-mail system.[16]

Like all other interorganizational arrangements, attention must be paid to security.

GLOBALIZATION[17]

We live in a global business world in which firms in every country are interconnected with firms in many other countries. At the large firm end, the world of multinationals is now more than just the major U.S. firms such as IBM. European and Japanese firms (such as Mercedez-Benz and Honda) are also multinational. What hasn't changed is that the country of origin is still the lead firm. The lead firm controls the information system and uses it to control the total entity. Nonetheless, control

---

[14] Source: *McKinsey Quarterly* 4, 2000.

[15] Source: *International Herald Tribune,* http://www.iht.com/articles/542182.html.

[16] Source: *International Herald Tribune,* http://www.iht.com/articles/542182.html.

[17] Source: R. Heller, "Connect the Dots," *CIO,* March 1, 2001.

is not absolute because local middle managers make decisions for their country or region and these decisions tend to change the overall strategic direction of the larger firm.

In a few firms, centralization of information and hence strategic direction is absolute. A good example is Cisco Systems, the network hardware supplier. Its customer support processes and centralized wired supply chain create operational efficiency and effectiveness. Another important aspect is the firm's ability to close the books once a day. By itself, daily closing is not important; what is important is that the information system provides timely and accurate data to the entire firm and allows decisions to be delegated locally with full assurance that they will be consistent with policy from the top.

A global firm can gain more than sourcing worldwide, coordinated marketing, and integrated operations. Firms that can interchange information across national boundaries so everyone has the same data and can then get their managers to cooperate and collaborate will gain strategic advantage.

As trade barriers are eliminated, supply chains stretch across the world, and businesses use the Internet to develop presences in multiple countries, firms that used to be only domestic become involved in globalization.

Globalization, while expanding a firm's horizons, also introduces new problems, many of which involve the firm's information systems. Consider the following, which are only a few that must be dealt with:

1. The world is a Tower of Babel with multiple languages, cultures, and customs. Simple words mean different things when translated into or used in different languages. For example, in most of the world football refers to soccer. Even simple things like measuring systems (pound and inch versus kilo and centimeter) get in the way.

2. Although the quality of technology of communications keeps increasing around the world, communications systems (e.g., telephone, videoconferences, and Internet meetings) do not yet do the whole job. Communications networks worldwide can be unreliable and of differing qualities.[18] Travel is still required.

3. In doing business abroad, particularly e-business, the technology of the country must be considered. For example, in Japan, postal workers collect money for goods; credit cards are rare. Europe and South Korea are far ahead in using cellular phones for Internet access. The logistics of shipping goods differ because transportation systems differ, changing the rules for how well and how quickly you can deliver. Where communications are problematic, such as in Ecuador, firms may require virtual private networks (VPNs) to be able to communicate.

4. Although wage scales may be lower in some parts of the world with high education levels (e.g., India, Russia), wages by themselves do not guarantee lower costs of projects such as software development. The transaction costs include, among other things, language translations, differences in the speed in which things get done, different regulatory environments, and brokerage costs. Brokerage refers to the idea that an intermediary takes responsibility for negotiating, managing, and even running the offshore operations, whether they are B2B (e.g., software outsourcing) or B2C. Brokerage fees tend to be high and easily eat up half or more of the anticipated gain from the overseas operation.

5. Standards differ across the world. Purchase orders in Europe are different than those in the United States. As discussed in Chapter 15, Europe imposes much more stringent standards on revealing personal information than does the United States.

---

[18] Remember that many other countries are ahead of the United States in telecommunications because they don't contend with legacy infrastructure. They can leapfrog to current technology because they never built the previous infrastructure.

6. Another aspect of the lack of standards is in the exchange of data. No international rules exist for doing e-business worldwide. Something simple like data format can be critical. For example, Asian languages require 2 bytes (16 bits) for a character where English requires 1 byte.

7. Globalization also implies sensitivity to mores and to ethics differences from one country to the next. For example, humor does not travel well. The author recalls an evening after a dinner in China with professional counterparts. Each side tried to tell funny stories to the other and every one of them drew laughs from their own side but fell flat on the other.

8. Local events can have global implications. For example, the outbreaks of the disease SARS suddenly removed portions of Asia from both export and import markets.

Bringing in Immigrants, Moving Work Abroad

Many issues in globalization become political. An example is the globalization of IT personnel. Many companies believe that it is cheaper to outsource IT overseas (or to bring foreign workers to the United States) than to hire local workers. The lure is twofold: (1) the lower labor cost per hour for workers in such countries as India who speak English well and (2) the perceived shortage of domestic workers. However, as indicated in item 4 above, wage rates are not the total picture. Just as a firm must consider the total cost of ownership of its PCs, so it must look at the true total cost involved in bringing foreign workers to the United States or for outsourcing jobs overseas.

Outsourcing, as discussed in Chapter 9, involves having another firm doing a job previously done in-house. The concept is well established. However, where outsourcing to a domestic company implies that the total number of jobs in the country remains about the same, outsourcing globally implies moving jobs from one country to another. Inevitably, the domestic jobs go away. The number of jobs in the outsourcing country decreases since local workers do not move overseas to take lower paying jobs. The observed result is an increase in unemployment among knowledge workers. While that reduces wage costs for new hires, it also creates a climate of fear and a sense of disloyalty among remaining employees. IT professionals worry "Am I next?" It also creates a virtual brain drain. As discussed in Chapter 7, Knowledge Management, when employees leave or are displaced, the knowledge that they carry in their head (procedures, company ways of doing things, technical skills) leaves with them. In sum, major globalization outsourcing activities imply knowledge loss.

A major issue on which Congress is lobbied is H1B and L1 visas. At the time of writing, these visas allowed overseas programmers and other IT professionals to enter and work in the United States. Despite strictures in the law about equal pay, imported workers were often paid much less than domestic workers. The net effect was that when the IT market stopped growing, reducing the number of jobs, many U.S. workers were displaced.

A loophole in the law allows foreign workers to come to the United States to be trained. That is, a firm can set up shop abroad, hire foreign workers, and then bring them to the United States for training. The backlash is an understandably high level of resentment by U.S. workers who spend time training people who will take their jobs. One possible outcome of these visa policies may be unionization by IT workers, a group that, like engineers, is usually opposed to unions.

Privacy Rules and Transborder Data Flows

Privacy is discussed in more detail in Chapter 15. It is important from a globalization viewpoint to recognize that privacy regulations differ from country to country and that, in particular, strong regulations exist on transborder data flows. Simply put, other countries don't like American companies to share their country's data with strangers. Here is an example. SAS, the Scandinavian airline, points out that if someone orders a Kosher meal, his or her religion is revealed, which can be dangerous in today's world.

The European Parliament and the Council of 24 in October 1995 passed the strictest privacy regulation. They introduced a Europeanwide privacy standard through Directive 95/46/EC. The directive restricts businesses in collecting, processing, and sharing personal information about individuals and moving data across borders. Under the regulations, you can't share data about a person without their permission. The rules, in effect, barred United States companies from moving data that their operations generated in Europe back to headquarters in the United States. After extensive negotiations with the Clinton administration, a "safe harbor" provision was agreed to. The safe harbor provision allows moving data to the United States but requires that you treat the data moved according to regulations that apply in its home country. Many firms agree with and implemented this compromise.

INTEGRATION CASE STUDY: *Owens & Morton*[19]

Owens & Morton, a Fortune 500 firm located in Richmond, Virginia, distributes name-brand medical and surgical supplies. Over a 4-year period the company completely changed its business model by integrating supply chain management, e-business, data warehousing, and Internet technologies. It changed both its physical distribution system (to improve service and decrease cost) and its internal information system (that provides information to its trading partners). It created a software system called WISDOM[20] for use by its suppliers and customers as a supply chain extranet that is used as well by its employees. With WISDOM, suppliers can better understand what products are selling and customers what products they are buying. The result is a software system that is a key component of corporate strategy, a source of revenue, and a basis for competitive advantage. As a result of WISDOM, the major systems at Owens & Morton communicate with one another in an integrated fashion.

Owens & Morton's business strategy called for three components:

    a. Operational excellence

    b. Supporting patient care

    c. Turning information into knowledge and then profit (the role of WISDOM)

The core for operational excellence was its customized ERP system. It added (1) Manugistics supply chain management software to automate its order forecasting process, (2) Cost Track, a software package which separated its cost of product from the cost of delivery, and (3) a data warehouse. These packages were integrated with the ERP system and improved order fulfillment rates from 91% to 96% and decreased credits issued for incorrect pricing and orders by a factor of 2.

Supporting patient care was a new initiative. It used an Internet-based inventory management system and a set of software built internally, called eMedExpress, to serve new customer bases, particularly customers and suppliers whose volumes were small, acute care facilities, and departments within hospitals.

Owens & Morton's data warehouse was central to its knowledge initiative. A Business Objects business intelligence package is tied to the warehouse. The warehouse, in turn, is connected to the ERP system. External suppliers and customers can gain access to the integrated system at a fee. This fee structure helps pay for the ongoing costs of WISDOM.

---

[19] Based on D. Stoller, B. H. Wixom, and H. J. Watson, WISDOM Provides Competitive Advantage at Owens & Morton. Competing in the New Economy, 2000, http://www.simnet.org. Note: This paper was an honorable mention in the Society for Information Management (SIM) Annual Paper Awards Competition 2000. SIM is the national professional society for chief information officers.

[20] WISDOM is an acronym for WebIntelligence Supporting Decisions from Owens & Morton.

GLOBALIZATION CASE STUDY: Capital One[21]

Capital One Financial of Falls Church, Virginia, is a bank whose principal operation is credit cards. It uses an information-based strategy for rating credit cards and for product development. It goes through terabytes of data using data mining (Chapter 5) looking for good credit risks and offers credit cards with interest rates, conditions, and fees customized to the individual. Its approach is a sophisticated form of customer relationship management (see Chapter 6).

This case study is not about Capital One's CRM approach but about how it began to expand globally. Capital One chose the United Kingdom (England, Scotland, Wales, and Northern Ireland), abbreviated UK. With its English-speaking population and the largest percentage of credit card holders in Europe, the UK was the natural place to expand. It began operations in 1995. Capital One's approach was to repeat its information-based strategy that was successful in the United States. It turned out a stream of new products to attract new customers. By 2001, it had 2400 employees and 2 million customers. Although the firm grew over the years, its principal overseas operation is still in the UK.

The basic challenge faced by Capital One was in moving from the United States, where the credit card market is well established, to countries where the notion of credit cards is strange and, because of various restrictions on data dissemination and often the lack of a credit rating agency, credit data is scarce.[22] Even to make its move into the UK, with its relatively credit card-friendly environment, required Capital One to think through the practicalities of operating in foreign countries. To move to continental Europe would require, for example, considering such issues as language and whether to have a central call center for the continent (requiring people speaking multiple languages) or geographically dispersed call centers for each country.

ANSWERS TO MANAGERIAL QUESTIONS

What is systems integration and why is it important?

Systems integration involves making sure that computer hardware and software systems can talk to one another and can work together seamlessly. With most firms operating computer solutions obtained at different points in time, creating seamlessness is a difficult and often expensive task. Often integration requires outside consulting help. However, failure to integrate incurs larger costs and longer times to complete processes.

Don't ERP systems solve the integration problem?

Although ERP systems perform a multitude of processes that are highly integrated with one another, they do not yet cover all the computing needs of a firm. As a result, ERP systems, like other computer systems, require integration if they are to work with the rest of the company's IT infrastructure.

What is involved in systems integration?

Systems integration typically involves making multiple systems work together. Maintaining standards helps. So does the use of middleware that stands between two systems and allows them to interchange data and results.

What are interorganizational systems?

Interorganizational systems, as their name implies, serve more than one firm or more than one business unit. They allow firms to exchange data and results. They give a firm access to information (such as inventory levels, sales forecasts) of partner firms so that they can smooth out their production and inventory.

What are their risks and rewards?

Inter-organizational systems improve the work flow between organizations, smoothing production, reducing inventory, and enhancing other interactions. However, they introduce additional security risks (Do you really want to give someone else carte blanche access to your computer data?) that must be handled. They also

---

[21] M. Wheatley, "Charging Into Europe," *CIO,* November 1, 2001.

[22] For example, France at the time did not even have a credit bureau.

tie firms more closely together, which becomes a problem when firms decide to go their separate ways for whatever reason.

How do alliances work?

In an alliance, two firms agree to work together on particular projects. Alliances are believed to be superior to mergers and joint ventures because they can be started and dissolved much more quickly and cheaply. Firms may form an alliance on one project and compete against each other on another. Alliances, from an IT point of view, require all the safeguards of interorganizational systems.

What are the criteria for entering or avoiding an alliance?

Because nearly half of all alliances fail, due diligence must be exercised when entering into one. Even if an alliance partner has the know-how or computer programs to solve a critical part of a project, they may not be suited for the problem at hand.

How can information technology help me in globalizing my business?

Globalization requires communications and the exchange of data worldwide. The Internet helps in this regard. Globalization also makes it possible to source work at its cheapest location. However, the backlash against moving jobs outside the United States is a continuing problem.

PROBLEMS

1. INTEGRATION

    Consider your own firm or a firm that you worked for previously. To what extent are systems integrated? Are there any processes that require manual transcription of data? Are there stand-alone systems that do not need integration? Is it possible for your firm's computers to communicate with computers at other firms?

2. INTERORGANIZATIONAL SYSTEMS

    Find 3 case descriptions of interorganizational systems on the Internet or from other sources. Describe each briefly and then present a table that compares and contrasts the various systems described.

3. ALLIANCES

    Discuss the advantages and disadvantages of alliances compared to mergers or acquisition in your industry. Describe examples either in your industry or in related industries. Consider the problems associated with communicating data and knowledge between the firms involved. If possible, find examples of where an alliance failed or where the partners in an alliance received different benefits from the arrangement.

4. GLOBALIZATION

    Globalization requires working across time zones, languages, cultures, and worker skills. Discuss the problems associated with making computer systems work across these dimensions. Find additional case studies (beyond Owens & Morton and Capital One) to illustrate how these problems are (or are not) handled.

Chapter 11

IS in Managing Business Operations: The Supply Chain

MANAGERIAL QUESTIONS

What is supply chain management?
What are the five components of supply chain management?
What is the goal of supply chain management?
How is supply chain software used?
What is the role of collaboration?
What is the relation to ERP?
What are the resistances to supply chain software?

INTRODUCTION

Businesses always dealt with their supply chain. That is, they bought raw materials, components, and supplies that they used to create their products or services and sold to a set of customers to whom they delivered their products. What is new is that the speed at which goods and services move through the supply chain increased considerably because improvements in computers and communications speeded the exchange of information.

Although a firm may see only its direct providers and its direct purchasers, as shown in Figure 1, the sets of suppliers and customers are much more complex. For example, auto manufacturers obtain almost every component of a car from someone else, although most components are built to the manufacturer's specification. The so-called manufacturer in this case is really an assembler. The suppliers (of doors, batteries, mirrors, engines, and hundreds of other pieces) in turn assemble these pieces from components bought from their own suppliers and so on back to the people who dig raw material out of the ground. If the firm is a producer of consumer products, it may sell directly to end users (e.g., acting as a retailer via e-commerce) or the goods may go through a distribution chain that can involve multiple levels of distributors and resellers. For business-to-business transactions, the sales may be direct through a sales force, through intermediaries such as jobbers, or more and more over the Internet. In other words, the supply chain extends from your supplier's supplier to your customer's customer.

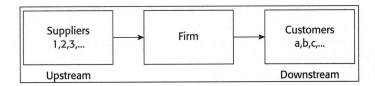

Figure 1 The supply chain as seen by the firm.

Note, too, that supply chain activities go on within the firm as goods are transferred among departments or from subsidiaries. In manufacturing, these operations are the assembly, manufacturing, and packaging that produce the finished product. Each of the subassemblies must be available to create the next level of subassembly or the finished product.

The supply chain is really a delicate mechanism that depends on everything working together at the same time. In real life, of course, everything doesn't always come together. A lot of the variables are random: the economy fluctuates; mergers and acquisitions happen upstream and downstream in the chain; suppliers and customers go in and out of business; natural and man-made disasters (e.g., hurricanes, strikes, blackouts) occur along the chain. However, decisions need to be made ahead of time, sometimes a considerable time ahead, on how many to produce and when to produce. Keeping a firm's supply chain going often seems more of an art than a science. Therefore, like an insurance policy, firms keep inventory (even with just-in-time delivery) to protect against uncertainty. They also engage in supply chain planning (SCP) to make their estimates of the future better.

THE SUPPLY CHAIN[1]

As described by the Supply Chain Council, managing the supply chain includes five components:

1. Planning
2. Sourcing
3. Making
4. Delivering
5. Returning

1. *Planning*. Planning involves assessing what demand will be (i.e., forecasting), finding and contracting for sources of supply, and measuring how well the supply chain is running. Metrics are used to determine whether your supply chain is being run efficiently, how well cost goals are being met, and the level of quality and value being delivered to customers.

2. *Sourcing*. Sourcing refers to choosing suppliers that provide the needed goods and services. Pricing, delivery, and payment are considerations, as are quality and value.

3. *Making*. In this step, the product to be delivered to the customer is produced. The product may be a physical object (a car, a toy) or a service (insurance policy, money market account). To create a sellable product and make a profit, it is necessary to schedule its production, test it for quality, package it, and prepare it for delivery. Measures include quality level, production output, and worker productivity.

---

[1] The discussion of supply chain management is based on information at www.supply-chain.org, the website of the Supply Chain Council.

4. *Delivering*. Delivery, also called logistics, refers to the activities that move the product to the customer. It involves coordinating shipments so they reach the customer on time, implementing warehousing strategies for storing products until they are ready to ship, selecting transportation carriers, and creating an invoicing system to get paid.

5. *Returning*. Because customers may return part or all of a shipment, either because it is deemed defective or an excess amount was ordered, a network for receiving returns and for supporting customers must be established. In addition, for expensive, complex products, support services (e.g., a help desk) are required. (See the Section on Returns, near the end of this chapter.)

SOFTWARE'S ROLE

Many software products are on the market to help improve supply chain operations. Unfortunately, although some software vendors claim to deal with the entire process, none do. The complexity of each of the five steps described in the previous section is such that dozens of tasks need to be performed. Specific software is available that deals with individual or groups of tasks, but these software packages are not integrated with one another. Integration (see Chapter 10) is a holy grail.

In thinking about supply chain software, it is convenient to divide it into

- software that supports planning and
- software that helps execute the steps after planning.

Planning Software

Supply chain planning is intertwined with the methods of management science. Much of the planning software imbeds advanced mathematical algorithms designed to reduce inventory and improve both the efficiency and the flow through the supply chain. Being mathematical, these methods can only provide good answers if the input data from customers (e.g., present and future orders, sales by the customer to its clients, inventory on hand) and from within the organization (e.g., production, warehouse, and delivery capacity still available to commit) are current and accurate. The key parameter is demand, because if the demand estimate is right, the rest of the results will usually be right. If not, you can overproduce or underproduce, hire too many or hire too few, and make other errors. Demand forecasting turns out to be the most complex and the most likely to be wrong in quantity in the planning process.

Execution Software

Execution software automates supply chain operations. The idea is to complete steps more quickly so that the delay between the receipt of an order and its delivery to the customer is shortened. Some execution software is quite simple. For example, by sharing your estimates of demand with your suppliers, your suppliers can organize their production to meet your production needs. In theory, all that is needed is to decide which information to share, sending it regularly to suppliers, and receiving data from suppliers on their performance and their capacity. As discussed later in this chapter, coordination with suppliers is not an easy task.

WHY INSTALL SUPPLY CHAIN SOFTWARE?

Supply chain software makes it possible to gain visibility about demand. Interchanging supply chain information up and down the supply chain became easier as the Internet grew in speed and capacity, telecommunications networks expanded, and communications costs went down. In theory, supply chain software can connect the firm with its suppliers and customers in a large, optimized network. In practice, information is exchanged in only a few industries (e.g., automobiles, high technology, supermarkets, and drugstores) and even then not among all firms.

When they share demand estimates:

- suppliers don't have to guess how much material or how many subassemblies to order for meeting a particular client's needs,

- manufacturers reduce the inventory they need to keep to meet sudden or unexpected demand, and

- retailers are not out of stock of specific items in a store because the manufacturer's production falls behind the store's demand.

COOPERATION

A part of the problem is getting firms to collaborate. Most firms trust no one[2] and therefore prefer not to give anyone information about their plans. Thus, while it is technically relatively easy to share information, the culture (both in the United States and in most other countries) is not to do so, even though sharing information helps everyone. As a result, inventories all up and down the supply chain expand to guard against contingencies.

Cooperation is easier if a large firm insists on it as a condition for doing business with it. Two classic examples, Wal-Mart and Cisco Systems, are described in Sidebars 1 and 2.

SIDEBAR 1   *Wal-Mart*

Wal-Mart is, by some accounts, the gorilla of retailing. Specializing at the low cost end of the retail market, it insists on large volumes of information from suppliers who want to do business with it. They do so even with large suppliers. For example, Proctor & Gamble is connected to Wal-Mart distribution centers and, via satellite uplinks, can tell when a single unit of theirs passes through a scanner at a store. When a distribution center drops below a preset level of inventory, Wal-Mart sends an alert to Proctor & Gamble to ship more product.

The nearly real-time information (see the discussion of business activity monitoring in Chapter 8) helps Proctor & Gamble to coordinate its production and shipments with Wal-Mart's demand. In effect, Proctor & Gamble is managing Wal-Mart's inventory. The claim is that Proctor & Gamble is able to reduce its own inventory because of better knowledge of Wal-Mart's demand. Through this process, Wal-Mart, of course, shifted a large portion of its own inventory management and physical inventory costs to its suppliers.

---

[2] Some firms stamp everything company confidential. It is said that if you wrote force = mass times acceleration (Newton's law), some firms would consider it private information.

SIDEBAR 2   *Cisco Systems*

Cisco Systems Inc. creates network hardware for connecting to the Internet, to corporate intranets, and to extranets (see Chapter 3). By linking its own network to its suppliers, contract manufacturers, and distributors, Cisco created a just-in-time supply chain. When an order is received for a network router, for example, messages are sent to contract manufacturers (e.g., of circuit boards, final assembly) and to distributors of standard components (e.g., power supplies). That is, these firms in Cisco's supply chain receive advance warning of what demands are coming because they are logged on to Cisco's intranet and linked to Cisco's manufacturing execution system.

Once an ordered item is assembled by a subcontractor,

- Cisco receives a bar code identification,
- Cisco checks the assembly's compliance with its customer's order, and
- the unit is connected to a centralized facility for automated quality control testing.

At that point, Cisco provides the customer name and the shipping instructions to its contractor.

The foregoing process is used for items that are custom-built in response to orders. For some products, whose demand is steady, parts are built to forecasts and, if necessary, stored in warehouses.

Ideally, for custom orders, Cisco needs no inventory and hence no warehouses. Furthermore, no paper invoices (remember it is all done over the Internet) are required among members of its supply chain. If events don't happen according to plan, management by exception kicks in.

The system was set up under the assumption that demand would continue to increase. It didn't in the economic downturn of 2001 to 2003. Cisco and its supply chain partners wound up producing more units than needed and creating warehouses of unsold products. At that point, supply chain planning had to be revised to cope with the situation.

MANUFACTURING

An enormous amount of software and hardware is available to improve both engineering and manufacturing operations in a firm. These two functions are the 'make' part of the supply chain.

Overview

Factory automation, long a dream of futurists, is coming closer and closer to reality. The idea goes back to the early twentieth century. For example, the Czech play RUR (the name is a crossword puzzle favorite) opened in 1920. It told the tale of Rossum's Universal Robots. Today, lights out factories and lights out computer centers are in the early stages of implementation. Many of these operations are part-time, such as plastic factories stamping out products on third shift. Information systems are central to making this change happen.

The reality for most companies is much less than full automation. We are at the stage of computer-aided design (CAD) and computer-aided manufacturing (CAM), where many functions previously performed by hand are automated. For example, in engineering, computer-aided design is standard.

CAD

The first CAD systems in the late 1960s were typically limited to producing drawings similar to hand-drafted drawings. Since then, CAD systems grew to include

- Reuse of existing design components and automatic generation of standard components of the design.
- Validation/verification of designs against specifications and design rules.
- Simulation of designs without building a physical prototype.
- Automated design of assemblies of parts and subassemblies.
- Creation of manufacturing drawings, and bill of materials.
- Output of design drawings directly to manufacturing facilities.

Realizing these benefits requires recognizing that CAD is not a universal solution. CAD will not automate all routine design tasks. It will not generally provide a three-dimensional rendering that can be viewed from all angles, with detailed cross sections, and used to create CAM data sets or solid models. The design process is still far from paperless.

CAM

Computer-aided manufacturing uses computers to communicate work instructions directly to manufacturing machinery. The technology evolved from numerically controlled machines. Today a single computer can control banks of robotic milling machines, lathes, welding machines, and other tools, moving the product from machine to machine as each step in the manufacturing process is completed. Such systems allow easy, fast reprogramming of the machines from the computer, permitting quick implementation of design changes. As we will see below, these capabilities make customized and just-in-time manufacturing possible. The most sophisticated CAM systems, often integrated with CAD systems, can manage tasks such as parts ordering, scheduling, and tool replacement. Analysis of CAM systems indicates three critical success factors:

- a technology champion who is effective,
- systems integration (see Chapter 10), and
- cross-functional steering and implementation teams.

Just-in-Time Manufacturing[3]

Just-in-time (JIT) manufacturing, done right, is a means for increasing the return on investment by reducing the amount of inventory needed. JIT differs from traditional manufacturing in that it takes a different approach to work flow. In traditional manufacturing, production planners schedule production of a batch, that is, a fixed number of units of a given product. The key parameter is the "economic lot size," determined by trading off the cost of setup[4] and the cost of inventory. A large amount of in-process inventory (and hence cost) is created to make sure that raw materials and subassemblies are available as needed.

In just-in-time manufacturing, individual products are built from beginning to end and traditional inventory is largely eliminated. However, in just-in-time manufacturing not having materials or parts available at the time they are needed stops the entire production line. Therefore, to make

---

[3] Just-in-time is also discussed in the next subsection on inventory.

[4] Setup refers to making the changes needed to move from one product or model to another. If a production run is too short, more setups are required. If it is too long, too much inventory is produced and must be stored.

just-in-time work, you need to store data on where each piece of material and part is located and to make sure that parts and components arrive at the place where they are needed at the correct time.

Conversion to just-in-time means keeping accurate track of raw material and in-process inventory, including materials issued and component scrap. The goal is to keep raw material and in-process inventory as low as possible while avoiding frequent setups.

Inventory

The idea in the supply chain is to make sure that goods are available when needed. For physical goods, that results in inventory—goods kept in reserve to meet demand when it occurs. Inventory, of course, incurs cost. It ties up capital, storage space (which costs money), and requires a good data system to keep track of what is currently in stock and what is scheduled to arrive.

The movement to just-in-time inventory as part of just-in-time manufacturing, that is, the attempt to minimize inventory so that supplies are obtained only at the moment they are needed, also acts as a device to push the storage of inventory up the supply chain.[5] For example, the auto manufacturer who plans to assemble 500 units of a given model tomorrow seeks to have its suppliers bring the exact number of components needed for the 500 cars to the factory floor in the early morning or, better still, at the very moment each car is assembled.[6] In practice, the goal can be approached but not reached because some spare parts must be available in case of a defect or to rectify a mistake in assembly.

Inventory shows up in two ways: in-process and finished. In-process inventory refers to goods that are stored between stages of production or service. For example, consider the service of creating an insurance policy. The sales information (input) comes in from the insurance agents. Sales pile up (inventory) at the receiving desk. From there they are routed to individual actuaries and/or risk assessors who determine whether the policy should be written or not and, if written, should it be at the price sold by the agent or at a higher or lower price. The actuaries usually have a stack of policies to act on in their in-box (in-process inventory). As they complete individual policies, the actuaries route them to a production department whose clerks create the needed forms and send them out. Of course, there is an inventory of policies waiting to be sent out by each of the clerks.

Reducing inventory is an example of where improving the supply chain pays off. A company aims to minimize its inventory. To do so, it must produce products as close to when it is demanded as possible. Two kinds of losses can be incurred:

1. Not producing enough goods to meet demand. The penalty comes from lost sales and profits.

2. Producing more goods than are demanded. The penalty is the cost of storing (or even destroying) excess goods.

One of the fundamental formulas learned in operations management courses in business schools is the idea of an optimum lot size, that is, the number of units to produce at a time and the frequency between starting successive production batches. The idea is to balance off the two kinds of losses.

The classic example involved hiring airline stewardesses.[7] Stewardesses were trained in classes. How big should a class be (the lot size in inventory theory) and how often should a new class be

---

[5] Just-in-time manufacturing, invented at Toyota in Japan where space for keeping inventory was at a premium, was originally devised to reduce the amount of inventory on hand.

[6] Your author observed an example of the unintended consequences of just-in-time inventory in Tokyo. Arriving around 11 P.M. because of a flight delay, he found the freeways crowded with giant trucks creating traffic jams as bad as rush hour.

[7] Today, stewardesses are called flight attendants and are no longer limited to female employees

started (time between setups)? Recognize that there is a lead time (from the time a class starts to the time it graduates) before newly trained stewardesses become available. Recognize too that there are two kinds of losses: (1) salaries to stewardesses who graduated but are waiting to be assigned to flights (excess inventory) and (2) airplanes that can't fly because too few stewardesses are available[8] (loss of sales). Clearly, the latter is more expensive.

ROLE OF ERP

The role of ERP (Chapter 4) is different for supply chain planning and for supply chain execution software.

Supply Chain Planning

Enterprise requirement planning systems, which gather information from throughout the company, contain large amounts of information that are used as inputs in supply chain management planning. For a firm with an ERP system in place, it can be of great help because the system assembles needed up-to-date planning information in one place and, conversely, the planning information serves as input to the ERP system. To be useful for supply chain planning, an existing ERP system must be compatible with the supply chain software selected.

The conventional wisdom is that if a firm plans to install both ERP and supply chain planning, it should install ERP first. Part of the reason is that the ERP installation forces the firm to regularize its data. As discussed in Chapter 4, ERP is expensive and difficult to install. Therefore, if supply chain is a major problem and funds are tight, it may prove appropriate to install the supply chain software separately. However, while it is possible, it is quite difficult to create a supply chain planning system from legacy systems because information is needed quickly and reliably from many places. To do so requires great skill in integration with legacy systems (Chapter 10).

Supply Chain Execution

Execution systems don't need as much information as planning systems. Therefore, it is easier to install such systems without ERP in place. However, even in this case, it is advantageous to create compatible ERP, supply chain planning, and supply chain execution capabilities so that orders, payments, delivery, and manufacturing status are available together.

ROLE OF DATA WAREHOUSING

For firms with a large number of items in their supply chains, a data warehouse is a necessity both for planning and for execution. Wal-Mart, discussed in Sidebar 1 in this chapter, is an example. Its data warehouse in 2004 was 400 terabytes. It contains every transaction in every store, recorded within a few minutes of purchase. Data are available on new merchandise as it arrives and as it is put on the shelves. Thus, Wal-Mart is able to keep track of inventory available to sell, to plan orders, and (since they run on just-in-time deliveries) determine when goods should arrive at the stores. The data warehouse thus is the key to integrating their supply chain. Many firms also give access to selected parts of their data warehouse to their trading partners, both their suppliers and their customers.

---

[8] The problem can be ameliorated to some extent by using retired stewardesses who work part-time.

CHALLENGES TO IMPLEMENTATION

The three major challenges in implementing supply chain software are

- Gaining trust from suppliers, partners, and customers.
- Overcoming resistance to change by employees.
- Going up the learning curve.

Trust

Almost all the other large-scale software systems described in this book operate completely internal to the firm. Supply chain software, however, requires the cooperation of other firms to make it successful. Not only will your own people need to change how they work, but so will almost every one of your trading partners. That's a tall order. While large firms, simply because of their size, can force changes by threatening to replace a partner (and actually doing so, if need be), most firms do not enjoy enough market clout to enforce a behavior change. A firm embarking on improving its supply chain activities must coax, wheedle, and entice each of its trading partners to change their ways. That's a culture change, and like all culture changes, it is hard to implement. As described in Sidebar 1 for Proctor & Gamble, supply chain changes can move the management of inventory to the supplier, something suppliers did not do in the past and which they do not necessarily feel able to do.

Resistance

Not only will partners be difficult to bring on board, your own employees will resist change as well. As discussed in Chapter 12 on people issues, people don't like to deal with new ideas in their work. Precomputer supply chain operations involved long-term people-to-people contacts through phone, fax, and e-mail. People in the organization have tacit information (see Chapter 7, Knowledge Management) about likely sources in case of a crunch. Computer-based supply chain systems upset relationships and diminish individual importance. If the software doesn't perform as expected or runs into even minor problems, people return to their previous ways of solving a problem.

To overcome a lack of commitment within an enterprise and in the supply chain, it is important to provide specific, measurable goals for the effort and to make certain that the goals are clearly understood within the firm.

Learning Curve

When a commercial supply chain program is introduced, it behaves according to what the software vendor viewed as the standard way or the best practice for the purpose. Such programs do not include the company's practices and history. They follow the built-in algorithms and, as a result, seem dumb to the user. Thus, the initial forecasts often need to be modified.[9] Only after a while when a program is, in effect, trained does it develop the smarts that the vendor advertises.

---

[9] A classic tale, reported in CIO magazine, involved an auto industry supplier who received an unusually large order just after the software was installed. As a result, the program badly overestimated future demand because forecasts were based on this single order. Fortunately, a staff member who substituted his own estimate based on history caught the error.

A side effect is that initial errors reduce the trust in the program. People revert to working with their own data. Trust is only regained after the program becomes more accurate and when in-house expertise is merged into the system.

OTHER PROBLEMS ALONG THE SUPPLY CHAIN

Problems along the supply chain principally come from three sources:

- Uncertainties, particularly in demand. Decisions are made on the basis of a demand forecast, that is an estimate of what kinds of units and how many of each will be ordered and when they must be delivered.
- Difficulties in coordinating multiple activities, business partners, and internal units. That is, managing the nuts and bolts of the supply chain.
- Poor customer service, ranging from defective products to poor after-purchase support to early or late delivery.

As shown in Table 1, IT can help in reducing these sources of difficulty.

Demand Forecasting

Demand depends on competition, prices, weather (e.g., a warm or a cold winter), new technologies or fashions, the state of the economy, and much more. Modeling demand can be a tricky business. First, there is the bullwhip effect, discussed in Sidebar 3, that causes demand forecasts to escalate because of small errors made at various stages.

Table 1   IT SOLUTIONS TO SUPPLY CHAIN PROBLEMS

Supply chain problem	IT solution
Waiting times between chain segments are too long	Find reasons by using decision support software and/or groupware for collaboration
Non-value-added activities along the chain	Use supply chain management or simulation software
Slow delivery of paper documents	EDI, e-mail
Shipment errors, poor quality	Electronic verification, automation, quality alerts
Learn about delays after they occur	Shipment tracking systems, trend analysis
Excessive approvals	Work flow software, electronic approvals
Poor coordination, cooperation, and communication	Groupware, collaboration tools, e-mail
Parts obsolescence due to excessive time in warehouses	Tracking software, RFID[10]

---

[10] RFID is an acronym for radio frequency identification. Units are equipped with microchips in a tag or label with stored data such as unit number and date built. Transmitters send inquiries to a physical area and each unit responds with its identification information. Privacy issues for RFID are discussed in Chapter 15.

SIDEBAR 3   *The Bullwhip Effect*

The bullwhip effect is the name given to systemic problems that can arise in the supply chain where problems at one point can create problems at many others.

Originally found at Proctor & Gamble in its disposable diaper business, the bullwhip effect reflects the magnification of small errors into large ones. Specifically, Proctor & Gamble found that, while demand for its product at the retail level was relatively stable and hence predictable, the orders they received from their intermediaries, the distributors, fluctuated wildly. On investigation they found that poor demand forecasts, price fluctuations, and the batch size of orders were principal causes of the variations. The result was unnecessary inventories all along the supply chain because each firm was looking at its own interests, not the interests of the supply chain. Stockpiling against just-in-case scenarios occurred simultaneously at seven or more points, resulting in up to 100 days of inventory. The bullwhip effect can be overcome by sharing information between firms. As pointed out previously in this section (and in Chapter 7, Knowledge Management), corporate culture in the United States is ingrained against sharing. However, firms that do share, gain significant benefits.

Second, there is the issue of how the demand forecast is created. If the sales department makes it, there is a cultural tendency for salespeople to assume that only the best outcome will occur. Again, the forecast is badly overestimated. If a pessimistic manager who assumes the worst will happen makes the forecast, the forecast demand is much lower than the actual. A more neutral (and realistic) way to forecast is to run a computer model of the supply chain. Sidebar 4 describes this methodology briefly.

Note: If you are unfamiliar with simulation under uncertainty, feel free to skip Sidebar 4. It requires somewhat more mathematical understanding than the other sections of this book.

WHAT IS THE PAYOFF FROM INFORMATION SYSTEMS IN THE SUPPLY CHAIN?

The major benefits achieved from a successful supply chain software installation include

- a shorter supply chain (implying fewer suppliers to deal with),
- lower costs,
- shortened cycle times,
- ability to build to demand,
- use of more science in meeting customer demand,
- reduced overstock, and
- improved customer service.

SIDEBAR 4	*MODELING THE SUPPLY CHAIN*

Because of the uncertainties in the supply chain (e.g., in demand, in supplier performance, in manufacturing performance, in transportation, and in timing of customer payments) many firms use "stochastic risk analysis" based on simulation techniques. Stochastic is just a fancy word for saying uncertain. Simulation is the idea of creating a computer model that describes the phenomenon being studied. The idea is that you can run the computer program much, must faster than the real supply chain and that you can do so with much less expense. Thus, you can explore many more cases than by other means. Risk models fall into the class of simulation models in which randomness is represented by probability distributions.

A model allows you to create a simple generic framework that describes the supply chain. The framework is really a network with randomness in time and/or cost at many nodes and along many arcs. For example, you might consider the following uncertainties:

- Manufacturing: the time for process design, the capabilities of the resulting product design, the time to produce a component, and the quality of the product produced.
- Customer demand: the robustness of the economy, the stimulation of incentive programs.

- Customer delivery: time required to deliver the goods.
- Supplier performance: responsiveness of the supplier, cost of transportation

Figure 2 shows one distribution (a normal distribution) that an uncertainty may follow. You use your best estimate of what the distribution will look like for each uncertainty.

In a simulation, when an uncertainty is encountered, a single number is chosen from the probability distribution to represent what happens. For example, if the distribution of time for goods to reach you from a particular manufacturer is normally distributed as in Figure 2, you choose a value from that distribution.[11] By proceeding through the chain in this way, you create one possible outcome. But an individual outcome only has a small chance of occurring. Repeating this procedure many times allows you to obtain both the average and the standard deviation of the time from one end of the chain to the other. You can then do what-if analysis that allows you to see what proposed improvements in a node (e.g., time for a supplier to produce a component) or an arc (e.g., shipping time) can do to improve the average performance and the variability of your supply chain.

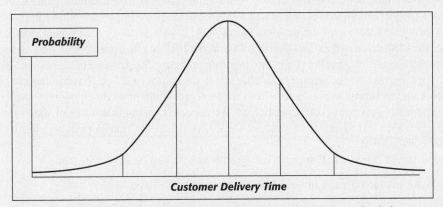

Figure 2 Normal distribution: One representation of uncertainty in a supply chain.

[11] The way the computer program is organized, it picks numbers from the probability distribution in proportion to the shape of the distribution. Thus, in a normal distribution such as shown in Figure 2, numbers from the middle are picked much more often than numbers from the end.

EXAMPLES OF SUCCESS[12]

Toy maker Mattel, who makes the Barbie doll among other products, uses supply chain optimization software in managing its seven distribution centers, seven factories, and other facilities around the world. In planning, it was able to move from monthly cycles to weekly ones and to align its production to reduce overproduction and, at the same time, meet customer demand on time. At the distribution end, it concentrated on moving product by installing a transportation management system that reduced less-than-truckload shipments and improved its shipping network.

Atari, a video game manufacturer, uses cooperative forecasting. It links its Oracle ERP system with the sales planning system to formulate weekly demand forecasts by SKU (stock keeping unit) and store. It obtains input data from customers such as Target and Best and feeds its analysis of the data to its suppliers who produce its games. Specific orders come in electronically via EDI and go through an order management system. When an order is shipped, the system sends an advance shipping notice and an invoice.

A McKinsey & Company study[13] concluded from a study of 63 high-tech companies that a firm can't and won't improve the flow of goods and information unless:

- the supply chain software is coupled with improvements in a company's most important supply chain processes,
- it improves training,
- provides clear accountability, and
- sets more realistic goals.

The difference between a successful installation and an unsuccessful one is a supply chain that is in good shape.

McKinsey & Company found that firms that didn't adopt any supply chain technologies fared better than low-performing adopters. This finding is in keeping with the idea that management must address flawed supply chain processes and practices before technology implementation can do any good. Simply throwing software at the problem won't help. It will, in fact, make things worse. It also reinforces the idea, discussed earlier, that it is wise to put ERP in place before undertaking supply change management. The ERP installation requires updating the firm's business processes so they are compatible across the firm. The McKinsey & Company study emphasizes the simple truth that implementing supply chain management technologies without a corresponding business process change makes you worse off than before. As expected, firms that adopted the supply chain technologies after improving their processes did better than the nonadopters and the low-performing adopters.

In summary, the McKinsey & Company survey found, as would be expected, that

- successful implementation occurs if broken processes are fixed first,
- rollout is incremental with repeated success rather than an all-at-once approach,
- what is promised is delivered,

---

[12] Examples appear in B. Bacheldor, "Steady Supply," *Information Week,* pp. 37-42, November 24, 2003.

[13] Source: McKinsey Quarterly e-mail version.

- training emphasizes improvement in decision making by using the technology, and
- a credible incentive program is instituted for adopters.

RETURNS

Returns are the last stage of the supply chain. They happen all the time. An individual receives a faulty unit (e.g., a lemon) or accepts the money back guarantee offered. A clothing store returns merchandise at the end of the season. A company upgrades its PCs to flat screens or replaces its portables with new ones that are wireless. In each case, the old merchandise must go somewhere. Usually it winds up being returned to the source. That is, returns create a supply chain in reverse.[14] Rather than pushing merchandise down the supply chain to the customer, the customer is pushing finished merchandise up the chain. The source firm's objective is to recover unsold or defective product and then resell it or send it to a liquidation outlet or a recycling center. The income derived from salvage offsets some of the losses on the returns.

In some cases, the product itself implies a reverse supply chain. A disposable camera, for example, is recycled with fresh film and resold. Manufacturers of laser printers encourage people to return their spent toner cartridge units back to the manufacturer. Recycling is being encouraged for more and more products.

Unfortunately, it is not possible simply to operate the supply chain in reverse. Forward supply chain management processes reduce transaction and transportation costs by minimizing the number of transactions in the system. For example, goods are shipped in standardized lot sizes (e.g., cases) for cost effective performance. In the reverse direction, moving unsold goods, say, from a store shelf, rarely results in standard lot sizes. That creates new problems in receiving, material handling, and stocking. Additional handling costs are incurred as individual items move to different locations in a warehouse. The computer must be able to account for small, irregular quantities.

Another technique at the retail level is to sell slow moving products at a discount either through markdowns or closeouts or outlet malls. Unfortunately, such tactics can send false signals into supply chain planning. A classic example is Volvo, whose dealers found that few people wanted their cars in green. When the dealers cut prices to move the cars, the factory took it as a signal that green Volvos were selling and started producing them in even greater quantities.

The conclusion is that reverse supply chains must be established separately from forward chains. They may take the form of third parties that act as accumulators of goods into standard lot sizes that are then shipped to the warehouse or to a plant that remanufactures the product. In either case, the goods are then treated as new product.

Computer software and infrastructure for reverse supply chains is still in its infancy. It is a business opportunity.

THE SUPPLY CHAIN MARKET

What you can do to improve the supply chain changes continually as new software comes on the market and additional supply chain functions are automated. The electronic supply chain is being credited with better customer service, more support from suppliers, and shorter production cycles.

---

[14] For a discussion of the reverse supply chain see, for example, R. Reddy, "Swimming Upstream," *Intelligent Enterprise,* p. 42, September 1, 2003.

Firms believe that they are creating ever greater levels of customer, supplier, and partner integration. To do so, however, involves challenges:

- Security
- Privacy
- Competition

Clearly, with hundreds of suppliers and customers, many of whom are small, a firm is not able to extend its supply chain end-to-end. A trade magazine, *InformationWeek*,[15] surveyed the 500 most innovative U.S. firms and found that a typical company in that cohort coordinated its supply chain in 2003 with 39% of its suppliers, 36% of its business partners, and 35% of its customers. These numbers are averages and vary by industry. At the high end is the automotive industry where the three numbers are 61%, 56%, and 54%, respectively. In some industries close connections are maintained with suppliers only.

InformationWeek found that companies provided different access to their suppliers depending on the application. The values ranged from 58% down to 35%. In rank order the applications were: order management, inventory, accounts payable, receivable status, product development specification, and production schedules.

Major Firms in the Supply Chain Market

Major vendors in the supply chain market include Manugistics and I2 which specialize in the area, and large software vendors such as SAP, Oracle, and IBM who offer supply chain software as well as ERP and other major systems. Table 2 lists the firms included in one supply chain management stock index.[16]

Table 2   COMPANIES INCLUDED IN A SUPPLY CHAIN STOCK INDEX

Company	Symbol
Amer Software A	AMSWA
Aspen Technology	AZPN
Clarus Corp	CLRS
Catalyst Intl	CLYS
Descartes Systems Group	DSGX
Exe Technologies A	EXEE
Frontstep Inc	FSTP
Industri-matematik Intl	IMIC
I2 Technologies	ITWO
Logility Inc	LGTY
Manhattan Associates	MANH
Manugistics Group	MANU
Made2manage Systems	MTMS
Qad Inc	QADI
SAP	SAP

[15] Source: *Information Week* pp. 108-110, October 27, 2003.

[16] Source: http://stocks.ittoolbox.com/ittoolbox/indices.asp?Symbol=$SCMDEX Last consulted 10-7-04. The list represents publicly traded vendors in October 2004. Some of these companies may disappear as mergers and acquisitions take place.

ANSWERS TO MANAGERIAL QUESTIONS

What is supply chain management?

Supply chain management refers to the use of the computer and analytic techniques to reduce the cost and improve the speed with which a firm obtains materials, components, and supplies for its products and services and is able to move those products to its customers.

What are the five components of supply chain management?

Supply chain management includes (1) planning to make it all happen, (2) sourcing to find the best (usually lowest cost, quickest response) vendors, (3) making the product or service, (4) delivering output, and (5) dealing with returns.

What is the goal of supply chain management?

Supply chain software allows firms to gain visibility about supplies and demand over time. As a result, they can reduce inventory, smooth out production and labor, and avoid being out of stock when a demand occurs.

How is supply chain software used?

Supply chain software is used to support planning and to help execute the supply chain steps after planning.

What is the role of collaboration?

To make the supply chain work effectively, both providers of input and consumers of output need to work together. Thus, for a given firm, vendors who sell to the firm work better if they have access to anticipated needs and clients can plan better if they can obtain accurate forecasts of what outputs will be available.

What is the relation to ERP?

Although ERP is not required, it usually makes it easier to manage the supply chain because an ERP system provides much of the data needed for managing the supply chain.

What are the resistances to installing supply chain software?

The resistance to supply chain software is similar to that for other innovations. People don't like to learn new things, and fear their job will be displaced.

PROBLEMS

1. SUPPLY CHAIN PAYOFF

   Discuss the supply chain in your current firm or a firm that you worked for previously. Describe what parts of the supply chain and inventory records were automated and which were not. Suggest ways in which the supply chain could be improved.

2. MATHEMATICAL AND COMPUTER MODELS (ONLY FOR STUDENTS WITH ANALYTIC BACKGROUNDS)

   A large amount of effort in creating mathematical optimization models and simulation models is underway by firms specializing in operations research and industrial engineering. Discuss the models and the firms building and selling them.

3. VENDORS

   For four of the vendors listed in Table 2, determine the extent of their offerings of products for supply chain management. Include the products produced, the market they seek to serve, what they claim their market distinction is, and (if available) the dollar volume of their shipments.

4. REVERSE SUPPLY CHAIN

   Discuss how your company deals with returns. Frame your explanation in terms of the reverse supply chain discussed in the section on returns.

Chapter 12

The Chief Information Officer, People Issues, Project Management, Change Management

MANAGERIAL QUESTIONS

What is a Chief Information Officer?
What does he or she do?
How does the Chief Technology Officer differ from the CIO?
Are people who work in IS different than other employees?
What is the role of the IS Project Manager?
How are change management and project management related?

INTRODUCTION

Although the previous and the following chapters all pay some attention to people issues, they are principally about managing and understanding the technology of information systems. Yet, information systems involve all the people problems studied and discussed in other functional areas, be they marketing, accounting, finance, or management. In this chapter, although the problems are the same, the focus and mix of people issues are somewhat different.

The popular notion is that information systems are populated by the introspective, people-averse geeks that were outsiders in high school and beyond. That image, while true for a few, is not true in general. Yes, there are people who speak only in computer jargon and are happiest when their face is buried in a screen. They are, however, the exception rather than the rule.

This chapter is about the role that information systems people play in the organization. It describes their organization, usually led by a person with the title Chief Information Officer (CIO) who may report to the CEO or to another C-level individual. It discusses the role of the Chief Technology Officer, a person charged with overseeing the firm's technology, usually found in firms in which the CIO is not a technical expert. Because most IT initiatives involve long-term, high cost projects, the chapter considers the important role of the Project Manager in coordinating and running major efforts. Finally, this chapter considers change management, that is, the need to manage the sociotechnical effects on people that occur in an organization as a result of changes in the way people work when computer system changes introduce new tasks, technology, and structure.

CHIEF INFORMATION OFFICER

American businesses are populated by a management group, each of whom bears the title "Chief" and "Officer," whether it be the Chief Executive Officer or the Chief Operating Officer or the Chief Information Officer. Collectively, they are known as CXOs. New CXOs keep popping up all the time. Several years ago the title of Chief Knowledge Officer (Chapter 7) became popular. More recently, Chief Strategy Officer came into vogue.

Each CXO is responsible for all or a portion of the business. The Chief Information Officer (CIO for short) is no different, being responsible for all the information operations of the business.

The CIO's portfolio of responsibilities spans a broad range, including

Operations	Running the corporate information center and managing the company's computing efforts and its computing group.
Project management	Running large-scale, high cost, time-constrained projects involving acquisition and installation of hardware and software.
Technology	Determining what technologies to invest in.
Planning	Aligning the direction of IS with that of the business.

Good Chief Information Officers are a scarce talent because the holder of this position must possess credibility in both the business and the technical world. CIOs who are good at one but not the other do not survive. As it is, the half-life of a CIO is of the order of 3 to 5 years. This turnover comes from many causes, ranging from conflicts over decisions to changes at levels above them to a lack of understanding of what the role of IT is in the organization. Major problems for the CIO are managing expectations and communicating.

Managing Expectations

Managing expectations turns out to be critical for the career survival of a CIO. If the IT group doesn't deliver what other senior managers expect, the CIO's job is often on the line. The problem is exacerbated by the "seat pocket dilemma." This dilemma occurs when a senor executive travels on an airplane and, to pass the time, reaches into the seat pocket and pulls out the airline magazine. Here the under-informed executive reads about the fantastic results some other firm achieved through an IT investment. The system might be quite simple in that environment but very difficult or expensive in the firm's own. Yet, on return, the executive asks, "why don't we have one of these?"

Expectations, unfortunately, often don't meet reality. They tend to be vague and impressionistic. Most senior managers have little training or knowledge in technology, and may have avoided it in school. The expectations can be too high (in which case the CIO can't possibly meet them) or too low (in which case, even if the IT department creates great information systems, the CIO is seen as providing little but costing a lot). In general, expectations and reality don't match and fairness is not involved.

With little knowledge of what is being done, surrogate measures are used. Unanticipated outcomes, cost overruns, scope creep, and large failures are remembered. When things go right, it is assumed to be the normal state of things and little credit is given.

SIDEBAR 1	*An Experience*

I experienced the seat pocket phenomenon several years ago when the General Manager of a large, nearby aerospace division, came home after having read an airline magazine and asked why the firm did not have an executive information system (EIS) to support him and his senior staff. The situation is similar to the one where the executive walks into the plant and remarks that the paint in the ceiling looks grimy. By the next morning, a dozen painters are applying a fresh coat. In this particular case, the IT group immediately called me in as a consultant and asked how they should create an EIS to meet the request. They had neither the infrastructure nor the data they needed.

Another problem with expectations is that little attention is given to the process of approving projects. A department or IT proposes a project. The senior management decides it should be done. The Chief Financial Officer looks at the budget and slashes it.[1] Then others in the line of signatures cut or remove the budget for one feature or another or for training or quality control or consulting that goes with it. Similarly, the time to completion is chopped (that also cuts budget) because the end product is needed or wanted on a shorter timescale than proposed. The IT department is then expected to produce the original project with the funds and time left in the approved project plan.

A variant of this scenario is the one in which the time and budget are adequate, but the company's needs change between the initiation and the completion of the project. Requirements are determined at the start of the project and then frozen while the work is done. When the project is delivered (particularly for long projects), the situation is changed and IT is told "this system is interesting, but it doesn't meet our needs."

How can the expectation problem be resolved? The conventional wisdom is that a mutual feeling of trust must be achieved between the CIO and the other senior executives. Such trust requires a track record by the CIO. It also requires extensive communications among the parties involved. The CIO must keep expectations in line with what can be done.

Even here there can be problems. Where the CIO sits in the organization is important. A CIO who reports, as they often do, to the Chief Financial Officer or the Chief Accountant, finds layers between their position and that of the CEO. They receive little face time from the CEO and their boss filters all that they say. In such a position, they are expected to align IT with the business,[2] yet have little input to the strategic process.

Face time with the CEO can be important. However, some CEOs offer little face time to anyone in the organization, and the CIO is no exception. In troubled companies, the CEO (and other executives) turns over rapidly. One story is told of the CIO who worked for a firm that appointed four different CEOs in a year. She was let go by the last one, who was bringing in his own CIO. In such an environment, trust and communications are difficult to build.

CHIEF TECHNOLOGY OFFICER

Many firms appoint a Chief Technology Officer (CTO). These individuals usually take on the technology part of the CIO's job. That is, they are technically skilled people responsible for advising on technical decisions such as the selection of infrastructure hardware and software, computer systems

---

[1] That's what a CFO is supposed to do.

[2] Alignment with the strategy of the business is discussed in Chapter 2. That discussion points out that, because businesses change strategy from time to time, departments such as IS often become out of alignment when such a change occurs.

architecture, the technical design of projects, and sometimes security. The CTO is also responsible for setting technology standards and taking the visionary view, keeping track of future technologies (such as nanotechnologies) that may be of future value to the business. In such firms the CIO is responsible for the business alignment of computing, and the CTO worries about both the nuts and bolts of computing operations and the future.

It would be reasonable to assume that the CTO reports to the CIO. That, it turns out, is not the usual case. A survey by the Cutter Consortium, a research group, indicates that over 60% of CTOs don't report to the CIO but do report to the Chief Financial Officer or the CEO.

Because their responsibilities overlap to a certain extent and their objectives are different, the jobs of CIO and CTO in the same firm can create conflict. For example, they may compete for portions of the same budget. The CIO is responsible for ongoing operations and the CTO for the future. Thus, the CIO typically wants funds to keep the existing systems patched up so that the business continues to operate, whereas the CTO is a visionary who wants to create new architectures and expand the use of the Internet.

GOVERNANCE AND STEERING COMMITTEES

Although the term governance is often used synonymously with the term government, in organizations it describes the processes and systems by which a function or the firm as a whole operates.

Information systems are unique in that, in many firms, its governance involves steering committees staffed by senior people who are appointed to oversee IT. To talk about steering committees for accounting, or finance, or marketing would seem ludicrous. Yet, steering committees are common in IT. A typical steering committee helps link IT with corporate strategy, establishes priorities for scarce resource allocations, reviews IT's operations and performance, selects a new CIO when needed, and acts as a communications link between IT and other branches of the firm.

Steering committees involve both good features and bad. A good feature is that if resources are limited, the CIO can turn to the steering committee to resolve competition among departments for major projects. It should not be up to the CIO alone to make decisions arbitrarily that affect the needs of various parts of the business. For example, if a data warehouse and an ERP system are proposed but capital funds are inadequate for both, the steering committee should make the choice. Another good feature is the steering committee's communications role. Once a project is decided on, members of the steering committee can (and should) act as champions and cheerleaders of the new system, encouraging people in their own areas to make the changes needed.

WHAT DO IS PEOPLE NEED TO KNOW?

As we saw in the earlier chapters of this book, information technology can change the way a business works by introducing new classes of applications. Some, such as keeping track of payroll and recording transactions, are now mundane. Others, such as ERP and data warehousing, are still near the leading edge. To make information technology happen requires skilled people. These people may work for your firm or for firms that provide services; most likely your firm will have both insourced and outsourced functions.

In this section we discuss some of the skills that are needed, either inside the firm or outside, to make it all happen. Note that in small firms, with only a small IS staff, individual people are expected to provide multiple capabilities, whereas in large firms, several people may be available for each function.

Create Programs

Initially, the main task of IS people was to write computer programs that could be run to meet specific needs. In the days of batch processing, the mainframe computer was given programs to run one at a time. The programming task was relatively easy because most programs simply digitized tasks that were performed previously by hand. The result was stand-alone programs that did not communicate with one another. Even minor modifications to reflect changes in the business or external environment were major undertakings. Over time, a variety of programming languages and tools and a number of programming methodologies were developed to improve the process. Nonetheless, creating programs still occupies a significant portion of resources at some firms.

Even though many software packages are used, IS people still need to maintain their programming skills and keep current on new programming languages and techniques.

Manage Vendors and Outsourcers

In today's environment, companies don't create most programs on their own but buy them from software vendors or use the services of outsourcers (see Chapter 9). Here, IS people are in the role of purchaser. They evaluate the alternatives available in the marketplace and make recommendations for purchases.

Customize Programs to the Firm's Needs

Buying and installing a program is usually not sufficient to make the program useful to a firm. Most vendor programs are generic, containing many features (some of which you do not need), but missing specifics that apply to you. Therefore, in-house IT staff (or the vendor's people, hired as consultants) needs to initialize programs (as in ERP) or write additional code so that the program fits your firm precisely. The main problem with such customization is that it is a recurring rather than a onetime cost. That is, if the vendor upgrades to the next version of a program, the upgrade does not include the customizations. Therefore, additional code needs to be written each time a commercial program upgrades to a new version.

KNOW THE NEEDS OF THE BUSINESS

Programmers, being professionals, try to create the most elegant code possible. However, elegant code does not guarantee that the program meets the business's needs. IS people need to be aware of the (continually changing) needs of the business and be able to respond to them in the software that they create. As we discuss in the subsection The Role of Educational Institutions, later in this chapter, it is of great help if people in the IS group know about how a business works and are able to translate this knowledge into the needs of their own firm.

Business Processes

As part of knowing about their own firm, IS people need to know about the firm's business processes. What are the steps in recording a transaction (e.g., sales, returns, inquiries)? What are the steps in accounts payable? What are the steps in maintaining inventory? Over the years, more and more business processes become embedded in software. The IS staff responsible for the software need to know the steps in the process and must be able to make changes as business needs and regulations change.

Communicating with the User Community

The ultimate success of the IS group depends on how well they relate to the general user community in their firm. Although some aspects of this relationship are determined by how well the IS group meets schedules and budgets and keeps the firm competitive in its IT capabilities, a large part of the relationship is the result of one-to-one interactions between IS people and the rest of the firm. Here, interpersonal skills become central. And, like most technical groups, the issues are what C. P. Snow called the "two-culture problem." That is, the IS people come out of a computer culture with its own technical jargon and the rest of the firm comes out of business and other cultures. As in most two-culture situations, the technology people need to communicate in nontechnical terms since (even in these days of nearly universal computer ownership among knowledge workers) most people don't understand the computer jargon.

Part of the relationship is attitude. Where IS people view themselves as being apart from the rest of the firm, they encounter resistance. Where they see their role is to help improve the business and to assist people in their work, the relationship becomes cooperative.

Maintaining the Corporate Data

In addition to their role in programs, IS people are responsible for corporate data stored digitally. In Chapter 5, for example, we discussed data warehouses that fall within this category.

Typically, the IS group will have one or more "database administrators" whose job it is to manage the organization's databases. Among the roles involved in database administration are monitoring trends in size and activity of existing databases, planning for expanding (and contracting) existing databases and for creating new databases, enforcing standards and procedures for keeping databases accurate and backed up, making sure that only authorized people gain access to specific data (e.g., salary information), and monitoring response time so that users don't wait long if they want to gain access to specific data. Some database administrators specialize in managing the data warehouse.

Maintaining Corporate Telecommunications

Although some firms separate telecommunications from information systems, the two functions are highly interrelated. Historically, telecommunications only involved the telephone. But, with the introduction of e-mail and networks and the Internet, an ever-larger portion of the telecommunications budget goes for information systems functions. Even where telecommunications functions are organizationally separate, IS people need to know about them because of the interconnected nature of the computers.

Integrating Systems

Systems integration was discussed in Chapter 10. As the number of applications and the amount of hardware grows, so does the need for systems integration and for IS people skilled in it. Even when a company hires consultant firms to perform their systems integration work, some internal systems integration skills are needed to handle changes that occur. When consultants are used, internal people need to look over their shoulder to make sure that they perform the job properly and to retain as much of that knowledge as possible.

Managing E-mail and Internet Usage

E-mail is still a blessing and a growth industry. The blessing is the speeding of communications that makes distributed organizations possible. The growth is in the ever-increasing number of e-mails, much of which comes from increased traffic volume but also from the viruses, worms, and spam (see Chapter 15). E-mail turns out to be a favorite way of hackers sending malevolent programs to the unsuspecting. The courts ruled that, because the firm provides the storage and the programs for e-mail, it has the right to determine how its employees use it. Firms also face legal responsibilities for the content that goes over their system (Chapter 15). It is IS's role to monitor the flow and use of e-mail and the Internet and to recommend both usage and security policy. Above all, because of the importance of e-mail to the firm, IS is responsible for keeping the e-mail functioning.

The use of the Internet by employees is in the same category as e-mail. Here issues include such factors as what is being accessed (company business? private business?), what cookies are being placed on the system, and protecting the organization's website. Keeping both the e-mail and the website running is part of what IS staff does.

Managing the Firm's Web Presence

If a firm uses one or more websites to communicate with its clients, IS people work with graphic designers, marketers, and others to provide the website and to update it as needs change. If the website is used for e-commerce transactions, it is the IS staffers who make sure that the website is connected to the transaction system and that it functions 24/7 every day in the year.

Managing Computer Security

IS is responsible for managing computer security. One person acts as Chief Security Officer for the firm, with a staff that depends on the size of the firm's computing efforts. He/she worries about attempts to breach security from outside and from inside the firm. As discussed in Chapter 15, keeping the data on the computer safe involves recognizing that disgruntled employees are a likely source of disruption. Activities carried out by IS people range from developing security policies to frequent checks for security breaches to initiating and running countermeasures if an incident occurs.

Documentation, Updates, and Training

As new applications (such as programs) and policies are developed or acquired, IS people make sure that innovations and changes are properly documented and that the documentation is available. For packaged software, the vendor usually provides documentation. A more complex case is when the software is developed in-house or customized. In this case, the person who did the work or a technical writer is given the responsibility for turning out the necessary documentation. In either case, IS must make sure that the documentation reaches the end user. Similar considerations apply when software is updated.

For major upgrades and for acquisition of new software, training is usually required. The training may be given by IS people or by training department staff (if the firm is large enough) or by a combination of IS and training people. Training, if handled right, is an opportunity to overcome resistance to change by showing people how the new software can make their job easier.

MAINTAINING AND RUNNING THE COMPUTERS

The day of white-coated computer operators working in glass-enclosed, air-conditioned rooms is pretty well past. But firms still run mainframes, servers, and desktop computers, as well as peripherals such as printers and scanners. IS's role is

- to keep track of all of it,
- to keep it working through maintenance,
- to replace obsolete equipment, and to provide new equipment to meet expanding needs.

Running computer operations is a very different specialty than creating new programs. Here the focus is primarily on the hardware but also requires consideration of the software running on the computer.

Help Desk

Help desks are the place to call if a PC goes down or software crashes. Internal help desks are usually run by the IS department (although some firms outsource them). Users in the organization need someone they can talk to if they encounter computer problems. Help desks are run in two ways:

- by people in the IS staff taking turns answering the help phone,
- by people who spend their time at it full time.

The method used depends to a certain extent on the size of the desktop population.

The role of the help desk is to determine the source of hardware and software problems and then to share the knowledge they have about solutions. Companies find it useful to create a knowledge base (Chapter 7) of past failures and solutions. Such a knowledge base is targeted to specific problems that are expected to recur and is therefore used. It reduces the time for handling routine calls and, over time, builds up histories on what was tried and what worked.

| SIDEBAR 2 | *Desktop Management* |

An example of operations is desktop management, which deals with the PCs on peoples' desks and the portables that they carry around. The issues include

- inventory management: keeping track of what is owned and where it is;
- configuration management: knowing what hardware and software each unit contains;
- software distribution:[3] upgrading operating systems, security patches, and installing new software;
- fault and performance management: early warning on failures, fault correction, capacity planning;
- help desk assistance: (see above);
- security management: unauthorized changes in configuration, theft prevention, virus intrusion;
- software metering: keep track of number of licenses and of concurrent usage since firms are billed on usage.

---

[3] Software distribution can be quite labor-intensive for a firm with many personal computers because replacements are made one machine at a time. To mitigate these costs, many firms automate large portions of the process. Some upgrades, such as fixing security holes, must be done quickly for all machines. That imposes massive spikes in demand that are difficult to cope with.

ROLE OF EDUCATIONAL INSTITUTIONS

The people in IS departments typically start out with a college education in either computer science (CS) or management information systems (MIS) [also called computer information systems (CIS) and, in a few cases, information science]. Computer science departments tend to be in liberal arts or engineering schools whereas management information systems tend to be taught in business schools. Computer science tends to focus on learning to program in several computer languages and on learning the underlying technology and science, whereas management information systems programs focus on the business aspects of computing. Both talk about systems analysis, database, and telecommunications but from different viewpoints.

The outcomes of the two approaches are quite different. Computer science graduates are more technically skilled than management information systems graduates but know much less about the nature of business and its use of information systems.

A major problem is the difference in perception of what graduates should know and be able to do. Companies talk about wanting generalists who know a little about everything. However, when it comes to hiring decisions the bottom line is whether the graduate knows the specifics of the particular opening that the firm is trying to fill. Universities argue that they can't predict what specific jobs will be available (and demands for skills do change from year to year).

The situation is changing, however. A July 2003 poll by *Computerworld* of 244 IT people[4] showed that the top skills that employers said they look for are

1. Communications/people skills

2. Business skills

3. Real-world/hands on experience

4. Troubleshooting

5. Project management

6. Analytical skills

7. Integration

Five of these seven skills are part of the Master of Science in Information Systems (MSIS) curriculum[5] defined in 2000 and now adopted by several hundred schools at the master's level.[6] The only missing items are 1 and 4. Communications and people skills are notoriously difficult to teach by the age people graduate college, even at the master's level, and troubleshooting is a matter of experience. Real-world/hands-on experience is offered by most of the MSIS programs in the form of "practicum" projects in which students are organized into small teams to work on a real problem against a time deadline for a real client firm.

PROJECT MANAGEMENT

Project management is

> *"the application of knowledge, skills, tools, and techniques to project activities to meet the project requirements."*

Project Management Institute [2000][7]

---

[4] T. Hoffman, "Preparing Generation Z," *Computerworld* 37(4): pp. 41-42, July 2003.

[5] J. Gorgone et al., "MSIS 2000," *Communications of AIS* 3(1): January 2000.

[6] A revision of the MSIS curriculum is scheduled to be issued on January 1, 2006.

[7] Source: A Guide to the Project Management Body of Knowledge (PMBOK), Project Management Institute, 2000.

Much of IS work involves projects which, of course, must be managed. IS projects can range from a simple update involving one programmer to major development and installation of new software or hardware that changes a firm's capabilities.

The following are the characteristics of a project:

- Its objective is to produce a unique product or service. Before starting, the goal is defined and outputs are agreed on.

- It is temporary. The project involves a beginning, a middle, and an end.

- It requires resources dedicated to it. These resources include budget, people, software, hardware, and office or other space.

- It involves risk, particularly when undertaking tasks that were not done before.

- It should have a sponsor in the firm. That is, a person of sufficient importance in the organization who wants the project accomplished and who has the "clout" and controls the resources needed to complete the project.

In a sense, project management for IS projects is similar to that for a firm's other projects. What differs for IS projects is the strong dependence on both the technical and people skills of the Project Manager and the long history of low success in completing projects on time, within budget, and within the scope and quality originally set for them.

At one level, the numbers are truly appalling. Only around 25% of IS projects satisfy the combined criteria of time, cost, scope, and quality, while about another 25% are considered failures. The middle 50% are completed with one or more of the criteria violated. That's not necessarily bad. Forecasts for projects are notoriously bad. Scope creep (adding new tasks to the project) is endemic. Because the lead time between approval and implementation of a project is often long, solutions that appear to be correct at project initiation become irrelevant when they are completed. The realities are such that advocates tend to overpromise to obtain approval to get the project started. Things change as corporate managers, IS managers, and sponsors turn over and company policies and markets change.

IS projects run into trouble when, after the requirements are determined and the resources allocated, the IS group works on the project without consulting with the people who will use the end product. The net result is that, while the product delivered meets its specifications, the users respond with "that's not what I wanted" or "I don't need that anymore." What happened is that the IS group and the users did not communicate with one another.

Projects cannot run in isolation. Rather, they must integrate with their organization's environment and be in context. If the project is unique and designed to change the way the organization works, then it is necessary also to make changes in the portions of the organization with which the project intersects to create a new context. That, of course, implies change management, which is discussed later in this chapter.

From a management point of view, it is important to divide the project into phases and perform management reviews after each phase. An appropriate management style is to allocate resources on a phase-by-phase basis rather than all at once. The management reviews offer the opportunity to look at a project and determine whether it should be continued, modified, or terminated. At these reviews senior managers can check to see whether the project is still aligned with company needs. The reviews thus serve as points at which major revisions can be made.

Project management can and does help reduce the failure rate. However, remember that project management is not a panacea and does not always result in success.

The Project Manager

The key person in a project is the Project Manager. It is the reason we discuss project management under people issues. The requirements for a Project Manager can be daunting because the individual must meet many requirements. Table 1 shows some of the work the Project Manager does.

These job characteristics need to be complemented by personal traits which are rarely all found in a single individual. These traits include technical competence, being a good communicator and motivator, a visionary yet decisive, a supporter of team members, an encourager of new ideas, and a person who stands up to senior managers when necessary.

In a typical project, the Project Manager is responsible not only for the work of people in his or her own specialty but also for people from other disciplines. Thus, a large project may involve people from IS, from manufacturing, from engineering, from marketing, and from human relations. Part of the Project Manager's skill is the ability to work across disciplinary boundaries.

The organizational structure, be it functional, project, or matrix, determines where the Project Manager and his/her reports are located. Since projects usually involve cross-functional teams, in a pure functional organization the Project Manager has the least authority whereas an organization that is organized around projects provides the most. A matrix organization involves people who report both to their function and to the project. People working in matrix organizations typically hate the arrangement because they find it difficult to serve two masters.[8]

Whatever the arrangement, a project requires that people assigned to it actually spend time on the project. In some firms it is found advantageous to create a "team room." That is, a separate space for use by team members while working on the project. By having project members come to the team room, they have an opportunity to exchange knowledge with one another. The team room also becomes a place where the team's knowledge is stored for easy retrieval—including charts, documents, and outputs. By restricting access to the room, the team room also provides a secure place where charts and drawings can be displayed and where the project team can meet for presentations, reviews, to exchange knowledge among members, and for conferences.

The project members and the team must recognize early that a new or updated computer system implies that changes will occur in the organization and in the way that individuals work. Thus, to implement their work, project team members, led by the Project Manager, must participate in change management, which is the subject of the next section.

Table 1   SOME OF THE PROJECT MANAGER'S JOB FUNCTIONS

- Define project scope
- Develop detailed work structure
- Estimate time
- Identify and obtain needed resources, budget
- Evaluate project requirements
- Evaluate risks
- Identify interdependencies
- Track critical milestones
- Manage change control
- Report project status and participate in project reviews

[8] At least that is the experience reported to the author over the years by executive and evening MBA students.

CHANGE MANAGEMENT

Changes in information systems are a highly political and technical process. Each change in an organization's information system changes what people do and how they work. For example, if inventory changes from a paper-based system to a computer-based one, data are keyed into the computer and no longer recorded on paper files with pen or pencil. If bar codes are added, much (but not all) of the data entry is no longer required. If RFID (radio frequency identification[9]) devices are introduced, taking inventory can be done from a distance rather than by getting close to the item with a bar code reader. Thus, as each level of automation is introduced, the whole inventory process changes. Like inventory, for most knowledge workers, what they do is determined to a large extent by the capabilities of their computer system and how it works.

When a project becomes operational it introduces change and people tend to resist the change. Their reasons to resistance range from not wanting to modify what they are currently comfortable with doing to fear of being fired because the computer will replace them. People resist change in many ways. At one extreme is a labor strike, although that is rarely observed among knowledge workers. At the other extreme is putting up a series of arguments, such as "Yes, but now is not the right time," that appear to agree but really don't.

Change in an organization has much more to do with the flow of information, new business practices, and customer expectations than with the technical details of IT. Yet it is IT that most enables the changes to occur. The actual changes involve work flow, culture, and management much more than they involve technology.

Over the years, a number of people in both consulting firms and academia started understanding the need to manage change, particularly technology induced changes. The quality movement was perhaps the earliest harbinger of the need to manage change. Gradually, expertise was developed. Today, it is generally agreed that managing sociotechnical changes, for that is what they indeed are, involves task, technology, people, and structure.

Tasks. Tasks are what people do. Technology can imbed the task changes and force people to work according to the new software. When tasks are changed by technology to improve productivity, people must learn new ways of doing work. Selecting the tasks to be changed requires analyzing not only each task but also its interaction with other tasks.

Technology. Technology can promote or hamper change. When the IT people believe that technology is the only important factor, it tends to hamper change. When users criticize the change, they often blame the software rather than the concepts that it embodies that may be at fault. That is, the technology becomes an excuse for not confronting the underlying problem.

People. "Information systems increasingly alter relationships, patterns of communication, and perceived influence, authority, and control."[10] As a result, it is important to obtain buy-in from the workers whose lives will be affected.

Structure. Structure refers to creating organizational and technical infrastructure that makes the change possible.

The four areas of task, technology, people, and structure all depend on there being a vision of what needs to happen. The vision must be simple enough and compelling to people that they can

---

[9] Examples of RFID technology are Speed Pass (used to record auto tolls) and swiping a card at an Exxon or Mobil gas station to record purchases.

[10] Peter G. W. Keen, *Information Systems and Organizational Change,* Cambridge, MA: MIT Center for Information Systems Research, paper 55, 1980.

agree that the change should be made. The idea is that rather than imposing the change from the top down, the demand should come from the frontline people who are most affected.

Change can come in response to a crisis or be incremental. It can be radical and revolutionary (as was advocated by business process reengineering in the 1990s) or evolutionary. It can be opportunity based or emergent (i.e., spontaneous in response to long-range or medium-range plans).

Important actors in change management include

The Information Systems Steering Committee. As discussed at the beginning of this chapter, some firms appoint an information systems steering committee to review the activities of IS and to make decisions on prioritizing projects if resources are limited. An important function of committee members is to communicate and advocate coming changes in IT and in work practices to their constituencies and thereby smooth the transition from old systems to new.

The Project Champion. The project champion is an individual with stature and budget control in the organization who actively promotes a project. It is argued that, for a project to succeed, it must have a champion. The champion, like the steering committee, acts as an active advocate for the project and the changes it implies. Champions are usually people outside the IS department who are listened to by the people whose jobs will change.

The Training and Human Resources Departments. These departments working together with the IS department, do the work of training existing people on new systems and of hiring people with new skills if they are required.

Like all changes, technology changes need to go through three successive phases first advocated by the psychologist Kurt Lewin:

Unfreezing. If people are used to doing a job a certain way, that is, they are frozen, they first have to be convinced that there is a better way of doing the job than the way they are doing it now. This motivation for change can be the result of the promise of substantial improvement or the arguments of a charismatic leader (i.e., a champion).

Moving. This phase involves installing the change in such a way that it is accepted. It involves a well-defined objective, good communications with the people affected, a plan that provides leadership and resources, and managing the stakeholders.

Refreezing. Once the change is made, it must be institutionalized so that it becomes the way everyone works. At the beginnings of this stage, some resistance will still be present. For example, some people still keep and maintain their own customer database on spreadsheets or on card files rather than using the new corporate database. Often resistance is a desire to keep power that was lost when the new system came online. In this phase, managers need to work actively to overcome resistance to change or the people who are malcontent will stir up the rest to return to "the good old days."

The unfreezing, moving, refreezing paradigm assumes that the change is successful technically and is implemented. Of course, many things can go wrong along the way. For example, the change may fail, as was the case with many ERP systems and early data warehouses. Resistance that is not handled effectively may undercut it. It may be too little and too late.

EXAMPLE[11]

Outsourcing, particularly outsourcing of IS functions, is a major change in an organization. Many of the issues on whether or not to outsource are people issues.

On the positive side, as discussed in Chapter 9, outsourcing functions that require specialized skills but are used intermittently makes more sense than hiring full-time staff. Staffers who are transferred to outsourcers whose primary business is IT obtain expanded career opportunities. Outsourcing also reduces the number of nonperforming staffers that need to be managed or fired.

The positives are more than offset by the negatives. Outsourcing too much of IT results in losing needed skills within the organization and makes it difficult, if not impossible, to manage the outsourcer. Problems can result

if, for example, the outsourcer brings people onsite whose culture is hard driving into a company with a conflict-avoiding style or vice versa. Problems can also be created by fear in the remaining employees, many of whom start looking for ways to bail out. Finally, outsourcing involves legal problems of employment regulations, layoff notices, compensation, and benefits continuation. Advance notice of layoffs, such as an announcement by IBM that it would outsource to India, creates serious morale issues.

Most of the negatives associated with personnel issues are rarely considered in the outsourcing decision yet they must be factored in to make reasonable assessments of the savings that the change will bring.

CONCLUSIONS

Although information systems are usually thought of as technology, they are part of a sociotechnical system that involves people from throughout the organization. The people range from senior management and the Chief Information Officer at the administrative end, through the people in the IS department, to the users at the working level of the systems they create or purchase.

This chapter is written as though all IS people and functions report to the Chief Information Officer in some sort of hierarchical way. Although such organizations exist, they are not the rule. For business units of any size, people skilled in information systems perform many of the functions locally. The variations seem almost endless. For example, in some cases, the local people report on a dotted line basis to the CIO. In others, the staff is completely distributed and only a small planning staff reports to the CIO who sets the governance rules and policy the distributed people are expected to follow.

Because of the time and money required to create and install new systems, they are usually managed as projects with their own Project Manager and dedicated staff. New systems modify the way people work, which results in resistance to change. To be successful, new projects must use change management methods to overcome resistance if the system is to be considered a success.

ANSWERS TO MANAGERIAL QUESTIONS

What is a Chief Information Officer?
The title of Chief Information Officer (CIO) is typically used for the person responsible for information systems in an organization. The CIO may report to the Chief Operating Officer, the Chief Financial Officer, or other senior manager.

---

[11] Based on B. Perkins, "The Forgotten Side of Outsourcing," Computerworld, September 8, 2003.

What does he or she do?

Their job, similar to that of other people with the title Chief, is to be responsible for all aspects of their function (information systems) in an organization. People in the organization with hardware and software responsibility report to the CIO, either directly or indirectly. The CIO usually is also the person who advises senior management on which technology and applications the company should invest in and is responsible for implementation.

How does the Chief Technology Officer differ from the CIO?

Some firms create the position of Chief Technology Officer. This person usually (but not invariably) reports to the CIO, is technically skilled, monitors advances in technology, and provides the CIO (and often other senior managers) with advice on technology.

Are people who work in IS different than other employees?

People attracted to working in information systems tend to come more from a technical background, such as computer science, than a business background. They begin their career with the idea, gained in college, that computing is free. To be successful in a business environment, they require acculturation to the norms of the firm.

What is the role of the IS Project Manager?

The IS Project Manager supervises the team that undertakes a particular project. The job requires a mixture of technical skill, project management skills, and change management skills.

How are change management and project management related?

Because IS projects inevitably change the information people work with (and hence the nature of their jobs), change management is an important consideration in each IS project. Successful projects require that the people who will be affected by a project's changes buy in to it and that resistance to change is overcome early in the project development cycle.

PROBLEMS

1. CIO

   Interview the Chief Information Officer (or whoever is the head of the information systems group) or the Chief Technology Officer (if your firm has one). Prepare a report on what his or her duties are. Compare their responsibilities with those discussed in this chapter.

2. DESKTOP MANAGEMENT

   Explain how your company manages its collection of desktops and portables. If desktop management is outsourced, describe the arrangements followed. Explain how desktops are depreciated; how decisions are made on when to replace or add one or more desktops; how maintenance is handled; and how (or if) environmental conditions affect how desktops are disposed of.

3. PROJECT MANAGEMENT

   Suppose you are hiring a Project Manager (either from your existing IT workforce or from outside your organization) for a large IT project. What characteristics would be required, important and unimportant, in evaluating the candidates?

4. CHANGE MANAGEMENT

   Installation of new computer software usually involves some change management. For example, people must buy into the change and must be trained in the new system. Discuss two examples of information systems change in your organization, preferably a success and a failure. Use the change management concepts discussed in the text.

Chapter 13

Information Systems in Mergers and Acquisitions

MANAGERIAL QUESTIONS

Why merge?

What are the stages in mergers?

What are the information systems problems in mergers and acquisitions?

What are the security issues?

What are the cultural issues?

INTRODUCTION

Information technology is often a forgotten element for the people in a firm responsible for mergers and acquisitions. Because Chief Information Officers are often located at the second tier of management, such as under the Chief Finance Officer, they may have little input to the merger decision processes involved. Yet, the inability to combine the information systems of the two firms involved often leads to much poorer results from the merger or acquisition than had been hoped, and in some cases dooms the merger completely.

The purpose of this chapter is to explore the role of information systems in the merger and acquisition process. We recognize that information systems represent a one digit, not a two digit percentage of each company's expenditures. Therefore, information systems generally won't make or break a deal. However, the medium and long-term effects of a botched information systems merger can be significant (Sidebar 1).

WHY MERGE?[1]

Companies merge or acquire for a number of economic reasons, including achieving economies of scale, complementing resources, tax shelters, making capital investments, improved management effectiveness, and strategic opportunity. Savings after merger or acquisition come from eliminating redundancies in information systems and/or workforces.

---

[1] This section and the next two are based on B. Chatham, "Mergers, Acquisitions and Saving IT Dollars," *CIO,* March 15, 1998. The author was with Forrester Research, Inc.

SIDEBAR 1   *The Penn Central*

In 1968, the New York Central and the Pennsylvania railroads decided to merge. The logic was impeccable. The two railroads were both losing money. They served the same general areas, competing on many routes. The union of the two railroads should have reduced costs and made operations more efficient. The deal, first proposed several years previously, was agreed to by the Interstate Commerce Commission in 1966 and was consummated in 1968. Within 876 days, the merged railroad went into bankruptcy.

Part of the problem was financial; the management, thinking they had large amounts of cash, started buying airlines and New Mexico real estate. These deals were money losers. Meanwhile, the two railroads had very different corporate cultures, operational practices, and computer systems. The net effect was that they were not able to integrate their computer systems. The results were catastrophic. Railroad cars piled up at yards, some shipments were lost, and the merger became a laughingstock.

Unfortunately, people don't learn from mistakes, they repeat them. When the Union Pacific acquired the Southern Pacific in 1998, the same problems of culture, operational practices, and incompatible computer systems led to exactly the same operational results, even though the merged railroad did not go bankrupt.

Mergers can be classified into four categories:

1. *A Marriage of Equals*. Companies are about the same size and are in the same industry. The merger is designed to increase market share and take advantages of economies of scale.

2. *Acquisition*. One company is much larger than the other (say, twice the size) and both are in the same industry and perform similar roles. The acquisition creates a larger version of the acquiring company.

3. *Vertical Integration*. The companies are in the same industry but perform different roles. For example, a manufacturer and a distributor.

4. *Conglomeration*. Companies are in different industries and the acquired company becomes a separate division of the conglomerate.

EFFECT OF MERGER ON INFORMATION SYSTEMS

The implication of each category of merger is different from the point of view of information systems. Specifically:

In a pure merger, there is no reason for redundancies. The new IS merges both infrastructure and applications into a single organization. Some of the benefits forecast for the merger are elimination of duplication.

In an acquisition, the IS group of the acquiring company absorbs the parts of the target company it finds valuable (people, software) but typically replaces the acquired IT infrastructure.

In a vertical integration, since the two companies support different industry functions, the amount of overlap will be minimal except for administrative applications such as e-mail, office suites, and financials. The result is two linked systems with a smaller but unified staff.

In conglomeration, the two parties operate independently, and hence only a few administrative functions become common. Integration occurs through an IT council chaired by the conglomerate's CIO.

MERGER PRINCIPLES

1. *Choose One Portfolio*. The best results seem to be obtained when one of the two merging portfolios of applications is selected. It is tempting to try to pick the best technology from each firm, but this approach runs into problems. Criteria for selection include compatibility with the postmerger strategy, ability to scale to the larger firm that the merger brings, and total cost of ownership.

2. *Treat the People Well*. Don't treat the merger as the victory of one culture or one staff over the other (Sidebar 2).

3. *Spend Money to Make the Merger Happen*. Forrester claims that the average merger results in a 19% savings on the merged companies' budgets. However, in the first year, about half of that savings is lost as infrastructure costs (e.g., PCs, servers, networks) and transition personnel costs (severance packages, retention bonuses) are incurred.

4. *Bring the CIO into the Merger Discussions Early*. Forrester claims that only about a third of CIOs are involved in the merger decision process and can help plan the merger. The rest are brought in later to clean up messes that would have been avoided with the right premerger planning.

5. *Prioritize*. Select projects that involve business rules and management preferences as your first priorities. Communicate the changes to people.

THE MERGER PROCESS

Most completed mergers go through three stages:[2]

1. Strategy
2. Valuation
3. Transition

SIDEBAR 2   *Security Pacific National Bank and Bank of America*

In 1992, Bank of America acquired Security Pacific National Bank, a major competitor in California, with headquarters in Los Angeles. At the time, Security Pacific was renowned for the quality of its computer operations and Bank of America was known for a failure of its computer-based trust system. When the acquisition occurred, it was decided that each of the programs available in the two banks would be evaluated and, where there was duplication, the better of the two systems would be selected. The net effect was that, despite Security Pacific's higher reputation, only one of its programs was selected. From the outside, it appears the problem was the attitude of the acquiring company (often encountered in acquisitions) that its way of doing things was better because it was the acquirer. However, simply picking the better application suite may, in fact, not be optimal. In this particular case, one bank was much larger than the other, and the cost of conversion would have been much larger if Security Pacific's systems had been chosen.

---

[2] The stages concept is described in P. Glasser, "Secrets of the Merger Monster," *CIO,* April 15, 1999 [based on a study by E. M. Roche of Concourse Group (a consulting house) and N. Venkatraman of Boston University].

The strategy stage is like a ritual mating dance. The two firms eye each other and try to determine whether a merger or acquisition is the appropriate action. Discretion is vital. For example, if software developers and other personnel find out a merger is coming, the best of them (who are mobile) may decide to leave to avoid the uncertainties of the merger, thereby costing the firm intellectual capital and decreasing its value. However, the CIO or his/her representative needs to be at the table at this stage to make sure that the two systems can be integrated (see Sidebar 1).

In the valuation stage (also called due diligence), each function examines its counterpart in detail. In the case of IS, the readiness for merger is assessed by looking at questions such as:

- How easy or difficult will integration be? (For example, what happens if one firm has SAP and the other Oracle as its ERP system?)
- Are there opportunities for growth?
- Potential savings and liabilities.
- The effect of the merger on IT labor and on outsourcing.

At this stage, some expertise will need to be brought in and rumor control is essential. People in the negotiation may be more concerned with their own job than with the merger. Some people may need to be given guarantees on how long they will be kept and some given retention bonuses. Information exchanged includes critical applications, organization of the IT department, vendors, budgets, and current projects both in-house and outsourced The quicker the merger is completed at this stage, the better. People tend to do almost nothing while the discussions go on because they don't know which projects will be important, which will be delayed, and which will be dropped. Some of these actions are rational. For example, a project for marketing may be put on hold because no one knows what postmerger marketing will look like.

In the transition stage, the detailed decisions are made. Teams meet and make choices. The actual cutovers occur and, hopefully, the merger becomes a success.

All three stages are needed. Without planning, chaos can result.

SECURITY ISSUES[3]

Computer security issues need to be resolved in these days of viruses, worms, spyware, and worse. Computer security is more than a physical issue; it also reflects company culture. It is a risk that needs to be attended to. Even if each of the two firms' networks are secure, joining the two of them may create new risks that did not exist before.

Risks from security breaches include reputation loss, legal liability, and financial loss. The risk will differ depending on what the networks are used for. For example, the risk is greater when financial data are involved than for general administrative announcements to all employees.

Here are some indicators to looks for:

- *Attitude*. How is information handled? Is security taken seriously or is it an afterthought?
- *Security Program*. Are security responsibilities clear? Is there a budget for security? Are the people who handle security capable? Is there an effective antivirus program in place?

---

[3] Based on B. L. Murphy, "Managing Mergers and Acquisitions," *CIO,* September 19, 2002, http://www.cio.com/research/security/ed9t/091901_mergers.html.

- *Emergency Response*. Is there a credible plan in force? Is monitoring being done to recognize attacks? Was the emergency response plan tested recently?

Security is discussed further in Chapter 15.

CULTURAL CONSIDERATIONS

A merger implies that two corporate cultures as well as two financial statements become one. The two cultures may differ considerably. In Chapter 9 we discussed the outsourcing of Kodak's IT to IBM and to DEC. In the case of IBM, its top-down, centralized culture matched Kodak's. However, DEC was a decentralized, bottom-up culture and it didn't match. The long-term result was that IBM still handles Kodak's work but DEC was not renewed after its initial 5 year contract. The same considerations apply in mergers. In the case of the IS function, some are centralized, mainframe operations while others are distributed among the departments and divisions. Some IS organization are command-and-control, while others are team-oriented. Some look only at results while others are sticklers for process. Some work entirely in-house while others are totally outsourced (Chapter 9).

IS culture becomes important in a merger because the people in IS interact frequently with each other and with other functions. Whatever your IS culture, the people in the firm learned how to deal with it. Bringing in a new culture creates disturbances that require management attention.

The two case examples, below, illustrate the cultural as well as the technical problems associated with mergers.

CASE STUDY: *TransCanada Pipeline*[4]

The merger of two Canadian wholesale natural gas suppliers, TransCanada Pipeline and Nova Corp., in July 1998, was the largest in Canadian history at the time. The statistics for the merged company are shown in Table 1.

The information systems groups in the two companies at the time of merger were quite different, as shown in Table 2.

With the exception of desktop software, the companies diverged in approach (in-house vs. outsourcing), organization, and technology. The key was to meld these disparate groups into a single organization.

Russ Wells, formerly customer service vice president for Nova, was appointed Chief Information Officer. Although Wells appointed a transition team from both firms and planned to integrate the two groups after a year, rumors quickly flew that the merger plan would either outsource everything or cut the outsourcers out completely. As a result, it became necessary to integrate the groups within 4 months after the merger. A number of steps were taken. The agreements with the outsourcers were renegotiated, but service level agreements were left for future negotiation. About 100 people were transferred to an outsourcer and 40 people were brought in-house from an outsourcer. The new IS group was centralized but included four directors, one for each business area in which the merged company organized. Solution teams still lived within the business units. Commodity services (desktop, server, telecommunications support) would continue to be outsourced, as would IT resources. However, internal IT people would supervise the latter.

After 2 years, the major problems that remained involved tying down service levels and other outsourcing details that were not resolved at the beginning of the merger. For example, users were unhappy with the service levels, with IT being blamed for the performance of the outsourcers. Achievements included

---

[4] Sources: K. Melymuka, "Rules of Engagement," *Computerworld,* July 24, 2000, and C. Koch, "Russ Wells on Merging IS Departments," *CIO,* June 15, 1999.

- completing the Y2K modifications on time,
- using decision teams to choose between the two companies' existing applications,
- solving most of the communications problems with in-house and outsourcing staff, and
- only a few people leaving and no people laid off.

The first year's total IT costs exceeded the premerger expenditures, but savings of over 12% were achieved in the second year and costs were expected to decline in future years.

Table 1   TRANSCANADA PIPELINES IN 2000

Location	Calgary, Alberta, Canada
Asset base	$26 billion (Canadian)
Revenue	$17 billion (Canadian)
Net income	$425 million (Canadian)
Employees	4500
IT employees	266 internal, 600 outsourced

Source: K. Melymuka, "Rules of Engagement," *Computerworld*, July 24, 2000. Note that by 2002, as a result of divestitures of portions of the merged company to concentrate on its core business, the workforce had shrunk to 2500 and the revenue to $6 billion (Canadian).

Table 2   PREMERGER IT ARRANGEMENTS

	TransCanada PipeLines	Nova Corp.
Number of employees	250	18 plus 600 outsourced
Organization	Centralized in one group reporting to a CIO.	Distributed, with each business unit having its own IT organization. Nova was in the first year of a 7 year outsourcing agreement with two firms
Standards and architecture	Centralized	Centralized with the 18 internal employees
Desktop software	Windows NT, Office	Windows NT, Office
Infrastructure	Forte, Java, Sybase, Netscape	Oracle, Internet Explorer
ERP system	Best of breed applications	Multiyear SAP R/3 implementation

Sources: K. Melymuka, "Rules of Engagement," *Computerworld*, July 24, 2000 and C. Koch, "Russ Wells on Merging IS Departments," *CIO*, June 15, 1999.

CASE STUDY: Cingular Help Desk[5]

SBC Communications and Bell South, two giant regional telephone companies, jointly formed Cingular, the second largest wireless company in the United States, in 2000. These companies were themselves the results of mergers and acquisitions over the years. When they merged, they operated

- 60 call centers
- 1400 IT systems
- 11 major customer billing systems

[5] Source: D. Slater, "Call Together Now," *CIO*, May 1, 2002.

These assets needed to be rationalized. Service is the key in the consumer wireless business, where customers can switch relatively easily from one carrier to another.

The basic approach was to create 20 new call centers with staffs of 600 to 1200 people, located in smaller cities (Lubbock, Texas, Ashland, Kentucky) where wages are lower and where Cingular could become the employer of choice through its personnel policies. It took nearly a year to make all 20 operational. In the transition, the old systems were left online until it was clear that the new systems that were replacing them were working properly. There was a need for technical and managerial problems to be solved so that, for example, power supplies were available and telephone circuits were assigned to centers as needed. Ten thousand new employees had to be hired for the call centers. To improve call center operations, networks were put in place to allow calls to be picked up by other centers as a particular center became loaded or when knowledge about a particular query was concentrated somewhere else. At a more sophisticated level, knowledge bases (see Chapter 7) using neural network technology were installed that could search for relevant information so that operators could give answers for complex problems that were beyond simple scripts.

An inventory was taken of the 1400 overlapping software packages in use. Teams from both the business and information technology groups were then formed to recommend packages as standards for the merged organization. Trade-offs were made between functionality and cost. Their location in the life cycle was determined. The extent of revision needed to make them universal was considered. And, most important, their relevance to where the company was going over the next several years needed to be estimated.

The billing system, like the call center, is the interface with the customer and turned out to be a crucial element of the merger. Sending a bill that was wrong or could not be understood lost business. Cingular was able to get down to two billing systems within 2 years but was still a year away from a single billing system for the whole company.

IMPLICATIONS OF CASES

As can be seen from both the TransCanada PipeLine and the Cingular mergers, combining the information systems of two organizations successfully is not a trivial task. It involves extensive planning, considerable work, and considerable initial investment. The long-term payoff is actually realizing the savings anticipated from the merger or acquisition.

The conventional wisdom at this point is that merged firms do this job right by forcing the two partners into a single combined information system. Data for banking show that letting separate computer systems continue working as they did in the past generally leads to the merged companies being acquired in the future.

ANSWERS TO MANAGERIAL QUESTIONS

Why merge?

Mergers are almost always undertaken for reasons other than information systems. The parties believe that they will function better together than apart. They also believe that savings will occur because redundancies (such as in people and information systems) can be eliminated, that better market position will be achieved, or that the merger presents a strategic opportunity.

What are the stages in mergers?

Mergers go through three stages: strategy, valuation, transition. In the strategy stage the two firms try to determine whether they will be better off merged than alone. Once they answer in the affirmative, they need to determine the value of each firm so that an equitable deal can be struck. This due diligence stage is important because the partners need to understand what they are getting into. Finally, in the transition stage, the details of the merger take place and choices are made as to which systems and policies will remain and which will disappear.

What are the information systems problems in mergers and acquisitions?

It is rare that the two companies' information systems are identical or even compatible. Differences, for example, can occur in the hardware, in the software, in what is in-sourced and outsourced, in centralization versus decentralization of the IT function, in the relationships between the IT function and the user community, and in the extent to which existing systems can be scaled up to handle the work for the combined firm. Usually, a large amount of work is needed to create a single information system that can be used by the new firm. Unfortunately, the issues and costs of combining information systems are rarely considered. Examples of mergers that fail because of information systems abound. The case examples in this chapter show that, with work and with investment, information systems can be merged.

What are the security issues?

Even if both partners in a merger or acquisition operate their computer networks securely, integrating them can lead to security problems. The security of the new, larger system must be checked before it goes online.

What are the cultural issues?

Rarely, if ever, are the cultures of the merger or acquisition partners identical. As a result, attention must be paid to resolving cultural conflicts in all parts of the organization, including information systems and technology.

PROBLEMS

1. IMPACT OF IS ON MERGERS—CASE

   Find a case example of the details of a merger in which IS compatibility played a major role. Describe the case as either a success or a failure.

2. SPIN-OFFS AND SALES

   Companies often spin off a subsidiary or sell a portion of their business to someone else. For example, AT&T sold its wireless business. Conexant, in Irvine, California, first spun off several portions of the firm and then merged. Find and describe a case of the effect of managing information systems where such a spin-off or sale occurred.

Chapter 14

Work Systems and Infrastructure

MANAGERIAL QUESTIONS

What is infrastructure?
Why should I spend money on it?
What is the risk of not investing?
What is a work system?
How does information technology relate to work systems?
Is the work system the right unit to evaluate?

INTRODUCTION

In this chapter we consider two topics, work systems and infrastructure, which may seem to be quite disparate at first glance. However, they describe the two major aspects of information systems that cut across specific applications.

Work systems are the processes that a firm uses to accomplish its objectives. Examples range from recording transactions at the point of sale to maintaining inventory records, to accounting, to knowledge management, to business intelligence. The information system is built into each work system and it is really the work system that managers care about.

Infrastructure is the portion of the firm's information systems (e.g., hardware, software) that support many people in the organization and their work systems. Infrastructure supports the entire firm, rather than just supporting a particular application.

The two pieces are related. Infrastructure underlies everything in a firm's information capabilities. For example, if a firm doesn't have database hardware and software, it can't use a database (or a data warehouse) to keep track of anything, be it receivables or inventory. Work systems depend both on the available infrastructure and the software, hardware, and rules that are built for a specific application. As pointed out in Chapter 12, from a people point of view, how work is performed depends on what the technology can do and how individuals use it.

Work System

A work system is defined[1] as a system in which people and/or machines perform work by using information, technology, and other resources to create products or services. The customers may be internal or external to the firm.

To understand a work system, you have to recognize that these systems include nine components as shown in Figure 1. These components are

- Customer
- Product and services
- Infrastructure
- Work practices
- Participants
- Information
- Technologies
- Environment
- Strategies

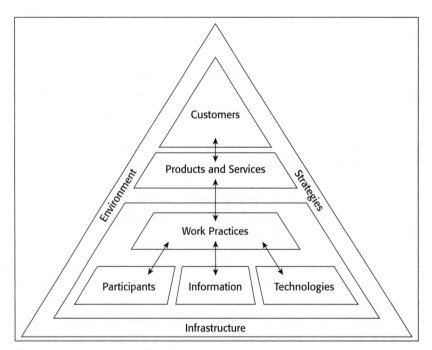

Figure 1 The work system framework.

Source: S. Alter, "18 Reasons Why IT-Reliant Work Systems Should Replace 'The IT Artifact' as the Core Subject Matter of the IS Field," *Communications of AIS* 12(23): Figure 1, p. 8, October 2003. Used by permission.

---

[1] S. Alter, *18 Reasons Why IT-Reliant Work Systems Should Replace " The IT Artifact" as the Core Subject Matter of the IS Field.* Communications of Associations for Information Systems 12(23), pp. 366–395.

Information systems, projects, and supply chains are all special cases of work systems. Work systems are discussed in detail in the second half of this chapter.

INFRASTRUCTURE[2]

Infrastructure is the hardware and the software needed to make applications run. It is also the services that are provided centrally. Because elements of infrastructure usually apply to multiple applications and are often quite expensive, the question is who is to pay for it. No one wants to pay for information infrastructure out of his or her budget. Not the departments, not the divisions, and usually not the top management. People are perfectly willing to spend resources on applications such as ERP or CRM or data warehouses because they can see the direct benefits that they will accrue. However, infrastructure is a much more ethereal thing. When a firm installs infrastructure, it is not usually clear whether what it buys will be used either in the short or long term.

Like with many capital improvements, there is a sense that it is possible to go without improvements in infrastructure another 6 months or a year before making the expenditure. (The "yes, but now is not the time" argument again.) When coupled with IS's reputation for not delivering projects on time or on budget (Chapter 12), managers fear that they are writing a blank check with unknown return. Furthermore, while IS infrastructure is only one of many claimants for capital budgets, it is often a very large and visible claimant.

What Is Infrastructure?

A broad definition of infrastructure is that it is hardware and software that supports the flow and processing of information. The *Merriam-Webster's Collegiate Dictionary* defines infrastructure as the resources (including facilities and people) required for an activity. These are only two of many definitions. What the definitions include is that infrastructure:

- is a large-scale system,
- involves a technological dimension,
- consists of physical components,
- delivers essential services that are both necessary and hard to replace.

Table 1 lists some examples of IT infrastructure. Note that, what is considered infrastructure is company dependent. Hence there are differences of opinion on whether some of the elements listed are infrastructure or not. One viewpoint is that infrastructure refers only to systems that are a pure cost. Classifications become messy for a system such as video conferencing that generates no revenue, per se, but can result in large travel cost avoidance.

Looking at Table 1, each of the infrastructure examples are systems or management processes that require expenditures that support the firm as a whole (or multiple departments), rather than an individual department or product.

---

[2] The best source on infrastructure is by P. Weill and M. Broadbent, *Leveraging the New Infrastructure,* Boston: HBS Press, 1998. Many of the ideas in this section are based on that source.

Table 1   EXAMPLES OF IT INFRASTRUCTURE

Type of infrastructure	Examples
Applications	A common systems development environment, electronic data interchange, point of sale systems, video conferencing
Communications	Enterprisewide networks, e-mail, and messaging services
Data	Data standards, data warehouse
Education	Training, help desk
Services	Mainframes, project management, managing outsourcing
Research and development	Developing new technologies
Security	Data security, software security, physical security of computer equipment, disaster planning
Standards	Enforcing IT architecture and standards

Another way of looking at infrastructure is given by Weill and Broadbent[3] who group infrastructure into:

- Commodities such as operating systems, printers, and routers
- Humans with knowledge, skills, standards, and experience
- Stable services such as shared databases, e-mail, and Internet access
- Shared applications that change slowly, such as budgeting or human resource management

Example: Telecommunications Infrastructure

Every time you pick up the telephone, send a fax or e-mail, or download from the Internet you use the telecommunications component of your company's infrastructure. Yet to most of us, unless the communications links go down, this infrastructure is almost invisible. Like the lights and the water, we take it for granted.

From a management point of view, you need to make periodic decisions about investing in telecommunications infrastructure. You are continually facing cost vs. capability trade-offs. Should you use more expensive private leased lines or public carriers? How does that affect security and privacy (Chapter 15)? Should you increase the bandwidth for your Internet connections? The more bandwidth you have, the faster your messages go out and come in. But bandwidth costs money. If you decide to outsource information systems work to India or the Ukraine, you need communications contact with them. The cost is a function of the communications tariffs to those countries, and the reliability needs to be checked. If you engage in B2C e-commerce (Chapter 3), you need communications for people to contact you via the Internet and an 800-number to call your help desk. If you do B2B e-commerce, you must be able to reach suppliers and clients via EDI or its equivalent. Adding wireless communications, be it phone or computer access, keeps salespeople in touch no matter where they are. But wireless introduces risks, adds cost, and exacerbates security concerns. The list goes on. The only favorable news is that telecommunications prices have been dropping in recent years.

---

[3] P. Weill and M Broadbent, op. cit.

The Infrastructure Portfolio

At each budget cycle (and often in between), senior managers are faced with making information infrastructure investments that will shape their firm's long-term capability to compete. Some of these investments are in response to strategic initiatives that require additional infrastructure; others are to replace existing infrastructure or to make use of new capabilities that would help the company's current position.

What the manager is really being asked to determine is whether and/or how the firm's technology portfolio should be changed. Like financial portfolios, the technology portfolio must be managed and the relation of risk to return must be balanced.

Information technology investments tend to be the largest individual investments that a firm makes. Failure to make them can result in the firm being unable to undertake specific initiatives. Yet, often the technology investment cannot be justified based only on the expected return on investment from the technology and/or the project. Here it is necessary to look at the other ways the infrastructure improvements, which are assets, can be expected to be used and to credit the project with these additional gains. On the other hand, the high failure rate for information projects (e.g., Chapter 12) introduces risk that must be factored in. The bottom line is that investment in the information technology portfolio is like any other investment that a company makes. A firm therefore needs to know how much it is investing[4] and what it expects to get back.

An Infrastructure Example

Consider a company bidding on a contract worth $50,000 that will last 3 months, and is estimated to provide a $5,000 contribution to profit. The project will require buying or leasing a heavy-duty, industrial strength color laser printer that costs $2,000. The project expects to print 6000 pages on this printer for the project. The printer, if bought, will clearly last much longer than the project and can be used for many other projects now and in the future. If charged fully to the project, it either makes the bid noncompetitive or reduces profitability. The decision, then, is whether to charge the expenditure to project or to the capital budget.

Thus far we considered only the firm's central infrastructure, which supports corporate. The business units also use specialized infrastructure. Where business units are diverse, several (or all of them) may need local IT infrastructure to manage their unit. In addition, firms buy services from public infrastructures that serve many clients. Examples are the Internet, telecommunications networks, external service providers, and industry networks. Thus, the total infrastructure portfolio includes both internal investments and purchases of infrastructure services. It is the total infrastructure that makes it possible to deal with suppliers and customers.

Because of the size of the investments and their interrelations with the short- and long-term strategic posture of the firm, investments in the infrastructure are the responsibility and challenge of senior management. Yet, senior managers are often ill prepared to undertake this task. In part this difficulty is an age phenomenon; many of the people who went to business school 25 or more years

---

[4] Determining how much is invested is not a trivial accounting task. The IS department can usually estimate the amount of investment in terms of its own expenditures. However, an information system requires expenditures around a firm such as the training department, the time learning the new system, hiring personnel who will use the new system, outplacement of redundant employees, and much more. It is the total cost that is difficult to determine.

ago simply did not take IS courses. However, even if they did, a lot happened in the interim while they were engaged in other functional areas or responsibilities. In part it is due to managers not being involved in information technology expenditures for many years. Yet the decisions about IS capital budgets cannot be delegated to the CIO or the Chief Technology Officer. Their viewpoint is often parochial to their function and to IS's own agendas, not that of the firm.

Infrastructure Architecture

Information systems people talk a lot about the architecture of their hardware and software. Architecture is a fancy word for planning. Just as your architect draws a set of plans for your new house that serve as a guide to its construction, so do computer architects draw plans for a new information system that specifies the design specifications. Common to all forms of the use of architecture is the idea that there is a set of principles and objectives that define design.

Within the computer field, architectures are defined for the computer hardware, the software, and the information, among others. Even within computer architecture, the term is used at several levels:

- the instruction set, ways of addressing, degree of parallelism,[5]
- the requirements for speed and interconnection for parts of the computer (the central processing unit, the motherboard, the memory, and the peripherals), and
- the arrangement of arrays of computers, such as clusters of machines[6] or grid computing.[7]

Just as there is no single preferred architecture for a house, there is no single architecture for infrastructure. Infrastructure grows over time. There may have been an initial plan for a firm's computing environment, but as the size and needs of the firm change and as technology advances, the architecture of the infrastructure also changes. The idea is analogous to the architecture of a house or an office complex that changes over time as new rooms or cubicles are added or areas refurbished.

Infrastructure Investment Strategies

In their book, Weill and Broadbent[8] define four ways (listed in Table 2) in which companies decide on firmwide infrastructure investment, the specific choice depending on the management objective.

In moving from "none" to "enabling" in Table 2, the investment in infrastructure increases as do the services provided centrally and the "range" and "reach" of the services. Firms can move from one view to another as their circumstances, their strategies, and their leadership changes.

No single view is considered best by all firms. Of 27 firms studied by Weill and Broadbent, 10 used a dependent view, 8 were enabling, 8 treated infrastructure as a utility, and 1 was rated as none.

---

[5] Parallel computing refers to the idea that in large computations, rather than performing computer instructions one at a time in sequence, several are done simultaneously by different computers. In practice, the multiple computers are kept working together by software that balances the loads among them. Computer clusters and grid computing (described in the next two footnotes) are examples of computing systems that use parallelism.

[6] A computer cluster is a group of locally connected computers that work together as a unit. An example is the "Beowulf" cluster that uses the Linux operating system and free software to implement the parallelism.

[7] Grid computing refers to solving massive problems (particularly in engineering and science) by making use of the unused resources (CPU cycles and/or disk storage) of large numbers of different, often desktop, computers treated as a virtual cluster within a distributed telecommunications infrastructure.

[8] P. Weill and M. Broadbent, op. cit.

Table 2 INFRASTRUCTURE OBJECTIVES, INVESTMENT VIEW, AND INFRASTRUCTURE

Name	Management objective	Investment view
None	Local independence, not economies of scale	The firm is made up of independent business units with little in common and with little control from headquarters. The firm makes a trade-off between autonomy and economies of scale in favor of autonomy.
Utility	Cost savings through economies of scale	The infrastructure is not strategic. Information technology is not strategic; rather it is viewed as an administrative cost to be reduced. Economies of scale are obtained by sharing infrastructure among business units.
Dependent	Business benefits for life of a specific strategy	Infrastructure is obtained to support specific strategies already decided on.
Enabling	Current and future flexibility	Infrastructure is an asset that can provide competitive advantage. It is OK to over-invest for current needs to gain future flexibility.

Source: P. Weill and M. Broadbent, *Leveraging the New Infrastructure*, Boston: HBS Press, 1998.

The investment strategy has implications for the range and reach of the information technology.[9]

- Reach refers to the people that can be connected through the infrastructure.
- Range refers to the activities that can be completed across a given level of reach.

Ideally, using the Internet, a firm should be able to reach anyone in the world who has a computer and suitable communications, and complete any kind of transaction or information exchange with them and their firm. With the Internet it is possible to send and receive messages even to those customers and suppliers with minimal IT infrastructure. For more complex interactions, involving multiple applications, the infrastructure needs to be able to coordinate the outputs of the applications and update all the databases involved.

Reach and range are a good way to communicate between management and IT about infrastructure capabilities. When a new strategy is proposed that requires IT in its implementation (and most of them do), then managers need to know whether the customer base for that strategy can be reached and whether the portfolio of infrastructure and applications needed to implement the strategy are available. If they are not, investments need to be made and rollout schedules adjusted. Honest assessments need to be made. Often significant challenges exist and they can't be swept under the proverbial rug.

Making Infrastructure Investment Decisions

As indicated in the previous section, infrastructure investment decisions should reflect the organization's strategy. They also depend on the existing infrastructure. Since both opportunities and investments can be large and their outcomes are not certain, senior management needs to be involved.

---

[9] Peter G. W. Keen defined the concepts of range and reach in his book *Shaping the Future: Business Redesign through Information Technology,* Boston: Harvard Business School Press, 1991.

As indicated earlier in this section, costs are usually better known in advance than benefits, which are often intangible. Cost estimates tend to be on the low side because information projects are exposed to both scope creep (adding features, changing objectives) and unanticipated overruns as projects prove more difficult than anticipated. Cost estimates for outsourcing may seem firmer because contracts are involved, but outsourcing projects require exact specification beforehand (difficult to do) and cannot be changed in midstream when business needs change. Information technology decisions tend to become political because implementing a project can change the way work is done, with concomitant winners and losers.

Choosing an infrastructure is the result of choices and trade-offs. The objective is to find infrastructures that are compatible with the firm's strategy, offer the possibility of strategic advantage, and hence are hard to copy by competitors.

In appraising choices, standard investment techniques such as discounted cash flow, payback time, or breakeven analysis are used. However, these methods generally assume that the cash flows (e.g., expenditures, returns, savings) are known precisely. Since that is rarely the case, some subjective judgment often needs to be applied. In general, business managers should make these judgments.

The subjective measures often include the "risk of not investing" (RONI), that is, the expected loss if an investment is not made. A classic example is computer security, including protection of assets, defense against hackers and viruses, and business continuity. As indicated in Table 1, security is a form of infrastructure. Examples of investments in security offering a positive ROI are believed to be few. However, failing to invest in security usually exposes the firm to unacceptable risks. The management decision then becomes not whether to invest in security or not, but on which threats to counter, how much to invest, and when to make the investment.

Infrastructure Capabilities[10]

How much infrastructure does your firm need? Although the needs are situational, it helps to know that there are certain trends. Basically, on average more infrastructure is provided by firms that change products quickly, try to gain synergies among their business units, plan information and technology needs together, and track the implementation of long-term strategies. Conversely, less infrastructure is provided if a firm is in manufacturing rather than finance or retail or when resource investments are based primarily on current needs.

WORK SYSTEMS[11]

At the beginning of this chapter we defined a work system as one in which people and/or machines perform work by using information, technology, and other resources to create products or services for internal or external customers. To understand a work system, you have to recognize that these systems include the nine components shown in Figure 1.[12]

---

[10] The data in this section are based on M. Broadbent et al., "Firm Context and Patterns and IT Infrastructure Capabilities," Proceedings of International Conference on Information Systems, Cleveland, Ohio, December, 1996.

[11] This section on work systems uses, with permission, copyrighted material originally published in Communications of the Association for Information Systems, "Sidestepping the IT Artifact, Scrapping the IS Silo, and Laying Claim to the IS Organization," Volume 12, Article 30 by Steven Alter, Professor of Information Systems at the University of San Francisco, 494–526.

[12] The nine components shown in Figure 1 are customers, products and services, work practices, participants, information, technologies, infrastructure, environment, and strategies.

Typical business organizations contain work systems that procure materials from suppliers, produce products, deliver products to customers, find customers, create financial reports, hire employees, coordinate work across departments, and perform many other functions.

Organizations are best viewed as consisting of multiple work systems. The concept of work systems applies to organizations whether or not IT is involved. The work system concept is broader than IT since it examines how IT fits into what the organization does. Thus, IT is a subsystem that provides IT infrastructure (discussed in the previous subsection), the software for the work system, and the human interfaces that employees use to do their work.

Work systems can be thought of in both a static view of a current (or proposed) system in operation and a dynamic view of how a system evolves over time through planned change and unplanned adaptations. The static view was shown by the framework in Figure 1. This framework describes the system being studied, identifying problems and opportunities, describing possible changes, and tracing the likely impacts as those changes propagate to other parts of the system. As used in Figure 1, the term "work practices" covers both business processes (prescribed sequences of related steps) and other activities that occur within work systems but are not well described as business processes. Such activities include communication, nonsystemized decision making, sense making, improvisation, work-arounds, and exception handling.

Managers (and IT people) in discussing the nine elements of a work system should avoid focusing solely on information needs, computerized information, or IT. They should also avoid focusing solely on an idealized work flow or business process, ignoring the deviations from prescribed methods that occur frequently because of errors, exceptions, and work-arounds motivated by personal incentives. Instead, they should view all elements of the work system in terms of what happens in reality.

The dynamic view is based on the work system life cycle model (Figure 2), which shows how a work system may evolve through multiple iterations of four phases.

Note that work system is a general case of systems operating within or across organizations. Special cases of work systems include information systems, projects, value chains, supply chains, and totally automated work systems. Most properties of work systems also apply to the special cases.

The purpose of most information systems is to support one or more work systems. Although information systems and the work systems they support were often quite separable decades ago when most business computing was still card-based and batch-oriented, today many important information systems overlap significantly with the work systems they serve. In extreme cases such as highly automated manufacturing, the information system and work system overlap so much that the manufacturing is largely controlled by the information system. Turn off the information system and this type of manufacturing grinds to a halt.

Fundamental Concepts of Work Systems

This subsection discusses each of the elements of the work system framework presented in Figure 1. The framework defines the nine elements that should be included in even a superficial understanding of a work system (which might be an information system or a project in an organization). In Figure 1, the trapezoid surrounding the work processes, participants, information, and technology indicates that those four elements constitute the system performing the work. The work system's outputs are the products and services received and used by its customers. Including the products and services and the customers in Figure 1, even though they are not part of the system, reflects the notion that a work system exists to produce outputs for its customers. Regardless of whether a work system is operating consistent with its initial design or its formal documentation, it is not fully successful unless it generates products and services the customers want. The framework also includes the related infrastructure, environment, and strategies that are outside of the work system because any system's operation and success depends to some extent on external factors beyond the direct control of its participants and managers.

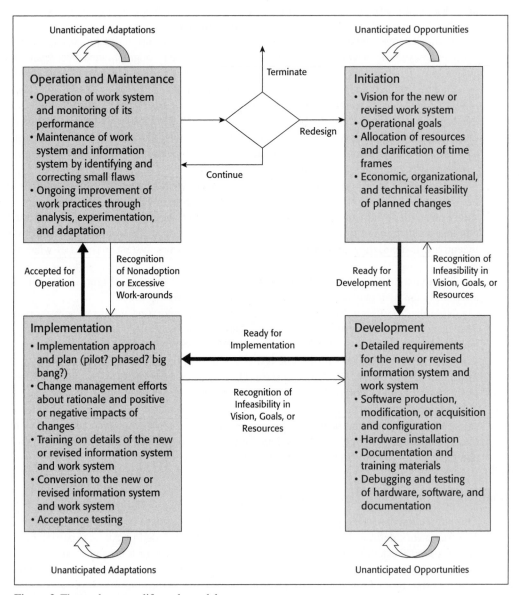

Figure 2 The work system life cycle model.

Source: S. Alter, "18 Reasons Why IT-Reliant Work Systems Should Replace 'The IT Artifact' as the Core Subject Matter of the IS Field," *Communications of AIS* 12(23): Figure 2, p. 9, October 2003. Used by permission.

1. *Customers*. Customers are the people who receive, use, and obtain direct benefits from the products and services produced by the work system. They may include both external customers who receive the organization's products and/or services and internal customers inside the organization.

2. *Products and Services*. Products and services are the combination of physical things, information, and services that the work system produces for its customers. The work system exists to produce these products and services.

3. *Work Practices*. Work practices are the set of work steps or activities performed within the work system. These steps may be precisely defined in some situations or relatively unstructured in others. In some situations, the same steps may be performed differently, based on differences in the participants' skills, training, and interests.

4. *Participants*. Participants are the people who perform the work steps in the business process. Some participants may use computers and information technology extensively, whereas others may use little or no technology.

5. *Information*. The specific information used by the participants to perform their work. Some of the information may be computerized, but other important information (such as unstructured information in a report) may never be captured on a computer.

6. *Technology*. Technology includes the hardware, software, and other tools and equipment used by the participants while doing their work. The technology considered to be within a work system is dedicated to that system, whereas technical infrastructure is technology shared with other work systems.

7. *Infrastructure*. Infrastructure, discussed at the beginning of this chapter, is shared human, informational, and technical resources that the work system relies on even though these resources exist and are managed outside of the work system. Infrastructure typically includes human infrastructure such as support and training staff, information infrastructure such as shared databases, and technical infrastructure such as networks and programming technology.

8. *Environment*. Environment is the organizational, competitive, technical, and regulatory realm within which the work system operates. These external factors affect the system's performance even though the system does not rely on them directly to operate.

9. *Strategies*. Strategies refer to the overall organizational direction set by management. Work systems are affected by strategies because strategies determine the products, services, and customers the firm will pursue. Thus, for example, work systems for back-office operations such as billing, will differ for a manufacturer with less than 50 distributors as customers than for a direct sales manufacturer such as Dell dealing with hundreds of suppliers and hundreds of thousands of customers.

Relations among the Concepts

Note that the term "work system" is different than a business process, business function, organization, and other terms commonly used to describe business operations. A work system is smaller than an entire organization or business function because organizations typically contain multiple work systems and operate through them.

A work system is larger than a work practice because it explicitly includes the participants, the information, and the technology. Looking at the entire work system does not diminish the importance of the work process, which is viewed as the core of the work system. Considering the entire work system is useful, however, because the same work practice can be performed with drastically different levels of efficiency and effectiveness, depending on who does the work and what information and technology they use. For example, the best programmers are many times more productive than mediocre programmers.[13] The same may be true of the best salespeople, fashion designers, and athletes. Just as different participants usually produce different results when performing the same work practice, different (or better) information or technology can affect the results generated by a business process.

Looking at the entire work system also helps in seeing whether the work practices actually operate as they were designed. In some cases the difference between the idealized practice (how it was designed) and the work that actually occurs (the real work practice) stems from a mismatch between the idealized practice and the participants. For example, a website user who is both the customer and a participant in a self-service process may be unable or unwilling to follow the designer's intentions. Aside from serving people with different knowledge levels, the site might also need to support different work practices related to different goals for using the site.

> *Customers*. Although every work system should have at least one customer, many work systems involve both internal customers (within the enterprise) and external customers. Even the term customer involves some ambiguity, however. In addition to the people who directly use or benefit from the products and services, "customer" is sometimes construed to include other stakeholders, especially people who do not receive or use the products and services but do authorize or pay for them.

> *Products and Services*. What term(s) should denote the outputs produced by a work system? The term "output" contains too many connotations related to computers. If the product went to an external customer, it might be considered an "offering" but offering didn't seem satisfactory for internally directed work systems.

> *Participants*. Participants are the people who perform the steps in a work practice. It is not clear whether the managers of the organizational unit should be included as participants because managers may not perform business process steps. The term participant was chosen instead of "user" because business process participants have different roles, some of which may not involve technology use at all. Furthermore, from a participant's viewpoint, issues about being a user of a particular technology are only a subset of the issues about being a participant in the work system. In many cases, issues about being a user of a particular technology are minor compared to work system factors such as the organization and management of work, working conditions, and incentives.

> *Information*. Based on the frequently cited distinction between data and information, one might wonder whether data or information are the fundamental concept. Data might be the fundamental concept for a computer scientist looking at how computer programs process data, but information is the fundamental concept within a work system because the information cited is actually used or created by the work practice; irrelevant data is therefore not included in the description of the work system. The information might include hard information (precisely defined, often computerized) or soft information (poorly defined, typically noncomputerized, but often important).

> *Technology*. The concept "technology" includes information technology and any other technology that matters within the work system. For example, in the widely publicized Denver International Airport baggage system fiasco, part of the technology is the physical methods for moving baggage between locations in the airport.

---

[13] E. Yourdon, *Decline and Fall of the American Programmer*, Englewood Cliffs, NJ: Prentice-Hall, 1992.

Example: Budget Planning

Consider a firm undertaking its annual budget planning cycle. It uses a budget planning software package to record inputs, to consolidate budget numbers, and present outputs to managers throughout the organization. Table 3 shows the interpretation of budget planning in work system terms.

Table 3   WORK SYSTEMS ANALYSIS OF BUDGET PLANNING

Elements of a work system	Elements of the budget planning work system
Work practices	Budget planning involves two work processes: The formal enterprise budget planning process and Institutional budgeting policies, rules, and practices
Participants	The budget process in most organizations involves inputs from employees throughout the firm. Some are users of the formal budgeting programs; others communicate inputs through e-mail memos and other means that are not part of the computer-based budgeting system.
Information	Budgeting depends on the information available to the firm (such as staffing and skill levels, sales forecasts, project proposals, economic conditions) and its objectives. Much of this information changes from month to month without changing anything about the structure of the computer-based budgeting system.
Technology	Technology is the budget planning software. Unless specifically dedicated to budgeting, other hardware and software (e.g., Microsoft Excel) would be part of the infrastructure.
Products and services	The budget planning work system exists to produce a corporate budget. Other products of that IT-reliant work system include documentation of the budget, verbal agreements, and greater understanding of the rationale for the budget.
Customers	The customers of budget planning include the department managers whose budgets are being determined and other managers and stakeholders who may be affected directly by the outcome or may have some other stake in it. Some, but not all, of the customers are also participants in the work system.
Environment	Environment includes the organizational, cultural, competitive, technical, and regulatory environment within which the budget and planning work systems operates.
Infrastructure	Infrastructure is resources shared across different work systems and typically owned and managed outside of those work systems. PCs, LAN, and database software can be considered part of technical infrastructure or part of the technology within the work system depending on how they are used.
Strategies	Both corporate and work system strategies are relevant to the budgeting work system because strategies designed into the work system should be consistent with corporate strategies. For example, if the corporation has a strategy of extremely rapid response to external conditions, then the budgeting system should operate consistent with that strategy.

Source: S. Alter, "Sidestepping the IT Artifact, Scrapping the IS Silo, and Laying Claim to "Systems in Organizations," *Communications of the Association for Information Systems* 12, pp. 517–518, 2003. Used by permission.

Example: Project Management

Building and maintaining a work system (or information system) can be viewed as a project in an organization.[14] Work system projects, particularly those that generate behavior change mostly through influence, power, and reorganization and those in which the behavior change can occur only after acquiring or developing substantial information and physical resources, go through four phases:

1. **Initiation.** Define the need to change an existing work system. Identify the people who should be involved in deciding what to do. Describe, in general terms, how the work system and any related information systems should operate differently.

2. **Development.** Build or acquire and configure hardware, software, and other resources needed to perform both the required IT-related and non-IT-related functions.

3. **Implementation.** Make a new work system operational in the organization. This phase starts from the point when development is complete and the system is installed and tested. It ends at the point when the new work system is truly operational.

4. **Operation and Maintenance.** The ongoing operation of the work system. Includes efforts to enhance the work system and related information systems and to correct bugs.

The four phases (or their synonyms) apply to a wide range of situations including major planned changes in organizations, moving to new work sites, creating e-business applications, major modifications of legacy information systems, selection and installation of vendor-supplied application software, and end-user development projects. When used in relation to information system projects (a special case of work system projects), this common denominator, which covers all work system projects, can help in comparing different approaches for system design, system testing, cutover, acceptance testing, and so on. For example, starting with a common denominator helps in understanding how terms such as "requirements" might be treated in many different ways. They might be determined and recorded formally in the typical methods prescribed for creating an information system, modifying an information system, or selecting a vendor package; they might be implicit, as in development through prototyping without ever defining an explicit requirement; or they might be nonexistent, as in selecting a software package without doing a complete analysis and just hoping it fits.

One level of detail greater than the four phases are the items listed in Table 4 that reflect specific actions with respect to the work system. The first several deal with the entire work system while the rest are associated with a specific aspect of the project, such as the business process or information that is used.

Table 4 SPECIFIC ACTIONS FOR THE PROJECT WORK SYSTEM

Project plan	One of the first products produced in the project, the project plan is especially important for achieving project goals related to cost and schedule. The project schedule is part of the project plan.
Project budget	The staff time and direct and indirect expenses that the project is expected to consume.
Anticipated benefits	Project costs are included in the project budget, but the anticipated benefits are an important part of the rationale for doing the project.
Project justification	The formal or informal statement explaining why the project should be undertaken. It considers such factors as costs, benefits, risks, and the project plan.
Sponsor	A special type of customer that funds the project but may not be directly involved in the use of the output (unlike most other work system customers).
Deliverables	The completion of deliverables marks the completion of major steps identified in project plans
Critical path	The critical path is the set of tasks whose timing and interdependencies determine the earliest time the project can be completed.
Analysis	The analysis effort to understand the current situation.

[14] See Chapter 12 for a discussion of projects from an IT point of view.

Design	The design effort related to how the new work system will operate, what tools are needed, and exactly how those tools should be configured for the work system to operate as desired. Analysis and design are sometimes done simultaneously and sometimes in sequence, but it seems appropriate to separate them because both need to be done.
Debugging	Part of the business process in almost any work system project should include identifying and fixing design errors and other errors that occurred earlier in the project.
Conversion/cutover	The actual change from the previous way of doing the work to the new way of doing the work.
Outsourcing	Most work system projects encounter issues about what should be done by the group in charge of the project and what should be outsourced to other groups inside or outside of the enterprise.
Requirements	How the new work system and each of its components should operate. The requirements may exist in many forms and with different degrees of formality.
Inertia	The tendency for an organization to continue doing things the way they are currently being done or were done in the past. Overcoming that inertia is often a key challenge.

Infrastructure. Infrastructure includes technical infrastructure, information infrastructure, and human infrastructure. The distinction between technology within the work system and technical infrastructure is admittedly hard to pinpoint because different people define the boundary differently. Explicit inclusion of external infrastructure is usually important because the operation of most work systems relies on technology, information, and human services that are external to the work systems themselves. For example, technical infrastructure such as the Internet is essential for the operation of an e-commerce work system even though it is not owned or controlled by the work system participants or their managers or their organization.

Environment. Environment is everything that matters enough even though it is outside of the work system and does not contribute directly to the work system's operation. The importance of the environment runs throughout the frequently cited story of the Challenger disaster, in which a rocket launch was not called off even though engineers knew that subfreezing ground temperatures might cause catastrophic failure of a critical component. The environment also included funding disputes, delays, and political pressures that influenced the launch decision.

Technical Considerations for IS Work System Projects

The list in Table 4 applies to projects in general. For information systems projects, a number of additional considerations apply principally to these specific systems:

User Involvement. As with the term user, the term user involvement takes on many meanings. For example, Ives and Olson,[15] identified six different levels including no involvement, symbolic involvement, involvement by advice, involvement by sign-off, involvement by weak control, involvement by doing, and involvement by strong control. The "user" in these various levels of involvement might include people who work directly with the technology or information and managers who are not direct users. Regardless of its many meanings, user involvement is fundamental because it is almost always an important issue in information system projects.

---

[15] B. Ives and M. Olson, "User Involvement and MIS Success: A Review of Research," *Management Science* 30(5): pp. 586–603, May 1984.

Internal Design vs. External Design. For information system projects it is necessary to distinguish between external design (what the information system will look like to users) and internal design (how it operates internally).

Documentation. While work system projects sometimes require careful documentation, documentation is an important deliverable of almost any project that creates or modifies an information system that will survive over time.

Programming. Programming creates, modifies, or configures the software needed prior to the implementation of the information system in the organization.

Unit Testing vs. System Testing. For an information system project, debugging is often more complicated because program modules[16] must be tested and then the entire computerized part of the information system must be tested as a system to make sure that the modules operate correctly together.

Software Change Control. Information systems that include a large number of computer programs written and modified by different people at different times use formal methods for checking out source code, verifying changes, checking in the modified code, and tracking the changes.

Acceptance Testing. Formal acceptance testing occurs in some implementations, and others would probably benefit from it.

Programmers, Analysts, Technical Writers, Trainers. These four job roles are common for the people involved in information system projects.

Test Data. Testing of programs and entire information systems requires test data, particularly for complex programs.

Database Management Systems (DBMS). Most information system projects use DBMS to keep track of the operational data.

Programming Tools. The efficiency of programming depends partially on the programming tools that are available.

ANSWERS TO MANAGERIAL QUESTIONS

What is infrastructure?

Infrastructure is the hardware and the software needed to make applications run, particularly applications shared by many people in the organization belonging to different strategic business units (SBUs) or departments. It also includes IT services, such as e-mail, help desks, and equipment maintenance that are provided centrally.

Why should I spend money on it?

Because elements of infrastructure usually apply to multiple units and are often quite expensive, units within the organization are naturally reluctant to pay for it out of their own funds. It is also often difficult to show a return on investment. Unfortunately, for infrastructure, what is everyone's responsibility can become nobody's responsibility. However, by examining its portfolio of infrastructure investments and by trying to align its infrastructure with its strategic plan, it usually becomes evident to a firm where its infrastructure is behind the competition and where investments can lead to strategic advantage or satisfy a strategic necessity.

---

[16] Most programs are designed modularly; that is, they consist of subprograms that have specific inputs from, and outputs to, other modules. Some modules can be reused from one program to another.

What is the risk of not investing?

Infrastructure is a clear case of the risk of not investing (RONI). If needed elements of infrastructure are not provided and then kept up to date, it becomes difficult for an organization to do its work. The firm loses competitive position and tends to fall further and further behind.

What is a work system?

At the beginning of this chapter we defined a work system as a system in which people and/or machines perform work by using information, technology, and other resources to create products or services. The customers may be internal or external to the firm.

The tasks in organizations are organized into work systems, be they selling product, deciding on and placing advertisements, customer relationship management, building specific products, recording orders, shipping goods, or creating financial consolidations.

How does information technology relate to work systems?

In today's workplace, almost all work systems involve use of information technology. However, the converse is not true. That is, the mere existence of an information system does not create a work system because work systems include the people, the procedures, and the physical movement of paper and products. In short, most information systems are embedded within work systems.

Is the work system the right unit to evaluate?

Given the ubiquity of work systems and the embedded nature of work systems, the appropriate criterion for measuring whether goals were achieved in implementation is at the work system level. If the information system fails, the work system likely will also fail; however, examples abound where the information system succeeded but the work system failed for reasons unrelated to the information system.

PROBLEMS

1. WORK SYSTEMS COMPARED TO OTHER WAY OF DESCRIBING THE ROLE OF INFORMATION SYSTEMS

   Alter's view is that information technology should be evaluated in terms of its contribution to improving work systems within the organization. Develop one or more alternative ways of thinking about the role of IT in the organization. Compare the alternatives to the work system concept. Use standard books and magazine articles to support your argument.

2. INFRASTRUCTURE

   Create a catalog of the shared infrastructure in your firm that you use to do your work. Explain how it is funded. Look at issues such as chargeback (the allocation of costs to business units or projects) for services. If specific infrastructure is provided that is used solely by your work group or your project (e.g., a CAD or CAM system), discuss how the infrastructure was obtained and how it is managed.

3. INFRASTRUCTURE AVAILABILITY

   The infrastructure available in most organizations often lags the state of the art, in part because infrastructure rarely has a champion. Consider the infrastructure available in your organization. Determine when each major component of the infrastructure was last updated (e.g., when was the Internet made available for general use). Evaluate the elements of the current infrastructure with current standards in your industry. Are you a leader or a laggard?

Chapter 15

Privacy, Security, Copyright, Patents, and Other Legal and Ethical Issues

MANAGERIAL QUESTIONS

How does privacy affect my business?

What are the risks and the rewards?

What risks and threats do I face from outside if my computers are not secure?

What risks and threats do I face from inside if my computers are not secure?

How much should I worry about disaster recovery?

How do the HIPAA and Sarbanes–Oxley legislation affect my computer resources?

How is copyright and patent law being used?

What is UCITA about and what can it do to me?

Are there special legal and ethical considerations for e-business?

How should I set policy for e-mail use? For Internet use?

What other legal risks do I run?

What ethical risks do I run?

INTRODUCTION

This chapter is about the legal and ethical aspects of computing. Studying for an MBA introduces you to the many hazards that the businessperson faces in the law and the ethical minefields that they must traverse. Most of these hazards apply in computing as well. However, a number of additional issues come to the forefront because your firm is involved in computing. It is the aim of this chapter to introduce you to these issues.

Most if not all customers are like the legendary Swedish movie star, Greta Garbo, best known today for her famous line "I vant to be alone." Each person's view of privacy differs. However, most people believe that in a democracy what they do is their own business. This attitude differs from that of firms who would like to know as much about customers as possible so that they can determine, for example, what to sell them and whether they are a credit risk worth taking.

The opposite side of the coin is computer security. Just as consumers don't want to give companies data about themselves, companies don't want to give access to their data to anyone and everyone. Furthermore, just as they protect their physical assets and their goods, firms want to protect their intellectual assets such as, for example, customer lists. They realize that outsiders, such as hackers, can wreak havoc with their digital information to such an extent that the firm cannot function for a period of time. Thus, security from invasion of privacy is important, but of course it is not cost free.

Copyright, patents, and trade secrets can protect information and processes. These approaches (which differ from one another) are defenses against competitors or consumers copying or adapting your firm's intellectual property. The law is a two-edged sword here. On the one hand it can protect what you have. On the other, others can use it against you. An example is the attempt to pass UCITA, legislation that would give software vendors the right to change the terms of licenses at will and would allow vendors to go into a corporate (or personal) computer and remove software.

In this chapter we will deal with each of these issues. In addition, we will deal with the ethics of computing. Just as the early 2000s saw revelations of unethical accounting practices, computing has been dogged over the years by ethical issues. The ethics of computing in many ways are extensions of business and personal ethics. Yet, the capabilities of computers, and the issues of privacy, security, and the law each affect ethics as well.

The issues discussed in this chapter could easily fill several volumes by themselves. Therefore, we will discuss only some specific examples to provide a feel for what the shouting is about and what managers must be aware of.

PRIVACY

"You Have Zero Privacy Anyway."

Scott McNealy, CEO of Sun Microsystems

The desire for privacy comes in a variety of forms:

- The Greta Garbo customer who wants to be left alone.
- The employees who do not want their e-mail read by their superiors.
- The company that does not want the government to subpoena their computer data.
- The consumers who do not want their e-mail address made available for spam.[1]
- The people who put their money in unnumbered Swiss bank accounts.

Personal Level

Personal privacy refers to the idea that what is on your machine is your business and no one else's. Although a simple principle, it creates a large number of issues when implemented.

---

[1] Spam refers to unwanted e-mail, typically containing advertising that is equivalent to a cold sales call.

SIDEBAR 1   *Personal Privacy and Your PC*

At the personal level, if you own a PC, this principle states that you should have absolute rights to what you put on it. Yet, even though the principle is simple, a series of issues need to be examined. Here are some of them:

- What if the material is about an illegal act? Is the right analogy that keeping an incriminating note on your computer's hard disk is the same as keeping paper notes of the same information? The courts argue that the analogy is correct.
- Is the right to privacy on your e-mail as sacred as your right to privacy for first class mail? Many corporations do not think so, arguing that the computer equipment and software that you use to receive or store the e-mail is their property. The government and the courts back up the organizational view. They read the law as being quite explicit in stating that companies own the mail sent or received on the firm's computers.

- Can your Internet service provider (ISP) censor your e-mail? Should they delete spam for you?
- Your visits on the Internet can be tracked and often are. Technology, known as "spyware," can be imbedded in very small spaces (the size of a period on your screen). Should such tracking be legal?

SIDEBAR 2   *Contents of Typical Information in a Privacy Statement*[2]

1. What information is collected at the website that identifies the individual customer.
2. What information that is collected about an individual person is shared with third parties.
3. What organization and/or who collects the information.
4. How the information is to be used.
5. With whom the information collected may be shared.
6. What choices are available to the users about collecting, using, and distributing the information.
7. What security procedures are used to ensure against losing, misusing, or changing the information collected.
8. How users can correct any inaccuracies in the information.

Privacy Statements

Most websites now contain "privacy statements." These statements are a set of rules in which the firm assures consumers (be they business or individuals) that their data will not be (or will be) used for any purpose other than within the company. These statements are in a state of flux, as some companies try to give absolute assurances of privacy while others try to get enough wiggle room so they can share the data with their branches, subsidiaries, or suppliers or can sell the data. It is the latter to which consumers object.

---

[2] Based on Model Privacy Statement (www.truste.org/webpublishers/pbu_modelprivacystatement.html).

Item 6, for example, refers to whether the policy is "opt-in" or "opt-out". In an opt-in policy the customer must specify that the website owner is given permission to use the information and for which purposes. When carried to its extreme by some companies, all customers have to opt-in to receive any communication from the company. In opt-out, the website owner maintains the right to use the information for any purpose; including selling it or giving it to others unless the customer specifically asks that the information not be disseminated. Costs are incurred in both cases. In the opt-in mode, lists of permissions must be kept; in the opt-out mode the names of the people who opt-out must be kept and, if people can opt-out at various levels, which information can be shared and which cannot.

Surveillance

RFID

Technology now makes it possible to track people and goods more efficiently than in the past. An example is RFID (radio frequency identification) technology. This technology is exemplified by the devices that people put on their windshields to pay tolls. The technology solves problems of needing toll takers, the honesty of toll collection, and maintaining tollbooths. The driver does not need to carry change or to stop at the tollbooth. However, a driver's movements can be traced as they move from place to place.

SIDEBAR 3   *RFID Technology*

RFID technology is composed of four major components:

1. *E-Tags*. These electronic radio frequency tags are essentially tiny computers (smaller than a "D" on a penny). They are tiny, lightweight, and cheap (predicted to eventually be less than 5 cents for a basic tag). They can be easily and invisibly embedded in most product packaging, clothing, or parts. Tag readers, based on cellular technology, can scan products as needed so that a system can identify what products are located in a particular physical space. Unlike bar code scanning, line of sight is not required and readers can deal with hundreds of tags at the same time.

2. *Electronic Product Code (EPC)*. New universal standards will identify individual product items (e.g., cans of soft drinks) uniquely through an EPC. This new naming scheme, based on a 96-bit code, will enable identification of 1.5 quintillion objects. Additional information about the product will reside on a server accessed through the EPC.

3. *Object Name Service (ONS)*. Based on its EPC, an item can be associated with one or more networks either on the Internet or a virtual private network where information about it resides.

4. *Physical Markup Language (PML)*. This standard is used to describe product items.

SIDEBAR 4 *Cookies*

The World Wide Web is built on a very simple, but powerful premise.

- Everything on the Web is formatted in a common computer language called HTML (Hypertext Markup Language),
- All information requests and responses conform to a standard protocol.

The user requests information when accessing a Web address (i.e., a server on the Web). The Web server responds to the request and sends an answer back. The user's browser displays the information received on the screen.

When answering, Web servers also generate pieces of information (the cookies) that are stored in the user's computer, ready for future access. For example, cookies allow personalizing Web search engines and storing lists of items a user looked at while browsing through a virtual shopping mall.

Essentially, cookies make use of user-specific information transmitted by the Web server onto the user's computer so that the information might be available for later access by that or other servers. Usually, storing personal information into a cookie goes unnoticed as does access to it. Web servers automatically gain access to relevant cookies whenever the user establishes a connection to them by typing in a URL.[3]

Cookies are based on a two-stage process. First the cookie is stored in the user's computer without the user's consent or knowledge. For example, with customizable Web search engines like My Yahoo!, a user selects categories of interest from a Web page. The Web server then creates a specific cookie, which is essentially a string of text containing the user's preferences, and it transmits this cookie to the user's computer. The user's Web browser, if cookie-aware, receives the cookie and stores it in a special file called a cookie list. This process happens without any notification or user consent. As a result, personal information (in this case the user's category preferences) is formatted by the Web server, transmitted, and saved by the user's computer.

During the second stage, the cookie is automatically sent from the user's browser to a Web server. Whenever a user displays the Web page from the server, the browser will, without the user's knowledge, transmit the cookie containing personal information to the Web server.

PC users can disable cookies. Although eliminating unwanted contacts, this process also eliminates contacts with companies that individuals want to keep. For example, newspapers such as the *New York Times* put a cookie on a PC so that individuals do not have to register every time they seek access.

Source: http://www.cookiecentral.com/content.phtml?area=2&id=1, a page by Victor Mayer Schonberger.

Cookies

Individual movements can also be traced when people surf the Internet. Here "cookies" and similar devices are used. Sidebar 4 is a simple explanation of cookies.

Anonymity

In a computer world, where every keystroke is recorded, anonymity depends on "the kindness of strangers."[4] In some situations, such as computer-based group support systems used for idea generation, participants are offered anonymity as an inducement to give their true opinion, although even there, the people running the conference can reconstruct authorship of contributions. In commercial situations, however, anonymity is rarely observed.

---

[3] As explained back in Chapter 1, URL is the abbreviation for universal resource locator, which is the name or number given to a server.

[4] The phrase "kindness of strangers" is from *A Streetcar Named Desire,* a play by Tennessee Williams.

Profiling[5]

Profiling involves recording and classifying behavior. It is an old art, practiced by firms and governments over the years. In dictatorial states they are known as "dossiers." For example, when filling out a warranty, people are asked where they live, what sports they like, what products they buy or intend to buy, and much more. Commercially, for example, the objective is to obtain a picture of who buys a product so that advertising can be targeted. With the ever-increasing data capacities of computers (e.g., Chapter 5) and their ability to correlate and combine information, a huge amount of detail can be obtained on individuals and on firms.

The firms that specialize in creating and selling profiles aggregate information from online and off-line purchases, surveys, contest entries, financial records, the U.S. Census records, credit records, warranty cards, and public records. Their work is done behind the scenes and the people profiled cannot opt-out. The dossiers compiled are sold. The dossiers themselves can contain 40 different pieces of information ranging from social security number, date of birth, and race to extensive medical information, contributions, memberships in organizations, and book preferences. The data can be sliced by categories and subgroups within them. For example, one firm offers 15 categories, such as urban midscale, that is then divided into urban achievers, big city blend, old Yankees, and mid city residents.

Sets of profiles are relatively cheap. Prices of $65 per million names are reported. On the other hand, their reputation is that significant portions of the information correlated may be wrong.

Privacy versus Convenience

Although privacy is highly desirable and desired, people are also faced with the trade-off between privacy and convenience. People make these trade-offs all the time. For example, they use a company supplied key chain accessory or similar device that can be scanned when they check out in order to obtain a tiny discount on their groceries. Of course, data for computer storage are generated on their buying habits, habits that they might prefer to be private. Similarly, people give information about themselves when they make online purchases, apply for loans, fill out warranty cards, or perform other tasks that generate computer data. In those cases, reward or convenience trumps privacy.

CRM, Data Warehousing, and Other Large Databases

Companies maintain large databases in their data warehouses (Chapter 5) for CRM (Chapter 6), and their transaction systems. Government keeps records on individuals ranging from social security and Medicare, to police records, to driving licenses, to military personnel records, and much more. Privacy comes into conflict with the need to know, particularly when records from different sources (particularly the mixing of public and private sources) are correlated.

Security

The biggest security problem for businesses is their own employees. The foregoing statement may seem strange. However, disgruntled employees and employees who give notice, are laid off, or are fired often can and do harm to a firm's computing equipment, its software, and its data files. This problem is particularly severe for people who are computer professionals or heavy computer users.

---

[5] Source: http://www.epic.org/privacy/profiling. This source on profiling is 12 pages long in small type. The site is maintained by the Electronic Privacy Information Center.

The best policy to apply to employees who leave the firm is to remove their access to computers immediately and to escort them out the door.

Computer crime can result in the loss of privacy, loss of data, loss of money, and loss of service. Because a firm's records are centralized in ever-larger systems (such as ERP discussed in Chapter 4) and computers are interconnected in networks, computer crime can magnify the scale of the losses. Think of the losses that are caused if the firm's data warehouse is erased or the accounts payable and receivable files are compromised, or if e-mail, Internet, or communications services are interrupted. FBI data indicate that the average size of the loss from a computer crime is of the order of $600,000, much greater than from typical white-collar crime that averages $25,000.

Harm can be done to computers is many ways. Some of the threats are in common with other property, such as physical theft of equipment. However, others are specific to computers. Among the many threats are

- Unauthorized access to databases to gain information (e.g., to manager's salaries, or by hackers) or change data either by adding or deleting.
- Copying data sets and giving them to outside parties (e.g., competitors).
- Unauthorized entry into central computer facilities.
- Intrusions by viruses, worms, and Trojan horses[6] and similar hostile programs from hackers.
- Disasters (e.g., power outages, hurricanes, tornados, earthquakes).

Computer crimes are mostly people issues. They are also a growth industry.

To deal with crimes and other potential calamities, most information systems groups maintain one or a group of security specialists whose job it is to monitor the level of security being maintained and to implement new security measures as threats change.

Controls

Be aware that security measures cannot eliminate all problems. They do reduce the risk. As we discuss at the end of this section, the analysis to determine whether particular countermeasures and controls should use a criterion such as "risk of not investing" rather than trying to estimate a return on investment.

Controls fall into five categories:

- Preventing accidents
- Deterring intentional hostile acts
- Finding problems as soon as possible
- Improving recovery if damage does occur
- Correcting problems

Controls can also be divided according to whether they are installed for a particular application or physical installation, or are to apply to all software. Table 1 describes some of the available control measures.

---

[6] Viruses, worms, and Trojan horses are three of several forms of computer programs that can do malicious damage. A virus alters or destroys data; a worm replicates itself and spreads throughout a network; a Trojan horse stays in the computer until it is triggered (e.g., at a set time) and then acts like a virus or a worm.

Table 1   COMPUTER SECURITY CONTROLS

Type of control	Measure
Physical	Prevent damage to computers and computer centers.
Access	Prevent people from gaining access to computer centers. Require authorization and authentication (e.g., name and password; fingerprints and other biometrics).
Data	Prevent disclosure of data or of altering them maliciously.
Network	Limit access, provide encryption, firewalls.
Administrative	Select people with access carefully; make frequent changes.
Application	Procedures for creating, running programs, and obtaining outputs.

Data Controls

Involves three kinds of issues:

- Confidentiality of the data
- Criticality of the data
- Preserving the data for their intended use (integrity)

Networks

With companies operating both internal networks [Local area networks (LANs)] and external networks [Internet, e-mail, wide area networks (WANs)], network security becomes crucial. Protective measures include encryption and firewalls. Encryption is coding the data so they are unreadable by someone who does not have the key. A firewall is a barrier, typically used for external networks, that controls which sources can enter the internal network. Firewalls do not, by themselves, protect against viruses.

Administrative Controls

The idea is to frequently change the rules for using systems to make it less likely that previous knowledge can be used forever. For example, most facilities change passwords regularly. They run computer audits frequently and at random times. They rotate people through multiple jobs and separate duties[7] so that a single person does not control an entire process. And, of course, they remove fired and resigned employees from both central computer and network access.

Applications Controls

Applications controls are concerned with content, specifically, input, process, and output.

- Input includes making sure the data format is correct, that data are within allowable ranges (e.g., no salary below minimum wage and none more than the CEO), and internal consistency (no pregnant males).
- Process makes sure that the people who access a program or run it are authorized to use it.
- Output controls look for output consistency and make sure that the output is shown only to those authorized to view it.

---

[7] A classic tale is the lady who was stealing from the computer accounts by having company checks made out to her. She never took vacation or sick leave. She controlled the entire check writing process. She was discovered when she was called to jury duty, was selected for a sequestered jury, and her duties were taken over by someone else.

New Technologies

Computer security, like competitive intelligence (Chapter 8), is a game of measure, countermeasure, counter-countermeasure, ... (counter)^n-measure. A basic rule of engineered systems is that no matter how you try to protect them, someone will try to find a way to break the security. Furthermore, as you introduce new technologies, consideration needs to be given to how to secure them. Consider, for example, a company that decides to reduce paper by scanning all incoming documents and storing them digitally. In one such company in the insurance business, a manager who received a layoff notice went through the steps in the work flow management process and randomized them and then took a file of incoming claims and randomized the order in which the steps were assigned to clerks. The result was chaos, and huge goodwill losses.

The Risk of Not Investing

Unfortunately, like many other aspects of information systems, it is difficult to determine the return on investment from specific security. Some argue that security is an overhead cost and hence the minimum possible should be spent on it. Certainly, faced with adding a new information system with high expected return or investing in better security, security will almost always lose if ROI is the only criterion. However, when it comes to security, ROI is not the appropriate criterion. The prime criterion should be the risk of not investing (RONI).

Basically, in assessing RONI, the evaluation should begin with assessing the likelihood of the threat or threats occurring (P) and the magnitude of the loss (L) if the threat materializes.[8] In technical terms, the expected loss is $P \times L$. (For example, if during the life of the proposed countermeasure, P is estimated to be 5% and L is \$1 million, then $P \times L = 0.05 \times 1,000,000 = \$50,000$.) The RONI criterion is, in effect, the appropriate amount of insurance that should be bought either by investing in security measures or by buying an insurance policy.

Risk Management

The foregoing subsections discussed various ways of mitigating risk, both physical and through insurance. We enumerated the various strategies that can be followed without evaluating either their cost or their effectiveness. Prudent firms will, of course, make such evaluations, using the tools of risk management. Risk management is the process of measuring, or assessing, risk and then developing strategies to manage the risk. Usually, the cost of investing in risk mitigation is compared to the expected cost of the risk.[9]

---

[8] For simplicity, the calculation given here does not include present value.

[9] The expected cost of a risk is the probability of incurring the risk multiplied by the cost if the risk occurs. Thus, high losses with only a minute chance of happening may sometimes be ignored, whereas a medium cost risk that happens frequently may lead to installing a countermeasure. For a more detailed discussion of risk, see Chapter 6.

HIPAA: THE INTERSECTION OF SECURITY AND PRIVACY

HIPAA[10] (Health Insurance Portability and Accountability Act of 1996) is an example of the intersection of privacy and security. This act required health care providers to be compliant with its provisions by April 14, 2003. This date was later shifted to April 1, 2005. It is typical of the legislation that the U.S. Congress passes which creates major record keeping and security requirements for firms. Here are some of HIPAA's provisions and their implications.

1. Health care plans and providers must use standard formats for electronic data interchange (EDI, discussed in Chapter 3) for transferring claims and other data.

    Implication: HIPAA mandates that organizations become as computer-efficient as, say, banks, in handling transactions. The paper records that many kept need to be replaced with computer-based records. Computer-based patient records are still a work in progress for many.

2. Records can only be shared for treatment.

    Implication: Computer security must be tightened.

3. Patients can access their records and correct errors.

    Implication: This mandate creates a conflict between providing people the ability to access the computer to obtain their own data and the organization's need to maintain privacy and not allow access to others (including employers and insurance companies) to see people's records.

4. Patients must be told how their information will be used.

    Implication: This requirement is important at the beginning of working under HIPAA and at the time that rule changes are attempted. From a computer viewpoint, it is a mailing to all clients.

5. Health care plans and providers must document privacy procedures.

    Implication: Unlike transactions (Item 1) that occur daily, procedures change rarely. It is the interaction between procedures and transactions that is the key. If the procedures result in transactions that are not transparent, satisfy the requirements for privacy and patient access, and are documented, then the firm becomes liable for HIPAA's penalties.

6. With lots of restrictions, people can keep health care coverage when changing jobs, although they must enroll in the new employer's plan rather than keep the one they had.

    Implication: Records must be kept on who is covered under which plan and the dates of their coverage. Such data is kept routinely now.

---

[10] HIPAA is usually used to refer to four laws, of which the Health Insurance Portability and Accountability Act of 1996 is one. The others are MHPA (The Mental Health Parity Act), NMHPA (The Newborn's and Mothers Health Protection Act), and WHCRA (The Women's Health and Cancer Rights Act). While slightly different rules are associated with each of them, the four are sufficiently alike from the information systems view, that the HIPAA discussion is representative of all four.

The penalties for HIPAA violations, although seemingly benign for a single failure to comply with a single violation, are quite severe if data are disclosed since they include imprisonment. Specifically,

- Failure to comply
  - $100 per violation
  - $25,000 maximum for all violations of a single requirement

- Wrongful disclosure
  - $50,000 and/or imprisonment for up to 1 year
  - $100,000 and/or imprisonment for up to 5 years if under false pretenses
  - $250,000 and/or imprisonment for up to 10 years if intent is to sell information

The bottom line is the need to keep data records both more accurately and more securely than in the past.

The costs of compliance with HIPAA, Sarbanes–Oxley, and other legislation that increases the requirements for record keeping compliance can be quite high. For example, *Information Week*[11] reports that Guardian Life spent 3% of its IT budget on compliance in 2004.

ANNOUNCING SECURITY FAILURES[12]

Whenever a security breach occurs, a company is faced with the issue of whether to go public with the breach or attempt to hide it. The general approach has been to keep a security failure secret. However, when customer records are involved, customers generally demand that they be informed. It is usually much more costly to maintain secrecy because failures eventually are found out. At that point, the reputation of the company is seriously damaged. For example, if a break-in results in personal data (such as credit card numbers) being stolen, the people affected believe they have a right to know that the loss occurred, what was done to control the damage, what new countermeasures are being taken, and what they need to do to protect themselves.

DISASTER RECOVERY AND BUSINESS CONTINUITY[13]

Disaster recovery and business continuity are at the extreme end of the security spectrum. Recovery presupposes an event that causes a failure, while continuity implies avoiding (or minimizing) the impact of a failure. Although continuity planning and management is not just about information systems, information systems are a major component of the process of ensuring that critical business functions can continue. The more sophisticated a firm's information technology, the more important the requirement for business continuity management.

---

[11] http://www.informationweek.com/articleID=20301021 "Rules, Rules, Rules," May 17, 2004.

[12] Source: http://www.informationweek.com/story/showArticle.jhtml?articleID=60402273.

[13] This section is based on a J. A. Hecht, "Business Continuity Management," *Communications of AIS* 8(30): 2002.

An Example

One of the periodic earthquakes that hit the Los Angeles area was centered at Whittier, which is close to El Monte, a town with a number of large data centers. Southern California Edison, which is the main electricity supplier for the region, and many commercial banks, did all their computing in the suburb of El Monte some 25 miles from downtown. When the earthquake hit, the computers at Southern California Edison survived beautifully, but the building was damaged and the law enforcement people ordered everyone out. The only communications that were working were cell phones. The nearby bank computer centers were also shut down, forcing them to close their ATM networks. One bank estimated it must get their ATMs and the computers that controlled them up in less than 72 hours or their customers would switch banks and they would be out of business. In this particular case, they were able to do it by applying extraordinary effort.

This example illustrates the need to know the recovery time window. A bare-bones plan might lead to requiring getting the mainframe or the servers back up in 48 hours. That is not adequate if, for example, your firm needs to maintain near continuous operations and the cost of being down is, say, $50,000 per hour.

Who Is Responsible?

In most companies, disaster recovery and business continuity issues are left to the information systems department, even though the responsibility really involves the entire senior management. Basically, most companies assume that their most critical danger is from losing the information in their computers, and assign the task to their chief information officer. Unfortunately, most of what needs to be done is outside the CIO's traditional skills and responsibility. To be successful, disaster recovery requires a senior sponsor in the firm and a commitment of resources.

The Threats

The threats to be countered are those that can affect the entire business. As indicated earlier in this chapter, they include

- Intentional human threats (hacking, terrorism, sabotage, product tampering)
- Unplanned human threats (e.g., an error such as a check without a decimal point disburses $10 million rather than $100,000).
- Natural threats (floods, hurricanes, earthquakes)
- Unnatural environmental threats (blackouts, arson, Internet and extranet outages)
- Reputation threats (unfavorable publicity, product problems)

Some IT Measures

Just being able to keep the mainframes going is not enough. Internet, e-mail, customers, suppliers, and trading partners are needed to keep the business going. For many firms, acceptable recovery times are minutes, not hours. Data can't be lost. Therefore, most information systems organizations standardize on techniques for keeping operations going.

SIDEBAR 5   *September 11*

Perhaps the ultimate test of business continuity management was the attack on the World Trade Center on September 11, 2001. Some firms in the Trade Center maintained their off-site facilities only a few blocks away. Although fine for a fire or flooding, these nearby backup facilities proved useless because they were also affected. However, firms whose backup sites were around the country found they could not be used because all travel was suspended. Tapes, people, and hardware could not be moved.

A number of firms who did have comprehensive plans (e.g., American Express, Merrill Lynch) were able to be back in business in a few hours. NASDAQ took 6 days.

Recognizing these problems, IS groups routinely send backup tapes off site, rent space at "hot sites" (i.e., facilities with the same computing equipment as their own who will act as temporary outsourcers for operations), and dry run plans for moving computing operations off site until the crisis is resolved.

Some Lessons

The September 11 experience resulted in some lessons learned.

- You need a business continuity plan that is communicated, rehearsed, and kept up to date.
- A well-designed plan can really work.
- Continuous availability strategies with real-time changeover capabilities kept the ability to serve clients going.
- Companies with clearly defined crisis strategies mobilized their employees and kept major business functions operating.
- Critical e-mail and messaging systems were slowed.

Since many corporate functions are outsourced (Chapter 9), specifying business continuity in outsourcing agreements is important. Outsourcing vendors who did not guarantee service contractually sometimes just terminated their services when hit with a disaster.

In summary, business continuity is about keeping the company going. Keeping the technology and the software systems going is only part of it.

LEGAL ISSUES

Over their 60 year history, computers increasingly became entangled in the law. Particularly in the last few years, as Congress and the Administration people became more computer savvy and as corporations saw the advantage of legal protections or exclusions, both the amount and the extent of the Federal law on computing and communications increased rapidly. The rise of the Internet is an integral reason for this extension of scope. It would be impossible to discuss all aspects of computer law in a short section. Our discussion is limited to some aspects of the law in 2005 so that business people can understand the risks that the law imposes.

Privacy

Just as we began this chapter with privacy, we begin this section on legal issues with the same subject. Many people in Congress are particularly sensitive to privacy because the issues resonate with constituents who want protection and with lobbyists who want exemption. Here are some of the privacy laws that affect businesses:

HIPAA. The Health Insurance Portability and Accountability Act, discussed earlier in this chapter, deals with the way health insurers handle customer data. It includes standardization of health care transactions, security of personal information, unique identifiers of patients and health care people, and the right of patients to access their own information and obtain data on who accessed their records. HIPAA was discussed earlier in this chapter under security since it is a good example of where security and privacy interact.

Financial Modernization Act. Also known as Gramm–Leach–Bliley, this act limits financial firms on what they can do with data and specifies ways customers can opt out.

Security Breach Notice Law. Although enacted by a state (California), this law requires companies to notify people in California if a database containing personal information about them was compromised. Because all customers in California are covered, even firms with only a few customers in California must reveal security breaches.

Taxation of E-commerce

A continuing battle is whether sales to consumers made in e-commerce should be subject to local sales tax. Congress exempted such sales taxes for a period of years. However, large firms like Target and Wal-Mart started charging sales taxes for B2C e-commerce in May 2003.

The situation on sales taxes is murky because these taxes differ from state to state (e.g., Oregon has none) and by counties and cities within states (e.g., New York City charges more than its suburbs). Furthermore, states make distinctions between use and excise taxes. Companies argue that determining the right tax and distributing the monies is an unnecessary burden. Governments complain that people use e-commerce as a way of avoiding taxes.

CASE STUDY: Identity Theft

In October 2004, ChoicePoint, which bills itself as "the leading provider of identification and credential verification services for business and government," was tricked into revealing 145,000 consumer profiles to identity thieves. The company was just recovering from allegedly giving access to its files to bogus firms. It wasn't until 4 months later, February 2005, that the company notified 35,000 of the victims who lived in California of the theft. They were required to disclose the incident under California SB-1386, an act of the California legislature that took effect on 1 July 2003. Massachusetts has a similar law and others states were expected to follow suit. Basically, the law says that "Any person or business that conducts business in California, that owns or licenses computerized data that includes personal information, is to disclose any breach of the security of the data to any resident of California whose unencrypted personal information was, or is reasonably believed to have been, acquired by an unauthorized person."[14] The company also announced that it intended to notify the other 110,000 victims.

---

[14] Source: SB-1386 http://info.sen.ca.gov/cgi-bin/postquery? bill_number=sb_1386 &sess=0102 &house=B&site=sen. The quote is from the *Legislative Counsel's Digest*.

CASE STUDY: Sarbanes–Oxley

The Sarbanes–Oxley Act is an example of the effect that legislation can have on a firm's information systems. The law was passed in an effort to prevent a recurrence of the Enron accounting scandal.[15] The result was the imposition of new requirements on companies, particularly large companies, that they certify the accuracy and veracity of their financial reports. The act is quite stringent. It requires senior managers to sign off on their financial reports. Companies have to show how they compute their financials. The information technology group is accountable for the quality and integrity of the information they generate. They cannot afford to be wrong, since senior executives and directors can go to jail and pay large fines. In examining the expected impact of Sarbanes–Oxley, AMR Research found that 85% of the companies they surveyed would have to change their information systems and their applications infrastructure [16]

Here are some of the things that Sarbanes–Oxley (also known as SOX) requires

• Management to certify the adequacy of internal financial controls in the company. This certification must be based on testing the system (which involves IT), not just a vague "in the opinion of management."

• Real-time disclosure (i.e., on a "rapid and current basis") of problems that affect the company's finances.

• Maintaining computer-based records for 7 years as well as paper records.

• System integration (see Chapter 10) for detecting fraud.

• Ongoing audits and security checks to maintain information quality.

And all that is just the beginning of the list. The Sarbanes–Oxley Act, like HIPAA and Gramm–Leach–Bliley (see above) before it, increases the requirements on firms. In a world where an ever-increasing fraction of the transactions and other records of a firm are computerized, it is inevitable that the requirements of the law will tighten and ever more complexity will be introduced.

UCITA

UCITA is the abbreviation for Uniform Computer Information Transactions Act, a law pushed by software vendors as part of the Uniform Commercial Code.[17] It gives vendors extraordinary rights about how their software is used. It was passed rather rapidly in two states (Virginia and Maryland) and then ran into a buzz saw of opposition from both business and consumer software buyers. In essence, the act shifts risk from vendors to buyers.

Opponents made the following arguments about the initial form of the statute:

• UCITA allows software publishers to change the terms of the contract after purchase without notice and to make terms of the license unavailable until after the goods are purchased.

• UCITA allows restrictions that prohibit users from criticizing or publicly commenting on software they purchased.

• UCITA allows software and information products to contain "backdoor" entrances, potentially making users' systems vulnerable to infiltration by unauthorized hackers.

---

[15] As indicated in Chapter 3, Enron and other electronic market makers manipulated the price of electricity by making sales to themselves and/or by moving electricity (on paper) out of California and then selling it back to California at a higher price. A classic scam.

[16] J. Surmacz, "Financial Fallout," *CIO,* May 28, 2003, http://www2.cio.com/metrics/ 2003/metrics552.html Current August 10, 2004.

[17] By mid-2004, UCITA seemed to be dead. However, its terms are sufficiently enticing for vendors that it will appear again in some other form. This discussion is designed to sensitize you to the issues involved.

- UCITA allows software publishers to sell their products "as is" and to disclaim liability for product shortcomings.

- UCITA allows the vendor to specify which state's law should apply. By choosing a state in which UCITA passed, it makes people in all states liable. Some states counteracted this provision by passing laws that invalidate this option.

Some of the most egregious of these features were later deleted. However, if UCITA is passed by states, individual firms will be at a substantial disadvantage with their software vendors.

Copyrights and Patents

Copyrights and patents are two aspects of intellectual capital discussed in Chapter 7. They are discussed here because they are part of the legal framework around computers. The idea is to use copyrights, patents, trademarks, and trade secrets as a way of protecting intellectual capital. The importance of the role of these approaches can be seen, for example, in Microsoft, who owns 3000-plus patents and maintains a corporate VP and deputy general counsel for intellectual property.

Copyright

Copyright law originally was designed to protect authors with a term of 14 years and a renewal of 14 more. The length of a U.S. copyright is now 75 years. At this point copyright violations are civil, not criminal matters, although some believe that may be coming. A copyright holder has the right to sue and have the courts enforce the copyright, including awarding damages if the copyright is violated. The 75 year protection extends to computer programs that are treated as literary works. As a result, the newspaper business pages and the computer press are filled with discussions of computer copyright infringement claims. Often firms will make copyright claims about their software as a way to extract money or competitive advantage. One such case apparently was over whether the LINUX operating system contained computer code owned by a UNIX operating system vendor.

Perhaps the most controversial aspect of copyright is The Digital Millennium Copyright Act, passed in 1998. This law was intended to protect the record and movie industries but, since these industries are going digital, the act has strong implications for computer software. The main features of the act, according to the University of California at Los Angeles,[18] include the following provisions:

- It is a crime to circumvent antipiracy measures built into commercial software. But non-profit libraries, archives, and educational institutions can do so under certain circumstances.

- Outlaws devices used to copy software illegally. However, you can use such devices for encryption research, to assess product interoperability, and to test computer security systems.

- Internet service providers are not liable for copyright infringement if they simply transmit information over the Internet.

- Requires "webcasters" to pay licensing fees to record companies.

---

[18] The UCLA Online Institute for Cyberspace Law and Policy "The Digital Millennium Copyright Act," http://www.gseis.ucla.edu/iclp/dmca1.htm.

A number of simple explanations of copyright can be found on the Internet. Internet postings are, of course, copyrighted. For example, one such explanation is entitled "10 Big Myths about Copyright Explained"[19] Among the points made are[20]

- Almost everything is copyrighted, included posting something on the Internet, as soon as it is written. A copyright notice (usually found with the symbol ©) is no longer required.

- You can violate a copyright even if you don't charge money.

- Under limited conditions (such as a book review) you can quote a small amount of copyrighted material under a complex doctrine called "fair use." In general, it is not worth the trouble.

- Unlike a trademark, you don't lose copyright protection if you don't sue about it.

- Because copyright law is mostly civil law, you don't have the rights that apply in criminal law.

- Forwarding e-mail is technically a violation, but since e-mail rarely has commercial value, the law doesn't do much to protect works with no commercial value.

Patents

A U.S. patent grants an inventor or his/her assignee the right to own an invention for 20 years and bars others from using the invention in the United States. In recent years, the idea of a patent was extended to include business processes and in some cases software. For example, Amazon.com patented "1-click" technology, which allows people who shopped at that site previously to make purchases without reentering either personal information (e.g., address) or credit card information. Amazon.com then sued Barnes&Noble.com, who used the same technique, claiming its patent had been infringed.

The use of patents in computers and in software is increasing. Firms can unwittingly violate these patents in their products. Perhaps most troublesome is the growth of patents in procedures for electronic commerce where relatively simple things are being patented, often to keep others out or to extract extortionate royalties.

ETHICS

Much of what is discussed in this chapter falls under the heading of ethics. Ethics is a concept from philosophy and deals with whether something is the right thing to do with respect to other people. Questions of right and wrong are always difficult because individual and societal beliefs enter into the decision. Something may be entirely within the law but, in the opinion of some, may not be ethical. Consider an employer who reads all his organization's incoming and outgoing e-mail. Although that is within the law, is it the ethical thing to do? Take it one level further. Suppose the employer reads all e-mail but does not tell employees that it is being done. Or, the employer deliberately deletes or alters messages without telling an employee. Different people will have different views as to whether each action is justified.

---

[19] Brad Templeton, 10 Big Myths about Copyright Explained, http://www.templetons.com/brad/copymyths.html.

[20] The items have been paraphrased.

The issue of ethics can be formulated[21] in terms of:

- *Privacy*. What information is public and what is not?
- *Accuracy*. Is information about individuals correct?
- *Property*. Copyright and patents are examples.
- *Access*. Ability to access computers and to use them.

This grouping goes under the name PAPA, based on the first letters of these four issues. Some of these aspects, such as privacy and property were discussed previously.

Privacy

Privacy was discussed at the beginning of this chapter. The ethical issues about privacy can be divided into physical and information privacy. Physical privacy refers to the "I want to be left alone" syndrome such as freedom from spam and other solicitations by e-mail. Information privacy is about the use and the sale of information about an individual such as their finances, health, social security number, and credit card numbers.

Accuracy

Accuracy includes both the correctness of information (was the mortgage payment made last month?) and the misrepresentation of information (calling a product safe when it isn't). From your customer's point of view, having the wrong information about them in your computer system can be devastating because of the decisions you make, such as refusal to grant credit or write a mortgage. A particularly serious problem is identity theft in which someone claims to be a person they are not and uses stolen information to commit fraud (see above).

Property

Intellectual property is protected by copyrights and patents (see above), which require the information to be made public, and trade secrets that rely on enforcing contracts to ensure confidentiality. The basic ideas carry over from the noncomputer world. Computing, however, introduces some new aspects. Once information is digital it can be manipulated in a large number of ways. For example, photo-editing software allows changing images and sound equipment allows rearranging sound. Thus, existing creative work can be manipulated to such an extent that it is no longer recognizable. Aside from the question of whether it is legal, there is the question of whether such manipulation is ethical.

Other ethical issues revolve around hiring someone from a competitor who knows trade secrets. Examples include such questions as whether it is ethical (and/or legal) to hire an employee who knows a firm's marketing plans or to let them use a set of business cards collected from their previous company's customers.

---

[21] This formulation was developed by R. O. Mason in "Four Ethical Issues of the Information Age," *MIS Quarterly,* March 1986. It has become the standard in the discussion of information ethics.

Access

The previous parts of PAPA dealt with information content. Access refers to a completely different set of issues: the ability of people, particularly handicapped people, to be able to access computers and the information they contain.

The ability to deal with computers is not uniform. Although almost all students were exposed to computers in elementary and high school in the last 10 to 20 years, skilled older workers with low education levels (such as machinists) or the inability to adjust to new ways of working often encounter difficulty in converting to the computer world. They are, in effect, frozen out.

A second group with difficulty is the people with physical impairments such as vision or hearing, or those confined to a wheelchair. For many, their impairments are being overcome by applying technologies such as voice synthesizers, voice instructions, and audio-to-text conversion. For others, however, even these technologies are not enough to overcome their problems. Microsoft, among others, has been in the lead to provide computer capabilities for handicapped people, but the efforts are far from complete.

The third form of access is access to the information itself. People without the skills needed to find computer-based information are cut out from participation in vast portions of economic life. They literally live on the other side of the computer divide. Even people with computer skills can be deprived of access. For example, it is difficult both for an individual and a firm to find all the information contained in databases about themselves.

Codes of Ethics

Since ethics is about right and wrong, various professional groups created codes of ethics for computer personnel. These groups include the Association for Computing Machinery (ACM) (80,000 members), the Association for Information Systems (4000 information systems faculty people), and others. Sidebar 6 shows the code developed by ACM. It is typical of such codes. They are useful as guidelines for individuals working in a company's information systems groups.

In summary, many of the ethical issues around computer-based systems are similar to those that have been around for many years. However, the computer introduces new issues that both individuals and firms must cope with.

ANSWERS TO MANAGERIAL QUESTIONS

How does privacy affect my business?
The general tenor of the times makes privacy a serious issue. People prefer privacy and fear that personal data will be revealed to others. They are afraid of identify theft and other mischief. Privacy codes that protect the consumer are desired by a majority of the general public.

What are the risks and the rewards?
A reputation for lax privacy standards can hurt an organization, whereas strict privacy standards with evident enforcement can help differentiate a company from its competitors.

What risks and threats do I face from outside if my computers are not secure?
Corporate computers are attacked for motivations that range from kids on a lark trying to show that they are able to affect operations, to people who want to injure a firm by stealing money or changing its data or obtaining competitive information. In any of these cases, successful attempts can (and do) result in large monetary losses.

| SIDEBAR 6 | *ACM Code of Ethics and Professional Conduct 1992* |

1. GENERAL MORAL IMPERATIVES
I will...

1.1 Contribute to society and human well-being.

1.2 Avoid harm to others.

1.3 Be honest and trustworthy.

1.4 Be fair and take action not to discriminate.

1.5 Honor property rights including copyrights and patents.

1.6 Give proper credit for intellectual property.

1.7 Respect the privacy of others.

1.8 Honor confidentiality.

2. PERSONAL RESPONSIBILITIES
I will...

2.1 Strive to achieve the highest quality, effectiveness, and dignity in both the process and products of professional work.

2.2 Acquire and maintain professional competence.

2.3 Know and respect existing laws pertaining to professional work.

2.4 Accept and provide appropriate professional review.

2.5 Give comprehensive and thorough evaluations of computer systems and their impacts, including analysis of possible risks.

2.6 Honor contracts, agreements, and assigned responsibilities.

2.7 Improve public understanding of computing and its consequences.

2.8 Access computing and communication resources only when authorized to do so.

3. ORGANIZATIONAL LEADERSHIP IMPERATIVES
I will...

3.1 Articulate social responsibilities of members of an organizational unit and encourage full acceptance of those responsibilities.

3.2 Manage personnel and resources to design and build information systems that enhance the quality of working life.

3.3 Acknowledge and support proper and authorized uses of an organization's computing and communications resources.

3.4 Ensure that users and those who will be affected by a system have their needs clearly articulated during the assessment and design of requirements; later the system must be validated to meet requirements.

3.5 Articulate and support policies that protect the dignity of users and others affected by a computing system.

3.6 Create opportunities for members of the organization to learn the principles and limitations of computer systems.

Source: (http://www.acm.org/constitution/code.html, current as of January 20, 2003)

What risks and threats do I face from inside if my computers are not secure?

The same problems are faced from inside as from outside. In particular, people with grudges against the company or their bosses, people who are laid off or fired, and people with character disorders may take out their animosity by hurting the computer systems.

How much should I worry about disaster recovery?

A lot. Disasters come in many forms and their occurrence often cannot be predicted. If your firm doesn't plan for business continuity in the event of a disaster and doesn't make the necessary investments, it can result in the firm going bankrupt.

How do the HIPAA and Sarbanes–Oxley legislation affect my computer resources?

These and similar laws result in the need for additional record keeping and, if violated, for notification and/or restitution. The costs involved can be significant.

How is copyright and patent law being used?

More and more vendors and competitors are using copyright and patent law as a way of trying to reduce competition, to make customers dependent on them, and to establish monopoly or near-monopoly positions. The trend of increasing both copyright and patent protection and of granting patents for simple business processes makes it possible for firms to rake in money for licenses and from lawsuits.

What is UCITA about and what can it do to me?

UCITA is a uniform code written to benefit vendors rather than buyers of software and other computer products. It is an attempt by vendors to restrict use of their software and to prevent competition. Some of its uglier provisions, such as vendors going into your computer to remove software without telling you about it, were eliminated, but many provisions remain that make it a matter of high controversy.

Are there special legal and ethical considerations for e-business?

E-business differs from ordinary business in that it requires a larger level of trust than conventional shopping. Although e-business seems to be well worked out for large company business-to-business transactions, the occurrence of spam and scams is rampant in business-to-consumer transactions.

How should I set policy for e-mail use? For Internet use?

These decisions depend on the culture of the organization. The trade-offs are among security, use of employee time, and giving access to needed information. Although employers have the right to monitor e-mail and Internet use, severe restrictions can damage employee morale.

What other legal risks do I run?

The number of legal requirements for ethical behavior and privacy are increasing. So are specific requirements for record keeping. For example, companies are required to retain e-mail just as they are required to retain correspondence. These growing requirements, usually imposed because some firms behave badly, not only increase cost but also increase the legal exposures that companies face.

What ethical risks do I run?

A firm that loses its reputation for ethical behavior can expect severe repercussions in the marketplace.

Appendix

The Computer Industry

By Marlene Davidson[1]

MANAGERIAL QUESTIONS

What is included in the computer industry?

What are in-house shops? What are outside shops?

How does the industry charge for its products and for maintenance?

What categories of people and jobs are involved?

How do computers and telecommunications interact?

What is open source?

What about new technologies such as Wi-Fi and RFID?

Where can I find current information on computers in business?

DEFINITION OF THE INFORMATION INDUSTRY

Defining an industry is a nontrivial task. What is to be included? What is to be excluded? What are the boundaries? Do you look at the economics? At the role of consultants? The role of customers?

For purposes of this appendix we focus our discussion on those parts of the industry that interact with business computing in both the private and public sector. We will not discuss other aspects of computing such as scientific computing (e.g., in physics or in space) or computing built into products (such as the many computers in your automobile). We will also not consider the news or entertainment industries although they contain aspects of computing.

We could start with the dictionary definition of information and of industry, but such analyses tend to be meaningless because dictionaries treat the terms information and industry separately rather than in combination. We can, however, talk about three definitions, given below. Unfortunately, none of them is completely satisfactory for this book.

---

[1] I am indebted to Dr. Marlene Davidson, Assistant Professor of Information Systems at Bradley University, who prepared this Appendix. Her finding of the Houghton framework, defining the components of the industry, and creating what follows is gratefully acknowledged.

U.S. Census Bureau[2]

Recognizing the growing importance of the information sector of the economy, the U.S. Census Bureau included a new subsector called the "Information" sector in its 1997 census statistics. The definition for the "Information" sector provided by the U.S. Census Bureau (2004a) is

> *The Information sector comprises establishments engaged in the following processes: (a) producing and distributing information and cultural products, (b) providing the means to transmit or distribute these products as well as data or communications, and (c) processing data.*
>
> *The main components of this sector are the publishing industries, including software publishing, and both traditional publishing and publishing exclusively on the Internet; the motion picture and sound recording industries, the broadcasting industries, including traditional broadcasting and those broadcasting exclusively over the Internet; the telecommunications industries; the industries known as Internet service providers and web search portals, data processing industries and the information services industries.*

Earlier, the U.S. Census Bureau (2000) added

> *The expressions "information age" and "global economy" are used with considerable frequency today. The general idea of an "information economy" includes both the notion of industries primarily producing, processing, and distributing information, as well as the idea that every industry is using available information and information technology to reorganize and make themselves more productive.*

Clearly, like the dictionary definition, the Census Bureau's definition is too broad in scope because it accounts for both the service and manufacturing segments. In 2002 based on this definition, the U.S. Census Bureau valued the information industry at $905 billion with an annual payroll of $190 billion (U.S. Census Bureau, 2004a).

Shapiro and Varian

Shapiro and Varian of the School of Business at the University of California Berkeley are the authors of an important book, *Information Rules: A Strategic Guide to a Network Economy* (Shapiro and Varian, 1999). Their definition is

> *"Essentially, anything that can be digitized—encoded as a stream of bits—is information."*
>
> *"Infrastructure is to information as a bottle is to wine: the technology is the packaging that allows the information to be delivered to end consumers."*
>
> *"Content providers cannot operate without infrastructure suppliers, and vice versa. The information economy is about both information and the associated technology."*

Again the definition is broad and includes more than what we are interested in. It does not try to specify industry segments.

Hoover's Online[3]

Hoover's Online breaks the computer industry down into two main subsegments:

- hardware, and
- software.

---

[2] The Census Bureau data tend to lag events. Thus, the 2002 data reported here were the best available in 2004.

[3] Source: http://www.hoover's.com.

Hoover's defines these areas as:

Computer Hardware
Companies that design, manufacture personal and large-scale computers, peripheral devices, data storage systems, networking equipment, point-of-sale (POS) devices, automated teller machines (ATM), and other computer-based systems.

(Hoover's, 2005a)

Computer Software
Companies that design, develop, market, and support systems and application software used in personal computers, servers, embedded systems, and mobile devices.

(Hoover's, 2005b)

With an additional key segment, computer services, which is defined as:
Computer Services
Companies that provide services related to computers and other information technology, including consulting, distribution, installation, maintenance, and support.

(Hoover's, 2005c)

Based on the three definitions of the information industry, we can conclude that the information industry consists of two overarching components:

1. an infrastructure component (companies that provide the structure for the information flow to take place); and

2. a content component (companies that supply and manage the information flowing through the infrastructure).

The infrastructure (discussed in Chapter 14) is centered around the hardware—computers, networks, peripherals such as printers—and the software to run them such as operating systems (e.g., Windows). The content component is principally software designed to make the infrastructure useful to businesses. Most of the systems discussed in this book deal with content and hence software. Even data warehousing, which sounds like hardware, is really software.

A FRAMEWORK FOR ANALYZING THE INFORMATION INDUSTRY— THE HOUGHTON MAP

In a publication of the Centre for Strategic Economic Studies in Australia (Houghton, 1999), John W. Houghton provides a framework for analyzing and measuring the information industries. Houghton aptly points out that the information industry "encompasses a range of industry and market statistics" (Houghton, 1999). The framework, or "map" as Houghton refers to it, is based on a technological approach to the industry, which "focuses on information and communication technology (ICT) as the key driver of change" (Houghton, 1999). The map is shown in Figure 1.

Houghton's two-dimensional technology map focuses on the information infrastructure. The map is segmented into four main areas.

1. Communication services

2. Information services

3. Information and communication equipment manufacturing

4. Content

Services

Basic Telephony Services	**Call/Telephony Services**	**Higher Level and Network Services**	**Professional Services**
Voice: Local, STD, ISD	Resale/aggregation	EFT and transactions	Consulting
Mobile: Voice, paging	Callback	EDI, voice/e-mail	Systems integration
Data	Account mgmt.	Video conference	EDP account/audit
Equip. rental and repairs	Call completion	Video broadcast	Engineering services
etc.	Centrex, etc.	News and directory svcs, etc.	Education and training, etc.
Communication Services		**Information Services**	
BCS and Transmission	**Leased Line and PSDN Services**	**Networks and Services**	**Computer, Comms. and Software Services**
Interconnect (ends)	Leased lines	ISP/IAP	Bureau/data proc.
Transmission services	Data network services	MSN, Compuserve, etc.	FM
etc.	VANs, VPNs, IVANs	Pay-TV nets	Outsourcing
	etc.	Broadcast nets, etc.	Maintenance, etc.
Line, Transmission and B'Casting Equip.	**Switch, LAN/WAN and Data Equip.**	**Network Software**	**Packaged Software**
Cable and wire	COS	Net operating systems	Applications
Line, cellular, radio,	Bridges, routers,	Net mgmt./diagnostics	Tools
Microwave and satellite	Hubs, mux	Navigation tools	etc.
transmission equip.	Multiplexers	OSS	
etc.	Modems	etc.	
	etc.		
Information and Comms. Equip.		**Information Products**	
Terminal and Peripheral Equip.	**Computer Equipment**	**Systems Software**	**Networked Content**
CPE	PCs		Online publications
Mobile and paging	Workstations	Systems	News services content
I/O devices	Small-scale	Utilities	Database content
Components	Mid-range	etc.	Programming
Printers, etc.	Large-scale		Multimedia, etc.
	etc.		

Form/Conduit ← → **Substance/Content**

Products

Figure 1 The information technology map (Houghton, 1999).

Source: Reprinted from: *Telecommunications Policy* 23, J. W. Houghton, "Mapping Information Industries and Markets," pp. 689–699, copyright 1999, with permission from Elsevier.

In turn, each of these major segments is further broken down into four areas, creating a total of 16 segments.

The horizontal and vertical axes represent, respectively:

a. product–services (vertical) differentiating the items by whether they are closer to the network end users and therefore final consumption, or whether they are parts of the network.

b. form–substance (horizontal) differentiating items based on whether they are a conduit or medium, or more informational content.

The segmentation of the information industry is constructed for use with official industry and market data, such as the North American Industry Classification System (NAICS). The aim of the map is to provide a tool for analyzing the industries that make up the computer industry and to explore the relationships among the various industries and market sectors.

Postal and courier services; accounting, financial, and legal services; magazines and books; business forms and greeting cards, and paper and filing cabinets, are not included in the framework, although the map is arranged so that these businesses border the items in the map. Furthermore, Houghton's map does not take into account many of the segments identified by the U.S. Census Bureau as being in the Information sector. These segments would include: motion picture, sound recording industries, book publishers, and greeting cards, among others. Conversely, the Houghton map includes data on professional services (such as consulting and systems integration), which are accounted for by the U.S. Census Bureau's statistics in their "Professional, Scientific, and Technical Services" sector rather than in the Information sector.

The Houghton framework is comprehensive and it provides a structure that can be used to determine the size of the information industry and its segments. Because we are interested specifically in the computer and computer-related segments of the information industry as outlined by Houghton, the scope of the areas explored in this Appendix focuses only on these portions of the map.

COMPUTER AND COMPUTER-RELATED SEGMENTS

Identifying the components of the computer industry and then determining its approximate size provides a foundation for understanding the magnitude of the resources and relationships in this industry. These data provide an understanding of the vast size of the information technology field and indicate the range of some of the components that have to be managed and the range of competition in the industry. Individual suppliers in the industry compete in multiple sectors and therefore are involved in multiple marketplaces.

Portions of the Houghton framework define the computer and computer-related segments. Shading on the Houghton map in Figure 2 highlights these segments.

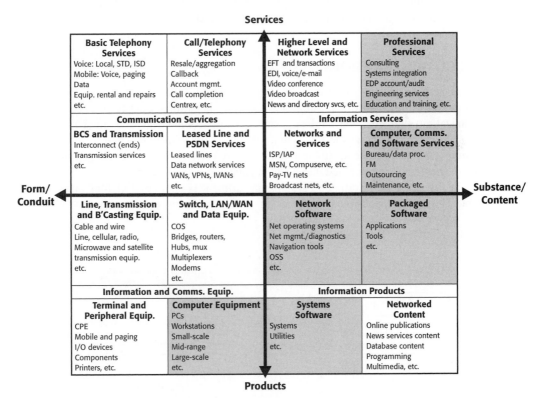

Figure 2 The Houghton map highlighting the computer industry segments.

Source: Reprinted from: *Telecommunications Policy* 23, J. W. Houghton, "Mapping Information Industries and Markets," pp. 689–699, copyright 1999, with permission from Elsevier.

Figure 2 shows that this segment of the information industry is itself a complex structure. The complexity arises because of the overlapping goods and services that are produced (many of which are needed to support one another), in addition to the infrastructure needed to sustain the industry. It can be seen from Figure 2 that the computer and computer-related components fall into various portions of the IT map. These segments include computer communication and software services, systems software, computer equipment, and packaged software. Additional elements such as input/output devices, modems, systems, and integration services can be found in the adjacent segments on the map.

To place the size of these industries into perspective, the sales revenue of the top 15 computer hardware manufacturers totaled $426 billion in 2003 (Plunkett, 2003b) and $70 billion for computer software companies (Plunkett, 2003c). The Software Industry Association (SIIA) estimated the package software industry at $179 billion worldwide for 2003 (SIIA, 2003). International Data Corporation (IDC) estimated the worldwide market for information technology products at $872 billion in 2003 with the software market at an estimated $200 billion globally (Plunkett 2003a). In March 2002, NDP Intellect, a market tracker, identified the market for personal computers at $154.3 billion. The number of PCs marketed worldwide in 2003 is 168.9 million (Plunkett, 2003a).

The computer industry segments can be further divided in terms of the location of the supply of the resources outlined by Hoover's (hardware, software, and services). The industry consists of resources, which are based

- within the organization (called "in-house computer shops"), and
- external to the organization (called "outside shops").

IN-HOUSE COMPUTER SHOPS

Figure 3 shows how a typical complex, centralized information systems department is structured and the functions it performs. Information systems departments are responsible for supplying the organization with both the hardware and software components and the services described by Hoover's. Figure 3 shows the first few levels of the organizational chart for a typical large information systems department. All these functions are performed in a given department, although several of them may be combined into a single person in a small shop.

In Figure 3, the information systems department is composed of four main units (shown in Table 1) that are responsible for addressing specific problems for the organization.

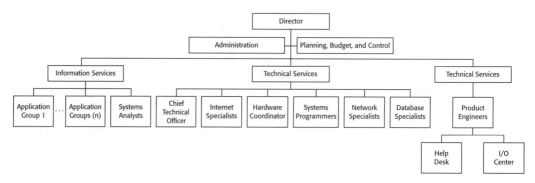

Figure 3 Organizational structure of a complex information systems department.
Source: Updated from Ahituv et al., 1994.

Table 1   STRUCTURE OF A COMPLEX INFORMATION SYSTEMS DEPARTMENT

Information systems department area	Focus	IS personnel within area
Information services	Users	Systems analysts Application groups
Technical services	Handles hardware/software technology	Chief technical officer Programmers Database specialists Network specialists Hardware coordinators
Operations	Mass production of information	Production engineering Computer operations staff Remote computer centers coordinators Help desk Input/output center (includes Internet and e-mail)
Management	Management and administration	Executives Administration personnel Planning/budget & control personnel

Although Figure 3 and Table 1 imply information systems departments are clearly defined with sharp boundaries, that is not the case. Like many other areas of the information and computer industry, the distinction between the roles of individuals within the information systems department and among other functions within the organization became blurred over time. Also note that the titles given in Figure 3 are generic and vary from organization to organization.

EMPLOYMENT

Table 2 shows a breakdown by the Bureau of Labor Statistics of the number of people employed in computer professions across industries and also by industry for the computer systems design and related services. Based on these figures, in 2003 the total number of individuals employed in computer professions across industries (excluding the administrative staff) is 3.1 million at an estimated annual cost of $197 billion and in the computer industry, 625,000 at a cost of $44 billion.

Despite the apparent large number of individuals employed in these professions within organizations, many organizations do not possess the resources necessary to manage, maintain, or implement technologies efficiently for their businesses. The primary reasons are that in many organizations, the information systems resources or technologies needed do not fall within the organization's main area of expertise, or the staff is not large enough to meet all the firm's needs. For example, a university wanting to implement a technology to run its administration would not necessarily have the in-house expertise to do the implementation of an ERP system (Chapter 4), nor would it be interested in writing the software, or have the funding to buy a commercial system. The resources needed include personnel, systems, money, and time. In these situations, the organization usually turns to an outside firm (i.e., the outside shops) to help them meet their needs (Chapter 9).

Table 3 shows estimates of the total employment in computer organizations within organizations (i.e., in-house computer shops). The data are summaries of the numbers given in Table 2.

Table 2 COMPUTER INDUSTRY OCCUPATIONS AND STATISTICS

Occupation	Number employed 2003 across industries	Number employed 2003 computer industry*	Mean annual wage estimate 2003 across industries	Mean annual wage estimate 2003 computer industry	Annual payroll 2003 across industries (000)	Annual payroll 2003 computer industry (000)
Information services						
Computer and information scientists, research	23,210	5,810	$84,530	$87,350	$1,961,941	$507,504
Operations research analysts	58,080	5,200	$61,700	$70,860	$3,583,536	$368,472
Computer systems analysts	474,780	93,270	$66,180	$71,900	$31,420,940	$6,706,113
Technical services						
Database administrators	100,890	14,600	$61,440	$71,190	$6,198,682	$1,039,374
Computer programmers	431,640	113,130	$64,510	$70,330	$27,845,096	$7,956,433
Computer software engineers, applications	392,140	125,910	$75,750	$78,140	$29,704,605	$9,838,607
Computer software engineers, systems software	285,760	77,110	$78,400	$79,420	$22,403,584	$6,124,076
Network systems and data communications analysts	148,030	25,070	$62,060	$66,550	$9,186,742	$1,668,409
Network and computer systems administrators	237,980	36,470	$59,140	$63,290	$14,074,137	$2,308,186
Computer support specialists	482,990	82,950	$42,640	$43,930	$20,594,694	$3,643,994
Operations						
Computer operators	160,170	7,340	$31,870	$34,260	$5,104,618	$251,468
Management						
Chief executives	-	790	-	$188,870		$149,207
General and operations managers	-	1,820	-	$136,440		$248,321
Computer and information systems managers	266,020	34,690	$95,230	$107,590	$25,333,085	$3,732,297
Total	3,061,690	624,160			$197,411,660**	$44,542,451

Source: Bureau of Labor Statistics, 2003.

*Computer industry refers to computer systems design and related services.

**Figure excludes compensation for chief executives and general and operations managers.

Table 3   STATISTICS FOR IN-HOUSE COMPUTER SHOPS

Category	Number of people employed (000s)	Total salaries ($ millions)	Latest year
Information services	556	36,966	2003
Technical services	2,079	130,008	2003
Operations	160	5,105	2003
Management*	266	25,333	2003
Total in-house computer shops	3,061	197,412	

*Only includes management in the computer industry, not across all industries.

OUTSIDE SHOPS

When a company outsources (see Chapter 9) for computer or information technology services on a contract or customer basis, they solicit the assistance of one of the approximately 146,000 firms that offer services in the computer systems design and related services industry (Bureau of Labor Statistics, 2004a). The Bureau of Labor defines the services provided by outside shops to include

> *"prepackaged software, customized computer programming services and applications and systems software design; data processing, preparation, and information retrieval services, including on-line databases and Internet services; integrated systems design and development and management of databases; on-site computer facilities management; rental, leasing, and repair of computers and peripheral equipment; and a variety of specialized consulting services."*

(Bureau of Labor Statistics, 1998)

The Bureau of Labor reported in 2004 that there were about 1.2 million jobs in this area and an additional 116,000 self-employed workers (most of whom are independent consultants), making the computer and data processing services industry one of the largest in the economy (Bureau of Labor Statistics, 2004). It also points out that approximately 78% of the 146,000 establishments in the industry employed fewer than 5 workers, with the majority of the jobs residing in establishments that employ more than 50 workers (Bureau of Labor Statistics, 2004). The major areas for outside shops (and the services offered through them) can be classified into the following categories:

- application service providers (which are really outsourcers),
- Web services (which are also outsourcers),
- outsourcers,
- software development firms,
- hardware manufacturers, and
- communication services.

Application Service Providers

In simple terms, an application service provider (ASP)[4] (discussed in Chapter 9) is an outside firm that provides computer-based services to customers over a network. At this level, the ASP provides

---

[4] ASP is also used in the computing industry as an abbreviation for active service pages, which is an indication of a type of program used on an Internet server. The areas defined by the two abbreviations are not related.

access to a particular application program (such as payroll or billing at one end and full ERP and CRM systems at the other). A standard protocol, such as HTTP used for the World Wide Web, is used to connect the company to the ASP. In a sense, it is a "rent an application" market where a company lets an outsourcer run its programs for it. The company provides the data to be run and the ASP provides the computer, the program, and the computer operators.

A more formal definition of ASP is

> *"An application service provider (ASP) provides software-based service that hosts, manages, and provides access to an application from a centrally managed facility to its customers on a contractual basis."*

(Bureau of Labor Statistics, 1998)

> *"An application service provider (ASP) is a business that delivers and manages applications and computer services from remote computer centers to multiple users via the Internet or a private network."*

(Laudon and Laudon, 2004)

The first is a complex definition from the government bureaucracy. Let's break it down:

1. *Software-based service* means that the ASP rents out the use of software.
2. *Hosting* means that the service is performed on the ASP's computer.
3. *Manages* implies that the ASP performs the service for many clients and manages the requests so that they are all performed expeditiously. It also implies that the ASP takes care of buying and maintaining the latest version of the software.
4. *Provides access* means that the ASP can be reached via telecommunications links (usually the World Wide Web) to receive requests for service and the data to be run on an application and can send the results back to you, their customer.

Thus, an ASP is responsible either directly or indirectly for managing one or more software applications or set of applications by providing all the activities and expertise required. The ASP typically enables customers to access the applications through the use of Web-based browsers. In doing so, the ASP is able to offer a range of software and technology-related services to its customer that would otherwise have to be performed by the company's own information systems department.

The ASP market, which was growing in the 2000–2001 time period, started shrinking in the next several years and then rebounded. It is not clear whether the independent firms in this market will survive. However, many large outsourcers and vendors are still active.

ASP Types

Five forms of ASPs are

- A *specialist* or *functional* ASP delivers a single application, (e.g., credit card payment processing).
- A *vertical market* ASP concentrates on an industry, such as medicine.
- An *enterprise* ASP delivers many solutions, including ERP (Chapter 4) and CRM (Chapter 6) systems solutions.
- A *local* ASP provides small-business services within a limited area.
- A volume ASP is a website that provides a low-cost service, such as *PayPal*, that relies on large volume to cut costs of individual transactions.

Advantages and Disadvantages of the ASP Model

The advantages of the ASP model to the individual firm (i.e., the client) include

- Software integration issues (Chapter 10) are eliminated from the client site.
- Software costs for the application are spread over a number of clients.
- ASPs develop more experience with a particular software application than the in-house staff.
- Contracts with ASPs usually include a "service level agreement" (SLA) that specifies the quality, quantity, and schedule of what is to be delivered. If the contract is written well, the ASPs may be required to deliver a better product than can be obtained in-house.

Inherent disadvantages, include

- A small- or medium-sized client must generally accept the application as provided by the ASP since ASPs can only afford a customized solution for their largest clients.
- If the firm relies on the ASP to provide a critical business function, the firm is limited in how they can handle the function to what the ASP offers.
- Continuing consolidation of ASPs may cause changes in the type or level of service available.

Web Services

Web services are a variant on the ASP idea. In the ASP arrangement, the Internet is used primarily in a people-to-people way. Applications send data through Web browsers. If the applications differ between the parties involved, software called middleware has to be used to allow the applications to talk to one another. In Web services, computer-to-computer connections can be made between the company and its Web services vendor. Applications send data and instructions to one another using a universal language with no translation required. A whole alphabet soup of standards were developed, going by such acronyms as SOAP, WSDL, and UDDI.

To make Web services work, agreements have to be reached on what the Web service would require as input and what information would be returned. A Web services provider would want authentication (are you who you say you are?), access restriction (allow only customers to connect), prioritization (different customers may pay for different levels of priority for receiving services), and nonrepudiation (not being able to deny that you asked for the service).

A vendor may sell only specific services over the Web. In that case, a company may buy only specific modules from the vendor and combine their own calculations with those from one or more Web service providers. Web service providers may subcontract to other vendors who specialize in particular applications.

Outsourcers

ASP and Web services outsource operational tasks that involve running existing programs on hardware. As discussed in Chapter 9, outsourcing is broader than that. It may involve outsourcing processes, portions of work of the IS function (including hiring temporary workers who perform their duties either on site or remotely), or the entire IT function. The Outsourcing Institute[5] states that, according to IDC, one of the fastest growing areas for outsourcing in IT is e-commerce. The numbers for outsourcing most likely includes ASPs, which were discussed previously.

---

[5] http://www.outsourcing.com.

Outsourcers can be grouped into three main categories:

- information processors,
- consultants, and
- stand-alone outsourcers.

The total numbers and revenues for each type is difficult to estimate because the services offered by firms overlap and because serving as an outsourcer is only one of many activities for a given firm. An example is IBM, which provides both information processing and consulting services in its many product lines.

Information Processors

Information processors primarily support areas that focus on finance and operations, such as payroll and check processing. That is, specific operations are outsourced rather than kept in-house. One of the largest outsourcers is Automatic Data Processing (ADP), which claims to be "one of the largest global independent computing services firms in the world" and reports over $8 billion in revenue, approximately 42,000 employees worldwide, and 550,000 clients in 26 countries (InvestQuest, 2005).

Consultants

Consulting organizations are able to offer expertise in many areas that are not available to an information systems department in-house. Table 4 identifies several of the major consulting organizations. It should be noted that while the data show some of the largest consulting companies, they are not complete and they do not take into consideration the consulting practices of software development firms such as ERP vendors Oracle and SAP which employ sizeable numbers of people as consultants and generate large revenues from consulting.

Table 4   MAJOR CONSULTING FIRMS IN INFORMATION SYSTEMS

Company
IBM Global Services
PricewaterhouseCoopers
Deloitte Consulting/DTT
Accenture (formerly Andersen Consulting)
Computer Sciences
Capgemini (formerly Ernst & Young)
Bearing Point (formerly KPMG Consulting)
McKinsey & Company
Mercer Consulting Group

Stand-Alone Outsourcers

Because many information systems departments do not have or cannot attract the required staff to meet the needs of their organization, they turn to outsourcing organizations to handle specific tasks. People from the stand-alone outsourcers take the place of personnel within an organization. In some instances, a portion of the information systems department staff is transferred permanently to the outsourcer and the outsourcer provides the management and missing technical expertise. Electronic Data Systems (EDS) describes itself as "the world's largest outsourcing services company" (EDS, 2003). In 2002, EDS revenues were $21.5 billion and they employed 138,000 people (EDS, 2003). These numbers include the entire organization; EDS also is a consulting firm and information processor.

Some stand-alone outsourcers, such as Volt Information Sciences, are "body shops" that provide temporary workers. This arrangement allows a firm to keep a small core staff that it augments from the body shop whenever a large task is encountered.

Software Development Firms

Software development is one of the prime areas where companies go outside the organization to purchase solutions. Although companies may write computer code for small jobs, most new software is bought as packages and, if necessary, customized to the needs of the firm, and then installed. The internal shops gather requirements, evaluate packages (often jointly with user groups), and manage the purchase and installation of the software. They also provide a first level of support to users and help customize[6] the package to meet the company's specific needs.

International Data Corporation (IDC) reports that in 2003 the packaged software industry for all platforms was $169 billion worldwide (Software & Information Industry Association, 2004). When the software industry is broken down into three segments (application software, application tools, and systems software), the 2002 IDC market projections in billions of dollars were

- application software market $77 billion (2000) $149 billion (2005)
- application tools $46 billion (2001) $106 billion (2005)
- systems software $54 billion (2000) $95 billion (2004)

(*Business Week*, 2002).

IDC reports that the packaged software industry in the United States was an estimated $70 billion. This figure consisted of an estimated $5.5 billion in products related to home use, $64 billion in business software, and the remaining $600 million in software designed for schools. They also estimate that the packaged software industry in 2003 employed approximately 236,000 people with an annual payroll of almost $24 billion (Software & Information Industry Association, 2004).

---

[6] Software packages are generic and often try to include best practices. Customization involves a trade-off. The more customized the package, the less change is required in work systems when it is installed. However, the more customized it is, the more expensive it becomes both initially and later on when upgrades are made by the vendor or when work systems are changed. Customization has to be repeated and hence customization costs are incurred every time the system is changed.

The packaged software market includes all of the major applications discussed in this book including electronic commerce, enterprise resource planning, data warehousing, data mining, customer relationship management, knowledge management, business intelligence, supply chain management, logistics, and inventory as well as the market for conventional software such as word processing and spreadsheets. Many of the firms in the packaged software market, such as Oracle and Microsoft, also participate in other industries such as the ASP industry, consulting, and even aspects of the hardware industry (Microsoft, 2000).

HARDWARE MANUFACTURERS

The hardware market[7] provides goods and services ranging from personal computers to mainframes, from peripherals such as printers and displays to individual circuit boards (Hoover's 2004a). For example, the major firms in the PC market include Dell, Hewlett-Packard, and Gateway. These same firms also operate in other parts of the hardware market. Table 5 lists some of the firms and their total revenues. The numbers for the companies include all the company's products and services with the exception of IBM, which provides its information segmented by product line.

In addition to the computer and peripheral market, the hardware market includes network-linking routers and switches. Cisco Systems, 3Com, Nortel Networks, and Enterasys (formerly Cabletron Systems) dominate this market segment.

Table 5   HARDWARE MANUFACTURERS

Company	Number of employees worldwide	Revenue ($ billions)	Year ending
Dell	39,000	35.4	January 2003
EMC Corporation	17,400	5.4	2002
Gateway	11, 500	4.2	2002
Hewlett-Packard (includes COMPAQ)	141,000	73.0	2003
Hitachi Ltd.	321,500	68.3	Fiscal 2003
IBM*	315,900	81.2	2002
NEC	143,000	44.5	2003
Seagate	46,000	6.5	2002
Sun Microsystems	38,900	$11.4	2003

Source: SEC 10-K filings 2003 and annual reports.

* Note: IBM sold its PC business to a Chinese firm in 2005

[7] Dollar numbers for the hardware market are quite scattered and lag in time. Data for the largest firms unfortunately cover much more than their hardware sales.

Table 6   MAJOR MIDDLEMEN

Company	Type of service	Number of employees worldwide	Revenue ($ millions)	Year ending
Ingram Micro	Wholesaler	11,300	22,613	2003
Tech Data	Wholesaler	8,400	17,406	2003
Avnet	Wholesaler	10,100	10,245	2003
Arrow Electronics, Inc.	Wholesaler	11,200	8,679	2003
Bell Microproducts	Wholesaler	1,294	2,230	2003
PC Mall, Inc.	Retailer	1,386	976	2003

Source: SEC 10-K filings.

RETAILERS AND MIDDLEMEN

Like any industry, the computer industry includes retailers, middlemen, and even firms that sell used hardware. At the retail level, PCs and some larger computer equipment can be bought at specialty chains such as Comp USA, Micro Warehouse, and more general-purpose chains such as Circuit City and BestBuy. In addition, manufacturers such as Dell, Gateway, and Hewlett-Packard sell direct via the Internet.

Firms such as Ingram Micro run a lively middleman business. These firms buy from manufacturers and sell to businesses. Some of the major firms in this part of the industry are listed in Table 6.

PRICING AND MAINTENANCE

The standard complaint about computer pricing and maintenance is that computers keep getting cheaper, yet the total cost of ownership for equipment keeps going up. This increase in cost is due in part to ever-expanding capabilities being offered. At a simple level, the cost of PCs dropped from $4,500 for a 1981 IBM PC with two floppy (not hard!) disk drives, 3 megahertz (not gigahertz) of speed, and a green screen display, to under a $1,000 for a PC with a gigantic hard drive, a gigabyte of speed, and a high resolution flat screen. Yet, a top of the line computer still goes for $2,500 to $3,000 dollars. Of course, software ballooned in size, so that all that storage and speed is needed. Mainframe computers and servers also declined steeply in price. Even though per-unit prices decreased significantly over the years, the demand for computing inside firms more than compensated, so that today most firms find that their total equipment budget keeps going up.

Unlike PC software, which is nominally owned, packaged software for larger computers is, in effect, leased. When the software is first acquired, a large up-front payment is made. This initial cost can run into the hundreds of thousands of dollars depending on the size of the package and the number of people who will use it. As part of the purchase, the acquiring firm agrees to pay the vendor an annual maintenance fee that runs in the 15% to 20% range of the initial cost. As part of the maintenance agreement, the vendor agrees to keep the software up to date by providing new versions and "bug fixes" (i.e., computer code to fix mistakes made in the original program). The argument made by the vendors is that upgrades are costs for them and the maintenance fees pay for that. Software maintenance, however, is a highly profitable business.

This arrangement contrasts with that for PCs, where software maintenance is not provided. Although upgrades are not mandatory, the existing software does become obsolete over time and upgrades need to be purchased. People who own a previous version usually receive a discount when upgrading from recent versions.

One of the (stranger?) aspects of the software business is that vendors continually revise pricing policies. There is a tug-of-war between the vendor who wants to maximize revenue and customers who want to minimize cost. Vendors keep changing from fixed price to prices determined by the number of people who will use the software (called the number of seats) to the maximum number of people using the software simultaneously, to a cost per use, and many more variations. Hardware vendors, like software vendors, charge annual maintenance fees

OPEN SOURCE

In the past, software firms produced software languages and applications. The products tended to be proprietary, with firms competing based on specific features. The proprietary structure locked customers into continuing to buy from the initial vendor they selected. In the 1980's and 1990s, a new movement of "free software" (which wasn't fully free, and mostly involved applications) arose as an outgrowth of the introduction of the PC and as a reaction against proprietary solutions. Eventually this movement also spawned an operating system called LINUX, where the Lin stands for Linus Torvalds who invented the system. The idea was that software would not be written in a corporate environment but would be contributed by people who worked for glory rather than money. A small group, in the case of LINUX a review committee headed by Torvalds, would approve adding new developments to the basic system. Thus, the term open source, which refers to the idea that the product is not proprietary and that anyone could contribute as long as the review committee accepted their work. Firms arose (like Red Hat) which commercialized Linux and, because they did not have the enormous overhead cost of paying the software creators, could sell the software at a price that is a small fraction of what conventional software vendors charge.

Many firms and governments are now adopting LINUX and other open source systems because they are quite cheap and seem to perform as well as the commercial products.

COMPUTING FOR NONBUSINESS APPLICATIONS

This book, being designed for business students, focuses on managing business computing applications in the firm. However, most business managers will become involved in making decisions about computing used throughout their firms, particularly in technical areas such as research, development, engineering, and manufacturing. The principles discussed throughout the book apply to computing in general. Be aware, however, that each area uses specialized software as well as standard items such as word processors. For example, engineering drafting used to be done by hand and is now done as computer-aided design. In manufacturing, there is computer-aided manufacturing software. The list goes on.

TELECOMMUNICATIONS AND NETWORKS

This appendix focuses primarily on the computer industry. However, the modern computer does not need to be a stand-alone unit. It can communicate with other computers worldwide through the Internet. Individuals communicate with people in their own firm, with clients, with customers, and even with spammers, through local area and wide area networks.

| SIDEBAR 1 | *Local Area and Wide Area Networks* |

The telephone system is a network. It allows two or more people to talk with one another. Its value comes from the fact that an individual can reach a large fraction of the people they want to deal with even though these people are widely scattered. A similar situation exists for computers. A personal computer that stands alone can do marvelous things for the individual. But as soon as the stand-alone computer user wants to communicate with someone else, they need a network for computers that is analogous to the telephone network.

As its name implies, a local area network allows a computer to communicate with other computers that are close by, usually within the same location in a firm. A wide area network expands the capability to communicating with people hundreds and thousands of miles away. Connecting all the computers in a home or in an office is an example of a local area network. The Internet is the ultimate wide area network.

Computers and telecommunications grew toward one another over the decades. Many organizations place their computer and telecommunications in the same organization. The cost of creating local area networks and connections to wide area nets can be considerable and must be included in estimating the cost of new computer initiatives.

SEARCH ENGINES

A search engine, as its name implies, is software for finding data in large databases by searching for it. Most people are familiar with search engines such as Google, or Yahoo, or Excite! which search the Web. Search engines are also available on most private and public websites. The idea is that, in response to keywords (e.g., computer manufacturers or IBM or data storage), the search engine provides a list of data resources available on the subject.

Search engines provide a quick way of locating information. The down side is that the information is limited to the domain searched. In the case of Google, for example, the domain is the Internet, with Google searching over 3 billion Web pages. However, if information is not in the search domain it will not be found. Thus, users of search engines cannot be assured they made a complete search. Nonetheless, search engines are an important phenomenon and, like a library, they often give you clues as to where to search next.

NEW TECHNOLOGIES

New technologies are continually being developed and integrated into the computer environment. In this subsection we describe two of them:

- Wi-Fi
- RFID

Wi-Fi

Wi-Fi was a technology intended to be used for wireless local area networks but is now often also used for Internet access. It allows a person with a wireless-enabled computer (usually a portable PC) or personal digital assistant (PDA) or even a cell phone to connect to the Internet by moving close to (e.g., less than 50 feet) an access point, called a "hotspot."

Hotspots can either be free or for a fee. They may be metered access or with a pass for a unit of time (e.g., a day, month, or year) valid for one or more locations. They are located in such places as coffee houses and airports around the world. Hotspots in public and semipublic places are provided by T-Mobile, Boingo, Wayport, and iPass. Compared to cellular telephones, however, the combined coverage of hotspots is currently still very spotty.

The advantages of hotspots include

- Commercial availability of reliable and bug-free Wi-Fi products on the market
- Ability to move around while connected on a Wi-Fi network without breaking the network connection.

Disadvantages include

- Wi-Fi currently operates in the 2.4 gigahertz spectrum, a crowded frequency band which can degrade performance.
- Devices consume a lot of power, making battery life and heat a concern.
- Many business and residential users do not bother to protect their network. Therefore, people just outside a building can use the system for free (or tamper with it!).

Wi-Fi is an outgrowth of the use of wireless computers within organizations. For example, wireless connections can be used by a workgroup. The 2004 version of Wi-Fi is probably an interim technology that will become more robust and more secure.

Wi-Fi is a trademark of the Wi-Fi Alliance (formerly the Wireless Ethernet Compatibility Alliance), the trade organization that defines the Wi-Fi standards.

RFID

RFID (radio frequency identification) uses computer chips that can be interrogated at radio frequencies to track pallets, cartons, and individual items in warehouses, stores, and other locations. In the near future, companies will be able to create a network of physical objects much as they now create networks of people and information. This network would mesh completely with other networks and open up new opportunities for product and supply chain management.

RFID technology uses e-tags and electronic product code:

E-Tags. These tags are essentially tiny computers (smaller than a "D" on a penny). They are tiny, lightweight, cheap, and versatile, enabling them to be easily and invisibly embedded in most product packaging, clothing, or parts. Tags range from simply identifying products (as bar codes do) to monitors that give such quantities as weight, temperature, and pressure. Tag readers, based on cellular technology, can identify what products are located where. Unlike bar code scanning, line of sight is not required. It is estimated that 100 billion e-tags will be needed to identify the global supply chain.

Electronic Product Code (EPC). Standards are being developed to identify individual product items (e.g., cans of soda) through an EPC. These standards create a unique identifier for an individual item. The coder can identify 1.5 quintillion objects uniquely.

RFID technology is superior to bar code technology because its user does not need to know where an object is and does not need to get close to scan it. Since tags can be read at a distance they lend themselves to many applications across a supply chain (see Chapter 11).

An early RFID application was the tags that identify and automatically debit the accounts of car owners whose vehicles go through toll road entrances. Applications are much, much broader than that, ranging from airport baggage handling, to keeping track of patients in hospitals, to libraries, to retail theft prevention, to auto parts and auto manufacturing.

The downside risk is cultural. RFID tags lend themselves to Big Brother invasions of privacy. Many people do not want information about them to be made public. For example, wearing an RFID tag in clothing would allow tracking every movement a person makes. The cultural dimensions may be the determining factor in the ultimate adoption of this technology.

FINDING OUT MORE ABOUT THE COMPUTER INDUSTRY AND COMPUTER APPLICATIONS: THE COMPUTER PRESS AND THE INDUSTRY OBSERVERS

For an industry whose main function is to move data, information, and explicit knowledge into digital form, the amount of written material available on paper is remarkable. Moreover, a large fraction of the publications come out daily, weekly, and monthly. Most are controlled circulation magazines that are free to people who work in the computer industry. They should also be available through university, college, and corporate libraries.

The following table lists some of the more influential publications and their URLs:

Publication	URL
Business 2.0	Business2.com
CIO	CIO.com
*Computerworld	Computerworld.com
CFO	Cfo.com
*Datamation	Datamation.com or http://itmanagement.earthweb.com/
*DM Review	Dmreview.com
Fastcompany	Fastcompany.com
Findarticles.com	findarticles.com/cf_0/PI/index.jhtml
Forbes ASAP	Forbes.com/asap
Fortune	Fortune.com
*Information Week	Techweb.com
*InfoWorld	Infoworld.com
*Intelligent Enterprise	Intelligententerprise.com
*KM World	Kmworld.com
*ZDNet	techupdate.zdnet.com

* Denotes publications that offered e-mail newsletter containing all or part of their content in 2004.

Many of these weekly and monthly publications offer daily or weekly updates as newsletters sent via e-mail. They are almost invariably free. The weekly and monthly publications usually offer online versions that can be searched.

CONCLUSION

This appendix presented an overview of the computer industry, its firms, and the functions performed. The process of defining industry boundaries, which are needed to estimate the size of the computer and computer-related segments of the information industry, is one that should not be taken lightly. In many areas industry segments and firms overlap and it is difficult to determine what part of a firm's sales come from a given segment. In addition, many estimates are made, but their validity or even the foundation upon which those numbers were developed are not available. Published figures are always out of date because much can, and does, occur between the time the data are gathered and the current date. Nonetheless, the data given in this appendix can be used to gain insight on the vast, worldwide computer industry.

ANSWERS TO MANAGERIAL QUESTIONS

What is included in the computer industry?

In this book, the computer industry includes not only the vendors of hardware and software but also the people who work in computer-related tasks in small and large companies.

What are in-house shops? What are outside shops?

Almost every company now uses one or more computers. To run them, most firms employ one or more people who specialize in the field. These people form what is called the in-house shop. Their work ranges from acquiring computers and software, to programming, to help desks, to setting companywide standards, to arranging for outsourcing. Outside shops are firms that specialize in information systems and perform services, including application service providers, Web services, and outsourcers.

How does the industry charge for its products and for maintenance?

Computer products usually incur "purchase" and annual maintenance costs. Products beyond the PC are typically licensed rather than owned. The maintenance costs are in the form of required annual contracts that provide maintenance service for hardware and upgrades for software. Maintenance costs are in the range of 15% to 20% of the purchase price per year.

What categories of people and jobs are involved?

The computer industry is a major employer. It requires people with college degrees and with specialized technical training. The jobs for in-house shops range from computer operators and programmers to specialists in fields ranging from databases to security to managers who can interact with the managers in other parts of the firm.

How do computers and telecommunications interact?

Whenever a computer needs to communicate with other computers, telecommunications are required. Whether it is a cable modem or DSL to the house or a local area or a wide area network or the Internet, telecommunications are used to tie computers (and hence people) together. Telecommunications and computers are intertwined, and in many cases it is not possible to tell where one ends and the other begins.

What is open source?

Open source refers to an arrangement in which a large number of people contribute to a particular software package rather than the package being developed by a specific company as a proprietary product. Initial costs are usually less for open source than proprietary software. Proprietary software makers claim that the total cost of ownership over the life of open source packages may be larger.

What about new technologies such as Wi-Fi and RFID?

It is a characteristic of information systems that it is a business whose technology is continually changing. This appendix describes two technologies that were emerging in 2004: Wi-Fi, which is an example of using wireless communications, and radio frequency identification (RFID), which is a replacement for bar codes for identifying what and where an object is.

Where can I find current information on computers in business?

A large business press exists for information systems. Many of the publications are controlled circulation, which means they are supported by advertisers and are sent without cost to people who are responsible for or influence computer purchases. Many of these publications also provide regular (daily, weekly) e-mail editions.

REFERENCES FOR APPENDIX

Ahituv, N., Neumann, S., and Riley, H. N. *Principles of Information Systems for Management*, 4th ed., Dubuque, IA: Wm. C. Brown Communication, Inc., 1994.

Bureau of Labor Statistics, *Occupational Employment Statistics*, U.S. Department of Labor, 1998, http://stats.bls.gov, 1998.

Bureau of Labor Statistics, *Occupational Employment and Wages, May 2003*, U.S. Department of Labor, 2003, http://www.bls.gov/oes/2003/may/oes151011.htm, 2003.

Bureau of Labor Statistics, *Career Guide to Industries, 2004–05 Edition, Computer Systems Design and Related Services*, U.S. Department of Labor, 2004, http://www.bls.gov/oco/cg/cgs033.htm, 2004.

Bureau of Labor Statistics, *Industry at a Glance—NAICS 51: Information*, U.S. Bureau of Labor Statistics, 2005, http://www.bls.gov/iag/information.htm, 2005.

Business Week, "Software," in *Business Week*, Business & Company Resource Center, p. 178, 2002.

E-Commatrix *eSolution*, e-Commatrix, Inc., 2003.http://www.e-commatrix.com, 2004.

Electronic Data Systems, "About EDS: Overview—Who We Are," *EDS*, 2003, http://www.eds.com, 2003.

Hoover's *Computer Hardware*, Hoover's, Inc., 2005, http://www.hoovers.com/computer-hardware/--HICID_1092--/free-ind-factsheet.xhtml, 2005a.

Hoover's *Computer Software*, Hoover's, Inc., 2005, http://www.hoovers.com/computer-software/--HICID_1121--/free-ind-factsheet.xhtml, 2005b.

Hoover's *Computer Services*, Hoover's, Inc., 2005, http://www.hoovers.com/computer-services/--HICID_1116--/free-ind-factsheet.xhtml, 2005c.

Houghton, J. W. "Mapping Information Industries and Markets," *Telecommunications Policy* 23: pp. 689–699, Special Issue November–December 1999.

IT Outsourcing Institute, *IT Outsourcing: The State of the Art*, The Outsourcing Institute, http://www.outsourcing.com, 2000.

InvestQuest *ADP*, InvestQuest, 2003, http://www.investquest.com/iq/a/aud, 2005.

Laudon, K. C., and Laudon, J. P. *Management Information Systems*, 8th ed., Upper Saddle River, NJ: Pearson-Prentice-Hall, 2004.

Microsoft, *Corporate Information*, Microsoft Corporation, http://www.microsoft.com, 2000.

Plunkett, *Computers, Software and Information Technology Trends & Market Analysis*, Plunkett Research, Ltd, 2003, http://www.plunkettresearch.com/technology/infotech_trends.htm, 2004a.

Plunkett, *Top 15 Computer Hardware Manufacturing Companies, by Sales: 2002–2003*, Plunkett Research, Ltd, 2003, http://www.plunkettresearch.com/technology/infotech_statistics_2.htm, 2004b.

Plunkett, *Top Computer Software Companies, by Sales: 2002–2003,* Plunkett Research, Ltd, 2003, http://www.plunkettresearch.com/technology/infotech_statistics_3_htm, 2004c.

Shapiro, C., and Varian, H.R. *Information Rules: A Strategic Guide to the Network Economy,* Boston: Harvard Business School Press, 1999.

SIAA, "Packaged Software Industry Revenue and Growth," Software & Information Industry Association, 2004, htpp://www.siia.net/software/resources.asp#stats, 2004.

Software & Information Industry Association, *Packaged Software Industry Revenue and Growth*, Software & Information Industry Association, 2004, http://www.siia.net/software/resources.asp#stats, 2004.

U.S. Census Bureau, *1997 Economic Census*, U.S. Census Bureau, 2000, http://www.census.gov/epcd/ec97/det/51.TXT, 2000.

U.S. Census Bureau, *2002 Economic Census: Table 1. Advance Summary Statistics for the United States—2002 NAICS Basis*, U.S. Census Bureau, 2002, http://www.census.gov/econ/census02/advance/TABLE1.HTM, 2004a.

U.S. Census Bureau, *2002 NAICS Definitions: 51 Information*, U.S. Census Bureau, 2002, http://www.census.gov/epcd/naics02/def/NDEF51.HTM, 2004b.

U.S. Census Bureau, *New Sectors in NAICS*, U.S. Census Bureau, 2004, http://www.census.gov/epcd/www/naicsect.htm#Information, 2004c.

Volt Information Sciences, Volt Information Sciences, Inc., 2000, http://www.volt.com, 2000.

Wikipedia, *Application Service Provider*, Wikipedia, 2004, http://en.wikipedia.org/wiki/Application_service_provider, 2004.

Glossary

24/7   A shorthand reference for working or operating 24 hours per day, 7 days a week.

A2A   Application-to-application.

Acceptance testing   Testing by the user that a completed system works in the way that they expect it to.

Access control   (1) Forbids people from gaining access to computer centers if not authorized and their identity authenticated. (2) The ability of people, particularly handicapped people, to access computers and the information they contain.

Accuracy   The correctness of information stored on computers.

Adapter   A program that connects application programs, databases, and middleware.

Administrative controls   Rules and measures to make certain that access rules are changed frequently; for example, changing passwords.

Ahmdahl   A manufacturer of mainframe computers.

Alert   Notification that a particular condition exists or will require action.

Alliance   A formal agreement between independent firms to cooperate in achieving a particular aim. The arrangement is limited to specific tasks rather than being a merger. Members of an alliance are equal.

Apple   One of the earliest PC manufacturers who is still in business. Known for its quality interface.

Application control   Limiting who can create, run, or obtain the output of applications.

Application service provider (ASP)   Firm that provides the software and computers needed to run an application based on data provided to it by a client firm.

Applications   Computer programs that solve specific problems such as payroll, supply chain management, or customer relationship management.

Architecture   A fancy word for plan. It describes the design specifications for a system in terms of principles and objectives.

Audio card   A card put in a PC to allow speakers to be connected for sound.

B2B   An abbreviation for business-to-business e-commerce.

B2C   An abbreviation for business-to-consumer e-commerce.

Back-office   Those functions which are internal to the firm such as payroll and billing.

Batch mode   Running multiple cases together at one time (such as an insurance company running a day's insurance payments) rather than as individual events occur. (See interactive mode.)

BI   Business intelligence.

BI for the masses   See Pervasive BI.

BPM   An abbreviation used for both business performance management and business process management. Although confusing, the meaning is usually evident from the context.

Bricks and clicks   A colloquial expression for a firm that sells both in stores (i.e., bricks) and over the Internet (i.e., clicks).

Browser   A program (such as Internet Explorer or Firefox) that accesses and displays files and other data available on the Internet and other networks. Usually referred to as Web browser.

BSP   Business service provider.

Buckman Laboratories   A chemical distribution firm that started using knowledge management in 1992 and sustained its efforts since then.

Bug   A mistake in computer software that causes the software to malfunction or give incorrect answers.

Build-vs.-buy   The option of creating software or services inside a company versus purchasing from a vendor.

Bullwhip effect   The magnification of small errors into large ones, such as occurs when everyone buys inventory to guard against small fluctuations in demand.

Bundling   Used to describe software that comes with hardware. For example, most PCs are sold with an operating system and other software included in the price.

Business activity monitoring (BAM)   BAM systems report business activity process outputs and key performance indicators to managers in near real time. BAM is a subset of BPM.

Business continuity   Avoiding or minimizing the impact of a failure so that the company can continue operating.

Business intelligence (BI)   Concepts and methods to improve the timeliness and quality of the input to decision processes. Typically involves the use of business intelligence systems.

Business intelligence systems   Combines data gathering, data storage, and KM with analytical tools to present complex corporate and competitive information to planners and decision makers to improve quality, timeliness of decisions.

Business performance management (BPM)   A set of processes to help organizations optimize business performance. BPM is focused on business processes such as planning and forecasting that help businesses discover efficient use of their resources.

Business process   A series of steps taken to accomplish a specific business purpose. For example, the steps performed in creating a bill for goods or services.

Business process monitoring (BPM)   Activities that organizations perform to optimize their business processes or adapt them to new organizational needs.

Byte   Numbers in a computer are represented in a base 2 arithmetic. In this arithmetic only the symbols 0 and 1 are allowed and are called a "bit." A byte consists of 8 bits and can represent numbers from 0 to 255.

C2B   Consumer-to-business e-commerce.

C2C   Consumer-to-consumer e-business such as eBay.

Call center   A group inside an organization that responds to questions and provides advice on how to solve hardware and/or software problems.

Capital budget   Money set aside, typically annually, for the creation or purchase of equipment or software that is expected to last for several years after installation.

Central processing unit   The part of a computer that carries out the instructions contained in the software.

Change management   Managing the sociotechnical effects that occur in an organization as a result of changes in tasks, technology, people, and structure.

Charge back   An accounting arrangement in which projects, departments, and SBUs are charged for the cost of the IT services that they consume.

Chat room   An online forum for broadcasting messages to people via the Internet or other network in real time. Distinguished from discussion groups that also operate on the Internet but not in real time.

Chief Information Officer (CIO)   The person responsible for all information operations in the firm.

Chief Knowledge Officer (CKO)   The title often given to the person in charge of a firm's knowledge management efforts.

Chief Technology Officer (CTO)   Responsible for technical decisions and standards. Usually (but not always) reports to the CIO.

Client-server computer systems   A distributed computer system in which software is split between server tasks and client tasks. A client sends requests to a server, asking for information or action, and the server provides the information. Clients and servers can be placed or located on different nodes in a network, and can even use different hardware and operating systems.

Code   Also referred to as computer code. The set of instructions in software.

Collaborative enterprise   A firm that links their systems with those of suppliers and customers.

Communications   The technology employed in transmitting and receiving messages.

Community of practice   Groups of people who share knowledge on a particular topic.

Competitive intelligence (CI)   A systematic and ethical program for gathering, analyzing, and managing external information that affect our company's plans, decisions, and operations.

Competitor profile   A description of a competitor.

Computer cluster   A group of locally connected computers that work together as a unit. Often used for parallel computing.

Computer divide   The separation between people who can access computers and use them from people without access or without skills to use them.

Computer Sciences Corporation (CSC)   A consulting firm with expertise in systems integration.

Computer security   The process of keeping the firm's and the individual's computer safe from intrusion so as to avoid loss of resources and privacy.

Computer utilities   Deploying IT as a utility-like service that can expand or contract quickly depending on customer needs. Customer pays only for the services used.

Computer-aided manufacturing   The use of computers to communicate work instructions directly to factory equipment.

Conjoint analysis   A statistical method of forecasting that starts with people asked to make trade-offs among conflicting considerations.

Content   Information such as schedules, products, price, provided by the computer.

Contract programming   Programming work done under contract for another firm.

Cookie   Information that is placed on computers by an outsider for later retrieval. Typically used to record that a firm was contacted previously by this computer.

Copyright   A way of protecting software by copyrighting the computer code. Copyrights treat software as literary works.

Core rigidity   Things companies do that they won't change when needed.

Corporate information center   The location of the central hardware, software, and supporting personnel for IT.

Custom software   Software, typically for a business process, that matches the way a company does business. Custom software generally can be used only in a single firm or department.

Customer relationship management (CRM)   Marketing to each customer individually based on information about customers (e.g., previous purchases, needs, and wants) to frame offers that are more likely to be accepted.

Customers   The people who receive, use, and obtain direct benefits from the products and services produced by the work system.

Cycle time   The average time before an event or situation recurs.

DARPA   Abbreviation for the Defense Advanced Research Project Agency. DARPA was the initial funder of the Internet.

Data   Items of information, such as transaction data, kept in a database.

Database   The collection of data in a firm or for use in a specific application. The data are arranged to make search and retrieval easy and quick.

Database administrator   A person responsible for one or more databases and their use.

Data control   Means for preventing, disclosing, or altering data maliciously.

Data cube   A multidimensional representation of data.

Data integrity   Preserving data for their intended use.

Data mining   Finding answers about a business directly that an executive or an analyst had not thought to ask. The information usually comes from data in the data warehouse.

Data storage   Physical means for keeping data such as hard disks, tape, and random access memory.

Data warehouse   Software for storing large amounts of data. The data are subject-oriented and integrated. They cover long time periods and do not change once put in the warehouse. Data in the data warehouse are used in support of management decision processes.

Decision support system (DSS)   A software system consisting of a database, a model base, and an interface that is programmed to help in making management decisions.

Delphi method   A method used in making estimates about events and trends that will take place in the future.

Desktop management   Managing the acquisition, maintenance, repair, and disposition of PCs.

Digital Equipment Corporation (DEC)   A manufacturer of mid-scale computers. Now defunct after a merger with Compaq which later merged with HP.

Digital Millennium Copyright Act   A law sponsored by the record and movie industries to protect records, movies, and software from being copied and resold.

Directive 95/46/EC   A directive on data privacy by the European Union.

Disaster recovery   The set of steps taken when a natural or other disaster strikes. Usually handled by IT because such disasters typically involve loss of computer capabilities.

Document management system   A program to track and store paper documents. Document management systems commonly provide check in, check out, storage, and retrieval of electronic documents.

Documentation   Descriptions of how a system works, how it is operated, and how it is repaired.

Documentum   A firm that creates and sells document management systems.

Domain   A communications address, such as a URL, that is used by one or more computers.

Domain registration   The process of obtaining a unique domain name.

Downstream   The connection by the firm to its distributors and customers.

Drilldown   Finding out more detail about the components of a number; for example, sales by region rather than total national sales.

Dumb terminal   A terminal tied to a mainframe or midrange computer or to a server that is not able to perform calculations or store information locally like a PC. It can request calculations from the computer to which they are attached.

Dynamic pricing   Allows pricing to fluctuate with supply and demand. Can be performed in real time, online.

E. F. Codd   Developer of relational databases and of online analytic processing (OLAP).

E-commerce   See Electronic commerce.

Economic lot size   The number of units to be produced based on a trade-off between setup and inventory cost.

EDS   A consulting firm with expertise in systems integration.

Electronic commerce Buying and selling goods and services using computers over networks such as the Internet.

Electronic data interchange (EDI) A formal system for transferring data between firms. Standards include X.25 in the United States and EDIFACT in most other countries. May use the Internet for data transfer.

Electronic document management system (EDMS) Computer application that manages the sharing of documents throughout the organization.

Electronic product code (EPC) A unique 96-bit identifier that replaces bar codes.

E-mail Messages addressed to specific individuals sent over a network such as the Internet.

Encryption Coding information so that it can only be read by people who are given the key to decode the encryption.

Enron A Houston-based firm whose accounting and computer scandal involved manipulating the price of electricity.

Enterprise application integration (EAI) Combining applications so they work seamlessly together.

Enterprise information integration (EII) Integrating data from multiple systems.

Enterprise requirements planning (ERP) A large, complex, typically enterprisewide software program in which multiple applications share one database. Data on transactions flow through the ERP system without manual intervention and automatically update information that uses the transactions as an input.

Enterprise systems Distributed information networks that work together.

Environment (work system perspective) Organizational, competitive, technical, and regulatory situations that a work system operates in.

E-tags Tiny computers embedded in products or carried by people that allow objects or people to be identified.

Ethics A concept from philosophy that deals with whether something is the right thing to do with respect to other people.

Exception report A report detailing deviations from plan and/or unusual occurrences.

Excite A search engine on the Internet.

Execution software Software used in supply chain management to automate operations.

Executive information system (EIS) A form of decision support system that contains only a database and an interface but not a model base.

Expertise Know-how plus creating new knowledge that influences a domain of knowledge.

Explicit knowledge Knowledge that can be written down and made available to everyone.

External design How the information systems look to the users.

Extract, transform, load (ETL) Three functions used to create data suitable for a data warehouse.

Extract: copying data from another database.

Transform: converting the data format in the original database to the format of the data warehouse.

Load: Moving the extracted, transformed data into the data warehouse.

Extranet A private Internet that connects the firm to people and organizations outside the firm.

Factory automation Using machines to replace humans for factory work.

Financial analytics Methods for determining the effects of alternative actions on a firm's balance sheet and other financial measures.

Financial Modernization Act Also called Gramm–Leach–Bliley. Limits what financial firms can do with data and how customers can opt out.

Financial planning systems Fourth generation language for use in financial calculations that typically allow users to write instructions in ordinary words.

Finished inventory Completed goods stored before they are sent to a customer.

Firewall   A software barrier that controls which sources can enter an internal network or a specific computer. Does not by itself protect against viruses.

Front-office   The portions of a business that deal with the customer.

Fujitsu   A Japanese manufacturer of mainframe computers.

Fusion   Forming a team of people with different perspectives to find a joint answer to a problem.

G2C   Consumer to government.

Gaming   A computer-based simulation in which two or more teams assume the roles of a firm and its competitors.

Generic software   Software that is not tailored to a specific client.

Geographic information system (GIS)   Software package that links databases and electronic maps. Also used to refer to the capability for analyzing spatial phenomena.

Gigabyte   A thousand megabytes.

GIS layer   A layer that presents a particular geographically based feature that can be overlaid accurately on a map.

Google   The most popular search engine in 2005.

Governance   The processes and systems by which a function or the firm as a whole operates.

Gramm–Leach–Bliley Act   See Financial Modernization Act.

Graphics   The use of visual representations on the computer screen. Can include graphs, pictures, and diagrams.

Grid computing   Solving massive problems (particularly in science and engineering) by making use of unused resources of a large number of computers in a distributed infrastructure.

H1B visa   A visa program that allows American companies and universities to employ foreign scientists, engineers, and programmers in the United States for up to 6 years.

Hacker   A person who is able to change computer programs by brute force. Most commonly used for people who seek to invade computers and distribute malware.

Handheld computer   Usually known as a personal digital assistant, a handheld computer is small enough to fit in the palm of a hand but is much more limited than a conventional PC.

Hardware   Physical computer equipment including electronics, displays, and storage.

Help desk   An organization that provides answers and assistance to users. Often uses a "call center" where people of different levels of expertise are available via telephone to give assistance.

Heuristic pattern analysis   Methods for finding and looking at the implications of patterns of data.

Hierarchy of knowledge   Skills, know-how, expertise.

HIPAA   Health Insurance Portability and Accountability Act of 1996.

Hitachi   A Japanese manufacturer of mainframe computers.

Home page   The first screen that appears when a URL is requested on the Internet.

Hosting   An arrangement in which an outsourcing firm provides IS services at its own facilities for one or more of its clients. The host gains economies of scale.

Hot site   A rented facility with the same computing equipment that can be used in case of a disaster.

Houghton map   A framework for analyzing and measuring the information industries.

Hub-and-spoke design   A computer architecture for systems integration in which interconnections occur at the hub and individual systems (spokes) communicate through the hub.

IBM   International Business Machines.

Identify theft   The theft of information about a person (e.g., social security number, drivers license data) that allows another individual to falsely assume that individual's identity.

Information   Data endowed with relevance and purpose. Information puts data into context.

Information portals   See Portals.

Information processors   Outsourcing firms that focus on finance and operations (e.g., payroll, check processing).

Information services   Systems analysts and applications groups in the information systems department that focus on user issues.

Information system   An automated or manual collection of people, machines, and/or methods to gather, process, transmit, and disseminate data. Information systems are used to acquire, store, manipulate, manage, display, transmit, or receive data. It includes both software and hardware.

Information systems department   The organization charged with managing and operating a firm's information systems.

Infrastructure   The hardware, software, and telecommunications needed to make applications run.

Infrastructure (work system perspective)   Shared human, informational, and technical resources that a work system relies on.

Infrastructure characteristics   A large-scale system with a technological dimension consisting of physical components that deliver necessary and hard-to-replace essential services.

In-house computer shop   The organization charged with managing and operating a firm's information systems. Usually referred to as the information systems department.

In-process inventory   Goods that are stored between stages of production or service.

In-sourcing   Using the in-house IS team to perform a task.

Integrity   See Data integrity.

Intellectual assets   Assets that result from knowledge.

Intelligent agents   Also known as bots, a shortened form of robot. Software that works without the assistance of people in making choices where the choices are rules that programmers built into the software. On the Internet they are used by search engines to find content on URLs.

Interactive mode   Computing in which results are fed back to the user as they are obtained. For example, records on a transaction.

Internal design   How a system operates internally.

Internet   A worldwide network of computer networks that use the TCP/IP network protocols to facilitate data transmission and exchange. A publicly available system of interconnected computer networks over which electronic mail, online chat, Web pages, and other documents are transmitted worldwide.

Interoperability   The ability of software and hardware on multiple computers from multiple vendors to communicate.

Interorganizational systems   Systems that span organizational boundaries.

Intervendor connection   An adapter that connects equipment from one vendor with that from another.

Intrabusiness   Transactions within a firm such as between departments or SBUs.

Intranet   A form of Internet used only within a firm.

Island of automation   A function that is computerized but does not communicate with other computerized functions.

ISP   Internet service provider. Most firms and individuals use ISPs for access to the Internet.

JIT   Just-in-time.

Joint venture   A form of cooperation between firms in which both firms invest in a project.

Just-in-time (JIT)   A system of receiving supplies and components just prior to the moment they are needed rather than warehousing them as inventory.

Just-in-time inventory   Minimizing inventory so that supplies are obtained only at the moment they are needed.

Just-in-time manufacturing   Building individual products from beginning to end. Requires materials and parts available at the time they are needed.

Key performance indicator   Any quantity, such as sales, that indicates how well a business is performing.

Kiviat diagram   A way of representing relations among multiple variables.

Know-how   Skills plus the ability to act in unforeseen circumstances.

Knowledge   Integrating information and data into ideas that lead to action. It differs from data (individual facts) and information (data put into context). Knowledge may be explicit or tacit.

Knowledge engineer   A term originally developed in artificial intelligence. A person who works with one or more individuals to make tacit knowledge explicit about a particular task or problem.

Knowledge management (KM)   The organizational process for acquiring, organizing, and communicating knowledge so people may use it to be more effective and productive.

Knowledge management system   Information systems to facilitate creating, organizing, gathering, and disseminating knowledge.

Knowledge repository   A collection of information and knowledge kept as a computer database for use by individuals and groups in the firm.

Knowledge sharing   The transfer of knowledge from one individual to one or more other individuals.

Knowledge transfer   Transmitting knowledge from one person or repository to another person or repository.

L1 visa   A nonimmigrant visa that allows companies operating both in the United States and abroad to transfer certain classes of employee from its foreign operations to the U.S. operations for up to 7 years.

Learning curve   The improvement that occurs as users become familiar with equipment and/or processes.

Legacy system   An information system that is not new.

LINUX   A freeware operating system in wide circulation that was developed by Linus Torvalds.

Local area network (LAN)   A network that connects computers in close proximity.

Logistics   Managing and controlling the flow of goods, energy, information, and other resources into and out of the firm's facilities.

Lotus   A Boston-area firm bought by IBM for its software to support groups (i.e., groupware).

M-commerce   E-business using mobile devices.

Mac OS   The operating system for the Macintosh personal computer by Apple. The latest version in 2005 was TIGER for Version X.

Mainframe computer   Large, expensive digital computers used for massive computing jobs. These computers are highly reliable, with good security and backwardly compatible with older software. They can support thousands of users simultaneously.

Malware   Software that does harm to a computer and/or its data.

Management by exception   An idea first popularized by Peter Drucker that managers should intervene only when things are not going according to plan.

Management information system (MIS)   Hardware and software that provides reports and answers queries for managers based on the transaction data available in the firm.

Management science   A field that uses advanced analytic techniques to solve managerial problems.

Materials resource planning (MRP)   A forerunner of ERP, it was concerned with planning and monitoring production schedules and inventory including requirements for materials used in the factory. MRP II extended MRP to include allocations of resources and costs associated with production.

McKinsey & Company   A large consulting firm.

Megabyte (Mb)   A million bytes.

Message board   The output of a computer conference on which people post messages to be read by others.

Middleware   Programs that allow interactions among applications that were designed independently.

Mid-range computer   Although the computer industry does not define mid-range computers, they are computers that fall between the PC and mainframe computers. Historically they were sold to small to medium-sized businesses as their main computer and to larger firms for branch or department-level operations.

Modem   A device that serves as a modulator–demodulator of digital signals so they can be carried over telephone lines.

Module   A subprogram that provides specific inputs from and outputs to other modules.

Moving   Installing a change so it is accepted.

MSP   Infrastructure management service provider.

NAICS   North American Industry Classification System. Replaced the older Standard Industrial Classification (SIC) codes. Issued by the Office of Management and Budget.

Near shore outsourcing   Outsourcing to Canada, Mexico, or the Caribbean.

Net Meeting   A Microsoft product that allows ad hoc groups to meet.

Network control   Limiting access to networks; providing encryption and firewalls.

Network effect   The value of knowledge, information, and data increases as more people connect to it. Originally used for telephones or computers. One phone is worth nothing because you can't talk to anyone else. The value of a telephone network increases faster than the number of people connected to the network.

Object name service (ONS)   Connects an item carrying an EPC with the location where information about it resides.

Office suite   A collection of software for office use in which the applications can work together. Typically includes word processing, spreadsheet, presentation, and a small database.

Offshore outsourcing   Outsourcing to an overseas firm.

Online analytic processing (OLAP)   Quick processing and analysis of multidimensional information retrieved through queries of data, usually from a data warehouse.

Online market maker   In e-commerce, a firm that handles the trading of specific goods, finding sellers and buyers.

Online transaction processing (OLTP)   Processing in which the computer responds immediately to user requests, such as sales terminals in groceries.

Onshore outsourcing   Outsourcing to a domestic firm.

OODA   The iterative steps in observe, orient, decide, and act.

OODA loop   The OODA loop is a way of learning because the faster the loop, the quicker and less costly the response.

Operating system   Software for controlling and managing a computer's operations. Provides means for running applications.

Operations   A group responsible for managing and running the firm's production of information.

Optimum lot size   See economic lot size. Optimum lot size is determined by the methods of management science.

Opt-in   The customer specifies that the website owner is given permission to use the information and for which purposes.

Opt-out   The website owner maintains the right to use the information for any purpose, including selling it and/or giving it to others unless the customer specifically asks that the information not be disseminated.

Outside shop   Resources external to the organization.

Outsourcing   Contracting work, such as information technologies, to other firms.

PAPA   An abbreviation for four properties of ethics: privacy, accuracy, property, and access.

Parallel computing   Performing several instructions simultaneously by several computers, using software that balances the load among them.

Participants   The people who perform the work in a business process.

Password   A personal identifier, used together with a user name, to authenticate a person. The weakest form of security.

Patent   A way of protecting business processes by patenting how they are performed. Example: Amazon.com obtained a patent on its 1-click logout procedure.

Personal computer (PC)   A small computer (called microcomputer) used by an individual for office tasks (see Office suite), programming, or playing games. PCs may be networked to access the Internet or other computers or used in combinations in grid computing. Characterized by low cost to purchase and simple operation.

Pervasive BI   Sharing business intelligence data and capabilities with large numbers of staff members rather than restricting it to a staff group and senior managers.

Physical control   Steps to prevent damage to computers and computer centers.

Physical markup language (PML)   A standard used to describe product items.

Plug and play   A shorthand way of describing software that can be installed and used immediately without modification of either the software or the computer.

Polyani   A Hungarian philosopher who originally made the tacit/explicit distinction.

Portable computer   A PC that is small enough and lightweight enough to be carried from place to place. Usually sells at a premium.

Portal   A Web page that contains links to other Web pages.

Predictive analytics   Statistical and other methods for forecasting.

Privacy   The ability to keep personal information away from others.

Privacy statement   A set of rules in which firms assure customers that their data will not be (or will be) used for any purpose other than within the company.

Process integration   Systems integration between processes. May be event or transaction oriented.

Products and services   The combination of things, information, and services produced by a work system.

Profiling   Recording and classifying behavior.

Programmers   People who create computer programs.

Programming   The work done by programmers.

Programming tools   Software designed to help programmers create new software.

Project champion   A person with sufficient power and budget who wants the project to succeed and works with people in the firm to make it happen. The project champion usually comes from outside the IS department.

Project development cycle   The series of steps followed from project initiation until a project is delivered to its client.

Project management   The art and science of running individual projects so that they complete on time and within budget.

Project management (formal definition)   The application of knowledge, skills, tools, and techniques to project activities to meet the project requirements.

Querying   Using the SQL language or other means to ask questions of data.

Radio frequency identification   A technology that uses tags that act as antennas and can be interrogated to obtain information about the location and characteristics of a product or person being queried.

Range   The activities that can be completed across a given level of reach (see Reach).

Reach   The people that can be connected through infrastructure.

Recovery time window   The time available for disaster recovery before losing a large amount of business.

Refreezing   Institutionalizing a change.

Remote computing   Computing done at a location some distance away (which may be across town or even across continents).

Retrieve   Find information in storage and display it on a user's computer screen.

Reuse   Some modules created previously can be used from one program to another.

Reverse supply chain   The supply chain in reverse. Goods are sent back to the vendor from the customer. Recycling is an example.

RFID   Radio frequency identification.

RFID technology   Radio frequency identification technology. Tags that allow people and things to be interrogated at a distance.

Rightsourcing   Creating an appropriate portfolio of outsourced and in-sourced work.

Risk analysis   The process of measuring and assessing risk, particularly for projects.

Risk management   Taking steps, based on risk analysis, to manage the risk associated with projects, including deciding not to undertake the project.

Risk of not investing   The potential loss multiplied by the probability of incurring that loss if an investment is not made.

Roll up   The opposite of drilldown. Data at a given level are combined into a total. Used for aggregating information such as the sales or profitability of a set of subsidiaries.

Rollout   The initial implementation of software or processes across an organization.

RONI   The risk of not investing.

Safe harbor   A trade provision that allows moving data to the United States as long as regulations that apply in the home country are followed.

Sales Force Automation (SFA)   Software that automates the functions performed by salespeople.

Sarbanes–Oxley Act (SOX)   An act that requires companies to certify the accuracy and veracity of their financial reports. Resulted in major changes in most companies' information systems. Requires real-time disclosure.

SBU   Strategic business unit.

Scenario   A possible, plausible, internally consistent description of an alternative future outcome.

SCIP   Society for Competitive Intelligence.

Scope creep   (1) Increase in the specific work (scope) to be done. Usually occurs a little at a time but tends to add up to major changes. (2) Adding features and changing objectives that increase the size of a computer software project.

SCP   Supply chain planning.

Screen scraper   An adapter that allows sharing input data from one application with other applications.

Security Breach Notice Law   A state law, first passed in California, that requires companies to notify people if a database containing information about them is compromised.

Server   In client-server systems, the physical computer on which the software runs. The server runs computer programs to carry out tasks requested by users (i.e., clients). Servers may be specialized to offer access to the Web, to e-mail, and to databases.

Service level agreement   A contractual specification of the quality, quantity, and schedule of what is to be delivered by an outsourcer or by an in-house computer shop.

Service provider   A firm that provides a particular service. The following are examples of service providers: ASP, BSP, ISP, MSP, SSP. See these abbreviations in this glossary for more detail.

SharePoint   SharePoint is a Microsoft product for Windows to assist collaboration. Allows users to create, manage, and build collaborative websites and make them available.

Simulation   A computer representation of a process that allows determining the effects of changes and uncertainty.

Skill   Ability to follow rules.

SKU   Stock keeping unit. An SKU is the smallest unit of an item that may be taken out of inventory or returned to a vendor. Typically assigned both a name and a number.

Slice and dice   A colloquial term that refers to the ability to analyze data cubes by subdividing them (slice) and by creating subcubes.

Software   Computer programs. These programs provide the operating system and the applications run on a computer.

Software change control   A formal method for checking computer code, verifying changes, and tracking changes over time.

Spam   Unwanted e-mail, typically containing unsolicited advertising.

Spreadsheet   A work sheet created by the computer with rows and columns in which data and text can be entered. Formulas can be applied to perform calculations. Typified by Excel from Microsoft.

SSP   Storage service provider.

Steering committee   Consists of senior people in the firm who oversee IT and who make allocations of scarce IT resources.

Stochastic   Uncertain.

Storage   The parts of a digital computer that retains data, programs, and other information. In PCs, storage includes hard disks, random access memory, and portable memory (memory sticks) that can be moved from one computer to another.

Store   To retain information for future use.

Strategy   The overall organizational direction set by management.

Structured information   Information such as numbers or key words that can easily be stored in relational or multidimensional databases.

Sun   A manufacturer of mid-range computers and the Solaris Operating System.

Supply chain management (SCM)   The use of analytic techniques to improve the functioning of the corporate supply chain.

Surfing   Searching the Internet for interesting URLs.

SWOT analysis   Acronym for strengths, weaknesses, opportunities, threats. SWOT analysis refers to determining these characteristics for one's own form and one's competitors.

System integration   See systems integration.

System testing   Testing to make sure that all components of a system work together.

Systems integration   The process of making disparate systems able to work together so that the boundaries between systems are seamless.

Systems integration (more formal)   Connecting the separate components of computers, software, storage, and telecommunications so that they work together and share resources.

Systemshouse   Systems integration contractors.

Tacit knowledge   Knowledge kept in people's heads that is difficult or impossible to make explicit.

Team room   A place where members of a project team can meet and work together. Such a room usually contains project materials and charts as well as a place to meet and confer.

Technical services   A group responsible for hardware/software technology in the information systems department.

Telecommuting   Working from a remote location, such as from home or from a "telecommuting center."

Terabyte (Tb) 2^{40} bytes. Roughly a million megabytes or a thousand gigabytes.

Test data   Data used to do module, system, and acceptance testing.

Time share   Running several computer programs simultaneously to gain computer operating efficiencies.

Total cost of ownership (TCO)   The cost of owning hardware or software over their entire life. Differs from purchase or lease price which deals only with initial cost.

Touch point   Any way in which a company maintains contact with a customer. Touch points include phone conversations, e-mails, advertising, and direct sales efforts.

Tracking software   Software that is used to determine where a particular item is right now.

Transaction processing   Recording and updating information about individual transactions.

Transmit   Send computer data or e-mail.

Trojan horse   Malware that stays in the computer until it is triggered and then acts like a virus or a worm.

UCITA   Uniform Computer Information Transaction Act. Legislation that would, if adopted, give software vendors the right to enter computers and remove software.

Unfreezing   Convincing people to change the way they do their job.

Unit testing   A method of using test cases to determine the correctness of a particular software module. Involves testing every function and/or method in the module.

Universal resource locator (URL)   The name or address of a file or a location on the Internet.

Unix   An operating system used almost exclusively on mid-range and large computer systems.

Unstructured information   Information that is not stored in a database because it does not fit the characteristics of databases. Includes text and graphics.

Upgrade   Replacing an existing computer, computer component, or software with a newer version or one with more capability.

Upstream   The connection by a computer to its suppliers in the value chain.

URL   Universal resource locator; the name or number given to a computer server.

User involvement   Can be no involvement, symbolic involvement, involvement by advice, by sign-off, by weak control, by doing, and by strong control.

Value-added tax   A tax, in many countries outside the United States, which is imposed at each stage of manufacturing and distribution.

VAT   Value-added tax.

Vendor   A firm that sells hardware or software.

Vertical market   A specific industry.

Virtual machine   Presents computing resources in ways that users and applications can obtain value out of them without relying on specific implementation, geographic location, or physical packaging. Provides a logical rather than physical view of data, storage capacity, and other resources.

VPN   Virtual private network.

Virtual reality (VR)   Simulation of an environment by a computer. Most VR environments are visual but some include audio. The VR environment can be similar or differ significantly (e.g., computer games) from the real world. In 2005, convincing VR experiences are difficult to create because of computer limitations.

Virtual server   Typically a server located at a host that acts as though it were located at the client's premises.

Virus   Malware that alters or destroys data.

Visualization   The process of presenting information as visual images rather than in text form that allows decision makers to use visual and spatial capabilities to solve business problems.

Volt Technical   One of the original outsourcing firms that offered contract programmers for hire.

Web (www)   See World Wide Web.

Web browser   See Browser.

Web hosting   Using the Web to communicate in a hosting arrangement. See Hosting.

Web services   A form of application service provider that uses the World Wide Web for communications. The applications send data and instructions to one another, with no translation required. By using the Internet, most of the connection and communications problems are eliminated.

Website   A collection of Web pages on the Internet accessed from a common URL. Usually reside on the same physical server.

WebEx   Software for running meetings over the Internet. Produced by WebEx Communications.

Website traffic analysis   Software that measures the number of visitors to a website.

What-if analysis   Analyses that explore the implications of alternative actions or alternative numeric values of particular parameters.

White paper   Usually a description of a development in IS by a senior staff member at a vendor describing a problem and the solution offered by that vendor. Useful for learning about the subject, but recognize that a white paper is usually biased toward the vendor's offering.

Wide area network (WAN)   A (typically) private network that covers a large geographic area. See also Local area network.

Win/loss analysis   An analysis of why a company (and its competitors) won or lost a particular project bid.

Wireless   Computer networks that do not require physical cables between nodes to operate.

Word processing   Software designed to create documents on a computer. Contains many features that allow people to create good looking documents on their personal computer.

Work practices   The steps or activities performed in a work system.

Work system   A system in which people and/or machines perform work by using information technology and other resources to create products or services for internal or external customers.

World Wide Web (www)   A service on the Internet, not the Internet itself. URLs of sites that belong to the World Wide Web are identified by the initial letters www. Example: http://www.wiley.com.

Worm   Malware that replicates itself and spreads throughout a network.

Y2K   An acronym for the Year 2000 problem. The problem referred to changing computer programs so that they could handle dates beyond December 31, 1999.

Yellow pages   A directory of people with specific knowledge.

Index